This is a further volume in a series of companions to major philosophers. Each volume contains specially commissioned essays by an international team of scholars together with a substantial bibliography and will serve as a reference work for students and nonspecialists. One aim of the series is to dispel the intimidation such readers often feel when faced with the work of a difficult and challenging thinker.

Descartes occupies a position of pivotal importance as one of the founding fathers of modern philosophy; he is, perhaps, the most widely studied of all philosophers. In this authoritative collection an international team of leading scholars in Cartesian studies present the full range of Descartes' extraordinary philosophical achievement. His life and the development of his thought, as well as the intellectual background to and reception of his work, are treated at length. At the core of the volume are a group of chapters on his metaphysics: the celebrated "Cogito" argument, the proofs of God's existence, the "Cartesian circle" and the dualistic theory of the mind and its relation to his theological and scientific views. Other chapters cover the philosophical implications of his work in algebra, his place in the seventeenth-century scientific revolution, the structure of his physics, and his work on physiology, psychology, and ethics.

New readers and nonspecialists will find this the most comprehensive and accessible guide to Descartes currently available. Advanced students and specialists will find a conspectus of recent developments in the interpretation of Descartes.

THE CAMBRIDGE COMPANION TO
DESCARTES

The Cambridge Companion to

DESCARTES

Edited by John Cottingham

CAMBRIDGE
UNIVERSITY PRESS

PUBLISHED BY THE PRESS SYNDICATE OF THE UNIVERSITY OF CAMBRIDGE
The Pitt Building, Trumpington Street, Cambridge, United Kingdom

CAMBRIDGE UNIVERSITY PRESS
The Edinburgh Building, Cambridge CB2 2RU, UK   http: //www.cup.cam.ac.uk
40 West 20th Street, New York, NY 10011-4211, USA   http: //www.cup.org
10 Stamford Road, Oakleigh, Melbourne 3166, Australia

First published 1992
Reprinted 1993, 1994, 1995, 1998, 1999

Printed in the United States of America

Typeset in Trump Mediaeval

A catalogue record for this book is available from the British Library

Library of Congress Cataloguing-in-Publication Data is available

ISBN 0-521-36623-2 hardback
ISBN 0-521-36696-8 paperback

CONTENTS

v

CONTRIBUTORS

ROGER ARIEW is Professor of Philosophy at Virginia Polytechnic Institute and State University; he is translator of Martial Gueroult, *Descartes' Philosophy according to the Order of Reasons* (1984–5) and Pierre Duhem, *Medieval Cosmology* (1985), co-translator of *Leibniz: Philosophical Essays* (1989), and co-editor of *Revolution and Continuity: Essays in the History and Philosophy of Early Modern Science* (1991).

JEAN-MARIE BEYSSADE is Professor of Philosophy at the University of Paris–Sorbonne. He is the author of *La philosophie première de Descartes* (1979) and translator of *L'entretien avec Burman* (1981); since 1988 he has been Chairman of the Centre d'Etudes Cartésiennes.

DESMOND CLARKE is Associate Professor of Philosophy and Vice-President at University College, Cork; he is author of *Descartes' Philosophy of Science* (1982), *Occult Powers and Hypotheses* (1989), and general editor of the Classics of Philosophy and Science series, which includes his translation of Poulain de la Barre, *The Equality of the Sexes* (1990).

JOHN COTTINGHAM is Professor of Philosophy and Head of the Philosophy Department at the University of Reading. He is the author of *Rationalism* (1984), *Descartes* (1986), and *The Rationalists* (Oxford History of Western Philosophy series, 1986), editor of *Descartes' Conversation with Burman* (1976), and co-translator of *The Philosophical Writings of Descartes* (1985–91).

DANIEL GARBER is Professor of Philosophy and Chairman of the Department of Philosophy at the University of Chicago. He is the author of *Descartes' Metaphysical Physics* (1992), the co-translator of *Leibniz: Philosophical Essays* (1989), and the coeditor of the forthcoming *Cambridge History of Seventeenth-Century Philosophy*.

STEPHEN GAUKROGER is Reader in Philosophy at the University of Sydney. He is author of *Explanatory Structures* (1978) and *Cartesian Logic* (1989), editor of *Descartes: Philosophy, Mathematics and Physics* (1980) and *The Uses of Antiquity* (1991), and translator of *Arnauld: On True and False Ideas* (1990).

GARY HATFIELD is Professor of Philosophy at the University of Pennsylvania. He is the author of *The Natural and the Normative: Theories of Spatial Perception from Kant to Helmholtz* (1991) and of numerous essays on philosophy and science in the seventeenth century.

NICHOLAS JOLLEY is Professor of Philosophy at the University of California, San Diego, and author of *Leibniz and Locke* (1984) and *The Light of the Soul* (1990).

LOUIS E. LOEB is Professor of Philosophy at the University of Michigan, Ann Arbor; author of *From Descartes to Hume: Continental Metaphysics and the Development of Modern Philosophy* (1981) and of numerous articles on the history of early modern philosophy.

JEAN-LUC MARION is Professor of the History of Classical Philosophy at the University of Paris X–Nanterre. He is the author of *Sur l'ontologie grise de Descartes* (1975), *Sur la théologie blanche de Descartes* (1981), and *Sur le prisme métaphysique de Descartes* (1986); and translator (in collaboration with P. Costabel) of *René Descartes, Règles utiles et claires pour la direction de l'esprit dans la recherche de la vérité* (1977).

PETER MARKIE is Professor of Philosophy at the University of Missouri–Columbia and author of *Descartes's Gambit* (1986), and of various articles on Descartes, and on ethics and intentionality.

GENEVIÈVE RODIS-LEWIS is honorary Professor at the University of Paris–Sorbonne, and author of numerous studies including *Nicolas Malebranche* (1963), *L'œuvre de Descartes* (1971), and *L'anthropologie cartésienne* (1990).

AMÉLIE OKSENBERG RORTY is Professor of Philosophy at Mt. Holyoke College. She is the author of *Mind in Action* (1988), editor of *Essays on Descartes' Meditations* (1986), and of *Essays on Aristotle's Ethics* (1980), *Essays on Aristotle's Poetics* (1992), and of numerous essays in the history of seventeenth- and eighteenth-century philosophy.

CHRONOLOGY

ABBREVIATIONS

Throughout this book, references to Descartes' works are made in parentheses in the main body of the text, by page and volume number of the standard Franco-Latin and English editions of Descartes (AT and CSM or CSMK, respectively). For full details of these editions, see the Bibliography, p. 424, below. Section I of the Bibliography also contains full details of other editions (such as Hall and Olscamp), which are occasionally referred to by the editor's name, followed by a page reference. In the case of Descartes' *Principles of Philosophy* and *Passions of the Soul*, references are sometimes given simply by the original part and article numbers (which are reproduced in all editions and translations).

For all other works cited in the Notes at the end of each chapter, full publication details may be found in the Bibliography.

Introduction

Descartes is perhaps the most widely studied of all the great philosophers. Students in countless introductory courses find that their imagination is captured by the lonely quest for knowledge described in Descartes' masterpiece, the *Meditations on First Philosophy*. The radical critique of preconceived opinions or prejudices (*praejudicia*) which begins that work seems to symbolize the very essence of philosophical inquiry. And the task of finding secure foundations for human knowledge, a reliable basis for science and ethics, encapsulates, for many, what makes philosophy worth doing. The excitement felt on first encountering Cartesian philosophy does not diminish as one delves deeper. Descartes' inquiries into the nature and structure of the material universe, his views on human freedom and the existence of God, and his account of the human condition and the relationship between mind and matter, all exert a powerful intellectual pull on us even today. And even when the details of the system are forgotten, Descartes' starting point in the quest for truth, his *Cogito ergo sum* ("I am thinking, therefore I exist") remains the most celebrated philosophical dictum of all time.

But despite the fame of Descartes' system, there is much about the Cartesian project that, from a twentieth-century standpoint, seems radically misguided. Many philosophers working today, whether in the theory of knowledge or the philosophy of mind, would probably define their position as systematically anti-Cartesian. The reasons for this go far beyond the fact that developments in physical science have rendered many of Descartes' scientific results obsolete. It is of course true that his theories of cosmology and astronomy are now little more than historical curiosities; his naively mechanistic account of gravity, for example, has long since been discarded by working scientists. But the philosophical worries about the structure of the Cartesian account of knowledge are of a deeper nature. Some of the worries began to be voiced less than a century after Descartes' death, and one central problem which seems to beset his ambitious program for reaching the truth was aptly summarized by Hume:

much inculcated by Des Cartes as a sovereign preservative against error [is a method proceeding] by a chain of reasoning, deduced from some original principle which cannot possibly be fallacious . . . But neither is there any such original principle, which has a prerogative above all others, . . . [nor] if there were, could we advance a step beyond it, but by the use of those very faculties of which we are already supposed to be diffident.[1]

Descartes enjoined philosophers to sweep all away and make a new start: *omnia semel in vita evertenda atque a primis fundamentis denuo inchoandum* ("Once in a lifetime we must demolish everything completely and start again right from the foundations" AT VII 17: CSM II 12). But Hume, many would now say, rightly exposed the pretensions of reason to reconstruct knowledge from scratch; and in our modern, post-Wittgensteinian world, the lesson seems to have been reinforced: human knowledge can only operate within the socially and linguistically conditioned forms of life we find ourselves inhabiting. Philosophers can no longer hope to step outside the boundaries of history and culture and construct a master language that "limns the ultimate structure of reality."[2]

Revolutions in philosophy, however, are seldom neat and tidy affairs; the true story is not one of unconditional surrenders but of continuing skirmishes, advances, and retreats. In the first place, Descartes' views on philosophy and science are often far more subtle and complex than is assumed by his post-Humean critics; to look at his actual writings on truth and knowledge is to realize that his system is very far from matching the caricature of "rationalist foundationalism" with which it is so often identified.[3] In the second place, we cannot properly comprehend the state of modern philosophy without studying the structures of thought, determined in large part by Descartes' ideas, that have generated the models of knowledge and understanding against which twentieth-century thinkers have reacted. Descartes is still rightly called the father of modern philosophy, not in the sense that our present-day belief systems lamely follow the Cartesian model, but in the richer and more interesting sense that, without

Descartes' philosophy, the very shape of the problems with which we still wrestle, about knowledge and science, subjectivity and reality, matter and consciousness, would have been profoundly different. Descartes' system, and the seventeenth-century philosophical framework in which it arose, richly repay serious study, both for their intrinsic fascination, and also because they mark out the broad territory within which our modern culture developed.

René Descartes was born in 1596 in the small town between Tours and Poitiers (formerly La Haye), which now bears his name. He was educated by the Jesuits at the newly founded college of La Flèche in Anjou, where he remained a boarding pupil for eight or nine years. The exact chronology of Descartes' time at La Flèche has long been the subject of scholarly dispute, and the problems of accurate dating are discussed in detail in Geneviève Rodis-Lewis's reconstruction of Descartes' early life (see Chapter 1). While Descartes' middle and later career is pretty well documented (partly as a result of his voluminous correspondence, much of which has survived), the accounts we have of his early years contain many gaps; we owe many points of interest to his biographer Baillet (whose *Vie de Monsieur Descartes* was published in 1691), although, as Rodis-Lewis demonstrates, Baillet was sometimes prepared to invent what seemed to him plausible details when he found the record incomplete.

At La Flèche Descartes studied classical literature, and traditional classics-based subjects such as history and rhetoric. Later, he took courses in mathematics, moral philosophy, and theology, as well as "natural philosophy," or physical science. Descartes' attitude toward the education he received at La Flèche was an ambivalent one: he later wrote that the college was "one of the best schools in Europe," but that he considered the philosophy he had learned there, "despite being cultivated for many centuries by the best minds, contained no point that was not disputed and hence doubtful" (AT VI 8: CSM I 115). As a mature philosopher, Descartes was to make the replacement of the scholastic philosophy he had imbibed as a schoolboy a major plank in his program for inaugurating a new method in the sciences; but we should be careful not to project back these later aspirations when interpreting Descartes' outlook as a young man. As Rodis-Lewis notes, Descartes' early correspondence shows that he did "recognize the value of the complete course in philosophy which the

Jesuits provided," and the point is reinforced in Roger Ariew's study of the scholastic influences that shaped the intellectual climate in which Descartes grew up (see Chapter 2). To understand Descartes' later outlook, it is important to know something of the principles of scholastic pedagogy in the sixteenth and seventeenth centuries, and Ariew's study sets out its most important elements: the allegiance to Thomist views on theology, and the broad assumption of the correctness of Aristotle's doctrines in the realm of logic, natural philosophy, ethics, and metaphysics. As Ariew shows, the conservatism implicit in the Jesuit educational program nonetheless allowed scope for cautious and subtle modifications of established doctrines in selected areas. As far as his later philosophy is concerned, there is no doubt of Descartes' ambition to develop a system that would avoid conflict with the received faith of the Church by relying only on the most general abstract principles, which, he believed, would command the universal assent of all human beings, irrespective of religious presuppositions: "I have written my philosophy in such a way as to make it acceptable anywhere – even among the Turks" (AT V 159: CSMK 342). These principles might seem to conflict with scholastic doctrines, but Descartes' strategy was a broadly reconciliationist one of emphasizing the points of contact: "as far as principles are concerned, I accept only those which in the past have always been common ground among all philosophers without exception, and which are therefore the most ancient of all" (AT VII 580: CSM II 392).

At the age of twenty-two (after taking a law degree at Poitiers), Descartes set out on a series of travels in Europe, "resolving" (as he later recounted) "to seek no knowledge other than that which could be found either in myself or in the great book of the world" (AT VI 9: CSM I 115). An important influence on Descartes in this early period was his friendship with the Dutchman Isaac Beeckman, who stimulated his lifelong interest in mathematics – a subject in which he discerned precision and certainty of the kind which genuinely deserved to be called *scientia* – reliable and systematic knowledge based on indubitable first principles. A great deal of Descartes' energy as a young man was devoted to pure and applied mathematics, and the first sample of his work, which he finally ventured to publish (anonymously) in 1637, – the collection of three essays prefaced by the *Discourse on the Method* – contained three notable examples of his success: the sine law of refraction (in the *Optics*), the calculation of the angles of the bows of the rainbow (in the *Meteorology*), and the solution of Pappus's problem, in the *Geometry*, (see Stephen Gaukroger's essay, Chapter 3). One of the most important general results to emerge from Descartes' work in these areas was, as Gaukroger shows, the emergence of the idea of a general algebra that would enable abstract relations to be exhibited in a way that was free from specific numerical interpretations. Descartes' achievement here represented, Gaukroger argues, a remarkable and substantial advance on earlier classical conceptions of geometry, which had largely relied on spatial intuitions. The invention of highly abstract structures of thought, neutral with respect to subject matter, is proclaimed by Descartes in his early work, the *Regulae* ("Rules for the Direction of our Native Intelligence"), as the hallmark of his new approach to knowledge:

> I came to see that the exclusive concern of mathematics is with questions of order or method, and that it is irrelevant whether the measure in question involves numbers, shapes, stars, sounds, or any other object whatsoever. This made me realize that there must be a general science which explains all the points that can be raised concerning order and measure irrespective of subject matter.   (AT X 377: CSM I 19)

The conception leads straight on to the famous Cartesian idea of science as the unfolding of abstract mathematical relations, an idea that remains to this day central to what we think of as the scientific enterprise.[4]

In Rule XII of the *Regulae*, Descartes outlined a model for all human knowledge as based, ultimately, on self-evident intuition of what he called the "simple natures." These included not only the "corporeal" natures (such as shape, extension, and motion), which were to be the building blocks for Cartesian physics, but also the "intellectual" natures, which enable us to understand fundamental mentalistic concepts such as those of doubt, knowledge, and volition. In his study of the role played by the simple natures in Descartes' system (see Chapter 4), Jean-Luc Marion argues that what is involved is no mere terminological innovation but an epistemological revolution. Descartes in effect banishes from metaphysics the Aristotelian realm of objective essence and nature (*ousia* and *physis*), which antecedently determines the objects of knowledge,

and substitutes the notion of intuitable objects directly and immediately accessed by the human intellect. It follows that, so far from
being (as is sometimes argued) a preliminary study in "method,"
the *Regulae* is a profoundly metaphysical work, containing (though
not in fully worked out form) all the elements necessary for the
deployment of Descartes' mature metaphysics. What is prefigured
here is a remarkably ambitious conception of the scope of philosophy, inspired by the simplicity and clarity of mathematical reasoning, but ranging far beyond it: "Those long chains of very simple
and easy reasonings, which geometers customarily use to arrive at
their most difficult demonstrations, gave me occasion to suppose
that all the things which come within the scope of human knowledge are interconnected in the same manner" (AT VI 19: CSM I
120). The task of linking together the simple natures in the appropriate way, so as to generate a unified system of reliable knowledge,
was the goal Descartes set himself. And it is a project he envisaged
in a way that was strikingly original in comparison with anything
that had gone before. The key to true knowledge was to be found
not from the deliverances of the senses or the received wisdom of
the past, but by turning inward to the resources of the human mind
itself:

I shall bring to light the true riches of our souls, opening up to each of us the
means whereby we can find, within ourselves, without any help from anyone else, all the knowledge we may need for the conduct of life, and the
means of using it in order to acquire all the most abstruse items of knowledge that human reason is capable of possessing.   (AT X 496: CSM II 400)

Descartes had already begun to work on metaphysics in the late
1620s (see Chapter 1), but it was not until much later that he published any systematic account of his views, first in outline form in
Part IV of the *Discourse* (published in French in 1637), and then in
rich and dramatic detail in his masterwork, the *Meditations on First
Philosophy* (first published in Latin in 1641; the definitive second
edition, with the full set of *Objections and Replies*, was published
in Amsterdam in the following year). Descartes chose the title to
make it clear that "the discussion is not confined to God and the
soul, but treats in general of all the first things to be discovered by
philosophizing" (letter to Mersenne of 11 November 1640). By this
time Descartes had been living in Holland for a considerable period

(though with frequent changes of address), and that country was to remain his home for most of the rest of his life.⁵

The Cartesian program for metaphysics begins with a systematic exercise of doubt, designed to clear out the rubble of preconceived opinions, often based on unreliable sources or unscrutinized presuppositions. The testimony of the senses is challenged, and doubt is then pushed further (by the various phases of the so-called dreaming argument), as the meditator questions the nature and existence of the world around him, and even the fundamental truths of mathematics (how do I know that a deceiving God might not make me go wrong "every time I add two and three or count the sides of a square"). Eventually, by the end of the First Meditation, Descartes conjures up the nightmare scenario of a "malicious demon of the utmost power and cunning" who employs all his energies in order to deceive: "I shall suppose that the sky, the earth, the air, colors, shapes, sounds and all external things are merely the delusions of dreams which he has devised in order to ensnare my judgment" (AT VII 22: CSM II 15). But the torrent of doubt is checked by the rock of certainty encountered at the start of the Second Meditation – the meditator's indubitable knowledge of his own existence as a thinking being: "I am, I exist, is necessarily true whenever it is put forward by me or conceived in my mind." Elsewhere expressed in the famous sentence *je pense, donc je suis*, this is Descartes' "Archimedian point," on which he proposes to build a new and reliable system of knowledge: "observing that this proposition, *I am thinking, therefore I exist*, was so firm and sure that all the most extravagant suppositions of the sceptics were incapable of shaking it, I decided that I could accept it without scruple as the first principle of the philosophy I was seeking" (*Discourse*, Part IV, AT VI 32: CSM I 127).

Descartes' "Cogito" (to use the label by which his first principle of metaphysics has come to be known) appears at first so simple and straightforward as to be entirely unproblematic. Descartes himself, indeed, claimed here to be doing no more than following the self-evident inner "light of reason," which "when it operates on its own is less liable to go wrong than when it anxiously strives to follow numerous different rules, the inventions of human ingenuity and idleness, which serve more to corrupt it than to render it more perfect" (AT X 521: CSM II 415). But despite Descartes' disarming appeals to the self-evident simplicity of the Cogito, its precise logical status, and the exact basis for its supposed indubitability, were subjected to close critical analysis even in his own day; moreover, what Descartes himself said when challenged about his first principle involves an implicit concession that a great deal more is needed in order to explain the basis for its certainty and the role it plays in the subsequent development of the Cartesian system. Perhaps no part of Descartes' philosophy has called forth more rigorous and exhaustive discussion in our own day, and Peter Markie's essay (see Chapter 5) sets out to examine the main interpretative and philosophical issues involved. Among the problems he discusses are the relation between intuition and deduction in Descartes' account of knowledge, the extent to which the allegedly "primary" truth of the Cogito presupposes various kinds of prior knowledge, and the relationship between our knowledge of the Cogito and Descartes' general claims about a class of "clear and distinct perceptions" that command assent. The suggested conclusion is that a defender of Descartes needs to show that the meditator's beliefs about his thought and existence are so well grounded in reason as to be certain; such grounding resists even the most exaggerated reasons for doubt that can be devised.

Once assured of the certainty of his own existence, the Cartesian meditator can proceed to the construction of a system of knowledge, moving 'from the inside outwards.' The crucial first step is to establish the existence of a perfect, nondeceiving God. In a much criticized causal argument, Descartes reasons that the representational content (or "objective reality") of the idea of God, which he finds within him, is so great that it cannot have originated from inside his own (imperfect) mind, but must have been implanted there by an actual perfect being, God (Third Meditation). The proof is later supplemented by a second demonstration (in the Fifth Meditation), that the idea of perfection logically implies existence (the so-called ontological argument). Once the deity's existence has been established, Descartes can proceed to reinstate his belief in the world around him: the strong propensity we have to believe that many of our ideas come from external objects must (since God is no deceiver) be in general terms correct, and hence the external world exists (Sixth Meditation). More important still, the knowledge of God generates a reliable method for the pursuit of truth: although human beings are often prone to error (particularly when they rely on the obscure and confused deliverances of the senses), provided they confine their judgments to the "clear and distinct ideas" God has implanted in each soul, and remember to withhold assent on matters where they do not have clear and distinct cognition, they can construct guaranteed chains of reasoning about the nature of minds and the material world. Genuine science is possible.

The importance of God in Descartes' system of knowledge can thus scarcely be exaggerated. But as Jean-Marie Beyssade argues in his essay on the idea of God (see Chapter 6), there is a paradox at the heart of Cartesian metaphysics. On the one hand, Descartes' whole system of science depends on our assured knowledge of God; on the other hand, the idea of God is explicitly stated by Descartes to be beyond our comprehension. Through a careful critical examination of what Descartes says about the idea of God, and the various versions of the proofs of His existence found in the *Discourse, Meditations* and *Principles of Philosophy,* Beyssade sets out to resolve the paradox. The infinite is indeed, by its very nature, beyond the *comprehension* of finite human minds, but for all that we can achieve genuine *understanding* of it, by a complex movement of thought from one divine attribute to another, which Descartes terms "induction." Further, the unity we experience within our own finite minds provides an analogy by which we can accurately glimpse the complete, perfect, and unitary uncreated thinking substance that is God. As Beyssade acknowledges, the chief problem for Descartes is to show how the (never fully comprehended) idea of God is nonetheless free of vagueness and inconsistency; what emerges is the resolute honesty with which Descartes grasped the problem, and the remarkably subtlety of his attempts to solve it.

The role of God as guarantor of the possibility of genuine human knowledge generates another deep tension in the Cartesian system, which was pointed out in Descartes' own day by Marin Mersenne and Antoine Arnauld, and has come to be known as the problem of the 'Cartesian circle'. If the reliability of the clear and distinct perceptions of the human intellect depends on our knowledge of God, then how can that knowledge be established in the first place? If the answer is that we can prove God's existence from premises we clearly and distinctly perceive, then this seems circular; for how are we entitled, before we are assured of God's existence, to assume that our clear and distinct perceptions are reliable? An enormous contemporary literature offers a plethora of solutions to this problem, but Louis Loeb in his essay on the Cartesian circle (Chapter 7) distinguishes these into two broad types of interpretation: the *epistemic* (according to which Descartes claims to provide a truth rule that gives us good reason not to doubt our clear and distinct perceptions), and the *psychological* (according to which Descartes' arguments are designed to show that it is psychologically impossible for us to doubt such perceptions). Loeb sets out to offer a detailed and carefully qualified version of the psychological interpretation that does justice to the central texts where Descartes discussed the circle problem – texts that provide some of the most complex and philosophically rich argumentation in the entire Cartesian corpus. Loeb's account yields the broader lesson that our understanding of the project of Cartesian epistemology needs to accord a greater place than is often allowed to the psychological role of our cognitive faculties in generating irresistible and unshakeable beliefs. This in a sense narrows the gap between the "rationalist" conception of knowledge often attributed to Descartes, and the "naturalized" epistemology of Hume and the post-Humeans. That said, there remains a crucial divergence, which Loeb hints at at the close of his paper, namely, that for Descartes reason is, par excellence, the generator of irresistible assent, while, for Hume, other aspects of our human nature take over where reason fails. The issue is but one instance of the extent to which Cartesian concerns feed through into central philosophical problems about the validation of human knowledge that are still very much alive today.

Perhaps the best known result to come out of Descartes' metaphysical reflections is his theory of the nature of the mind as a sui-generis substance, whose nature is utterly alien to that of matter. This doctrine (the doctrine of "Cartesian dualism," as it is generally known today) is announced with a flourish of confidence in Part IV of the *Discourse*: "this 'I' by which I am what I am is entirely distinct from the body and could exist without it" (AT VI 33: CSM I 127). The doctrine is markedly out of step with most (though not all[6]) modern approaches to the phenomenon of consciousness, and in Descartes' own day it marked a break with the traditional Aristotelian account of the soul, which resisted the reification of the mental as a separate substance, and tended to treat reason and thought as attributes, grounded (like other functions such as sensation, locomotion, and digestion) in the organic operations of the whole human being. In my essay on Cartesian dualism (see Chapter 8), I outline various types of motivation – theological, metaphysical, and scientific – that appear to have led Descartes to his uncompromising insistence on the incorporeal nature of the thinking self. I suggest that, while Descartes clearly saw his views as serving the cause of religious faith by facilitating belief in personal survival of bodily death, his version of dualism is not, in fact, necessary for that belief, nor does it provide unambiguous support for it. As far as Descartes' purely metaphysical arguments for dualism are concerned, there seems no escaping the conclusion that they are irreparably flawed (for reasons his contemporary critics had no difficulty in exposing). But when Descartes approached the nature of thought and its close concomitant, language, from the standpoint of a scientist concerned as far as possible to reduce complex phenomena to simple descriptions of matter in motion, he deployed quite different arguments to show why semantic and linguistic operations were radically resistant to such physical explanation. Some of these arguments depend on what were (at the time) plausible empirical claims (though they are vulnerable in the light of what is now known about the workings of the nervous system), while others seem to rest on somewhat cavalier pronouncements on the limitations of "mere matter," which are harshly out of tune with the vigorous ambitions of Descartes' reductionistic program for science in general. As for the general status of Descartes' account of the mind, its detractors and defenders alike must admit that it constitutes an awkward lacuna in his organic conception of knowledge as an interconnected system of truths. The unitary metaphor of the "tree of knowledge," with metaphysics as the roots, physics as the trunk, and the practical sciences as the branches (AT IXB 15: CSM I 186), masks the reality of a Cartesian universe containing disparate and incompatible elements – mind and matter – whose operations cannot be brought under a single set of explanatory principles.

Although his views on the nature of the mind led Descartes to posit firm limits to physical science, in all other areas he displayed remarkable confidence in the scope and explanatory power of his scientific program. In 1633 he had ready for publication a treatise on cosmology and physics, *Le Monde* ("The World" or "The Universe"), but he cautiously withdrew the work on hearing of the condemnation of Galileo for advocating the heliocentric hypothesis (which he too supported). But by 1644 Descartes had completed, in Latin, a mammoth exposition of his system, the *Principia Philosophiae* ("Principles of Philosophy"), divided into four parts: Part I dealt with metaphysics, Part II covered the general principles of Cartesian physics, Part III gave a detailed explanation, in accordance with those principles, of the nature and motions of the sun, stars and planets, and Part IV explained the origins of the earth and a wide variety of terrestrial phenomena. Descartes divided each of these parts into a very large number of short "articles," each about a paragraph long, and his hope was that the work would be adopted as a university textbook that would eventually replace the standard scholastic handbooks based on Aristotelian principles. Though Descartes did not see this hope realized, it remains true, as Desmond Clarke observes in his essay on Descartes' philosophy of science and the scientific revolution (see Chapter 9), that Descartes occupies a pivotal role in the transition from the widely accepted scholastic view of science to its complete rejection, and the emergence of what we think of as modern scientific methodology. The transition, as Clarke notes, was neither abrupt nor clear-cut, and there are some aspects of Cartesian science which reveal that its author could not entirely escape the presuppositions embedded in his cultural and intellectual inheritance. But several characteristic elements of a distinctively new approach are manifest. First, there is the "parsimonious" assumption that the size, shape, and motion of small particles of matter would be adequate to explain all physical effects; and second (and closely connected with the first), there is an insistence on jettisoning the traditional apparatus of substantial forms and real qualities as redundant, and amounting to nothing more than pseudoexplanations.

When it came to expounding the precise status of his scientific theories, however, Descartes' position was determined by conflicting aspirations. On the one hand, he was in large measure prepared to adopt what we think of as the modern approach to science – the adoption of hypotheses whose value lay in their providing plausible (in Descartes' case, mechanical) explanations of phenomena, even though their truth could not be demonstrated in any watertight manner. On the other hand, as regards the central principles of his physics, and the metaphysical foundations that lay beneath them, Descartes insisted on altogether more rigorous standards of certainty. Clarke argues that this latter insistence is best seen as a kind of hangover from Descartes' scholastic upbringing, and that his efforts to describe the degree of certainty that resulted from his scientific practice are a "doomed attempt to classify the probability produced by the new scientific method in the language of the scholastics." One moral here is the need to uncover the intellectual background in which Descartes operated, if we are to gain a proper understanding of his actual scientific practice and the (often misleading) way he described that practice.

The moral is underscored in Daniel Garber's essay on Descartes' physics (see Chapter 10), which begins by reminding us that "well into the seventeenth century, throughout Descartes' life, Aristotelian philosophy was very much alive and relatively well." Garber discusses the rationale for Descartes' conception of matter or "body" as extension – a conception that lies at the heart of his physics, and shows how this connects with two important Cartesian doctrines – the impossibility of atoms in the void, and the falsity of scholastic theories of substantial forms. He then proceeds to a detailed analysis of what is perhaps the most fascinating and problematic element in Cartesian physics – the nature of motion. Given that matter consists simply in extension, it follows that the only way bodies can be individuated is by motion (which determines the shape and size of individual particles – *Principles*, Part II, art. 23). But despite the crucial role motion plays in Cartesian science, Descartes vacillated in his accounts of motion, sometimes defining it in a complex way that allowed for a nonarbitrary distinction between motion and rest, and sometimes treating it simply as local motion (movement from place to place). When Descartes came to formulate the laws of motion, his approach greatly influenced the subsequent development of science; particularly important were his principle of conservation (that the quantity of motion, measured as size times speed, is conserved), and what Garber terms the "principle of persistence" (that everything remains in the state it is unless changed by external causes). The first of these principles turned out to be radically wrong in detail, and was later superseded by the modern concept of the conservation of momentum (mass times velocity), but nonetheless, Garber argues, it "defined an important way of thinking about how we do physics." As for the second (which prefigures the Newtonian law of inertia), it marked a clean break with the Aristotelian doctrine that all bodies naturally tend to come to rest.

The most important general feature of Cartesian science was its rejection of occult powers and qualities, and the proclamation of a program for "mathematicizing" physics: "I recognize no matter in corporeal things apart from what the geometers call quantity, and take as the object of their demonstrations, i.e. that to which every kind of division, shape and motion is applicable" (*Principles*, Part II, art. 64). Descartes was not entirely consistent here: he sometimes speaks in a way that suggests that bodies have powers, for example to impart motion, or to resist change in motion. But his considered view seems to have been that the only ultimate cause of all such transactions involving change and motion is God himself. This notion looks forward to the "occasionalism" of Nicolas Malebranche, later in the century; shorn of its theological trappings it forms the basis of the later Humean view that rejects the notion of causal efficacy in objects, and reduces causality to nothing more than a series of constant regularities.[7] Again we see here the pervasive influence of Cartesian ideas on central aspects of subsequent philosophical thought.

Descartes had originally planned to include in his *Principles of Philosophy* a fifth and a sixth part, dealing respectively with plants and animals, and man, and throughout his working life he was concerned to extend his general program for science to the principal manifestations of animal life and the bodily conditions for psychological phenomena such as sense perception and memory. As Gary Hatfield points out in his essay on Descartes' physiology and its relation to his psychology (see Chapter 11), every one of Descartes' major works, both those he published and those printed posthumously, contains some discussion of topics in physiology or in the physiology and psychology of the senses (though the terms "physiology" and "psychology" are themselves problematic, and need to be interpreted with sensitivity to differences between seventeenth-century and modern usage). Descartes' overall aim (a good example is his treatment of the movement of the heart and the circulation of the blood – see *Discourse*, Part IV) was, Hatfield argues, "to mechanize virtually all of the functions that had traditionally been assigned to the vegetative and sensitive souls." The general picture that emerges from Descartes' work is one that has been enormously influential in the development of the modern life sciences: the guiding model is that of an animal machine governed by stimulus–response mechanisms, whose complex behavior is to be explained purely on the basis of the structure and organization of the internal organs.

From a philosophical point of view, the greatest interest in the Cartesian account is how it proposes to tackle the relationship between the physiological workings so described and the mental occurrences in the "rational soul," which is, for Descartes, implanted in each human bodily machine. Hatfield distinguishes two distinct and conflicting aspects of Descartes' approach here: the *interaction conception* (according to which mental events are arbitrarily correlated with bodily events according to the divine will or the "institutions of nature"), and the *inspection conception* (according to which the content of a mental event is determined by the soul's directly "viewing" brain events). As Hatfield shows, the latter conception presented Descartes with serious explanatory problems: though he strove to avoid a naïve picture of the mind scanning little pictures in the brain which resemble external objects, it is not easy to make clear and unambiguous sense of his account of the relationship between, for example, visual sensations and images in the pineal gland (the tiny organ in the brain, which Descartes took to be the principal "seat" of the soul's activities – AT XI 352: CSM I 340). The issue is but one aspect of the intractable problem of the relationship between mind and matter in Descartes' philosophy. One crucial specific difficulty that emerges is a tension between the official Cartesian aim of reducing all animal physiology to "blind" mechanical interactions, and the need, when explaining how these mechanisms conduce to the health and survival of the animal organism, to revert to the Aristotelian notion of "final," or purposive causality. While officially maintaining that "the customary search for final causes is utterly useless in physics" (AT VII 55: CSM II 39), Descartes was compelled to acknowledge, in his physiological writings, that the beneficial functioning of the organism depends on the benevolent ordinances of God in nature, designed to ensure the health and welfare of the living creature. The tension remains in our modern world view, with the still not yet fully resolved issue of whether the teleological and functional language of the biological sciences is ultimately reducible to the mechanical and mathematical descriptions of pure physics.

Some of the problems associated with the relationship between mind and body were examined by Descartes in his last published work *Les Passions de l'âme* ("The Passions of the Soul," 1649), completed shortly before his ill-fated visit to Stockholm at the invitation of Queen Christina of Sweden. Descartes seems to have been restless and unhappy throughout his time in the "land of bears, rocks and ice" (AT V 349: CSMK 375), and the royal command to attend at five in the morning to tutor the Queen in philosophy obliged him to break his lifelong habit of "lying in" late into the morning; this disruption of his sleep patterns, coupled with the rigors of the Swedish winter, led to his catching pneumonia, from which he died on 11 February 1650, just over a month short of his fifty-fourth birthday.

In the *Passions*, Descartes makes the transition from physiology and psychology to ethics, which he envisaged as one of the crowning sciences sprouting from his philosophical system: the achievement of a fulfilled, healthy and satisfying life would be one of the fruits of a correct scientific understanding of the mechanisms of the body and its relation to the mind. The emotions and feelings which arise from the intermingling of mind and body constitute, for Descartes, one of the principal ingredients of the good life, and are responsible for some of the richest and most vivid experiences that humans can enjoy; moreover, by developing habits of thought and behavior whereby the passions can be controlled and appropriately channeled, we can become not the slaves but the masters of our passions, the attainment of which goal is the "chief use of wisdom" (AT XI 488: CSM I 404). Amélie Rorty, in her essay "Descartes on thinking with the body" (see Chapter 12), examines the contribution of bodily based thought both to the development of science itself and to the attainment of a worthwhile life; she uncovers, in the first of these areas, a crucial relationship between what she terms the *information system* (the external sense organs and all the bodily mechanisms involved in presenting perceptual ideas and the properties of physical objects to the mind) and the *maintenance system* (those bodily operations and mechanisms directed toward the survival and healthy maintenance of the body). One important result to come out of this analysis is that bodily sensations play, for Descartes, a vital role in identifying an epistemologically reliable body, and establishing the correlations that enable the body's information system to promote the development of genuine scientific understanding of the world. It is further suggested that, although the information system and the maintenance system are functionally interdependent, the criteria for the soundness of each system are logically distinct, so that we can, without circularity, identify a healthy body independently of the reliability of its information system.

But beyond these epistemological concerns, which demonstrate the intimate links that obtain between Descartes' metaphysical search for truth in the *Meditations* and the physiological and psychological work that occupied his later years, an analysis of the concluding section of the *Passions* uncovers what Descartes took to be the final goal of his system: the expanding (in Rorty's phrase) of medical health to moral soundness. Rorty shows how the habits of thought and feeling involved in the Cartesian virtues of self-respect and *générosité* provide (since divine benevolence underwrites the reliability of what nature teaches us) reliable guides to determine the will toward the good. What is generated here falls far short of a rigorous "geometry of ethics," because metaphysics can provide no ultimate tests for settling value disputes (for example the priority questions that may arise if the goals of high science conflict with the social and moral concerns of the community). But for all that, Descartes' ideas point the way toward a plausible and realistic grounding for ethics, which in turn shows that his aspiration to provide a unified and practically useful scientific system was no empty boast. The program Descartes proudly announced to the public in the final part of the *Discourse* was, as he himself acknowledged, very unlikely to be fully realized in the foreseeable future, but it could nonetheless claim to represent the richest and most exciting conception of what the philosopher–scientist of the new age could hope to achieve:

[Considering] the law which obliges us to do all in our power to secure the general welfare of mankind, my eyes were opened to the possibility of gaining knowledge which would be of great utility for life, and which might replace the speculative philosophy taught in the schools. Through this philosophy we could know the power and action of fire, water, air, the stars, the heavens and all the other bodies in our environment . . . and could use this knowledge . . . to make ourselves, as it were, lords and masters of nature. This is desirable not only for the invention of innumerable devices which would facilitate our enjoyment of the fruits of the earth and all the goods we find there, but also, and most importantly, for the maintenance of health, which is undoubtedly the chief good and the foundation of all the other goods in this life.   (AT VI 62: CSM I 142)

Noble as Descartes' aspirations may have been,[8] the critics of his system swiftly began, during the century following his death, the systematic demolition job that has continued down to the present day. As Nicholas Jolley observes at the start of his essay on the reception of Descartes' philosophy (see Chapter 13), Voltaire's witty and biting verdict on his celebrated compatriot already encapsulated many of the elements that are found today in the still commonly accepted caricature of "Cartesian rationalism." At a more detailed level, vigorous persecution of the "new philosophy" began during Descartes' own lifetime, both in the Protestant Dutch universities and in Catholic-dominated France. Much of the opposition came from a theological quarter, notably on the issue of transubstantiation in the Eucharist, which doctrine, despite Descartes' own efforts to demonstrate the contrary, was widely seen as threatened by the Cartesian account of matter; but as Jolley shows, theological hostility came not just from the Jesuits, whom Descartes had at one time hoped to recruit as supporters of his philosophy, but also from their arch rivals, the Jansenists (despite the sympathy for Cartesianism expressed by their brightest star, Antoine Arnauld). In the realm of science, however, Descartes' ideas proved immensely popular, notwithstanding official bans on its teaching, and a rich variety of philosophical schools, all owing something to Cartesian doctrines, rapidly proliferated. Among the most important of these developments was the occasionalist philosophy propounded, among others, by Arnold Geulincx and Nicolas Malebranche – a philosophy which (as suggested above) paved the way for the systematic Humean critique of traditional accounts of causation. In many quarters, however, there was strong philosophical resistance to Descartes' ideas, most notably from Thomas Hobbes and Pierre Gassendi, both of whom had contributed criticisms of his arguments in the *Objections* published with the *Meditations* in 1641. A third and even more determined critic was Pierre-Daniel Huet, whose *Censura Philosophiae Cartesianae* (1689) had, as Jolley shows, a powerful influence on the way Cartesian ideas were perceived in the closing years of the seventeenth century. The importance of all these developments, from a modern perspective at least, is transcended by the work of the three philosophical giants of the late seventeenth century, Spinoza, Locke, and Leibniz – all in different ways critical of Cartesian assumptions, whether in the areas of science or metaphysics or philosophical method, yet all subtly and pervasively influenced by the structures of thought which Descartes had deployed. The story continues down to the present day. Our modern world view, our conception of the philosophical enterprise, has in many respects developed in ways which Descartes could not for a moment have envisaged; but there remains much that he would recognize, much that he would see as the successful furthering of the program he inaugurated. If there is one lesson that should emerge from this volume, it is the extraordinary range and fertility of Cartesian ideas, extending over the entire field of philosophy, construed in the widest possible sense of that term. The boldly ambitious program, which Descartes described as "an infinite one, beyond the power of a single person" (AT X 157), is one that still arouses conflicting reactions; if we wish to understand the complex and tortuous history of the emergence of the modern age, there can be few more rewarding tasks than attempting to enlarge our grasp of that program, and of the philosophical system that remains its most accomplished embodiment.

NOTES

1 Hume, *Enquiry into the Human Understanding* (1748), Sect. XII, Part 1, pp. 150–1.
2 See R. Rorty, *Philosophy and the Mirror of Nature*, p. 357.
3 For this theme, see Cottingham, "The Cartesian legacy."
4 Though Descartes was prevented, for a number of complex reasons explored in Gaukroger's chapter, from extending the idea to the realm of formal logic.
5 For the reasons for Descartes' long self-imposed exile from his native land, see Chapter 1, p. 36–7.
6 Few modern philosophers have much to say for substantival dualism;

however, for antireductionist tendencies in present-day philosophy of mind that owe at least something to Descartes, see, for example, Nagel, *The View from Nowhere*, and McGinn, *The Subjective View*.

7 The term "Humean" is used here in accordance with what may be termed the "standard" reading of Hume's views on causality. For an alternative interpretation, see Wright, *The Sceptical Realism of David Hume*.

8 For a more sinister side to Descartes' aspirations, as seen from our present-day perspective informed by awareness of the danger posed to the environment by the controlling power of science, see Grene, *Descartes*, ch. 2.

1 Descartes' life and the development of his philosophy

"I resolved one day to . . . use all the powers of my mind in choosing the paths I should follow" (*Discourse* Part I: AT VI 10: CSM I 116). Thus Descartes introduces his account of his celebrated first solitary retreat during the winter of 1619–20. But he goes on to note that he decided to postpone actually embarking on his life's work until he had reached "a more mature age than twenty-three, as [he] then was" (Part II: AT VI 22: CSM I 122). Toward the end of the winter of 1619–20, then, he began to travel, and this occupied "the next nine years"; only after these "nine years" did he finally work out his philosophy, which was to be "more certain than the commonly accepted one" (Part III: AT VI 28, 30: CSM I 125–6). This period of Descartes' early life is obscured by the errors of his chief biographers, which have been repeated down the centuries. There is a marked tendency to bring forward his interest in science and the search for its foundations – an interest which in fact developed gradually and relatively late.

EARLY YEARS

It is to Adrien Baillet's biography that we are indebted for the preservation of many documents which have subsequently been lost.[1] He generally gives details of his sources, and sometimes treats them in a judiciously critical fashion. Unfortunately, however, when he has no access to the facts he simply invents them without warning. Everyone takes it that Descartes' family was an ancient and noble one. Baillet interviewed the philosopher's great nephews, who told him of Pierre Descartes, a soldier and nobleman who had fought in the defense of Poitiers in the sixteenth century. Baillet takes it that

Joachim (father of the philosopher), was this Pierre's son, and that he took up his duties of Counsellor at the Parliament of Brittany in preference to the "idle life" of a nobleman not in military service (*Vie* I 4). Or so Balliet makes bold to assume. But in fact Joachim was the son of a different Pierre Descartes, a doctor, whose tombstone is still to be found in the family home at Chatellerault. For some inexplicable reason Baillet mentions this doctor as belonging to another branch of the family that had fallen on hard times to the extent of being liable to the poll tax imposed on commoners and having to request an exemption.[2]

Joachim Descartes had, in 1589, married Jeanne Brochard, daughter of the lieutenant-general of the garrison of Poitiers. René Descartes was born on 31 March 1596 at his maternal grandmother's home at La Haye in the Touraine. (The town was named La Haye-Descartes in 1801, but since 1967 has been known simple as Descartes; the house of Descartes' birth is now a small museum.) He was baptised on 3 April at St. George's Church, and his godparents had administrative and financial responsibilities that put them in a position to benefit the child's future. The order of *noblesse de robe*, to be fully confirmed, had to be held for at least three generations, and the rank of *chevalerie* was finally granted to the Descartes family only in 1668. (Baillet sought in vain for evidence of the title in earlier generations.) In the course of his detailed research into the marriages of René's brother, sister, half-brother, half-sister, and all their offspring (apart from two in holy orders), Baillet is never taken aback by the absence of anyone of noble and military rank, though he does give details of various offices that were held, some of them quite important ones. The only connection of rank he cites is the marriage of René's sister Jeanne to a knight (the Chevalier du Crévy); the children were to become a baron and a count. Baillet was ignorant of the fact that René, like Joachim's two other sons, took his law degree at Poitiers; and his misunderstanding over the actual rank of the family led him to make various incorrect assumptions about Descartes' relationship with the army (cf. *Vie* I 41).

Like Descartes' niece Catherine (whom he cites as one of his sources), Baillet believed that René was "conceived in Brittany," not knowing that the parents lived at Chatellerault. But at the end of March 1596 his father was indeed at the Parliamentary sitting at Rennes, and earlier his mother would have been able to leave for La

Haye, where she gave birth to all her children. Baillet follows Descartes' widely accepted story that his birth cost his mother her life, and that she died a few days after his birth "from a disease of the lung caused by distress."[3] But in fact she died at La Haye in May of the following year after giving birth to a son who died three days later. René had a nurse, who was to survive him; on his deathbed he sent a message to his brothers to continue her pension. Was he put out to board with this nurse, or did she live at his grandmother's? At all events the young René, "born among the gardens of Touraine" (to Brasset, 23 April 1649: AT V 349) spent the best part of his childhood there, perhaps visiting or being visited by his father from time to time. He probably grew up with his brother Pierre, until the latter's departure for La Flèche at the start of 1604, and his sister Jeanne who stayed on at La Haye until their grandmother's death in 1610. Baillet, thinking that René lived with his father, who was "astounded by the questions the philosopher–infant used to ask him" (*Vie* I 16) has René enter college at the earliest possible moment after Pierre's admission in January 1604. Because of his delicate health he was entrusted to the care of the rector, Father Charlet, "once winter and the Lenten season were over" (*Vie* I 28).

What Baillet was unaware of is that Charlet did not arrive at La Flèche until October 1606; this completely undermines the dates he gives for Descartes' period at La Flèche; namely, Easter 1604 to September 1612. Yet Baillet's dates were accepted by Adam and Tannery in their edition of the correspondence of Descartes and used by Adam throughout the early sections of his biography (AT XII). Adam does not commit himself on the activities Baillet gives to Descartes to occupy the young man from 1612 until his departure to join the army; but suddenly, toward the end of the volume, he provides a note recording the fact that Charlet arrived at La Flèche in 1606 (AT XII 237). He then adds a brief appendix proposing the dates "1606–1614 (or even 1607 to 1615)" (AT XII 565). But the alternative dating added in parenthesis would in fact make a crucial difference to the name of Descartes' philosophy teacher: the system was for a given teacher to keep the same class for the full three-year course. Father Fournet is the name given in Monchamp's *Notes sur Descartes* (Liège, 1913) and this is followed by various editors, generating useless corrections in the Adam–Milhand edition of the correspondence and the revised edition of Adam and Tannery. Yet as early as

1928 Joseph Sirven had shown that the correct answer is Etienne Noël, who taught philosophy for the three academic years 1612–3, 1613–4, 1614–5.[4]

Descartes was later to praise the "equal treatment" which the Jesuits gave their pupils, "hardly making any distinction between the humblest and those of the highest birth" (letter of 12 September 1638: AT II 378). When the boarding accommodation was opened (the pupils had previously stayed in various lodgings) several private rooms were set aside for boys of noble birth, some of whom even had their own valets. Baillet justifies the privilege in Descartes' case by reference to his "fragile health." Father Charlet, he tells us, allowed him to "lie in" every morning, noticing that his mind was "naturally inclined to meditation" (even at this young age!); these "mornings spent in bed" were the "source of the most important philosophical results that his mind produced" (Vie I 28). At all events, the young schoolboy did have the leisure to do a lot of reading outside the classroom, a fact which Baillet promptly underlies (Vie I 20), citing the Discourse as confirmation: with the permission of his teachers he had "gone through all the books" that fell into his hands "concerning the subjects that are considered most abstruse and unusual" (AT VI 5). When Descartes recovered his health, he retained all his life the habit of staying in bed late into the morning "with the windows open." Until the discovery of antibiotics, such measures were the only available treatment for tuberculosis; and in the letter in which Descartes speaks of the "infirmity of the lungs" inherited from his mother, which gave him a "dry cough and a pale complexion," he says the cough lasted "until he was more than twenty years old" (AT IV 221). Had this eventual improvement in his condition not occurred, he would hardly have been allowed to leave for the army.

Baillet is in fact guilty of some misinterpretation on this last point, which he links with the conclusion of Descartes' studies and the disappointing curriculum which is outlined in Part I of the Discourse. There we find a contrast between what Descartes had been promised – a "clear and certain knowledge of all that is useful in life" (AT VI 4: CSM I 113), and his own verdict reflecting his disappointment at not having satisfied his "earnest desire to learn to distinguish the true from the false in order to see clearly into [his] own actions and proceed with confidence in this life" (AT VI 10:

CSM I 115). The historicity of these remarks has been questioned on the grounds that they reflect Descartes' later outlook.[5] Some of the language does indeed presuppose his more mature findings; for example, "I held as *well nigh* false . . ." (AT VI 8) prepares the ground for "I rejected as *absolutely* false (AT VI 31). But in fact when Descartes evokes the goals of his teachers and their shortcomings, the certainty found wanting is less of a theoretical than a practical kind. His weak constitution must frequently have led to a lack of resolve in the young schoolboy, even if he did not actually reach the conclusion, there and then, that one should not tie oneself down by promises,[6] or that the laws of virtue should be defined so as to include firmness of resolve. The critical reflections Descartes developed later, once he had found his true path in the search for truth, reflect the disappointment that made him abandon the study of "letters" (AT VI 9). Baillet talks instead of abandoning "books" (*Vie* I 34) – an apt change that implies a rejection of false science as well as literature. But the *Discourse* makes only the briefest of references to the underlying aspiration to achieve "glory" (AT VI 9), an aspiration he genuinely felt and which he contrasts with the "profession" he was expected to follow to gain "honor" or "riches" (ibid). And it is glory, at the end of Descartes' life, that is the goal of the "Volunteers" who appear in the ballet *The Birth of Peace.*[7]

The connection between the teaching of history that stresses noble deeds, and the "excesses of the knights-errant in our tales of chivalry" (AT VI 7) explains the attraction the young Descartes felt for the army. He was later, long after his health had recovered, to confess the "hot bile which had earlier drawn [him] to deeds of arms" (letter to Mersenne, 9 January 1639: AT II 480); Baillet stresses this in several places (*Vie* I 41, 51). But he muddles the chronology when he frequently reminds us that Descartes was a "spectator more than an actor" – a phrase Descartes himself connects with his travels after the decisive winter of 1619–20 (*Discourse* Part III: AT VI 28). Baillet takes it that Descartes' father was a soldier and a nobleman and that the young man was destined by his parentage to follow "the service of the King and the State in a military career" (*Vie* I 35, 39, 40, 219). In reality, Descartes' youth was colored by an ideal of what the culture of the time termed "generosity of spirit" (*la génerosité*) – an ideal that inspired him long before he succeeded, in his last work, in providing a philosophical foundation for this major virtue. Having learnt about the exploits of the heroes of history during his two years of study in the "humanities," Descartes came to love "oratory" and, still more "poetry" – such gifts as come from "inspiration rather than set rules" (AT VI 7). He reached the class in which poetry was taught just when the anniversary of Henry IV's death was being celebrated with various ceremonies and a grand anthology of poems (mostly in Latin). It has been suggested that Descartes may have written the sonnet (in French) hailing Galileo's discovery of the moons of Jupiter (which "brightened the gloom of the King's death . . ."). At all events, the students were taught about the new discoveries due to the development of the telescope – though without the problem of the heliocentric hypothesis being raised (the sonnet speaks of the sun circling the earth).[8]

The ideal of "generosity" also accounts for Descartes' interest in higher mathematics founded on algebra and geometry, detached as it was from the various applications of the subject taught in the general classroom. In his first essay, the *Compendium Musicae,* or "Summary of Music," written in Latin, and dealing with the mathematical ratios involved in harmony, he chose, as it were, the most disinterested application of mathematics that was available. Baillet makes a further error here when he connects with Descartes' childhood a remark that in fact relates to a much later phase: He could have been a craftsman, we are told, since "he had always had a strong inclination for the arts" (*Vie* I 35: "arts" here has the sense of "technical skills"). The philosopher's surprise that "nothing more exalted had been built on such firm and solid [mathematical] foundations" (AT VI 7) records an attitude that had long since been left behind when Descartes wrote the eulogy to technical skills in Part VI of the *Discourse,* and observed that in order to reach knowledge of practical utility in life, one must leave behind the "speculative philosophy taught in the schools," and establish a new philosophy modeled on mathematical demonstrations (AT VI 61). While he was still at college, by contrast, Descartes tells us, he "did not yet realize the true use of mathematics" (AT VI 7). It was during the few weeks they spent together in 1618 that Beeckman first interested Descartes in questions of mechanics and hydraulics, and weaned him away from his mathematical purism (and his lack of interest in empirical observation). Nonetheless, the first letter Descartes wrote on his return to Middelbourg still preserves a contrast between Beeckman's elevated studies and the applied subjects which he was then working on (perspective, and the techniques of fortification), and which he thought his friend would despise from the "exalted firmament of the sciences' (*ex edito scientiarum caelo*, 24 January 1619: AT X 151–2). During the later disputes with Beeckman, however, Descartes was to pour scorn on his "mathematico-physics" (*Mathematico-Physica*, AT I 164). Whether or not it was Beeckman who revealed to Descartes the "true use" of mathematics, there is no reference to him in the *Discourse*.[9]

Mathematics was taught in the second year of the philosophy course at La Flèche. If we follow Baillet's dates, Descartes would have completed the course in 1612, and would not have studied under the specialist teacher of mathematics, Jean François, who arrived at the college at the start of the academic year, 1612–13.[10] François published (after Descartes' death) works on arithmetic and geometry geared toward practical subjects – surveying and hydrography, and designed to expose the "superstitions of astrology."[11] It was he who must have lent Descartes, for his morning study-sessions in bed, various works of "obtuse sciences," while warning him against those that were "full of superstition and falsehood" (AT VI 5–6). Above all, recognizing his exceptional gifts, he invited him to join the higher mathematics course he gave to those future Jesuits destined to specialize in teaching mathematics. Descartes, who had no such vocation, later recalled the verdict then passed on his aptitude: "I knew how the others judged me, and I saw that they did not regard me as inferior to my fellow students, even though several of them were already destined to take the place of my teachers" (AT VI 5: CSM I 113).

As for moral philosophy, which was taught in the third year of the philosophy curriculum, and often entrusted to another teacher with a more literary background, Descartes' course of instruction had an anti-Stoic orientation (as was increasingly common at the time); hence his later condemnation of "insensibility" (the Stoic virtue of *apatheia*), "pride," "despair" (e.g. the suicide of Cato) and "murder" (*parricide:* the case of Brutus) (AT VI 8: CSM I 114). The final course in theology was reserved for those with a special vocation. For Descartes, heaven could be obtained even by the most ignorant (AT VI 6), and he later came to make a careful distinction between reason and faith, preserving the distinction even when he acknowledged that faith is needed to complete the demonstration of immortality, or when he employs reason to discuss various aspects of transubstantiation, while insisting on the "mystery" involved (letter to Mesland, 9 February 1645).

This separation of reason and faith enabled Descartes to reject the whole of scholastic "philosophy" together with the other sciences whose "principles" depended on it (AT VI 8–9). With heavy irony he recalls in the *Discourse* the claims made for that philosophy: "it gives us the means of speaking plausibly about any subject and of winning the admiration of the less learned" (AT VI 6). When he rejects as "well nigh false" everything that is merely probable (a formulation that prepares the way for hyperbolical doubt), there is an echo of the start of Rule 2 of the *Regulae*, which contrasts the certainty of mathematical demonstrations with the "disputes" resolved only by appeals to authority. Opinions formed on this latter basis can be wholly false (AT X 362). Nonetheless, Descartes did recognize the value of the complete course in philosophy which the Jesuits provided (letter of 12 September 1638: AT II 378); and when the *Discourse* and *Essays* appeared in 1637, he immediately (14 June) sent a copy to Father Etienne Noël, to be passed on to his less busy colleagues (Vatier, Fournier, Mesland). Noël was then rector of La Flèche.[12]

In the *Discourse* Descartes mentions not just philosophy but "jurisprudence and medicine" (AT VI 6). Here he is in fact recalling the "riches" that had enabled his father, a doctor's son, to attain the "honor" of being a parliamentary counsellor. But there is no need to suppose as Adam does (AT XII 39) that René might have extended his stay at La Flèche to start these two subjects, or even that he took both subjects while he was at Poitiers (AT XII 40). Gilson, rejecting the first suggestion, finds the second "obviously correct"[13]; and even Sirven, who reduces the stay at Poitiers to one year, states that "it is natural to suppose that Descartes supplemented his legal studies with some courses on medicine."[14] But when Descartes met Beeckman in 1618 (the latter having just received his doctorate in medicine), there is no hint that medicine figured in their discussions. Descartes began studying anatomy only in 1629, and a full development of his interests in this field was to await the securing of the foundation of science, of which medicine is one of the most useful skills (*Discourse*, Part VI: AT VI 62), or one of the branches of the tree of philosophy (Preface to the French edition of the *Principles: AT* IXB 14: CSM I 186). To follow Baillet in bringing Descartes' interest in medicine forward to the late 1610s is to risk reviving the old slander that he was a secret Rosicrucian; yet although he might have been keen to meet the Rosicrucians as early as 1619, to see "if they had any new knowledge worth acquiring," he affirms that he never in fact knew anything of them.[15]

The fabrications of Baillet to fill the time between 1612 and 1617 are even more incongruous. Baillet supposes Descartes was at Paris where he would have worked with Mersenne and the great specialist in optics, Mydorge; this happened only after his return from Italy in 1625, or perhaps shortly before his departure in 1623. Although we do not know exactly when Descartes' interest in optics began, Baillet is surely wrong in depicting the young man as fully devoted to science to the point where he had to avoid those who would interrupt his research.[16]

TRAVELS, MILITARY CAREER, EARLY PHILOSOPHY

Baillet produces an elaborate explanation for Descartes' choice to serve, not in the royal army, but with the forces of Prince Maurice of Nassau (*Vie* I 39–40). His general line is that Descartes "became a soldier only to study the customs of men" (*Vie* I 41). He refers to a much later letter in which Descartes talks of "those who regard a soldier's career as the noblest of all" but records his own view "as a philosopher" that "he can hardly accord it a place among the honorable professions, seeing that most young men today are attracted to it principally because of the opportunities for idleness and licence that it affords" (AT V 557). It may be that Descartes' disappointment with the soldier's life came early on, and was all the more acute because of his initial enthusiasm. When he met Beeckman accidentally on 10 November 1618, he thanked him for rescuing him from idleness and recalling his straying mind to serious thought (23 April 1619: AT X 162–3). Descartes was then beginning to learn Flemish (AT X 152) but would have questioned Beeckman in Latin. In his *Journal*, Beeckman mentions first "the man from Poitou" (*le Poitevin*), then "René le Poitevin," then finally "René Descartes" – sometimes adding "*du Perron*" (the name of a large farm Descartes had inherited from his mother and which he was to sell before his departure for Italy).[17]

Beeckman may have given Descartes the "Register," a small note-
book bound in parchment, to record his thoughts on scientific matters, as Beeckman himself had done in his *Journal*. The section
containing these reflections was entitled "Parnassus." Leibniz later
recopied some of these notes together with other reflections from
various other sections headed "Praeambula" ("Preliminaries").[18]
From the inventory found after Descartes' death at Stockholm (AT
X 8) and Baillet's comments (*Vie* I 51), we know that the motto
"The fear of God is the beginning of wisdom" followed the title
"Praeambula." Preparing to enter the stage (of the learned world),
Descartes comes forward "masked" (*larvatus prodeo*) as a simple
soldier.[19] After some initial personal reflections, the section called
Experimenta collects together various concrete observations, espe-
cially on the passions.[20] There then follows a reference to the famous dream of November 1619. We know from the *Discourse* that
Descartes was present at the "coronation of the Emperor" (Part II:
AT VI 11), and then found a quiet lodging where he had "ample
leisure" for reflection, "shut up in a stove-heated room" (*poêle*,
ibid).[21] Baillet, in the *Synopsis* of his *Vie de Descartes*, published in
1692, says, without giving his sources, that this winter retreat was
spent in Neuburg-on-Danube; this was a small independent princi-
pality allied to the dukedom of Bavaria, whose ruler was the new
Emperor.[22]

Descartes had promised Beeckman that as soon as he had the
leisure he hoped that he would finish the Mechanics and Geometry
of which he regarded Beeckman as the "original author" (23 April:
AT X 162). What we can reconstruct of the "marvelous discovery"
that filled Descartes with "enthusiasm" before his dreams on the
night of 10–11 November 1619, allows us to infer that geometry, and
its application to mathematics, played a central role. As early as 26
March 1619 (AT X 158) Descartes was working on various problems
leading to the technique for expressing equations by curves, a result
which "left almost nothing further to be discovered in Geometry."
The task was, however, a vast one beyond the capacity of any single
man (*nec unius*). In outlining his incredibly ambitious goal, Descartes says "I noticed amid the chaos of this science, a certain light
with the help of which I think I can disperse the thickest darkness."
Chanut's final epitaph gives an echo of this early confidence: the
young man (*adolescens*) "on his way to the army/ amid the calm of

winter/ combining nature's mysteries with the laws of *mathesis/*, dared to hope/, with one single key, to unlock the secrets of both." (AT XII 391). Such was the "enthusiasm" that preceded the turbulent night of 10–11 November.[23]

It is most unfortunate that Leibniz, who later criticized Baillet's misinterpretation of Descartes' "enthusiasm," did not copy the original account.[24] What Baillet provides is very far from an exact translation of Descartes' original Latin. And his introduction confirms how far he fails to grasp that what happened to Descartes was a revelation of the path he should follow. He talks of the "decision to get rid of preconceived opinions," taken at college and strengthened during an (invented) "retreat" taken during a first visit to Paris. He insists on Descartes' difficulty in "escaping oneself," driven on by the love of truth "whose pursuit would be his lifelong preoccupation" and he concludes: "he became so fatigued that a fire gripped his brain and he fell into a state of inspired excitement (*enthousiasme*) that took such a hold on his exhausted mind that he was a prey to dreams and visions" (*Vie* I 80–1: AT X 181).

These "visions" were in fact ordinary sleeping dreams – albeit the first began with a nightmare of "phantoms" (*fantômes*). In my *L'Oeuvre de Descartes*,[25] I have proposed that the "melon" offered him by a stranger is a symbol of the world "in a ball" – a conception he spoke of much later to Chanut (1 February 1647: AT IV 609). Some lines earlier mention is made of the extravagant wish to become like the Gods in our knowledge – the temptation in the Garden of Eden. Descartes was assailed "by an evil spirit" (*malo spiritu*), and soon awoke with a sharp pain in his left side.[26] In the last, calmer, dream, various books appeared and disappeared. First was an *Encyclopedia* (this appears in a fragment cited by Father Poisson in connection with the interconnection of the sciences (AT X 225) and is incorrectly translated by Baillet as "Dictionary"); it is then replaced by an *Anthology* of Latin poets, opened at the poem by Ausonius beginning "What road in life shall I follow?" The only reference to this in the *Discourse*, just before the description of his winter of solitude, is Descartes' remark that he "resolved one day to . . . choose the paths [he] should follow" (AT VI 10). This is picked up later, at the end of the moral code in Part III: "I thought I could do no better than . . . devote all my life to cultivating my reason and advancing as far as I could in the knowledge of the truth" (AT VI 27:

CSM I 124). God alone possesses infinitely perfect, infinitely complete knowledge; the human "encyclopedia" must progress by linking the sciences together (AT X 225).

At the end of the last dream (and Descartes begins interpreting it before he is fully awake), the encyclopedia reappears, incomplete: before he has mastered the working of the sciences, man must progress slowly. Right up to his last letter to Elizabeth, Descartes will aim at "advancing in the search for truth, which is my principal good in this life" (9 October 1649: AT V 430). The *Discourse* implies that the development of Descartes' method started during the winter retreat, and the end of Part III presents it as the conclusion of his early progress toward the truth (AT VI 27); but the condensation into four maxims must surely belong to a later period.[27] As for the "treatise" that Descartes began soon after his night of dreams, its subject cannot be known. Baillet gives 23 February (1620) as the date of a promise to finish it "before Easter" (*Vie* I 86), and also mentions a separate vow to go to Loretto to give thanks to the Virgin.[28] But Foucher de Careil, editor of the *Cogitationes Privatae*, gives the date as 23 September, and does not separate the two promises. The latter date is much more likely: Descartes says that he began his travels when the winter was scarcely over (AT VI 28) and we do not know where he went in the spring of 1620, after his winter residence at Neuburg. Did he use his soldier's uniform "as a passport," as Baillet suggests (*Vie* I 99)?[29] Borel has Descartes go to the battle of the White Mountain; Lipstorp resists this suggestion, thus avoiding having Descartes take part in the victory of the Catholic army, which cost Princess Elizabeth's father the throne of Bohemia. Baillet, in turn, attacks Borel's inventions, and notes that Descartes could not have seen Tycho Brache's instruments at Prague, because they were no longer there (*Vie* I 74). But he does have Descartes follow the Emperors' army as far as Pressburg and the siege of Neuhausel – "an episode so grim that witnessing it made him wholly sick of the military life" (*Vie* I 97).

If we may pass over these shadowy episodes, it seems at all events that Descartes did make a promise, on the 23 September 1620, to visit Loretto before the end of November to give thanks for his dreams of 1619. He also proposed to finish his "treatise" by Easter 1621, this giving himself time for further travels. But none of this throws much light on the 'discovery' of November 1620, which is referred to in the early notebooks. It must have been made in a place that provided as much tranquillity as the retreat of the previous winter (which excludes Prague, where the battle of the White Mountain took place on 8 November, followed by a week of pillaging). The "discovery" must presumably have been related to the treatise Descartes was working on. A possible answer is that it dealt with algebra, and that the manuscript was destroyed after Descartes incorporated some of its results into a more complete work – the *Geometry*. We may also ask when Descartes began writing his (never to be finished) *Regulae*, which he undoubtedly continued to work on until his departure for Holland in 1628, and which aimed to "investigate every truth for the knowledge of which human reason is adequate" (AT X 395). Certainly some of these inquiries were begun at an earlier period, though it is going too far to try to fix all the details.[30] Apart from the title which refers to the "search for truth," we can find several elements that seem to reflect the ideal of the unification of the sciences which Descartes had glimpsed in his state of "enthusiasm" in November 1619. The *mathesis* referred to in Chanut's epitaph is one such prominent feature.[31] And the first rule corresponds aptly with Descartes' early reflections on the linking of the sciences by a simple inquirer using the natural light of "good sense."[32] Moreover, so far from aspiring to a God-like state, the *Regulae* defines *sapientia* (which denotes both wisdom and science) as something strictly "human" (AT X 359–61).[33]

Among the works now lost, Baillet also mentions a small "Treatise on Fencing" (*Traité d'Escrime*), which he assigns (far too early) to the period following Descartes' last year at La Flèche (incorrectly dated 1612), when the young man had been occupied with "military matters" (*Vie* I 35) before going to Paris. The duel Descartes fought, showing mercy to his disarmed opponent, is assigned to a period after 1621 when Descartes was indeed in Paris (*Vie* II 501).[34] But from March 1623 to May 1625, Descartes was traveling in Italy, a journey for which Baillet provides a detailed itinerary (*Vie* I 117–28). Baillet is aware (from a letter to Mersenne of 11 October 1638) that Descartes "never saw" Galileo, and he adds "we do not know what accident prevented the encounter from taking place" (*Vie* I 123). Whether Descartes went to Loretto, as he had earlier intended, cannot be known. But he did complain of the heat at Rome, despite the fountains (to Balzac 5 May 1631: AT I 204), and was later to describe an avalanche he had seen on his return via the Alps (*Meteorology:* AT VI 316, 320–1).

Descartes' desire to "acquire some experience of the world" as Baillet puts it, was one he had renounced by 1630 when he was invited to go to Constantinople with the French ambassador (to Mersenne, 4 November: AT I 173–4). After his return from Italy he quickly became famous, although we do not know exactly when he became involved with Mersenne's circle.[35] According to Baillet, Descartes would have been deeply affected by the death of Bacon in 1626; earlier in the biography he tells us that "the Chancellor Bacon had already established the foundations of a new philosophy," and he goes on to mention Clavius, Viète, Tycho Brahe, Kepler, Stevin, and the "emerging Galileo" (*Vie* I 10, 11). Echoes of Bacon (and Kepler) may be found in the *Regulae*,[36] and Descartes drew up a list of qualities "taken from Bacon" in 1630, (*tiré de Verulamio;* letter to Mersenne of January 1630: AT I 109), as well as praising his method in several places (AT I 195, 251). In his works, Descartes seldom mentions the names of other writers, but he does refer to Gilbert's work on magnetism (*Regulae* AT X 431; the latter's *De Magnete* had appeared in London in 1600). As for the research into refraction, discussed in Rule VIII, Leibniz later frequently accused Descartes of having borrowed his results from Snell, whose discoveries date from the same period. But Beeckman, whom Descartes visited in Dordrecht on 8 October 1628, testifies that Descartes had already defined the angle of refraction by means of a hyperbola (AT X 335–7).

Beeckman's *Journal* allows us, incidentally, to nail another of Baillet's errors. Baillet reports that after the ceasefire at La Rochelle on 3 October 1628 Descartes visited the English fleet, and then in November returned to Paris where he made a great impression at the papal Nuncio's residence at a meeting at which Cardinal Bérulle was present. The cardinal saw him in private and "laid on him a duty of conscience to consecrate his whole life to his philosophical studies" (*Vie* I 166). The dates of the meeting between Descartes and Bérulle, and Descartes' participation (or presence) at the siege of La Rochelle are matters that remain obscured by the conflicting reports of the biographers. Borel cites his informant, Villebressieu, as reporting that he accompanied Descartes to La Rochelle, where the art of fortification had reached a pinnacle. Perhaps the engineer's enthusiasm in describing his own visit, in the summer of 1628, was so catching that Borel could not resist sending Descartes to the siege itself; but we know from Beeckman's *Journal* that Descartes was in Holland from the autumn of 1628 onward and so can hardly have been present at the siege (cf. AT XII 99).

As for the meeting at the papal Nuncio's, Descartes mentions it in a letter to the aforementioned Villebressieu written in the summer of 1631, which describes the power of "good reasoning" from principles that are "better established and more natural than those of anyone else" (AT I 213). The conclusion of the letter refers, like the end of Part III of the *Discourse*, to the urging of his friends that he should devote himself to "seeking the foundations of a more certain philosophy than the one commonly practised" (cf. AT VI 30). In rejecting skeptical doubt,[37] and talking of "digging down to the bedrock" (AT VI 29) Descartes would, after his meeting with Bérulle, have sought "reasons for doubting many things which others regarded as certain" (AT VI 30): this would include mathematics, which his new metaphysics would make subordinate to God. But when did he conceive of this (more radical) project? On his return from Italy he must (in April 1625) have heard the reported last words of his former commander, Maurice of Nassau: Asked about his faith, he had replied "I believe that two and two make four."[38] In the *Regulae* we find a similar affirmation of the specially privileged certainty of mathematics, which Descartes' more radical metaphysics was shortly to question. Baillet tells us that in the summer of 1628 Descartes "wanted to write on matters concerning God" (*Vie* I 157, 170–1). Before setting up in Holland he passed a final winter in France, in the countryside, to enable him to concentrate in the perfect solitude he needed from time to time.[39] It is highly unlikely that Descartes went to see Beeckman, to make plans for a prolonged stay in Holland, *before* the decisive meeting at the papal Nuncio's. But if we bring forward the date of the latter meeting to November 1627, instead of 1628, everything falls into place – the winter in the French countryside, and the plan to write on "matters concerning God."

MOVE TO HOLLAND: *THE WORLD*, THE *DISCOURSE*, AND THE *MEDITATIONS*

The plan to write about God was one Descartes had communicated to the Oratorian, Gibieuf, who had promised to correct the work.

Descartes wrote to him on 18 July 1629 that he had not yet started it (AT I 17); but by the following year he reported that he had "begun it . . . in Frisia" (letter to Mersenne 15 April 1630: AT I 144). On 26 April 1629 he enrolled at the University of Franeker (north of the Zuydersee): "*René Des Cartes, Français, philosophe*" (his concept of "philosophy" now included both metaphysics and the explanation of the whole of nature). Apart from an interruption of "more than two months" before 8 October 1629 (when he renewed contact with Mersenne: AT I 23) he reported that he had devoted the "first nine months" of his time in Holland to the project (AT I 144). He let Beeckman believe that he was returning to Paris, and remained in the secrecy of his perfect solitude in which he worked out the subordination of the Cogito to God. To begin the task of writing, he chose a remote university where he would find the books he needed (he had left France with just the Bible and Aquinas). For relaxation he intended to pursue his research on optics, and it was the brother of Metius, professor of mathematics at Franeker, who is referred to at the start of the optics as having developed a magnifying lens. Descartes' first letter from this period is addressed to a craftsman, Ferrier, whom he invited to share his life "as a brother" (18 June 1629; AT I 14). Ferrier never came, but Descartes was probably still at Franeker when he wrote to Gibieuf in July. Soon afterward, however, he learnt of the observation of the parhelia, which had been made at Rome that spring; and he abandoned his metaphysical inquiries that had proved the "existence of God and of our souls when they are separate from our bodies – from which their immortality follows."[40] In Descartes' eyes, the distinction he had shown between two types of substance, thought and extended matter, was quite enough to establish "the foundations of physics" (letter to Mersenne, 15 April 1630: AT I 144: CSMK 22).

Shortly afterward Descartes moved to Amsterdam to enable him to keep in closer contact with the learned world and to gain a richer store of observations and experiments (some reported by incoming sailors whom he questioned at the docks). He remained there for several years, welcoming the "fruits" of a country "at peace," and the discrete manners of the population, among whom he could "lead a life as solitary and withdrawn as if [he] were in the most remote desert"[41] "In what other country could he enjoy such complete freedom?"[42] The motive for Descartes' choice had nothing to do with the restrictions of the Catholic Church on freedom of thought. Mersenne and Gassendi defended the new physics in France without being persecuted; and Descartes was to find himself subject to far greater attacks from the Calvinists in the Netherlands for his metaphysical system and his "papism." Throughout his life he was a practicing Roman Catholic.[43] Although he spent long periods in solitary concentration, he had several real friends like Huygens and Pollot, to whom he wrote letters of condolence which assert that philosophy must be supplemented by faith: "There is nothing in either reason or religion which should make those who have lived an honorable life fear any ill after this life."[44]

One of Descartes' chief friends was Plemp, a Catholic and a medical man, who introduced him to anatomy and the techniques of dissection.[45] As for his interest in parhelia, Descartes proceeded without delay to make a "systematic study of the whole of meteorology," including the "colors of the rainbow."[46] Before long he was investigating "all the phenomena of nature, that is all of physics" (13 November 1629: AT I 70).[47] On 18 December 1629, he announced that he was to "begin studying anatomy" (AT I 102), and asked Mersenne if the demands of faith and religion placed any restrictions on "the extension of created things" (AT I 80). To avoid all controversy with a theology that was excessively committed to the closed universe of Aristotle (ibid. 85), he set about describing, in an unlimited "imaginary" space, a "new world" that developed out of chaos (*Discourse* Part V: AT VI 42, 45). The idea of this "fable" gave him great delight, and he hoped to live long enough to complete the project (25 November 1630: AT I 179). From the start he planned to include physiology in the system; after concluding that his own account of the universe matched the "real world" (AT XI 63), he decided to leave a space for the transition from cosmology to physiology and provide an account of the human body as a ready-made machine.[48] But he thought it should be possible to "demonstrate effects from their causes" (AT VI 45) and apply to all possible worlds the "laws of nature," which have as their "principle" the "perfections of God" (ibid. 43).

To specify the laws of movement (*Le Monde*, chs. 6–7) Descartes had to have recourse to "several metaphysical questions" (15 April 1630: AT I 145). In an extended plenum, movement requires the action of the Creator that is unique and, for us, continuous in time;

the laws of mathematics, which make such action intelligible, were created simultaneously with the intellectual natures.[49] In virtue of divine action, movement occurs indefinitely along a straight line (the principle of inertia); but in the plenum this will generate vortices and various elements differentiated by the "subtle matter" impelled through all the interstices of matter.

At the end of 1630 Descartes had given up his plan of going to England (2 December: AT I 191). A later letter of 11 June 1640 confirms that he would have liked to go, but in spite of the subsequent invitations of his English friends, Digby and Newcastle (the brother of Cavendish), he never made the trip. In 1631 Villebressieu probably took him on a brief visit to Denmark. When they were both staying at Amsterdam, the engineer told Descartes of his discoveries, and Descartes urged him to put them to practical use: the "mobile chair" would be "very useful, especially for wounded soldiers." Descartes himself toyed with optical illusions, including a system of mirrors that made a whole army pass before his friend's eyes, inside his room (Baillet, Vie 258–9). The Meteorology opens by referring to various extraordinary phenomena of this kind, able to be explained by science; and the Search for Truth announces the grand project of astonishing the world by uncovering the secrets of "the most impressive illusions and subtle tricks that human ingenuity can devise" (AT X 505: CSM II 405). But the dialogue, possibly a late work, was never completed.

From time to time Descartes laid aside his World to pursue other research. At the end of 1629 he joined Golius, who was professor of mathematics, at the University of Leiden; he himself enrolled as a "mathematician" on 27 June 1630. At the end of 1631 Golius put to him the problem of Pappus, unsolved since classical times: squares and cubes could be matched to equations of the second and third degree, but no such equations could be found for "sursolids" (solids of revolution). Descartes succeeded in matching curves to equations of all degrees, and sent his solution (found in "five or six weeks": AT I 244) to Golius in January 1632 (AT I 235). He also enclosed the first part of his Optics, on refraction, a project that had been outlined earlier, in a letter to Mersenne, of 25 November 1630: the relevant section, containing the mathematical description of a curve, would be completed in advance of an account of "the nature of colors and light," which would "contain as it were a complete physics" (AT I

178–9). The same letter speaks of "looking for practical results in medicine" after he had completed the "Treatise," which would be called *Du Monde ou de la Lumière*. Subsequent work on this treatise included an account of astronomy and a description of all particular bodies (5 April 1632: AT I 243); but he needed more time (3 May: AT I 248). On 10 May he asked for details regarding comets (AT I 250–1), which were to be the subject of the last chapter before the break in the work. Descartes found he was unable to make the mechanical generation of living creatures follow smoothly on from that of inert bodies; he wrote on 10 May that he was trying to make the transition, and in June, that he was wondering if he could include it in the full treatise. But during the summer he decided to rest content with an account of the principal function of man in his finished state (AT I 263). But in the same letter in which he reckoned he would soon be ready to send the whole work to Mersenne (AT I 270), he reports having heard that Galileo's *Sistemi del mondo* had been banned at Rome. Although he knew that this condemnation lacked any scientific warrant, his desire to avoid all controversy led him to postpone his own plans for publication. But later, in the *Discourse* (Part V), he outlined the contents of his book and provided an example of its philosophical findings (the circulation of the blood), hoping to generate a demand for publication and perhaps even get the ban modified. Although his scientific method was not to be fully unfolded in the *Discourse*, but was concentrated instead into four rules (a mere "part of my method", AT I 339), Descartes had, virtually ready for publication, three *Essays* that would serve to illustrate the method's richness – the *Optics, Meteorology,* and *Geometry*.[50]

The *Discourse* was planned as a "preface" to the essays, and took two or three months to write. The idea of such a preface appears in a letter of November 1635 to Huygens, who was advising Descartes about his plans to publish. The preface would take the form of a "history of [his] mind" or intellectual biography – a project Descartes had already discussed with his friends in Paris (cf. letter from Balzac to Descartes of 30 March 1628: AT I 570). In the rather grand title he proposed to Mersenne in March 1636, Descartes highlighted, apart from the method, the proofs of "the existence of God and of the soul when separated from the body" (AT I 339); but in spite of this, he later claimed that the fourth, metaphysical, section of the work was written very quickly and at the last moment (letter to Vatier 22

February 1638: AT I 560). Descartes wrote the *Discourse* in a small isolated house near Utrecht. Reneri had been appointed professor of philosophy (i.e. physics) at the university there in 1635, and Descartes had already accompanied him to Deventer in 1632. When he chose J. Maire of Leiden as his publisher, Descartes moved there to supervise the printing of the diagrams (which were entrusted to the young Schooten, future translator of the *Geometry* into Latin). The "Privilege," or licence to publish, which Mersenne was trying to obtain in France had still not arrived; Descartes was later to shorten it, finding it too laudatory, and he eventually released his first publication anonymously. We have a letter of condolence to Huygens, who had lost his wife, sent from Alkmaar on 20 May 1637; but Descartes cannot have stayed there long, because in June he was in Leiden for the printing of the shortened version of the Privilege, and to dispatch copies of the book. He sent one to the Prince of Orange via Huygens, who was a diplomat, and one to the French ambassador for Louis XIII and Richelieu.

In October 1637 Descartes completed for Huygens a long description of various *"engins"*, mechanical devices such as the pulley, the lever, and so on. (AT I 431–47); this was posthumously published as Descartes *Mechanics* (*Mécanique*) by Poisson in 1668. At this time Descartes was living between Alkmaar and Haarlem; in May he had decided to rent a place where he could live away from prying eyes with his daughter Francine, whom he was to pass off as his "niece." She was born at Deventer on 19 June 1635, and was baptized in the Reformed Church as the child of Hélène Jans and "René son of Joachim."[51] The mother was a serving woman, but we do not know whether Descartes knew her from the time of his first stay at Deventer, or only in Amsterdam, where the child was conceived (Descartes recorded the fact) on 15 October 1634 in the house near the Western Church. In a letter to an unknown recipient on 30 August 1637 he made arrangements for the arrival of his "niece" together with Hélène, in a serving capacity. In 1640 he planned to take the girl to France to give her a good education; but she died on 7 September of scarlet fever. A letter of condolence to Pollot of January 1641 speaks of his own "tears of sadness" recently caused by the recent "loss of two people who were very close" (AT III 278).[52]

The three *Essays*, and the passage in the *Discourse* on the circulation of the blood had raised many questions among Descartes' readers. Those of the Jesuit Vatier on metaphysics have not survived, though we have Descartes' reply (22 February 1638: AT I 558–65). Pollot is one of the few to have questioned Descartes on morals, metaphysics and the doctrine of animals as machines (*Discourse* Parts III–V; letter of March 1638: AT II 34–6). Descartes wanted to avoid imposing crippling doubt on his nonspecialist readers (the book was in French) and had therefore shortened the arguments from doubt and avoided the supposition of a deceiving God, or no God – his purpose being to destroy atheism and doubt.[53] An idea Descartes considered at one time was to print his earlier work on metaphysics in place of Part IV of the *Discourse*, in an eventual Latin translation of the book (letter of March or April 1637: AT I 350). But no Latin version appeared until 1644, and in 1638 Descartes decided instead to "clarify" what had not been fully understood (to Vatier, 22 February; to Mersenne 27 July: AT I 561: AT II 267). The topic he had in mind was probably the cause of the various kinds of ideas. But he set himself, in addition, to complete his early unfinished metaphysics, to explain the errors of the mind in speculative matters: our will, which alone is active and infinite, is responsible for our judgments. This becomes the Fourth Meditation; in the metaphysical summary in the *Discourse*, we have merely the essential elements that are to form the Third and Fifth Meditations, without any intermediate phase. A further lacuna, to be filled in the Sixth Meditation, is the real distinction between mind and body (which in the *Discourse* had been too swiftly linked to the Cogito), and the proof of the existence of bodies; the transition from metaphysics to physics in the *Discourse* had not required this complex demonstration, because no person of "good sense" ever doubted the existence of material things (Synopsis to *Meditations:* AT VII 12). A further issue to be dealt with was the union of our soul to our own body: our sensations and passions inform us only of the interactions between our bodies and external objects, and are thus signals that conduce to the preservation of the union.

After the *Discourse* appeared, Descartes had wanted to publish the chief objections he had received, together with his replies; but one of the objectors, Morin, professor at the Collège de France, had refused permission. In the case of the *Meditations*, Descartes now proposed to circulate the Latin text prior to publication, so that he could present Michael Soly, his publisher in Paris, with a complete text, including objections and replies. The first set of Objections was by a Dutch priest Caterus (Kater),[54] and the second set was drafted or collected by Mersenne, who had received the manuscript at the end of 1640. The whole collection, together with Descartes' replies, was then passed on to Hobbes, who was then in Paris. The fourth set (by Antoine Arnauld) was the one Descartes most appreciated, though he kept back the last part of his reply, dealing with theological matters, for the second edition.[55] The fifth set (by Gassendi), in which Descartes is addressed by the phrase "O Mind", exasperated Descartes and in his reply he calls Gassendi "O Flesh". The sixth and last set, again collected by Mersenne, presents additional objections from "geometers" (perhaps Fermat who had discussed the *Essays*).[56] The deliveries of the book to the Netherlands were not satisfactory, and Descartes entrusted the second edition to Elzevier, at Amsterdam. For this edition he deleted from the title page the phrase "with the approval of the learned doctors of the Sorbonne." He had hoped in vain for such approval right up until the publication of the first edition, but Father Gibieuf had not been able to secure it. (Gibieuf's objections to Descartes are lost, but we have Descartes' reply of 10 January 1642: AT II 472–80.) The second edition also corrected the title of the first: Mersenne, after "Meditations on First Philosophy" had announced demonstrations of the "existence of God and the immortality of the soul." But Descartes had already indicated the limits of reason (in the Synopsis) and the need for faith to complement it (Second Replies: AT VII 152–3). The second edition bore a title closer to the themes he had referred to back in 1630: the existence of God and the distinction between the human soul and the body.

The second edition of the *Meditations* also added a seventh set of Objections from the Jesuit Bourdin, together with Descartes' replies and an open letter to Bourdin's superior, Father Dinet. In the letter Descartes deplores the attacks he has received, both from Bourdin and from the Calvinists of the University of Utrecht; at the same time he pleads his cause before his former teachers, having already begun a more accessible general presentation of his philosophy which he hoped would be used in the Jesuit colleges. Descartes was shocked that Bourdin had presented, for public debate at the Jesuit college in Paris, theses attacking the *Dioptrique*, without giving him any chance to defend himself. The tone of the Seventh Set of Objections and Replies is harsh, and they were not included in the French translation of the *Meditations Objections and Replies* (1647). By August 1641 Descartes was refusing even to read the objections of an Englishman called Huebner (AT III 438; Baillet calls him Huelner); he was sick of empty debates and angry about the quarrel that had broken out in Utrecht in 1641, and which was to become even more acrimonious.[57] The Calvinists, led by Voet, had attacked Descartes' "papism"; Descartes denounced Voet in the letter to Dinet, and finally replied to him directly in a long open letter of 1643. To refute the charge of atheism (based on the fact that he proves God's existence from the idea of God, which, it is objected, not all people have), Descartes recalls the way Socrates questioned the ignorant slave boy in the *Meno:* the boy had geometrical knowledge within him, but it had to be brought out and made explicit.[58]

The Utrecht quarrel arose from the excesses of Regius (Henri De Roy, or Le Roy), a disciple (albeit a rash and over enthusiastic one) whom Descartes had supported, but who had never understood his metaphysics.[59] Regius had been named professor of medicine at Utrecht in July 1638 (with the help of Reneri, who died in 1639), and caused a great stir by defending the circulation of the blood, but also by proposing a definition of man as an *ens per accidens* – a definition Descartes vigorously condemned.[60] In July 1645 an argument broke out when Descartes learnt "with sadness" that Regius had produced new theses affirming that the spiritual nature of the soul could not be demonstrated, and defining the soul as a "mode of the body" – a worse error, in Descartes' eyes, than the earlier one. Regius accused Descartes of dissimulating his true views, at which Descartes hotly protested, while sometimes still talking of their friendship (AT IV 256–7). At the end of 1647 Regius issued a broadsheet (*Programma*) listing twenty-one anti-Cartesian theses; Descartes replied in detail in the *Comments on a certain broadsheet* (*Notae in programma* AT VIIIB 349–69). And in the *Lettre-Preface* to the 1647 French translation of the *Principles* he added a formal disavowal of the views of his former disciple (AT IXB 19–20).

LATER YEARS

The publication of the original Latin text of the *Principia Philosophia* in Amsterdam in 1644, and the issuing of a French translation in Paris in 1647 (shortly after the French version of the *Meditations* appeared), each coincided with Descartes' visiting France. These were the first two occasions he had returned to his native land since his departure in 1628. One purpose of the first visit was to attend to the inheritance from his father, which was still not fully sorted out.[61] He had hoped to bring the newly published *Principles* with him to Paris, but the book arrived there a little later. He had, however, brought with him a printer's copy which lacked the diagrams, and his friend Picot (a priest of *libertin* inclinations with whom he was lodging) started translating the text straightaway. Now reconciled with Bourdin, Descartes entrusted him with the task of distributing various copies to the Jesuits[62]; by dividing the work into short articles he hoped to facilitate its use as a textbook in the colleges of the order. His failure to achieve this goal, and the more favourable reception the book had from non-specialist readers, made him more inclined to agree to proposals for translating his works into French – from Picot for the *Principles*, from de Luynes for the *Meditations*, and from Clerselier for the *Objections and Replies*.

The *Principles* aimed to avoid the condemnation Galileo had incurred by insisting on the truth of the earth's movement – a proposition Copernicus had presented merely as a hypothesis. Descartes lists several hypotheses for comparison (Part III, art. 15–18) and insists that all motion is relative and must be referred to the relevant coordinates: thus the earth is immobile in relation to its atmosphere. Nevertheless it is called a "planet," "carried along by its own heaven" (art. 26). The sun is often described as a "fixed star," and the "fixed stars" are mentioned at the end of the work (Part IV, art. 206) among the Cartesian theses endowed with "metaphysical certainty"; they come at the end of a list that begins with pure metaphysics (discussed in Part I) and moves on to the general laws of movement (Part II).

The first edition of 1644 was dedicated to Princess Elizabeth, eldest daughter of the Frederick, Count Palatine and Elector of the Holy Roman Empire, who had been deposed from the throne of Bohemia after his defeat near Prague in 1619.[63] Through Pollot's good offices Descartes had been to visit her at The Hague; when he left Endegeest in 1643 to move back to a more northerly location, at Egmond, they began corresponding. The subject of the letters was the union of soul and body, a fact experienced in everyday life even if its nature remains obscure (letters of 21 May and 28 June: AT IV

663–8, 690–5). From 1645 onward the correspondence became more frequent, especially after Elizabeth left to live with an aunt in Germany (August 1646). The princess encouraged Descartes to develop his own reflections on morality (at the start he had referred her to Seneca), and asked him to define and classify the passions. Descartes sent her a small treatise in May 1646, which was eventually to be augmented, by up to a third, and finally published by Le Gras in Paris in 1649.[64]

The French versions of the *Meditations* and the *Objections and Replies* had been prepared before Descartes' visit to France in 1644. Descartes made the acquaintance of the respective translators, the Duc de Luynes and Clerselier (and was put in touch with Chanut, Clerselier's son-in-law); he then took the translations away with him, reread them and added some small changes. The edition was ready by the start of 1647 (Paris: Veuve J. Camusat and P. Le Petit), and was entitled *Meditations Métaphysiques;* the subtitle announced the demonstrations of God's existence and the "real distinction between the soul and body of man." Since the original Latin edition, Gassendi had reacted against Descartes' replies by publishing in 1644 a lengthy *Disquisitio Metaphysica* of "Instances" (i.e. Counter-Objections). Clerselier had made a selection summarizing the essential points, and Descartes wrote (in French) a letter to Clerselier "serving as a reply to a selection of the principal objections produced by M. Gassendi against the preceding replies" (AT IXA 202). His intention was that this new material should replace the Fifth Set of Objections and Replies in the French edition. In the volume that eventually appeared in 1647, the Sixth Set of Objections and Replies follows straight after the Fourth Set; but at the last minute Clerselier added, at the end of the volume, the Fifth Set, followed by Descartes' letter. The Seventh Set of Objections and Replies, and the letter to Dinet, were not included; Descartes' relations with the Jesuits were no longer polemical, but neither had an accord been reached.[65] When he returned to Paris in 1647, Descartes composed a letter to the translator of the *Principles* to serve as a preface to the French edition. In it he compared philosophy to a tree that is rooted in metaphysics; the trunk (physics) nourishes the branches, the chief of which are medicine, mechanics, and morals. The first, medicine, was still in an inadequate state as far as Descartes was concerned; his interest in the second is shown by the project he was to undertake for designing a school for craftsmen (AT XI 659ff). As for the third – "the most per-fect moral system which presupposes a complete knowledge of the other sciences" (AT IXB 14: CSM I 186) – this remained an ideal. The end of Part II of the *Passions of the Soul* speaks of the resolve to "do one's best" to make continued progress; to "judge well in order to act well, and to judge as well as we can in order to do our best" are the maxims found as early as the *Discourse,* in the "provisional moral code" with which man must content himself (*Passions,* art. 148; *Discourse,* Part III: AT VI 28). The goal of perfection is still in view, but the *Lettre-Preface* in the *Principles* concludes that it may be many centuries before all the truths of science are attained (AT IXB 20). Nonetheless Descartes was certain that all such truths *would* be deduced from his principles (ibid.). His mechanist friends, like Mer-senne, failed to grasp the necessity implied by the metaphysical foun-dations Descartes had laid.

One result of Descartes' metaphysics was the theory of a material plenum identified with extension, and this led to a dispute in his exchanges with Pascal. Descartes was sorry that Mersenne had not provided him with a speedier report on the experiments in Italy on the "vacuum" that appeared at a certain altitude in an inverted tube of mercury. At Paris he learned that Pascal, thanks to the excellent glass factory at Rouen, had managed to reproduce the experiment using straight and curved tubes, and syringes. Pascal himself was planning to come to Paris to consult medical experts, and on 23 September 1647 Descartes visited him (Baillet has it that Pascal went to Mersenne's monastery, where Descartes received him). The meeting was not a success. A large group of people was present, and Pascal was tired; Roberval, always a strong opponent of Descartes, ridiculed his explanation of the experiment which involved "subtle matter" slipping through into the top of the tube.[66] After Mersenne's death (1648) Descartes chose Carcavi as his intermediary for ex-changing information with the scientific world; on the 11 June 1649 he wrote to him inquiring about an experiment he had heard about and which he himself had advised Pascal to perform after their meet-ing. "I assured him he would meet with success," he later wrote to Carcavi, "since the result conforms entirely to my principles; with-out my assurance he would never have taken the trouble to consider the matter, since his own views were quite opposed to mine."[67]

At the start of 1648 Descartes began to explain "the way in which

the animal is formed, going back to the start of its development"
(letter to Elizabeth, 31 January: AT V 112). Although Descartes could
not perform experiments on humans, the work he had started on
was a new *Description du corps humain* (later published in 1664 by
Clerselier, who placed it after *L'Homme* and subtitled it "The formation of the foetus"). Had Descartes finished the project he would
have used it to replace his earlier account of the fully formed human
being. He had envisaged such a goal as early as 20 February 1639;
while acknowledging the limits of his knowledge he was nonetheless sure that the generation of living things was a natural process,
"provided one supposes that this nature always acts in accordance
with the exact laws of mechanics imposed by God" (letter to
Mersenne: AT II 525).

In the letter to Elizabeth of 31 January Descartes also mentions a
further trip to France, where had been offered a royal pension.[68] The
trip was to be a long one (he would stay in France over the following
winter) and he planned to set out as early as March 1648 (letter to
Chanut, 21 February: AT V 131). But he actually left later than
planned, because we know that on 16 April 1648 he spent the day
being interviewed by a twenty-year old student, Burman. The two had
lunch together,[69] and Burman took notes of Descartes' replies to his
carefully prepared questions; the notes were subsequently written up
by Clauberg. The interview dealt chiefly with the *Meditations*, before
moving on to topics from the *Principles*; discussing the latter, Descartes adds some important comments on divine freedom and the
creation of the eternal truths.[70] In connection with Book I, art. 26 of
the *Principles*, Descartes underlines the originality of his position
regarding the positive conception of the infinite. Finally, Descartes
comments on the opening of the *Discourse*, and ends by modifying
the high hopes he had placed in medical science in Part VI: it is better,
as Tiberius said, to rely on one's own personal experience.[71]

Descartes left for France in May 1648, and soon made it up with
Gassendi (although Roberval continued to attack him). In France he
received a letter asking him about memory and the duration of the
soul, and invited the author to come and discuss the matter with
him in person, showing his continued respect for lovers of the truth
(4 June: AT V 194). The author was in fact the great Arnauld, already
forced to hide his identity, and Descartes wrote a further long letter
to him on 29 July (AT V 219–24). Descartes' voluminous correspon-

dence (published in part by Clerselier in 1657, 1659, and 1667) thus partly owed its bulk to his prolonged absence from France, and indeed his decision not to visit England. (The letters he exchanged with Henry More in February and April 1649 are full of philosophical interest.) His chief correspondent Mersenne fell ill in 1648, and was to die in September. But as soon as the uprising known as La Fronde broke out in August with barricades set up in Paris, Descartes left. The hope he had started to entertain that he could enjoy greater tranquility in France than in Holland had evaporated. Nevertheless, when, in February 1649, he was invited by the Queen of Sweden to visit Stockholm, he expressed his reluctance to Brasset, secretary to the French ambassador at The Hague, and remarked on his pleasure at hearing that France had escaped the storms that threatened her (23 April 1649: AT V 349–50). And when the Queen sent a ship with an admiral to bring him to Sweden he allowed the ship to leave without him (letter to Chanut, 23 April: AT V 350–1). An apt question that arises here is why, when he was invited to go to Stockholm for the summer, he nonetheless elected to "spend the winter" there (letter to Chanut, 31 March: AT V 324). Where was his instinct of self preservation? His reason for the delay was that he had business to finish (ibid. 325); and it may be that he was still finishing his treatise on the *Passions*. He delivered the manuscript to Elzevier when he passed through Amsterdam in September.

Soon after arriving in Sweden, he wrote to Elizabeth that he missed his solitude and the opportunities it gave for furthering the "search for truth."[72] While praising the Swedish Queen, he would have wished that she was less obsessed with studying Greek (AT V 430). Was it during this period that Descartes began his unfinished dialogue, the *Search for Truth by Means of the Natural Light*? In this work we find Descartes' spokesman Eudoxus ("Good Sense") showing the way to Polyander ("Everyman") – an ordinary man who has escaped being filled with preconceived opinions by too much study – and attacking the complacent confidence of Epistemon (the "man of erudition"). The project was a substantial one, and the composition of the dialogue went slowly, breaking off soon after the point where Polyander himself uncovers the truth that if I am doubting, I exist.[73] In December, the end of the Thirty Years' War was being celebrated, and Descartes wrote the text of a ballet, for the "Birth of Peace." The Queen was often occupied with other business but to keep her mind free of distraction she arranged for her philosophy lessons to be held at five o'clock in the morning. Descartes was staying at the French embassy opposite to the Royal Palace, but he had to cross a bridge to reach it. Although he went by carriage, he still caught cold and succumbed to fever. He was delirious for several days, refusing all medical assistance and then finally agreeing to it. He died on 11 February 1650, and his last words, to his servant, were *"il faut partir."*[74]

Translated by John Cottingham.

NOTES

1 Baillet's sources included the memoirs of Clerselier, and the manuscripts and letters that Legrand was preparing for incorporation into a larger edition than Clerselier's. See Baillet, *La Vie de M. Des-Cartes* (1691), Introduction, vol. I, pp. xxi–xxii. (References to Baillet are hereafter made in the text by volume and page number thus: *Vie* I, 20). A further source was Lipstorp's *Specimina philosophiae cartesianae*, published in 1653; an appendix to this work had included, without references or dates, Descartes' birth place, his studies at La Flèche, the meeting with Beeckman at Breda, names of friends in Paris and then Holland, and some of Descartes' places of residence. Also published in 1653 was Borel's *Renati Cartesii . . . vita*, which emphasized the sieges and battles in which Descartes would have taken part. (This first edition is lost; for details of the second edition of 1656, see AT XII vii). Tepel's *Historia philosophiae cartesianae* (1674) listed (though without any chronological ordering) the countries that Descartes visited or lived in.

2 *Vie* I 4. Baillet describes Descartes' family home as "one of the noblest in Touraine, stretching far into the province of Poitou." Barbier, in *Trois Médecins poitevins au XVIe siècle* (1897), p.36, could find no reference to Doctor Pierre Descartes' exemption from the poll tax. It is interesting that Joachim, a doctor's son, himself married the daughter of a doctor – Jean Ferrand. Ferrand was thus René's maternal grandfather (not great grandfather, *pace* AT XII 40)

3 Letter to Elizabeth of May or June 1645 (AT IV 220–1). Joachim Descartes remarried (perhaps around 1600; the first son was born in 1601). This second wife came from Brittany, in the Nantes region.

4 Sirven, *Les Années d'apprentissage de Descartes*. Sirven is followed by Gilson in the revised edition of his *Descartes, Discours de la méthode, text et commentaire* (hereafter referred to as *Commentary*), p. 479.

5 Cf. Gilson, *Commentary*, p. 101.

6 Cf. letter to Elizabeth, 4 August 1645: AT IV 265 and the notes (by Leibniz) entitled "Cartesius" (AT XI 650).

7 Staged at Stockholm on 19 December 1649. The text was rediscovered and published in the *Revue de Genève* in 1920 by Nordström; it is printed in the revised edition of AT V 616ff. For *la Gloire*, see esp. p. 620.

8 Though he recognized the value of the classics, Descartes had no wish to remain ignorant of the events of his own epoch (AT VI 6). And though he chose French for his first publication, he accorded equal value to well-expressed thoughts in "low Breton" – a language he would have heard when he visited his family near Nantes.

9 Beeckman, in his *Journal tenu par Isaac Beeckman de 1604 à 1634*, says that the young Descartes studied a great deal of mathematics with the Jesuits but found no one to unite this study with that of physics (AT X 52). See further my paper "Du doute vécu au doute suprême."

10 Descartes sent a copy of his *Principles of Philosophy* "to R.P.F., [his] former master" (letter to Bourdin, October 1644: AT IV 144).

11 Cf. Gilson, *Commentary*, pp. 120, 126, 129.

12 AT I 382–3. Commentators have become involved in a string of errors here, incorrectly following the early dates that Baillet gives for Descartes' time at La Flèche. In the Adam-Milhaud edition of Descartes' correspondence, the letter of 14 June 1637 is said to be addressed to Fournet (vol. I, p. 19). It seems that Fournet, who taught philosophy to the class above Descartes' and was known to Descartes through the combined discussions that were held for the students of all three final years, never gave his reactions to the *Discourse* (which was sent to him via Plemp: letter of 15 September 1637: AT I 399); he died early in 1638.

13 Gilson, *Commentary*, p. 119

14 Sirven p. 52

15 Cf. Baillet, *Vie* I 87, 91; AT X 193, 196. For Descartes' attitude to the Rosicrucians, see Gouhier, *Les Premières Pensées de Descartes* pp. 150–7.

16 Baillet, *Vie* I 38. Cf. *Vie* I 154. According to Baillet, Descartes was more attracted to science than to the army, which his father wanted him to join; "Descartes had no wish to become a great warrior" (*Vie* I 41).

17 Descartes mentions various problems put to him by Beeckman in the first section of the "Register," entitled "Parnassus." (Cf. letters to Beeckman of 24 January and 26 March 1619: AT X 153, 154.) The later row with Beeckman arose from the latter having sent to Mersenne various propositions from the *Compendium Musicae*, as if they were his own work. See Buzon's translation, *Descartes, Abrégé de musique, avec présentation et notes*.

18 This incomplete copy, which Leibniz made at Paris, was first published

by Foucher de Careil (Paris, 1859) under the title *Cogitationes privatae* ("Private Thoughts"); the title may or may not have figured in Leibniz's original manuscript, which has since been lost. Baillet is an invaluable source here, providing extensive extracts not to be found in the Leibniz manuscript (including the account of the dreams). But he often gives paraphrases rather than direct quotations. On the correct order of the sections, see Gouhier, *Premières pensées*, pp. 11–18. See also Rodis-Lewis, "Le Premier Registre de Descartes"

19 For this interpretation see Gouhier, *Premières pensées;* and his *La Pensée Religieuse de Descartes.*

20 This section apparently included a story (missing from Leibniz's copy) of an adventure at sea (Baillet reports it in the third person, *Vie* I 102f): thinking that some sailors were plotting to kill him, Descartes drew his sword and showed "the impression that a display of courage can make on those of a base spirit" (AT X 190). Baillet dates the story 1621; see, however, AT XII 62, where 1619 is suggested.

21 As early as the end of March, Descartes had decided to leave for Germany, where war seemed inevitable (AT X 151). See further Adam's comments at AT X 167 and XII 62. The celebrations for the Emperor's coronation, in Frankfurt, which Descartes attended in 1619, were held from 20 July to 9 September (AT XII 47). *Poêle* was the name given to a room heated by a large earthenware stove that was stoked in the kitchen on the other side of a partition wall, and thus could not have produced the "sparks" or "flashes" that Descartes saw during his night of dreams.

22 Neuburg is not mentioned in either the first or second edition of AT XII.

23 See Rodis-Lewis, "L'alto e il basso e i sogni di Descartes."

24 Leibniz, *Die philosophischen Schriften*, ed. Gerhardt, vol. IV, p. 315.

25 Rodis-Lewis, *L'Oeuvre de Descartes*, pp. 51–2 and notes pp. 451–3.

26 Baillet here cites the Latin for once, but then talks of the "evil demon" (*mauvais génie*), which reminds us of the "malicious demon" of the *Meditations*. But the latter is still far in the future, as far as Descartes was concerned. Baillet reveals his priestly preoccupations when he goes on to talk of Descartes' repentance for his "grave sin" – a notion that has given rise to even more dubious psychoanalytic interpretations. As for the "flashes" that Descartes then saw in his room (a hallucination more than a dream), Baillet says they were first feared like the thunderbolt (which strikes those who aspire to become like Gods), but were later interpreted (after the third dream) as the light of the spirit of truth.

27 Sirven, *Les années d'apprentissage de Descartes*, pp. 169f.

28 According to Baillet, it was on the morning after his dreams that Descartes made a "vow" (*voeu*) to go on a pilgrimage to the shrine of the Virgin at Loretto, and he left for Italy "before the end of November." But

it is hardly likely that Descartes would have planned to cross the Alps in the winter season.

29 For Descartes' military experiences, cf. his encounter with a soldier who thought he had been wounded in battle (*Le Monde* ch. 1: AT XI 6: CSM I 86). The ballet, *La Naissance de la paix*, describes the horrors of war.

30 Cf. Weber, *La Constitution du texte des Regulae.*

31 The translation "mathematics" for *mathesis* (*universalis*), which appears in Rule IV (AT X 378), has been questioned. Marion retains the original term: cf. his edition *Règles utiles et claires pour la direction de l'esprit,* p. 15 and note 31.

32 *Bona Mens;* cf. the "good sense" (*le bon sens*) of the *Discourse,* which is identified with reason.

33 Compare the treatise entitled *Studium Bonae Mentis,* some quotations from which are preserved in Baillet (AT X 191ff); this was perhaps written a little later, after Descartes' return to Paris.

34 Adam puts the episode in 1628 (AT X 536). In 1630 Descartes mentions that he has directed his studies "towards something other than the use of arms" (to Gibieuf via Mersenne, 4 November 1630: AT I 174).

35 Mersenne spoke of an "excellent mathematician" to one of his correspondents who expressed a desire to know more of "our des Chartes," his "fine method" his "discoveries," and his "explanation of refraction." Cf. Mersenne, *Correspondence* vol. I, pp. 418, 420, 429.

36 See the indexes of Marion's edition of the *Regulae* (note 31, above) for numerous parallels with Bacon.

37 Those who "doubt only for the sake of doubting" (*Discourse* Part III: AT VI 29). In following Montaigne's desire to test himself with the help of the "great book of the world," Descartes ended up by finding that the customs of men gave him "hardly any reason for confidence" (AT VI 10).

38 The anecdote appears in Guez de Balzac, *le Socrate chrétien,* pp. 255–6; Descartes was very close to Balzac at the time. See further my "Du doute vécu au doute suprême," p. 883.

39 Cf. letter to Balzac of 5 May 1631 for Descartes' distaste for being disturbed by "petits voisins" (AT I 203).

40 To Mersenne 25 November 1630 (AT I 182). The *Meditations* were later to deal with the self-same issues, discovered in a different sequence but ranked in the same ontological order. But we must not assume the two works to be identical in scope (cf. Millet, *Descartes, sa vie, ses travaux, ses découvertes,* p. 203; and AT XII 129–44); nor on the other hand should we suppose that the early work (which was "fairly long": letter to Mersenne of March 1637: AT I 350) was merely a matter of a few pages.

41 *Discourse* Part III: AT VI 31: CSM I 126. This peace in Holland coexisted

with the "long duration" of the Thirty Years' War. Cf. letter to Huygens of 18 September 1637 (AT I 396, 582).

42 Letter to Balzac, 5 May 1631 (AT I 203–4), which contrasts the pressures he suffered in France with the freedom and repose he enjoyed in Amsterdam, with all its comforts and its interesting atmosphere. The phrase quoted in the text is engraved on a plaque that G. Cohen had placed on the house, opposite the Western Church, which Descartes inhabited in 1634 (the exact address is known from a letter: AT I 229). In 1629 he chose a house in the Kalverstraat (Calf-street) so that he could have a supply of fresh organs to dissect from the butchers.

43 For details of this and of his various residences in Holland, see AT XII 103–5, 123–8.

44 Letter to Pollot, January 1641 (AT III 279); cf. letter to Huygens, 10 October 1642 (AT III 796–9). The latter text, in the revised edition of AT, gives the wording of the original letter that Clerselier had cut, including the words "I am one of those who love life most" (AT III 798).

45 During a visit to a hospital Descartes observed the phantom limb syndrome in a young girl (*Principles* Part IV, art. 196). In 1637 Plemp taught at Louvain and had an important exchange of letters with Descartes on the circulation of the blood.

46 Letter to Mersenne, 8 October 1629 (AT I 23). This is the first letter to Mersenne, who was to become his chief correspondent.

47 Hereafter, letters cited without the name of the addressee are to Mersenne. The correspondence of this period covers numerous issues in mechanics, music, and (20 November 1630) the question of universal language (AT I 76–82). The diversity of natural phenomena cannot be ignored, and Descartes' aim is to subsume all under his dream of a perfect science (AT I 76–82).

48 The full manuscript (which is now lost) envisaged a transition from ch. 15 (a universe similar to ours: AT XI 104, 118) to ch. 18, which begins the section *L'Homme*. By chance the two sections were published in 1664 by different editors within a few weeks of each other; Clerselier protested about the separation in his preface to *L'Homme*, but nonetheless the title "*L'Homme*" came, incorrectly, to be regarded as the title of a separate work. The edition of 1677 contained both texts, but printed *L'Homme* at the start of the volume, before *Le Monde*.

49 Cf. letters of 6 and 27 May 1630 (AT I 149–53). The thesis developed here leaves on one side the theological question of the uncreated "Word" (*Logos* or Reason).

50 In the light of his solution to the Pappus problem, Descartes had a further section to add to the *Geometry* during the proof stage: letter to Noel of October 1637 (AT I 458).

51 The documents are reproduced in Cohen *Les Ecrivains français en Hollande.*

52 From the end of 1637 to 1640 Descartes' Francine and Hélène probably lived "at Sandport, a small town near Haarlem in the direction of Alkmaar" (address given to Pollot, 5 May 1639: AT II 546). In Spring 1640 Descartes prepared to go to Leiden (thinking he could have his *Meditations* printed there), and it may have been this that led to Francine and her mother going to Amersfoort. On 20 October Descartes' father died (though René heard of the news sometime later (letter of 3 December: AT III 35). On 28 October he had written to him, from Leiden, that he had had to postpone his trip to France (AT III 228–9). Soon afterward he lost his sister Jeanne who had been his childhood companion. (in 1644 he was to visit her children and their father, du Crévy; AT IV 130). It is not clear whether the two losses evoked in the letter to Pollot are the two most recent family deaths, or whether Descartes is thinking about the death of his daughter and his father. Descartes' relations with his father seem always to have been somewhat strained. After the appearance of the *Discourse* the father complained of having a son who was so absurd as to have himself bound in calf (a comment of which Baillet was unaware: AT XII 433–4).

53 Cf. letter to Mersenne, 25 November 1630. To conquer doubt one needs an argument to push it to its furthest limits; hence at the end of the First Meditation and in the *Principles* Part I art. 5, the possibility that there is no God is raised.

54 The manuscript had been sent via two priests at Haarlem. In 1640 Descartes and Huygens were judges at a musical competition between the two and the French composer Boesset (AT III 255–6, 266–7). Only one of the two objectors, Bloemart, was living in 1649, and he arranged for a portrait of Descartes to be made before his departure for Sweden. The portrait in question is probably that by Frans Hals, a copy of which is in the Louvre. (What may be a preliminary study for it is in the Statens Museum for Kunst in Copenhagen.)

55 Arnauld is named in the second edition; in the first, Gassendi's was the only objector's name to appear.

56 Another set of objections that arrived too late for the first edition (and would appear only much later, when the correspondence was published) were those of "Hyperaspistes" – a pseudonym of a friend of Gassendi (July 1641: AT III 397–412); for Descartes' reply, in August, see AT III 421–35.

57 See further Verbeek (ed. and trans.), *René Descartes et Martin Schoock, La Querelle d'Utrecht.* The volume contains (in French translation) the letters to Dinet and Voet, the "Lettre apologetique" to the magistrates of

Utrecht; and Schoock's pamphlet, *Admiranda methodus.* Also included is a detailed historical introduction. See also Verbeek, *Descartes and the Dutch: Early reactions to Cartesianism.*

58 AT VIIIB 108–14. See the appendix of my Franco-Latin edition of the letters to Regius and the *Comments on a certain Broadsheet* for various other passages of philosophical importance. See esp. AT VIIIB 108–14 on the "laws of charity."

59 Regius was the first to read the manuscript of the *Meditations;* see Descartes' reply to his objections (letter of 24 May 1640: AT III 65–71). For Regius's defense of the threefold theory of vegetative, sensitive, and intellectual souls, see AT III 369–71.

60 An accidental, as opposed to an essential unity. "You could hardly say anything more offensive," Descartes commented (December 1641: AT III 460).

61 He must have received some of it when, in 1642–3, he rented a small Chateau at Endegeest, near Leiden, with a large staff of domestic servants. During the 1644 visit to France he planned to go to La Flèche, but it appears that family business prevented the visit. On his return from France he lived near Haarlem or Alkmaar. When he left for Sweden in 1649 he was living at Egmond den Hoef.

62 Two copies were sent to Father Dinet and one to "P. F. my former teacher." This was Father J. Francois, the mathematician who arrived at La Flèche in 1612, but he was not identified by Baillet nor by AT (IV 144), because of the continuing confusion over Descartes' dates at the College. Other copies went to Vatier (who had appreciated the *Discourse* and *Essays).* Fournier, who came to praise the *Meteorology* in his *Hydrography* (1643), and Mesland, who had written to Descartes about the freedom of the will (for Descartes' reply of 2 May 1644 see AT IV 110–20; the theme is taken up again in 1645, AT IV 172–5). Mesland also asked Descartes about the Eucharist (AT IV 161–9). Not long afterward Mesland was sent to the New World – not to Canada (a mistake in a manuscript from Chartres that has often been followed) but to Venezuela.

63 Elizabeth lived in exile at The Hague; apart from Latin, she knew five other languages, including German, Flemish, and probably English (her mother was the sister of Charles I of England). Cf. her letter to Descartes, 24 May 1645, and the reply of May/June: AT IV 209, 221.

64 I have proposed that the section on generosity (arts. 152–61) was added for the final volume published in 1649. See my "Le Dernier Fruit de la métaphysique cartésienne: la générosité," pp. 43–54.

65 The Seventh Objections and Replies and the letter to Dinet were included by Clerselier in his later edition of 1661.

66 Pascal's sister Jacqueline wrote to her elder sister (whose husband F.

Périer performed the Puy de Dôme experiment in 1648) as follows: "on the morning of 24 September Descartes returned to give Pascal his advice about his health, and suggested he should rest in bed in the mornings" (Pascal, *Oeuvres complétes*, ed. Mesnard, vol. III, p. 481).

67 17 August 1649, AT V 391. The "opposition" between Descartes' principles and Pascal's may perhaps have led Pascal to overlook the value of Descartes' suggestions. For this highly disputed point cf. Pascal, *Oeuvres complètes*, vol. II, pp. 655ff. In October 1647 Pascal replied to the criticism of E. Noel (Descartes' former teacher), who had invoked Aristotle and maintained that nature does not allow (*ne souffre pas*) a vacuum. Pascal, as Mesnard notes, may have too readily assimilated Descartes' position to that of the Aristotelians; in fact, since *Le Monde*, Descartes had rejected nature's supposed "fear of a vacuum" (*crainte du vide:* AT XI 20).

68 He never received the pension, the uprising of 1648 (the "Fronde") having intervened. The pension is mentioned in a letter of March or April 1648, which is probably addressed to Silhon rather than to Newcastle (AT V 133). Silhon was Mazarin's secretary, and Descartes knew him as early as 1628.

69 Cf. AT V 148. On the question of whether our thought can encompass more than one thing in a single instant Descartes observes, "I am now aware and have the thought that I am talking and that I am eating" (Cottingham [ed.], *Descartes' Conversation with Burman*, p. 6). A note of caution is raised by Wahl, *Du rôle de l'idée d'instant dans la philosophie de Descartes:* the text is not written by Descartes himself. A better title would perhaps be "Burman-Clauberg, *Conversation with Descartes*; see, however, Cottingham (ed.), *Descartes' Conversation with Burman*, pp. xvi ff.

70 The articles of the *Principles* that are discussed (Part I, arts. 22–4) supplement the argument of the *Meditations*.

71 Descartes says that one can rely on one's experience "once one has reached the age of thirty" (AT V 179); Montaigne makes it twenty (last chapter of the *Essays* entitled "De l'expérience"). Descartes had quoted Tiberius earlier, in October 1645 (letter to Newcastle: AT IV 329). In his last illness, in February 1650, Descartes refused to be bled for a week, then finally submitted and died the following morning, exhausted by two long blood-letting sessions.

72 Letter of 9 October 1649 (AT V 429–31). This was to be his last letter to Elizabeth; at the end he says, "I cannot completely guarantee the future." On 15 January 1650 he wrote to Brégy, "the desire I have to return to my remote solitude increases every day. . . . I am not in my element here" (AT V 467: CSMK 384).

73 AT X 521. The long first part of the dialogue (AT X 492–527) was published (in Latin) with the *Regulae* in 1701. The beginning of the original
   French version (up to AT X 514) was found among Leibniz's papers. The
   date is very much disputed, but several points seem to indicate that the
   Meditations had already been written.

74 On Descartes' temporary tomb, Chanut had a fine epitaph engraved; it is
   quoted by Lipstorp, Borel, and Clerselier (at the end of the preface to vol.
   I of his edition of the letters) and in AT XII 589–91. After Descartes'
   death and the abdication of Queen Christina, his body was brought to
   Paris, in 1667, to be interred at the Abbey of Ste. Geneviève, which was
   later destroyed in the Revolution. The Convention voted for the transfer
   of the body to the Panthéon, but this was refused under the Directoire.
   In 1819 the remains were laid in the church of St. Germain-des-Prés.
   The Swedish Chemist Berzelius, who was in Paris at the time, reports
   that fragments of bone were found, but no skull. Shortly afterward a
   skull bearing an old inscription "René Descartes" was put on sale in
   Stockholm. Berzelius bought it and offered it "to be placed with the
   other remains of the philosopher" (letter to Cuvier, 6 April 1821: AT XII
   618–19). Cuvier kept the skull for the Museum of Natural History,
   where it is frequently put on display.

2 Descartes and scholasticism: the intellectual background to Descartes' thought

The Cartesian system is standardly seen, as indeed it was in Descartes' own day, as a reaction against the scholastic philosophy that still dominated the intellectual climate in early seventeenth-century Europe. But it is not sufficient, when discussing Descartes' relations with scholastics, simply to enumerate and compare the various Cartesian and scholastic doctrines. To understand what set Descartes apart both from scholastics and also from other innovators, one has to grasp the reasons behind the various opinions, but beyond that, one has to understand the intellectual context in which these reasons played a role, to see what tactical measures could have been used to advance one's doctrines or to persuade others of them. In this essay I first attempt to contrast Descartes' attitude toward scholastic philosophy as seen through his correspondence, with his attitude as revealed through his published works. I then try to give enough background about Jesuit pedagogy and Jesuit philosophy to begin to understand Descartes' attempt to gain favor among those of that order. Finally, I depict a few skirmishes between Descartes and the Jesuits, to capture the flavor of such exchanges. Perhaps the most interesting lesson that can be learned by looking at Descartes' relations with scholastics is the sheer power and authority of Aristotelianism during the seventeenth century.

DESCARTES' ATTITUDE TOWARD THE TEACHING OF SCHOLASTIC PHILOSOPHY

For most, the topic of Descartes' relations with the scholastics brings to mind Descartes' disparaging comments, in the *Discourse on Method*, about the philosophy he was taught: "*in my college days* I discovered that nothing can be imagined which is too strange or incredible to have been said by some philosopher" (AT VI 16: CSM I 118).¹ Descartes, in the *Discourse,* seemed to find little worthwhile in his education, including his education in scholastic philosophy and sciences; at best, "philosophy gives us the means of speaking plausibly about any subject and of winning the admiration of the less learned," and "jurisprudence, medicine, and other sciences bring honors and riches to those who cultivate them" (AT VI 8: CSM I 115); but "there is still no point in [philosophy] which is not disputed and hence doubtful" and, "as for the other sciences, in so far as they borrow their principles from philosophy [. . .] nothing solid could have been built upon such shaky foundations" (ibid.).

Obviously, the Descartes of the *Discourse* represented himself as dissatisfied with school learning in general. However, one can catch a glimpse of a Descartes with a different attitude when reading his correspondence. In 1638, approximately a year after the publication of the *Discourse,* Descartes wrote a letter responding to a request for his opinion about adequate schooling for the correspondent's son. In the letter, Descartes attempted to dissuade the correspondent from sending his son to school in Holland. According to Descartes, "there is no place on earth where philosophy is better taught than at La Flèche" (AT II 378), the Jesuit institution in which he was educated. Descartes gave four reasons for preferring La Flèche. First, he asserted, "philosophy is taught very poorly here [in Holland]; professors teach only one hour a day, for approximately half the year, without ever dictating any writings, nor completing their courses in a determinate time." Second, Descartes advised, "it would be too great a change for someone, when first leaving home, to study in another country, with a different language, mode of living, and religion"; La Flèche was not far from the correspondent's home, and "there are so many young people there from all parts of France, and they form such a varied mixture that, by conversing with them, one learns almost as much as if one traveled far." Descartes then praised as a beneficial innovation the "equality that the Jesuits maintain among themselves, treating in almost the same fashion the highest born [*les plus releuez*] and the least [*les moindres*]." Most importantly, Descartes asserted that although, in his opinion, "it is not as if everything taught in philosophy is as true as the Gospels, nevertheless, because philosophy is the key to the other sciences," he believes that "it is extremely useful to have studied the whole philosophy curriculum, in the manner it is taught in Jesuit institutions, before undertaking to raise one's mind above pedantry, in order to make oneself wise in the right kind [of philosophy]" (ibid.).

Of course, preferring La Flèche to a Dutch university is not the same as giving an unqualified endorsement to La Flèche. On the other hand, some of Descartes' pronouncements, especially his last assertion, do seem inconsistent with those of the *Discourse*. How can the Descartes of the *Discourse* recommend learning scholastic philosophy as preparatory to the sciences and to his own philosophy? Is not the study of scholastic philosophy antithetical to the Cartesian project to cleanse oneself of the effects of years of dependence on the senses? Would not the study of scholastic philosophy merely reinforce those bad habits? Still, Descartes' advice in his letter seems open and frank. Descartes' first three assertions in the letter correlate very well with what one can discover to have been the case in seventeenth-century Jesuit education.

Descartes was right in suggesting that students would have been taught more philosophy, and would have been taught it more rigorously at La Flèche than at a Dutch university. The philosophy curriculum at La Flèche is fairly well-known, and the daily routine of its students well-documented.² At La Flèche, as in other Jesuit colleges of the time,³ the curriculum in philosophy would have lasted three years (the final three years of a student's education, from about the age of fifteen on). It would have consisted of lectures, twice a day in sessions lasting two hours each, from a set curriculum based primarily on Aristotle and Thomas Aquinas. During Descartes' time, the first year was devoted to logic and ethics, consisting of commentaries and questions based on Porphyry's *Isagoge* and Aristotle's *Categories*, *On Interpretation*, *Prior Analytics*, *Topics*, *Posterior Analytics*, and *Nicomachean Ethics*. The second year was devoted to physics and metaphysics, based primarily on Aristotle's *Physics*, *De Caelo*, *On Generation and Corruption* Book I, and *Metaphysics* Books 1, 2, and 11.⁴ The third year of philosophy was a year of mathematics, consisting of arithmetics, geometry, music, and astronomy, including such topics as fractions, proportions, elementary figures, techniques for the measurement of distances and heights, trigonometry, gnomics, geography and hydrography, chronology, and optics.⁵ The students would have been expected to study their professors' lectures thoroughly. Their daily routine would have included a number of hours of required study time. They would have had to show their work to a prefect daily and to repeat materials from their lectures to a *repetitor*; their learning would have been tested in weekly and monthly oral disputations in front of their professors and peers.

Moreover, Descartes was not exaggerating when he asserted that the student population of La Flèche was diverse, geographically and otherwise. La Flèche accepted boys from all corners of France and from all walks of life. During Descartes' days, its boarders numbered approximately one hundred, and it taught, in addition, about twelve hundred external, or day, students. Moreover, the equality of treatment practiced by the Jesuits, and referred to by Descartes, does appear to be an innovation in the context of seventeenth-century France; it seems to be verifiable by available documents. The sons of the most humble families lived in the same rooms as those of the most exalted. When arriving at La Flèche, one checked one's sword in the armory. "Without a sword, a gentleman forgot his birth; there would be no distinction between nobility, bourgeois, etc."[6] There is even the case of Jean Tarin, one of Descartes' contemporaries, born in Anjou during 1586, who came to La Flèche "in poverty, with feet bare, and nothing but an undershirt and a bag of nuts and bread"; he was first a kitchen assistant and sweeper of classes for about four years, but then he became lackey to the young Comte de Barrant, who gave him the means and leisure to study. In 1616 he became professor of grammar at the Collège Honcourt, Paris, and in 1625, he became its rector.[7]

One should conclude that the attitude toward scholastic education in philosophy displayed by Descartes in some of his correspondence more nearly represents Descartes' views on the matter; at the very least, the letter to the anonymous correspondent about his son's education should provide one with a corrective for interpreting Descartes' more negative views about scholastic education, from the *Discourse*.[8]

DESCARTES' REQUEST FOR OBJECTIONS: THE LETTERS TO NOEL

There is another letter written by Descartes about the time of the publication of the *Discourse*, which also casts doubts upon the reliability of any literal reading of that work. During June 1637 Descartes wrote to one of his old teachers, sending him a copy of the newly published *Discourse*. As Descartes put it, he sent the volume as a fruit that belongs to his teacher, *whose first seeds were sown in his mind by him*, just as he also owed to those of his teacher's order the little knowledge he had of letters (AT I 383).

Now, it is true that Descartes sent copies of the *Discourse* to a great number of people: close friends, the nobility, various intellectuals, Jesuits, and others.[9] It is also true that Descartes indicated in the letter that he had not kept in touch with his old teachers after he left La Flèche: "I am sure that you would not have retained the names of all the students you had twenty-three or twenty-four years ago, when you taught philosophy at La Flèche, and that I am one of those who have been erased from your memory."[10] Moreover, the attempt to promote his works by making them the focus of discussion was already part of Descartes' strategy. When, in 1641, Descartes published his *Meditations on First Philosophy*, he did so with a series of *Objections* and *Replies* to the work. He had hoped to do the same thing with the earlier *Discourse*. In Part VI of the *Discourse*, Descartes announced:

I would be very happy if people examined my writings and, so that they might have more of an opportunity to do this, I ask all who have objections to make to take the trouble and send them to my publisher and, being advised about them by the publisher, I shall try to publish my reply at the same time as the objections; by this means, seeing both of them together, the readers will more easily judge the truth of the matter.

(AT VI 75: CSM I 149)

Thus, the letter Descartes wrote to his old teacher should be read in the above context; the letter was part and parcel of Descartes' strategy to promote discussions of his views. And, of course, Descartes did request objections from his teacher and from others of his order in the letter: "If, taking the trouble to read this book or have it read by those of your [order] who have the most leisure, and noticing errors in it, which no doubt are numerous, you would do me the favor of telling me of them, and thus of continuing to teach me, I would be extremely grateful" (AT I 383). Still, it is curious to see the Descartes of the *Discourse* being so obsequious and sending his work to his teachers "as the fruit belonging to them, whose seed they sowed."

We do not have a response from Descartes' old teacher, but we can infer what he said, given that we have a second letter from Descartes to him, written in October 1637. Descartes thanked his correspondent for having remembered him and for giving his promise to have the book examined and objections forwarded. Descartes pressed his correspondent to append his own objections, saying that there are no objections whose authority would be greater, and none he desires more (AT I 454–6). Descartes added that no one would seem to have more interest in examining his book than the Jesuits, since he did not see how anyone could continue to teach the subjects treated, such as meteorology, as do most of the Jesuit Colleges, without either refuting what he has written or following it. However, at the end of the letter, Descartes seemed to recognize the reason why the Jesuits might not willingly take up his philosophy; he attempted to reply to the difficulty:

Since I know that the principal reason which requires those of your order most carefully to reject all sorts of *novelties* in matters of philosophy is the fear they have that these reasons would also cause some changes in theology, I want particularly to indicate that there is nothing to worry from this quarter about these things, and that I am able to thank God for the fact that the opinions which have seemed to me most true in physics, when considering natural causes, have always been those which agree best of all with the mysteries of religion.   (AT I 455–6: CSMK 75; emphasis supplied)

Descartes was clear that a stumbling block to friendly relations with the Jesuits would have been their distaste of novelty, because of their desire to safeguard theology, and that they would have rightly seen him as offering novelties. As in previous instances, Descartes seemed to understand his situation fairly well; he seemed to have a clear grasp of Jesuit educational practices and objectives during the seventeenth century.

JESUIT PEDAGOGY IN THE SIXTEENTH AND SEVENTEENTH CENTURIES

There was a renaissance in Thomistic philosophy during the second half of the sixteenth century. For the duration of the Council of Trent (1545–63), Thomas's *Summa Theologiae* was placed next to the Bible, on the same table, to help the council in its deliberations, so that it might derive appropriate answers. In 1567 Pope Pius V proclaimed Saint Thomas Aquinas Doctor of the Church. Saint Ignatius of Loyola, founder of the Jesuits, advised the Jesuits to follow the doctrines of Saint Thomas in theology.[11] Naturally, it would have been difficult to follow Saint Thomas in theology without also accepting much of his philosophy; and to follow Saint Thomas in philosophy would have required one to follow Aristotle as well. None of this was unexpected; Loyola's advice was made formal in the Jesuits's *ratio studiorum* of 1586: "In logic, natural philosophy, ethics, and metaphysics, Aristotle's doctrine is to be followed."[12] The flavor of the advice can be captured through a circular from the chief of the Order of Jesuits (François de Borgia) to the Superiors of the Order, written just after the end of the Council of Trent and imbued with the spirit of the Council and Saint Ignatius of Loyola's advice. I quote the circular in full:

THAT WHICH MUST BE HELD IN THEOLOGY AND IN PHILOSOPHY

Let no one defend or teach anything opposed, detracting, or unfavorable to the faith, either in philosophy or in theology. Let no one defend anything against the axioms received by the philosophers, such as: there are only four kinds of causes;[13] there are only four elements;[14] there are only three principles of natural things;[15] fire is hot and dry; air is humid and hot.[16]

Let no one defend anything against the most common opinion of the philosophers and theologians, for example, that natural agents act at a distance without a medium.[17]

Let no one defend any opinion contrary to common opinion without consulting the Superior or Prefect.

Let no one introduce any new opinion in philosophy or theology without consulting the Superior or Prefect.

OPINION THAT [JESUITS] MUST SUSTAIN, TEACH, AND HOLD AS TRUE

Concerning God. God's power is infinite in intensity; He is a free agent according to the true philosophy. His Providence extends to all created beings in general, to each in particular, and to all human things; he knows all things present, past and future, according to the true philosophy.

Concerning Angels. Angels are truly placed in categories and are not pure act, according to the true philosophy. They are in place and move locally from place to place, so that one should not hold that they are not in place and do not move, so also that their substance is present in some manner in one place and then in another.

Concerning Man. The intellective soul is truly the substantial form of the body, according to Aristotle and the true philosophy. The intellective soul is not numerically one in all men, but there is a distinct and proper soul in each man, according to Aristotle and the true philosophy.[18] The intellective soul is immortal, according to Aristotle and the true philosophy. There aren't several souls in man, intellective, sensitive, and vegetative souls, and neither are there two kinds of souls in animals, sensitive and vegetative souls, according to Aristotle and the true philosophy.[19] The soul, whether in man or in animals, is not in fuzz or in hair. Sensitive and vegetative powers in man and animals do not have their subject in prime matter. Humors are, in some manner, part of man and animals. The whole being of composite substance is not solely in form, but in form and matter.

Varia. The predicables are five in number. Divine essence does not have a single subsistence common to three persons, but only three personal subsistences. Sin is a formal evil and a privation, not something positive. We are not causes of our own predestination.

Let all professors conform to these prescriptions; let them say nothing against the propositions here announced, either in public or in private; under no pretext, not even that of piety or truth, should they teach anything other than that these texts are established and defined. This is not just an admonition, but a teaching that we impose.[20]

One might wonder whether Descartes' attempt to gain acceptance of his philosophy by the Jesuits was a quixotic endeavor, given the above. Descartes did try to indicate that his doctrines were not dangerous to the faith; but the Jesuits defined danger to the faith as any novelty in either theology or in philosophy, especially as it concerned the axioms and common opinions of scholasticism. And Descartes would not have fared very well in this respect. He rejected the four causes, arguing that final causes are not appropriate for natural philosophy.[21] He rejected the four elements and held that there was only one kind of matter, and that all its varieties could be explained as modifications of extension.[22] Moreover, Descartes did not accept the three Aristotelian principles of matter, form, and privation. Except for rational beings who have minds, Descartes rejected the doctrine of substantial forms.[23] Finally, though Descartes might have agreed that fire is hot and dry, and air is humid and hot, it would have been as phenomenological descriptions, and not as representing any basic reality; such statements would have been inconsistent with Descartes' mechanical philosophy, which required some kind of corpuscularianism, as well as the rejection of final causes (except for man's body as informed by a soul) and substantial forms.

On the other hand, Descartes would have agreed with the common opinion that natural agents do not act at a distance without a medium.[24] Interestingly, Descartes could accept all the theological and philosophical opinions concerning God, angels, and man that Jesuits were required to sustain and defend, including that God's power is infinitive in intensity;[25] that he is a free agent;[26] that the intellective soul in man is the substantial form of the body;[27] that the intellective soul is not numerically one in all men and that there is only one soul in man (AT III 369–71: CSMK 182); that sin is a privation, not something positive (AT VII 54: CSM II 38). The only notable exception was Descartes' denial of animal souls, both sensitive and vegetative (AT III 369–72; AT VI 56–9). Perhaps Descartes might have thought that his orthodoxy with respect to theological matters would have led to the acceptance of his philosophical novelties, once they were seen to harmonize with Catholic theological doctrines.

Perhaps also, during Descartes' time, there was a slightly more liberal interpretation given to Loyola's advice to follow Thomas. The traditional difficulty with the advice was that there were many divergent authorities, including those of the Church Fathers. This problem was handled straightforwardly in a circular by Claudio Aquaviva, 5th General of the Jesuits (1580–1615), to his Superiors, written in order to express clearly the basic tenets underlying the *ratio studiorum* of 1586:

No doubt we do not judge that, in the teaching of scholastic theology we must prohibit the opinion of other authors when they are more probable and more commonly received than those of Saint Thomas. Yet because his authority, his doctrine, is so sure and most generally approved, the recommendations of our Constitutions require us to follow him *ordinarily*. That is why all his opinions whatever they may be (except those concerning the immaculate conception of the Blessed Virgin), can be defended and should not be abandoned except after lengthy examination and for serious reasons.

This interpretation of Loyola's advice drew a fine line between following Thomas's opinions *ordinarily* and abandoning them for extraordinary reasons, after lengthy examination. Surely, Descartes would have thought that he had abandoned Thomas's opinions only for serious reasons, after lengthy examination. Descartes' task would have been to demonstrate his reasons, to show that they are more probable. But Aquaviva's circular continued: "One should have as the primary goal in teaching to strengthen the faith and to develop piety. Therefore, no one shall teach anything not in conformity with the Church and received traditions, or that can diminish the vigor of the faith or the ardor of a solid piety." Aquaviva's intent was clear. The primary goal in teaching is the maintenance of the faith, and nothing should be allowed to interfere with it. All teaching must conform to the faith; and since the received traditions are known to conform to the faith, they should be taught and novelties are to be avoided. The circular continued:

Let us try, even when there is nothing to fear for faith and piety, to avoid having anyone suspect us of wanting to create something new or teaching a new doctrine. Therefore no one shall defend any opinion that goes against the axioms received in philosophy or in theology, or against that which the majority of competent men would judge is the common sentiment of the theological schools.

Let no one adopt new opinions in the questions already treated by other authors; similarly, let no one introduce new questions in the matters related in some way to religion or having some importance, without first consulting the Prefect of studies or the Superior.[28]

The prohibition against holding or teaching new doctrines, against adopting new opinions, and even against introducing new questions in order not to diminish faith in any way would surely have made it difficult, if not impossible, for Descartes to have had his views accepted. Descartes' opinions went against many of the axioms received in philosophy. It would have been too optimistic an assessment to think that he might have gained acceptance with a majority of competent men in the theological schools.

Still, as conservative as the Jesuit practices seem, there was always the possibility that new doctrines might come to be accepted, especially those which did not seem to threaten the faith, those which appeared distant from theological matters. It is almost paradoxical that an order so outwardly conservative about philosophy and theology, with a pedagogy that rejects novelty, would have been able to produce novel works in meteorology, magnetic theory, geology, and mathematics.[29] On the other hand, the reasons why Jesuits avoided novelties were not dogmatic, but prudential. One might therefore have expected rigid adherence to official positions, with respect to doctrines considered dangerous to piety, combined with some tolerance of doctrines considered nonthreatening.

Just such a strange a mix of conservative and progressive doctrines can often be observed; for example, here are some doctrines from a public thesis in physics by a student at La Flèche, Jean Tournemine, in 1642.[30] In the section about the world and the heavens we are told that "the stars and firmament are not moved by an internal principle, but by intelligences." The thesis appears to be the rejection of some progressive elements of scholastic physics that could have blazed a path for the principle of inertia.[31] On the other hand, we are also told that "Apostolic authority teaches us that there are three heavens. The first is that of the planets, whose substance is fluid, as shown by astronomical observations; the second is the firmament, a solid body as its name indicates; and the third is the empyrean, in which the stars are specifically distinct from the heavens." This odd theory of the heavens breaks from the Aristotelian–Ptolemaic account of the heavens, fashionable in the seventeenth century, itself a modification of the Aristotelian system of homocentric spheres, adding Ptolemaic three-dimensional epicycles and eccentrics.[32] It is clearly at odds with Aristotelian principles about the heavens; the hypothesis of a fluid first heaven (and the theory as a whole) appears more suitable for the Tychonic scheme.[33]

Concerning the elements, it is asserted that "from the definition of element, it is obvious that four are to be posited, that is, earth, water, air, and fire, neither more nor less" and "heat, cold, wetness, and dryness are primary active qualities." These are extremely rigid assertions about the scholastic doctrine that seemed most under fire in the seventeenth century, especially the statement that the definition of element requires exactly four elements.[34] We are also told (as expected) that "the system of Copernicus on the daily rotation of the earth and its revolution around its own center, which is the immobile sun, is false and foolhardy"; but we are told that "none of the popular experiments are sufficient to assail it." This last admission seems to be very progressive (depending upon the reference to "popular experiments"), since it seems to indicate the acceptance of the relativity of motion.[35]

There is a palpable tension between the intellectual vigor of the new Order of Jesuits setting up a whole new educational system and the attempt to reject novelty. This tension is evident even in an important event in which the young Descartes must have participated, the first memorial celebration of the death of Henry IV, the patron of La Flèche, on June 4, 1611. For the occasion, the students of La Flèche composed and performed verses. The compositions were published for posterity as *Lacrymae Collegii Flexiensis* (La Flèche, 1611). One of the poems has the unlikely title, "Concerning the Death of King Henry the Great and the Discovery of Some New Planets or Wandering Stars Around Jupiter Noted by Galileo, Famous Mathematician of the Grand-Duc of Florence."[36] The poem has little literary merit, but in it the reader is treated to the image of the sun revolving around the earth, taking pity on the sorrow of the French people for the loss of their king, and offering them a new torch – the new stars around Jupiter. The poem combines a naive, poetic view of the sun with an announcement of Galileo's discovery of the moons of Jupiter during the previous year.[37] The poem suggests that the students at La Flèche were made aware of the discovery, but perhaps not its significance, its use as an argument for the Copernican system and against the Aristotelian.

EARLY OBJECTIONS AND REPLIES: THE MORIN CORRESPONDENCE

Descartes' request for objections and his sending out copies did not bear much fruit. Early on, Descartes was uncertain whether he would receive a favorable reaction from the Jesuits. He wrote to Huygens:

As for my book, I do not know what opinion the worldly people will have of it; as for the people of the schools, I understand that they are keeping quiet, and that, displeased with not finding anything in it to grasp in order to exercise their arguments, they are content in saying that, if what is contained in it were true, all their philosophy would have to be false. (AT II 48)

But he was hopeful; in the same letter he wrote:

I have just received a letter from one of the Jesuits at La Flèche, in which I find as much approbation as I would desire from anyone. Thus far he does not find difficulty with anything I wanted to explain, but only with what I did not want to write; as a result, he takes the occasion to request my physics and my metaphysics with great insistence. And since I understand the communication and union that exists among those of that order, the testimony of one of them alone is enough to allow me to hope that I will have them all on my side.   (AT II 50)

Ultimately, Descartes received a number of responses; among them was one from Libertius Fromondus, an anti-atomist, one from Fromondus's student, Plempius, and a third from the progressive Aristotelian, Jean Baptiste Morin.[38] Fromondus treated Descartes as an atomist and sent him a tract against Epicureans and atomists he had written earlier; but he did not respond to Descartes' reply. Descartes wrote to Huygens concerning the exchange: "As for Fromondus, the small disagreement we had is not worth your knowing about . . . In any case, this dispute between us was more like a game of chess; we remained good friends."[39] The correspondence with Plempius was lengthier, with many letters debating biological matters, such as the theory of the circulation of the blood, going back and forth.[40] But the most interesting exchange was that between Descartes and Jean Baptiste Morin, who wrote to Descartes on 22 February 1638, with some comments on astronomy and Descartes' theory of light.

   In the exchange, Morin engaged Descartes in some provocative metaphilosophical issues. First, Morin complained that since Descartes' mind was used to the most subtle and lofty speculations of mathematics, he closed himself off and barricaded himself in his own terms and manners of speaking, in such a way that he seemed at first almost impregnable (AT I 540). He then stated,

However, I do not know what to expect from you, for some have led me to believe that, if I used the terms of the schools, even a little, you would instantly judge me more worthy of disdain than of reply. But, reading your discourse, I do not judge you the enemy of the schools, as you are depicted. . . . The schools seem only to have failed in that they were more occupied by speculation in the search for terms needed to treat things, than in the inquiry into the very truth of things by good experiments; thus they are poor in the latter and rich in the former. That is why I am like you in this respect; I seek the truth of things only in nature and do not place my trust in the schools, which I use only for their terms.   (AT I 541)

Descartes' answer is interesting. First, he assured Morin that he did not try to close off and barricade himself in obscure terms as a defensive move, and that if he did make use of mathematical demonstrations, it is because they taught him to discover the truth, instead of disguising it (AT II 200–1: CSMK 108). He then stated, "As for my disdain for the schools that you've been told about, it can only have been imagined by people who know neither my habits nor my dispositions. And though, in my essays, I made little use of terms known only by the learned, not because I disapprove of them, but only because I wanted to make myself understood also by others" (AT II 201–2). Later on, in the same letter, defending himself against one of Morin's objections, Descartes accepted some scholastic distinctions; trying to impress Morin with his knowledge of scholastic terminology, he peppered his letter with such terms: "I freely use here the terms of the schools in order that you do not judge that I disdain them" (AT II 205). He insisted on responding to Morin *in forma*; he threw in some scholastic disputation terms and phrases, such as *distinguo, concedo totum, nego consequentiam*, and he even suggested that he was taking the term "infinite" *syncategorematice* "so that the schools would have nothing to object to in this matter."[41]

There is an amusing reply to Descartes' letter, as a marginal comment to a letter from Mersenne to Descartes:

You so reassured and enriched us by the excellent replies you made to Mr. Morin and I, that I assure you, instead of the 38 sols of postage on the package, seeing what it contained, I would have willingly given 38 écus. We read the reply together; and Mr. Morin found your style so beautiful that I advise you never to change it. For your analogies and your curiosities satisfy more than what all others produce . . . Moreover, you succeeded very well, in the reply to Mr. Morin, by showing that you do not disdain, or at least, you are not ignorant of Aristotle's philosophy. That is what contributed toward the increase in esteem Mr. Morin testifies as having for you. It is also what I assure those who, deceived by the clarity and precision of your style – which you can lower to make yourself understood by the common man – believe that you do not understand scholastic philosophy at all; I let them know that you understand scholastic philosophy just as well as the masters who teach it and who seem most proud of their own ability.[42]

The greater esteem Morin felt for Descartes did not prevent him from sending a second letter, in the style of Descartes' response, still objecting about the uses of terms, etc. Descartes responded to the letter, but with less enthusiasm. Morin wrote a third letter, but Descartes stopped the correspondence there. Descartes wrote to Mersenne, "I will not reply to Mr. Morin, since he does not want me to. Also, there is nothing in his last letter that gives me the occasion to reply with something useful; between us, it seems to me that his thoughts are now farther from mine than they were at the beginning, so that we will never come to any agreement" (15 November 1638: AT II 437).

The episodes of anticipated objections and replies to the *Discourse* seem to have failed completely. When Fromondus bothered to respond, it was not to start a dialogue. Worse yet, when a dialogue was started, as in the case of Morin, it did not result in any meeting of minds. How could Descartes have expected to succeed in winning over the more conservative members of the intellectual community, including those with a specific intellectual agenda, such as the Jesuits, when he could not convince someone like Morin of his views? Morin, a renowned optical theorist, astrologer to the king, and professor of mathematics at the Collège de France, at least styled himself a progressive thinker: "I am like you," he said to Descartes, "in that I seek the truth of things in nature and do not place my trust in the schools, which I use only for their terms." It is true that Morin was antiatomist and antiheliocentrist, as were the conservatives, but he was a mathematician of the Collège de France, not a theologian or faculty of a Jesuit College; at least he was willing to entertain a debate. The exchanges with Fromondus and Morin could not have pleased a philosopher who held that when someone has the truth he cannot fail to convince his opponents (*Regulae* Rule II: AT X 363: CSM I 11).

THE BOURDIN AFFAIR AND THE EUSTACHIUS PROJECT

Descartes' relations with the Jesuits took a new turn in 1640. On 30 June and 1 July, a Professor at Clermont, the Jesuit college in Paris, held a public disputation in which his student, a young noble named Charles Potier (who later became a Cartesian), defended some theses; among the theses were three articles concerning Descartes' theory of subtle matter,[43] reflection, and refraction. The professor,

Father Bourdin, composed a preface to the thesis, called a *velitatio* (skirmish), which he delivered himself. Mersenne attended the disputation and defended Descartes. He apparently chastised Bourdin for having attacked Descartes publicly without having sent Descartes his objections; Mersenne then forwarded Descartes the *velitatio*, together with the three articles concerning Descartes' doctrines, as if they came from Bourdin himself.[44]

Descartes wrote to Mersenne on 22 July 1640, thanking him for the affection Mersenne showed for him "in the dispute against the theses of the Jesuits." He told Mersenne that he had written to the rector of Clermont College requesting that they address their objections against what he had written to him, "for he does not want to have any dealings with any of them in particular, except insofar as it would be attested to by the order as a whole" (AT III 94). And he complained that the *velitatio* Mersenne sent him was "written with the intent to obscure rather than to illuminate the truth."[45] At the same time, Descartes wrote to Huygens, telling him, "I believe that I will go to war with the Jesuits; for their mathematician of Paris has publicly refuted my *Dioptrics* in his theses – about which I have written to his Superior, in order to engage the whole order in this dispute" (AT III 103: CSMK 151).

The Bourdin affair degenerated, Descartes consistently referring to Bourdin's objections as *cavillations*.[46] The period of this dispute was a particularly difficult one for Descartes, since it was the time of his publication of the *Meditations*, his work on "First Philosophy," or metaphysics, which he had only sketched in the *Discourse*, and which was certain to lead him into greater controversies, given that its content was yet closer to theology than was that of the *Discourse* and its appended *Essays* on physical and mathematical topics. The summer of 1640 was also the time when Mersenne was sending out Descartes' *Meditations* to the intellectuals of the seventeenth-century, requesting objections that would be published with the *Meditations*. Descartes even expected a set of objections from Bourdin himself.[47] One has to remember that this enterprise would be crucial for Descartes if he expected to win his war against the Jesuits. The whole affair should be put into the context of the failure of the requested objections and replies to the *Discourse*, the unsuccessful correspondence with Morin, and the subsequent open hostilities with the Jesuits.

On 30 September 1640, Descartes wrote to Mersenne: "the cavils of Father Bourdin have resolved me to arm myself from now on, as much as I can, with the authority of others, since the truth is so little appreciated alone." In this context he told Mersenne that he will not travel that winter, since he is "expecting the objections of the Jesuits in 4 or 5 months," and he believes that he "must put himself in the proper posture to await them" (AT III 184–5). He then made an unusual request and an interesting revelation:

As a result, I feel like reading some of their philosophy – that which I have not done in twenty years – in order to see whether it now seems to me better than I once thought. Toward that end, I beg of you to send me the names of authors who have written textbooks in philosophy and who have the most following among the Jesuits, and whether there are new ones from twenty years ago; I remember only the Coimbrans, Toletus, and Rubius. I would also like to know whether there is someone who has written a summary of all of scholastic philosophy and who has a following, for this would spare me the time to read all their heavy tomes. It seems to me that there was a Chartreux or a Feuillant who had accomplished this, but I do not remember his name.   (AT III 185: CSMK 154)

The scholastics Descartes remembered, the Coimbrans, Toletus, and Rubius, were all Jesuit textbook authors Descartes probably read at La Flèche. The Coimbrans (the Conimbricenses), were professors at the Colègio das Artes, Coimbra (Portugal), who published a series of encyclopedic commentaries on Aristotle's works between 1592 and 1598. The most noted of the Coimbrans was Petrus de Fonseca, who contributed to the *Ratio studiorum* and who published separately his own commentaries on the *Metaphysics* and the *De Anima*.[48] Franciscus Toletus was a professor at the Collegio Romano (1562–9) who published numerous commentaries on Aristotle's works, including an important *Logic* (1572), *Physics* (1575), and *De Anima* (1575).[49] And Antonio Rubius taught philosophy in Mexico; he published commentaries on Aristotle's *Logic*, the *Logica mexicana* (1603), *Physics* (1605), *De Caelo* (1615), and *De Anima* (1611).[50] We do not have Mersenne's reply, but presumably, he identified Eustachius a Sancto Paulo as the Feuillant that Descartes remembered having written a summary of all of scholastic philosophy in one volume, since in Descartes' next letter to Mersenne Descartes wrote: "I have purchased the *Philosophy* of Brother Eustachius a

Sancto Paulo, which seems to me to be the best book ever written on this matter; I would like to know whether the author still lives" (AT III 232).

Eustachius a Sancto Paulo (Asseline) entered the Feuillants, a Cistercian Order, in 1605, and was professor of theology at the Sorbonne. He published the *Summa philosophica quadripartita de rebus dialecticis, moralibus, physicis, et metaphysicis* in 1609. It was published again and again throughout the first half of the century, until 1648.[51]

We should make no mistake about the sense of Descartes' praise of Eustachius's *Summa* as "the best book ever written on this matter." In the same letter, Descartes says about the philosophy of the schools, "As for scholastic philosophy, I do not hold it as difficult to refute on account of the diversity of their opinions; for one can easily upset all the foundations about which they are in agreement among themselves; and that accomplished, all their particular disputes would appear inept" (AT III 231–2: CSMK 156). This judgment was reinforced, as Descartes read more scholastic textbooks, seeking a textbook as good as Eustachius's, but written by a Jesuit; Descartes told Mersenne, "I will also look at the Philosophy text of Mr. Draconis [that is, de Raconis], which I believe will be found here; for if he is more brief than the other and as well received, I will prefer it" (AT III 234).

Charles d'Abra de Raconis was born a Calvinist and converted to Catholicism. He taught philosophy at the Collège des Grassins and the Collège du Plessis, Paris. He then held a chair of theology at the Collège de Navarre, also in Paris. He published his *Summa totius philosophiae* in 1617, republishing it in parts and expanding it numerous times throughout the first half of the century, up to 1651.[52]

Later, Descartes wrote:

I have seen the *Philosophy* of Mr. Raconis, but it is not as suitable for my design as that of Father Eustachius. And as for the Coimbrans, their writings are too lengthy; I would have wished wholeheartedly that they had written as briefly as the other, since I would have preferred to have dealings with the society as a whole, instead of a particular person.[53]

Descartes seems to have gained confidence as he read scholastic philosophy; he told Mersenne, "I thank you for the letter you've transcribed for me; but I find nothing useful in it, nor anything that seems as improbable to me as the philosophy of the schools" (AT III 256). He also informed Mersenne of his new project, the "design" to which he referred in the previously cited letter:

My intent is to write in order a textbook of my philosophy in the form of theses, in which, without any superfluity of discourse, I will place only my conclusions, together with the true reasons from which I draw them – what I think I can do in a few words. And in the same book, I will publish an ordinary philosophy text [that is, a school text], such as perhaps that of Brother Eustachius, with my notes at the end of each question, to which I will add the various opinions of others and what one should believe about all of them, and perhaps, at the end, I will draw some comparisons between these two philosophies.   (AT III 233: CSMK 157)

Later, he informed Mersenne that he had begun the project (AT III 259: CSMK 161). He wrote to others about it; he floated a trial balloon with the Chief of the Jesuits, almost using the project as a threat, but also trying to determine the Jesuits's reaction to it. He even attributed the project to one of his unnamed friends (AT III 270). But the project was soon aborted: "I am unhappy to hear about the death of Father Eustachius; for, although this gives me greater freedom to write my notes on his philosophy, I would nevertheless have preferred to do this with his permission, while he was still alive."[54] Descartes continued to use the project as a threat or bargaining chip with the Jesuits, but he no longer seemed willing to produce the work. He wrote to Mersenne, concerning a letter from Bourdin, "I believe that his Provincial sent it in order to ask you whether it is true that I am writing against them. . . . It is certain that I would have chosen the compendium of Father Eustachius as the best, if I wanted to refute someone; but it is also true that I have completely lost the intent to refute this philosophy; for I see that it is so absolutely and so clearly destroyed by means of the establishment of my philosophy alone, that no other refutation is needed."[55]

The Eustachius project is instructive for many reasons. One of the inferences one should draw from it is that Descartes was not familiar with scholastic philosophy in the period of his greatest work, during 1637–40. When he finally formulated his mature works, he departed either dramatically or by degrees from a scholastic tradition he no longer knew very well. Of course, Descartes was taught scholastic philosophy in his youth at La Flèche, but he abandoned his study of it for twenty years, roughly between 1620 and 1640, and he picked it up again only in 1640, to arm himself against the expected attacks of the Jesuits. We should expect that Descartes was generally well-versed in scholastic philosophy[56] only when writing his earliest works, the *Rules for the Direction of the Mind* for example. (The remnants of scholasticism in Descartes' mature works, the *Discourse* and the *Meditations*, are therefore likely to be deceptive for the interpreter.) Finally, from 1640 on, in the *Replies* to the *Objections* to the *Meditations* and in the *Principles of Philosophy*, Descartes relearned scholastic philosophy (and scholastic terminology) and began the process of reinterpreting his thoughts (or translating his doctrines) to make them more compatible with scholasticism.[57] One can detect Descartes' subtle shifts in doctrine or terminology by contrasting his early and later writings – roughly, those before and after 1640.

It is well-known that Descartes refused to publish his *Le Monde* after being told of the condemnation of Galileo by the Catholic Church in 1633. The Church had declared the immobility of the sun to be foolish and absurd in philosophy and formally heretical, and the motion of the earth to merit the same censure in philosophy and to be at least erroneous in faith. Clearly, the Church was attempting to defend the faith, but it was also upholding a particular philosophy; the immobility of the earth and revolution of the sun around the earth were tenets of Aristotelianism. Descartes responded in characteristic style: "this has so astonished me that I almost resolved to burn all my papers, or at least not to let anyone see them. For I cannot imagine that Galileo, who is Italian and even well-loved by the Pope, as I understand, could have been made a criminal for anything other than having wanted to establish the motion of the earth" (AT I 270–1: CSMK 41). In his *Le Monde* Descartes was clearly committed to the motion of the earth: "I confess that, if the motion of the earth is false, all the foundations of my philosophy are also. For it is clearly demonstrated by them. It is so linked to all parts of my treatise that I cannot detach it without rendering the rest defective" (ibid). So Descartes withheld publication and measured his public utterances on this issue. He avoided all discussion of it in the synopsis he gave of *Le Monde* in his 1637 *Discourse* and, when he finally took a public stance on the issue, in his 1644 *Principles of Philosophy*, it was to claim that "strictly speaking, the earth does not move" (*Principles*, Part III art. 28).

Descartes' philosophical progress on the motion of the earth seems to have resulted in a politically more tenable position. One can see similar changes in Descartes' terminology with respect to related matters. Descartes was pessimistic in *Le Monde* about the possibility of a definition of motion; he even ridiculed the scholastics' definition: "To render it in some way intelligible, they have not been able to explain it more clearly than in these terms: *motus est actus entis in potentia, prout in potentia est.* For me these words are so obscure that I am compelled to leave them in Latin because I cannot interpret them" (AT XI 39: CSM I 94). For Descartes, the nature of motion is simpler and more intelligible than the nature of other things; it is used to explain other things – lines as the motion of a point and surfaces as the motion of a line, for example – instead of being explained by them. But, in the *Principles*, Descartes gave his own definition of motion, both in the ordinary sense of the word and in the strict sense, contrasting his definition with that of the scholastics (Part II, art. 24–5). Similarly, Descartes criticized the related scholastic doctrine of place in his early works: "When they define place as 'the surface of the surrounding body,' they are not really conceiving anything false, but are merely misusing the word 'place' . . ." (*Regulae:* AT X 433–4: CSM I 53). Descartes rejected the scholastics' concept of intrinsic place (ibid.) and ridiculed their concept of imaginary space (AT XI 31). But in the *Principles*, Descartes developed a doctrine of internal and external place clearly indebted to those he had previously rejected.[58]

One can multiply such instances, but perhaps one more example might suffice to show that these instances are not limited to the more scientific aspects of Descartes' philosophy. One of the Cartesian philosophical doctrines under attack was the doctrine of material falsity. In the *Meditations* Descartes characterized material falsity as "occurring in ideas, when they represent non-things as things" (AT VII 44: CSM II 30). Descartes' example of material falsity was his idea of cold, which, though it is merely the absence of heat, represents cold as something real and positive. As Arnauld rightly pointed out, in his *Objections* to the *Meditations*, "if cold is merely an absence, then there cannot be an idea of cold which represents it to me as a positive thing" (AT VII 207: CSM II 145). Descartes' response seems to have been a shift away from his initial position; that is, Descartes asserted in the *Replies* that the reason he called the idea of cold materially false was that he was unable to judge whether or not what it represented to him was something positive existing outside his sensation.[59] But there was also an interesting addition in Descartes' reply. Descartes seems to have used the occasion to show off his knowledge of scholastic philosophy in an ostentatious manner; the reply looks suspiciously similar to those given to Morin. Descartes, who did not usually cite sources, went out of his way to state that he did not worry about his use of material falsity, because Suarez defined material falsity in the same way in his *Metaphysical Disputations,* disp. 9, sec. 2, n. 4.[60] The response is even more curious, given that Descartes did not refer to Suarez anywhere else, even though his correspondents did refer to him. And Suarez's scholastic doctrine is yet a third notion of material falsity. Suarez's doctrine was basically an expansion of the Thomist doctrine that truth and falsity consist in composition and division.[61] Thus, material falsity as used by Suarez was about propositions, not ideas.

There seems to have been some vacillation in Descartes' mind between the material falsity of an idea as representing being as nonbeing and as having so little content that we cannot tell whether it represents something or not; but Descartes aggravated the apparent vacillation with an uncharacteristic and unprepared for reference to Suarez on material falsity as arising from composition and division. In the end, the doctrine of material falsity seems to have disappeared entirely. It did not recur in the *Principles,* possibly having been replaced by Suarez's account, which would assimilate the notion with formal falsity.[62]

RECONCILIATIONS AND CONDEMNATIONS

After the publication of the *Meditations,* Descartes became involved in philosophical controversies on a larger scale. He quarreled with Voëtius, rector of Utrecht University, and judgment was pronounced against him by the Utrecht magistrates in 1642.[63] Perhaps because of his greater problems with the Protestants in the Netherlands, Descartes sought to make peace with the Jesuits. In 1644, after Descartes published Bourdin's *Seventh set of Objections* and his *Replies,* together with his *Letter to Dinet,* complaining about how badly he had been treated, there was a reconciliation between

Descartes and Bourdin. Descartes visited Bourdin at the Collège Clermont, and Bourdin offered to play the role of Mersenne in Paris, to distribute Descartes' letters. Descartes also visited La Flèche itself, for the first time since he had left it. From 1644 to his death in 1650, the relations between Descartes and the Jesuits remained outwardly cordial.[64] However, in 1663, the works of Descartes were put on the *Index of Prohibited Works* with the notation, "donec corrigantur" – "until corrected."[65] But this did not prevent Descartes from having followers.

Descartes even picked up some followers among the Jesuits of La Flèche though very belatedly. For example, one can find support for various early modern doctrines in a student thesis (by Ignace de Tremblay) defended on July 1700 at Le Flèche.[66] One can also find a Malebranchiste and Cartesian Jesuit, the Père André, teaching at La Flèche, though not without some problems with his superiors.[67]

There was a final spasm of opposition to Descartes' work during the first decade of the 1700s.[68] Michel-Angelo Tamburini was elected General of the Order on January 31, 1706; his first act was the promulgation of thirty prohibited propositions.[69] Some of the propositions seemed to be condemnations of Malebranchian positions rather than those of Descartes. Regardless, the attempt at condemnation could not have succeeded for very long; as one can see, among the Jesuit propositions are even the denial of the relativity of motion and the denial of the conservation of inertia. Once again, however, the resiliency of Aristotelian ideas seems to have been demonstrated.

Moderns tend to think of Cartesianism as having dealt the fatal blow to scholasticism; and that, despite the surprising tenacity of Aristotelianism, has the ring of truth to it. However, the defeat of Aristotelianism was accomplished by tactical measures as well as by arguments and doctrines. Descartes, as we have seen, was keenly aware of this aspect of his relations with contemporaries and predecessors; in a letter to Beeckman, he wrote:

Consider first what are the things a person can learn from another; you will find that they are languages, stories, experiences, and clear and distinct demonstrations, such as those of the geometers, that bring conviction to the mind. As for the opinions and maxims of the philosophers, merely to repeat them is not to teach them. Plato says one thing, Aristotle another, Epicurus another, Telesio, Campanella, Bruno, Basso, Vanini, and all the innovators all say different things. Of all these people, who teaches me, that is, who teaches anyone who loves wisdom? No doubt it is the person who can first persuade someone with his reasons, or at least by his authority.   (AT I 156)

Descartes, winning some early battles by seeming to defy authority and losing others when trying to identify himself with conventional authorities, finally won the war, perhaps by persuading others with his reasons.

NOTES

1 My emphasis. The statement is ambiguous, of course, between Descartes having learned the Ciceronian phrase and coming to realize the matter himself. The pronouncements of the *Discourse* are formulae that echo standard skeptical assertions; for the literary background to the *Discourse*, see Gilson, *Discours de la méthode texte et commentaire.* Still, the point is that disagreement about philosophical matters, and even the strangeness of philosophical positions, are part of the common knowledge shared by Descartes.

2 For more information concerning La Flèche and its curriculum, consult Rochemonteix, *Un Collège de Jésuites aux XVIIe et XVIIIe siècles: le Collège Henri IV de la Flèche;* a more popular exposition of the same material can be read in Sirven, *Les Années d'apprentissage de Descartes.*

3 For other colleges, as well as for general Jesuit educational theory, consult Wallace, *Galileo and His Sources, the Heritage of the Collegio Romano in Galileo's Science; Monumenta Paedagogica Societatis Jesu* (Matriti, 1901); and Dainville, *L'Education des Jésuites;* also Brockliss, "Aristotle, Descartes and the New Science: Natural philosophy at the University of Paris, 1600–1740," *Annals of Science* 38 (1981): 33–69; and idem, *French Higher Education in the Seventeenth and Eighteenth Centuries: A Cultural History.*

4 Later, the second year became the year of physics and mathematics, with the third year being devoted to metaphysics.

5 See, for example, Gaultruche, *Institutio totius mathematicae* (1656), a good exemplar for what would have been taught in mathematics at La Flèche, because Gaultruche was a Jesuit who taught mathematics at La Flèche and Caens.

6 Rochemonteix, *Un Collège de Jésuites*, vol. II, p. 27.

7 Ibid., pp. 25–7. Similarly, Marin Mersenne, Descartes' principal correspondent, was one of the students of humble origins who studied at La Flèche and played a role in the intellectual life of the seventeenth century. For Mersenne's intellectual biography, see Lenoble, *Mersenne ou la naissance du mécanisme,* or Dear, *Mersenne and the Learning of the Schools.*

8 As I've already indicated, it is difficult to reconcile Descartes' enthusiasm for La Flèche with his attitude on scholastic education in the *Discourse*. Of course, Descartes is merely stressing the academic rigor of the teaching, the discipline, and the social ethos of La Flèche; on the face of it this is quite compatible with the *Discourse* thesis that the subjects taught there weren't much use. But why should one recommend a more rigorous school over a less rigorous one when that which is taught more rigorously is of little use? This question becomes more pressing when one realizes that, as early as 1634, Regius (Chair of Medicine, and from 6 September 1638 on, extraordinary Professor at Utrecht) was already giving private lessons on Cartesian philosophy and physics, having been taught it by Reneri. It is one thing to recommend La Flèche as the best of a sorry lot, but another to recommend it over Utrecht, where one might be taught Cartesian philosophy.

9 See, for example, the letter of 14 June 1637 to Huygens (?): AT I 387, in which Descartes indicates that, of the three copies of the *Discourse* enclosed, one is for the recipient of the letter, another is for the Cardinal de Richelieu, and the third is for the King himself.

10 AT I 383. This sentence enables one to guess that the recipient of the letter is the Père Etienne Noël, Descartes' *repetitor* in philosophy, especially since Noël was rector of La Flèche in 1637. See Rodis-Lewis, "Descartes et les mathématiques au collège," in Grimaldi and Marion (eds.) *Le Discours et sa méthode*, p. 190 n; see also idem, "Descartes aurait-il eu un professeur nominaliste?" and "Quelques Questions disputées sur la jeunesse de Descartes", in *Idées et vérités éternelles chez Descartes*, pp. 165–81.

11 Rochemonteix, *Un Collège de Jésuites*, vol. IV, p. 10, citing Loyola: "in theologia praelegendum esse S. Thomam."

12 Ibid., p. 8 n.

13 The four kinds of causes, as given in Aristotle's *Physics* II, chs. 3–10, are formal, material, efficient, and final; all four would be involved in a complete explanation of a change. For example, in the Aristotelian account of the reproduction of man, the material cause is the matter supplied by the mother, the formal cause is the specific form of man (that is, rational animal), the efficient cause is supplied by the father, and the final cause is the end toward which the process is directed.

14 Aristotle discusses the four elements in *De Caelo* III and IV. The elements, that is, earth, water, air, and fire, are characterized by pairs of the contraries, hot and cold, moist and dry (*On Generation and Corruption* I); in Aristotle's theory of motion, the elements move naturally in a rectilinear motion, the first two elements having a natural downward motion, toward the center of the universe, whereas the second two have

a natural upward motion, toward the periphery of the sublunar region. This creates a distinction between the sublunar world of the elements and the supralunar world of the heavens, whose ether moves naturally in a circular motion.

15 The three principles of natural things are form, matter, and privation, discussed by Aristotle in Book I of the *Physics*. The form of a thing is its actuality, whereas the matter is its potentiality; privation is what the thing is not. For example, in a change from water being cold to being hot, heat is the form that the thing lacks, but it is water, the matter or subject, that gains the form and becomes hot (cold itself or the bare matter does not change). Change is the gaining or losing of forms; but some forms are essential and cannot be lost (for example, man cannot lose the form, rational animal, and remain man). Thus, a form is accidental when it confers a new quality to a substance already formed – heat, for example. On the other hand, a substantial form confers being; there is generation of a new being when a substantial form unites with matter, and real destruction when one separates from matter.

16 These "axioms" are sufficient to banish Stoic, Epicurean, and atomist philosophies. Epicureans and atomists account for change by the substitution or rearrangement of basic particles, or atoms, not by the replacement of forms in a matter capable of accepting various forms. Moreover, for an Epicurean or an atomist, the particles themselves would be more basic than the elements, and an insistence on four elements would go against Stoic cosmology.

17 This "common notion" is sufficient to reject the philosophy of non-Thomist scholastics, such as Ockhamists. In his *Commentary on the Sentences* II, Q.18, Ockham accepts an account of magnetism as action at a distance, without the intervention of a medium, instead of accepting a medium as necessary for propagating a magnetic quality.

18 The target of this opinion is the Averroist doctrine of the numerical unity of intellective soul, that is, the doctrine denying the existence of individual souls and asserting that there is just one intellective soul.

19 The target of this opinion seems to be the Augustinian and Franciscan doctrines of the plurality of substantial forms. John Duns Scotus and William of Ockham held the thesis that man is a composite of forms (rational, sensitive, etc.), a thesis rejected by Thomas Aquinas, who argued that there is just one form or soul in man (the rational soul), which performs the functions that the other souls perform in lower beings.

20 Bibliothèque Nationale, mss. fond Latin, n. 10989, regist. ord. fol. 87, as transcribed in Rochemonteix, *Un Collège de Jésuites*, vol. IV, pp. 4 n–6 n.

21 See Meditation IV: AT VII 55, and elsewhere.

22 Rule IV: AT X 442, for example. If one wanted to draw Descartes closer to Aristotle (as does R. Le Bossu, in *Parallèle des principes de la physique d'Aristote et de celle de Descartes* (Paris, 1674), pp. 286–7) one could say that Descartes accepts three out of Aristotle's four elements, that is, fire, air, and earth. (See, for example, *Le Monde:* AT XI 25.) But that would be to disregard the important difference that Aristotle's elements are differentiated *qualitatively*, whereas there is only a quantitative difference among Descartes' elements.

23 See *Principles* IV, art. 198, and elsewhere; Descartes does not say (in a letter to Regius: AT III 491–2) that he does not reject substantial forms overtly, that he mereiy asserts they are not needed; the context of the assertion is an interesting letter in which Descartes counsels Regius to abstain from public disputes and from advancing novel opinions (that one ought to retain the old opinions in name, giving only new reasons).

24 Descartes is a mechanist; his world is a plenum. For the impossibility of void, see AT IV 329.

25 Meditation III, AT VII 45–50 (AT IX 32–40).

26 AT I 152 and elsewhere.

27 For the doctrine that the numerical unity of a body does not depend upon its matter but its form, which is the soul, see the letter to Mesland: AT IV 346: CSMK 278.

28 Bibliothèque Nationale, mss. fonds latins, n. 10989, in-4 Reg. ord., as transcribed in Rochemonteix, *Un Collège de Jésuites*, vol. IV, pp. 11 n–12 n.

29 Cf. Heilbron, *Electricity in the Seventeenth and Eighteenth Centuries: A Study in Early Modern Physics.*

30 Joannes Tournemyne (La Flèche, 1642), as edited in Rochemonteix, *Un Collège de Jésuites,* vol. IV, pp. 365–8.

31 Including the rejection of fourteenth-century scholastic doctrines such as a circular impetus for the heavens. Cf. Oresme, *Livre du ciel et du monde,* ed. and trans. Menu and Denomy; and Albert of Saxony, *Quaestiones super quatuor libros de caelo et mundo* (1516).

32 As depicted, for example, in Eustachius a Sancto Paulo, *Summa Philosophica Quadripartita* (1609), Part 3, p. 96. It is interesting to note that "Apostolic authority" is invoked for the theory. Cf. Bellarmine's *Louvain Lectures,* trans. Baldini and Coyne, *Studi Galileiani* 1 (1984).

33 The opposition between fluid and solid indicates that the thesis is not a version of the homocentric spheres made fluid. See Grant, "Celestial Orbs in the Latin Middle Ages." The reason why this theory of the heavens seems to be Tychonic is that solidity is attributed to the firmament, or the outermost heavenly body, containing the fluid universe of the planets. Fluidity is attributed to the world of the planets because of "astronomical observations." This seems to allude to the kind of observations of comets and novas that Tycho de Brahe used to argue against

the solidity of planetary heavenly spheres. The Tychonic system, in which the earth was the center of the universe, with the planets revolving around the sun as their center, was a perfect compromise between the old Aristotelian–Ptolemaic system and the heliocentric Copernican system; it did not require a new physics for the motion of the earth. It did require, however, a fluid planetary heaven, since the paths of some planets intersected. Descartes discusses astronomical systems, including Tycho's in *Principles* III 16–19, 38–41.

34 See Reif, "The textbook tradition in natural philosophy, 1600–1650."

35 It is difficult to tell what exactly was argued by the student in his thesis. But there were many "popular experiments" at the time claiming to refute Copernican astronomy; for example, cannon balls fired the same distance east and west were used as evidence against the rotation of the earth required by the Copernican system. According to modern principles of physics, these results cannot be counted against the rotation of the earth, so that the student's admission that "popular experiments" cannot defeat Copernicanism is interesting. During the same period, defenders of Copernicanism, such as Gassendi and Mersenne, used similar experiments in defense of Copernicanism: a stone falling from the mast of a moving ship falls parallel to the mast – *De motu impresso a motore translato* (Paris, 1642), reported by Mersenne in his *Cogitata* (Paris, 1644). It should also be pointed out that calling the Copernican system "false and foolhardy" is less harsh than calling it "foolish and absurd in philosophy and formally heretical," as did the Church in 1616. See below for Descartes' reaction to the Church's condemnation of Galileo's heliocentrism in 1633.

36 In Rochemonteix, *Un Collège de Jésuites*, vol. I, pp. 147 n–148 n:

> La France avait déjà repandu tant de pleurs
> Pour la mort de son Roy, que l'empire de l'onde
> Gros de flots ravageait à la terre ses fleurs,
> D'un déluge second menaçant tout le monde;
>
> Lorsque l'astre du jour, qui faisait la ronde
> Autour de l'Univers, meu des proches malheurs
> Qui hastaient devers nous leur course vagabonde
> Lui parla de la sorte, au fort de ses douleurs;
>
> France de qui les pleurs, pour l'amour de ton Prince,
> Nuisent par leur excès àtoute autre province,
> Cesse de t'affliger sur son vide tombeau;
>
> Car Dieu l'ayant tire tout entier de la terre
> Au ciel de Jupiter maintenant il esclaire
> Pour servir aux mortels de céleste flambeau.

[France had already shed so many tears/ For the death of her King, that the empire of the waves,/ Heavy with water, ravaged the flowers of the earth,/

Threatening the whole world with a second flood;/ When the sun, making its rounds/ Around the universe, moved by the near disaster/ Which hastened toward us in its wandering path/ Spoke to her in this manner, amidst her pain:/ France, whose tears for the love of your Prince/ Do harm all other provinces by their excess,/ Stop grieving over your empty tomb;/ For God having taken him wholly from the earth/ He now illuminates the sky of Jupiter,/ That he may serve as a heavenly torch for all mortals.]

37 Galileo, *Siderius Nuncius.*

38 Descartes was asked by Mersenne whether foreigners formulated better objections than the French. Descartes replied that he did not count any of those received as French other than Morin's objections. He referred to a dispute with Petit, which he dismissed, saying that he did not take Petit seriously but simply mocked him in return. He then listed the objections of the foreigners: Fromondus from Louvain, Plempius, an anonymous Jesuit from Louvain, and someone from the Hague. AT II 191–2: CSMK 105.

39 AT II 49. The correspondence between Descartes and Fromondus as well as that between Descartes and Morin is discussed by Daniel Garber in "Descartes, the Aristotelians, and the revolution that did not happen in 1637."

40 The correspondence between Descartes and Plempius is discussed by Marjorie Grene, "Animal mechanism and the Cartesian vision of nature," in Brophy (ed.), *The Cartesian and Newtonian Revolution: Essays on Matter, Motion, and Mechanism;* it was not always a pleasant exchange.

41 AT II 205–7. *In forma* means in logical form; *distinguo, concedo totum,* and *nego consequentiam* mean "I distinguish," "I concede totally," and "I deny the consequence," respectively. "Taking the term 'infinite' syncategorematically" alludes to medieval refinements of Aristotle's doctrine on potential infinity (versus actual infinity) from *Physics* III, chs. 4–8. The logicians distinguished between categorematic terms and syncategorematic terms, or terms that have a signification by themselves, and terms that have no signification apart (cosignificative terms). Examples of the first kind are substantival names and verbs, and examples of the second kind are adjectives, adverbs, conjunctions, and prepositions. A list of the syncategorematic terms would commonly include: every, whole, both, of every sort, no, nothing, neither, but, alone, only, is, not, necessarily, contingently, begins, ceases, if, unless, but that, and infinitely many. One might call these words logical constants (or perhaps connectives, functions, quantifiers) and distinguish them from predicative terms. The distinction is applied to infinity to yield both a categorematic and syncategorematic infinite. It allows one to solve

some logical puzzles, since it may be true that something is infinite, taken syncategorematically, and false that something is infinite, taken categorematically. For more on infinity as a syncategorematic term, see Gabbey and Ariew, "Body and the physical world," in the forthcoming Ayers and Garber (eds.), *Cambridge History of Seventeenth Century Philosophy*.

42 AT II 287. It is difficult to believe that Mersenne is being straightforward in his marginal comment – that he believes Descartes to understand scholastic philosophy as well as the masters who teach it. Mersenne himself can be said to understand scholastic philosophy very well, as his writings demonstrate, and to have kept up with the various disputes. On the other hand, as we shall see, even Descartes is aware of his own shortcomings in this respect, aware that he has not read scholastic philosophy for the last fifteen years or so.

43 Descartes' world is a plenum of subtle matter (ether, or First matter), whose action is used by Descartes to explain such diverse phenomena as gravitation and light. Bourdin is complaining about Descartes' use of subtle matter for the propagation of light in *Optics* I, pp. 5–7, "as a blind man can sense the bodies around him using his cane" (AT VI 84: CSM I 153).

44 Baillet, *La Vie de M. Des-Cartes* II, 73. Bourdin was professor of humanities at La Flèche (1618–23), of rhetoric (1633), and mathematics (1634). He was sent to Paris, to the Collège de Clermont (later known as the Collège Louis-le-Grand) in 1635. On a couple of occasions, Descartes asks Mersenne to tell him whether the *velitatio* sent by Mersenne was given to him by Bourdin, so that Descartes might judge whether Bourdin acted in good faith. See AT III 162, for example.

45 AT III 94. In another letter, Descartes tells Mersenne that he is shocked by the *velitatio* of the Bourdin, for he does not have a single objection to anything Descartes has written, but rather attacks doctrines Descartes does not hold. AT III 127–8.

46 That is, "quibbles" or "cavils." See AT III 163, 184, 250, for example.

47 Bourdin wrote the Seventh Objections, which were not received by Descartes in time for the first printing of the Meditations and Objections and Replies, but made the second printing.

48 See C. H. Lohr, "Renaissance Latin Aristotle Commentaries: Authors C," *Renaissance Quarterly* 28 (1975) and "Authors D-F," *Renaissance Quarterly* 29 (1976). See also Schmitt, Skinner, and Kessler (eds.), *Cambridge History of Renaissance Philosophy*, pp. 814, 818.

49 See Lohr, "Authors So-Z," *Renaissance Quarterly* 35 (1982) and Schmitt, Skinner, and Kessler (eds.), *Cambridge History of Renaissance Philosophy*, p. 838.

50 See Lohr, "Authors Pi-Sm," *Renaissance Quarterly* 33 (1980).

51 See Lohr, "Authors D-F."

52 See Lohr, "Authors A-B," *Studies in the Renaissance* 21 (1974).

53 AT III 251. Descartes never mentions one of the more interesting works in the genre, Scipion Dupleix's *Corps de philosophie contenant la logique, l'ethique, la physique et la metaphysique* (Geneva, 1627). Dupleix is more a historian than philosopher, summarizing the school learning of his day as succinctly as possible, for an audience that is not comfortable with Latin – meaning, an unschooled audience. Cf. E. Faye, "Le corps de philosophie de Scipion Dupleix et l'arbre cartesien des sciences," *Corpus* 2 (1986): 7–15.

54 AT III 280. Descartes had previously indicated that he only wanted to do the project "with the writings of a living person and with his permission, which it seems to me I would easily obtain when my intention, to consider the one I chose as the best of all who have written on philosophy, will be known" (AT III 234).

55 AT III 470. For Descartes' keeping open the option to write such a philosophy as a threat against the Jesuits, see AT III 470, 480–1.

56 But probably only the scholastic philosophy represented by the Coimbrans, Toletus, and Rubius, that is, a sixteenth- and seventeenth-century neo-Thomism.

57 For differences between Jesuit scholasticism and non-Jesuit scholasticism, see Ariew and Gabbey in Ayers and Garber (eds.), *Cambridge History of Seventeenth Century Philosophy*, Part IV, Ch. I.

58 Cf. *Principles* II, arts. 10–15. One can find these distinctions in Part III of Eustachius a Sancto Paulo's *Summa*.

59 AT VII 234: CSM II 164. M. D. Wilson, *Descartes*, pp. 115–16, argues that Descartes' reply to Arnauld is inconsistent with his doctrine in Meditation III.

60 Replies IV: AT VII 235.

61 Aquinas, *On Interpretation* I, lect. 1, n. 3.

62 Cf. M. D. Wilson, *Descartes*, pp. 116–17.

63 See Verbeek (ed. and trans.), *René Descartes & Martin Schoock, La Querelle d'Utrecht;* and idem, *Descartes and the Dutch: Early Reactions to Cartesianism, 1637–1656*.

64 See, for example, AT IV 156–8, 584. In AT IV 159, Descartes tells Dinet: "Having attempted to write a philosophy, I know that your Society alone, more than any other, can make it succeed or fail."

65 The likely reason Descartes was put on the Index was, ironically, his attempt to dabble in theology, his account of transubstantiation; see Armogathe, *Theologia cartesiana: l'explication physique de l'Eucharistie chez Descartes et Dom Desgabets*.

66 Rochemonteix, *Un Collège de Jésuites*, vol. IV, pp. 357–64.

67 Ibid., pp. 82–8, 94–8.

68 Cartesianism seems also to have been frowned upon by the civil authorities until 1715; see Brockliss, *French Higher Education*, p. 353.

69 Rochemonteix, *Un Collège de Jésuites*, vol. IV, pp. 89 n–93 n: 1. The human mind can and must doubt everything except that it thinks and consequently that it exists. 2. Of the remainder, one can have certain and reasoned knowledge only after having known clearly and distinctly that God exists, that he is supremely good, infallible, and incapable of inducing our minds into error. 3. Before having knowledge of the existence of God, each person could and should always remain in doubt about whether the nature, with which one has been created, is not such that it is mistaken about the judgments that appear most certain and evident to it. 4. Our minds, to the extent that they are finite, cannot know anything certain about the infinite; consequently, we should never make it the object of our discussions. 5. Beyond divine faith, no one can be certain that bodies exist – not even one's own body. 6. The modes or accidents, once produced in a subject, do not have need of cause to conserve them by a positive action; but they must last as long as they are not destroyed by the positive action of an external cause. 7. In order to admit that some quantity of motion that God originally impressed on matter is lost, one would have to assume that God is changeable and inconstant. 8. No substance, whether spiritual or corporeal, can be annihilated by God. 9. The essence of each being depends upon God's free will, such that, in another order of things he was free to create, the essence and properties, for example, of matter, mind, circle, etc., would have been other than they are at present. 10. The essence of matter or of body consists in its actual and external extension. 11. No part of matter can lose anything of its extension without losing as much of its substance. 12. The compenetration of bodies properly speaking and place void of all bodies imply a contradiction. 13. We can represent local extension everywhere to ourselves; for example, beyond the heavens, there really exists a space filled by bodies or by matter. 14. In itself, the extension of the world is indefinite. 15. There can be only one world. 16. There is, in the world, a precise and limited quantity of motion, which has never been augmented nor diminished. 17. No body can move without all those from which it gets farther and to which it gets nearer moving at the same time. 18. For a body to move is for it to be conserved by God successively in different places. 19. Only God can move bodies; angels, rational souls, and bodies themselves are not the efficient causes, but the occasional causes of motion. 20. Creatures do not produce anything as efficient causes, but God alone produces all effects, *ad illarum*

praesentiam. 21. Animals are mere automata deprived of all knowledge and sensation. 22. The union of the rational soul and the body is nothing other than the act by which God willed some perceptions in the soul be excited in relation to some changes in the body, and reciprocally, to produce in the body some determined motions following some thoughts or volitions of the soul. 23. This communication of motions and effects is not required by the nature itself of body and soul; it is the result of God's free decree. 24. Color, light, cold, hot, sound, and all properties called sensible are affections or modifications of the mind itself, and not of the bodies called hot, cold, etc. 25. Mixed bodies, even of animals, do not differ from each other except by variations of magnitude, shape, situation, texture, rest, or motion of atoms or particles of matter that constitute them. 26. In perception, the mind does not act; it is a purely passive faculty. 27. Judgment and reasoning are acts of the will, not of the intellect. 28. There are no substantial forms of bodies in matter. 29. There are no absolute accidents. 30. Descartes' system can be defended as a hypothesis whose principles and postulates harmonize among themselves and with their deductions.

3   The nature of abstract reasoning: philosophical aspects of Descartes' work in algebra

No one contributed more to the early development of algebra than Descartes. In particular, he was able to unify arithmetic and geometry to a significant extent, by showing their mutual connections in terms of an algebraic notation. This was an achievement that eclipsed his other scientific work, and Descartes believed that algebra could serve as a model for his other enterprises. The connection between algebra and his other scientific work was explored, via a consideration of the question of method, in Descartes' first published work, the *Discourse on the Method of rightly conducting one's reason and seeking the truth in the sciences, together with the Optics, the Meteorology and the Geometry which are essays in this method* (1637). What we are ostensibly presented with here is a general treatise on method, to which are appended three examples of the method. And three very successful examples they are, for in each case we are provided with at least one new fundamental result: the sine law of refraction in the *Optics,* the calculation and experimental confirmation of the angles of the bows of the rainbow in the *Meteorology,* and the solution of Pappus' locus problem for four or more lines in the *Geometry.* But it would be a grave mistake to see the *Geometry* as merely an exemplification of method. Descartes effectively treats the algebraic approach that he develops in the *Geometry* as a source of, rather than simply an exemplification of, correct method. Moreover, the methodological aspects of algebra do not in any way exhaust its interest, and although I shall touch on them, the focus of this paper will lie elsewhere.

The three principal themes that I want to take up are: what Descartes' algebraic work actually amounts to, what its originality consists in, and how the application of algebra to the physical world is possible. But underlying these themes is a deeper issue, namely the question of the abstract nature of algebra. One thing that I shall try to clarify is what this abstractness consists in for Descartes.

3.1. THE NATURE OF DESCARTES' ALGEBRA

Algebra, arithmetic, and geometry

The Greeks classified geometrical problems as being either plane, solid, or linear, depending on whether their solution required straight lines and circles, or conic sections, or more complex curves. Euclid had restricted himself to the two postulates that a straight line can be drawn between any two points, and that a circle can be drawn with any given point as center to pass through another given point. But the range of problems that can be solved purely on the basis of these postulates is very restricted, and a third postulate was added by later mathematicians; namely, that a given cone could be cut by a given plane. The geometry of conic sections that resulted was treated in antiquity as an abstruse branch of mathematics of little practical relevance. Aristotle had convincingly shown that the natural motion of bodies was either rectilinear (in the case of terrestrial bodies) or circular (in the case of celestial bodies), so from the physical point of view it appeared that we could get by without the more complex curves: these apparently had no basis in nature and were of purely mathematical interest. But by the seventeenth century the need to give some account of curves beyond the straight line and circle became pressing. The parabola, being the path taken by projectiles, was studied in ballistics, and astronomers were well aware of the fact that planets and comets described elliptical, parabolic, and hyperbolic paths. And in optics, which was one of the most intensely studied areas in natural science in the seventeenth century, a knowledge of at least conic sections was required for the construction of lenses and mirrors. The work of the Alexandrian mathematicians on conic sections left much to be desired, and many of their results were more often than not the result of ingenious one–off solutions of problems rather than being due to the application of some general procedure.

It is precisely such a general procedure that Descartes develops and puts to use in the *Geometry*, a treatise which had a revolutionary effect on the development of mathematics. The *Geometry* comprises three books, the first dealing with "problems that can be constructed using only circles and straight lines," the second dealing with "the nature of curves," and the third with the construction of "solid and supersolid problems." The first book is the most important as far as the fundamentals of algebra are concerned, and consequently I shall focus on this.[1]

From its title, which indicates that it concerns only those problems that utilize straight lines and curves in their construction, one might expect the first book to contain the traditional material, and the others to contain the new material. After all, Euclid had given a reasonably exhaustive account of problems which can be constructed using only straight lines and a circle. But in fact the purpose of the first book is, above anything else, to present a new algebraic means of solving geometrical problems by making use of arithmetical procedures and vice versa. In other words, the aim is to show how, if we think of them in algebraic terms, we can combine the resources of the two fields.

The *Geometry* opens with a direct comparison between arithmetic and geometry (AT VI 369). Just as in arithmetic the operations we use are addition, subtraction, multiplication, division, and finding roots, so too in geometry we can reduce any problem to one that requires nothing more than a knowledge of the lengths of straight lines, and in this form the problem can be solved using nothing more than the five arithmetical operations. Descartes therefore introduces arithmetical terms directly into geometry. Multiplication, for example, is an operation that can be performed using only straight lines (i.e. using only a ruler):

> Let AB be taken as one unit, and let it be required
> to multiply BD by BC. I have only to join the

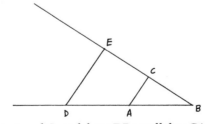

> points A and C, and draw DE parallel to CA; then
> BE to the product of this multiplication. (AT 370)

If we wish to find a square root, on the other hand, we require straight lines and circles (i.e. ruler and compass):

In order to find the square root of GH, I add, along the straight line, FG equal to one unit; then, divid-

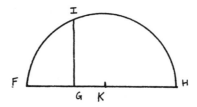

ing FH into two equal parts at K, I describe the circle FIH about K as a center, and draw from the point G a straight line at right angles to G extended to I, and GI is the required root. (AT VI 370–1)

Note that, given FG as the arbitrarily chosen unit, GI may well turn out to be irrational: this is not relevant in the geometrical construction.

Descartes next points out that we do not actually need to draw the lines, but can designate them by letters. He instructs us to label all lines in this way, those whose length we seek to determine as well as those whose length is known, and then, proceeding as if we had already solved the problem, we combine the lines so that every quantity can be expressed in two ways. This constitutes an equation, and the object is to find such an equation for every unknown line. In cases where this is not possible, we choose lines of known length arbitrarily for each unknown line for which we have no equation, and:

if there are several equations, we must use each in order, either considering it alone or comparing it with the others, so as to obtain a value for each of the unknown lines; and we must combine them until there remains a single unknown line which is equal to some known line, whose square, cube, fourth, fifth or sixth power etc. is equal to the sum or difference of two or more quantities, one of which is known, while the other consists of mean proportionals between the unit and this square, or cube, or fourth power etc., multiplied by other known lines. I may express this as follows:

$$z = b$$
or $$z^2 = -az + b^2$$
or $$z^3 = az^2 + b^2z - c^3$$
or $$z^4 = az^2 - c^3z + d^4 \text{ etc.}$$

That is, z, which I take for the unknown quantity, is equal to b; or the square of z is equal to the square of b minus a multiplied by z ... Thus all the unknown quantities can be expressed in terms of a single quantity, whenever the problem can be constructed by means of circles and straight lines, or by conic sections, or by a curve only one or two degrees greater.

(AT VI 373–4)

This is a novel approach to the question. Algebraic equations in two unknowns, $F(x,y) = O$, were traditionally considered indeterminate since the two unknowns could not be determined from such an equation. All one could do was to substitute arbitrarily chosen values for x and then solve the equation for y for each of these values, something that was not considered to be in any way a general solution of the equation. But Descartes' approach allows this procedure to be transformed into a general solution. What he effectively does is to take x as the abscissa of a point and the corresponding y as its ordinate, and then one can vary the unknown x so that to every value of x there corresponds a value of y which can be computed from the equation. We thereby end up with a set of points that form a completely determined curve satisfying the equation.

An example: Descartes' treatment of Pappus's locus-problem[2]

This procedure is exemplified in Descartes' resolution of one of the great unsolved mathematical problems bequeathed by antiquity, Pappus's locus problem for four or more lines. The problem had been posed by Pappus in terms of a three- or four-line locus problem. Essentially, what is at issue is this. In the case of the three-line problem, we are given three lines with their positions, and the task is to find the locus of points from which three lines can be drawn to the given lines, each making a given angle with each given line, such that the product of the lengths of two of the lines bears a constant proportion to the square of the third. In the case of the four-line problem, we are given four lines with their positions, and we are required to find the locus of points from which four lines can be drawn to the given lines, such that the product of the length of two of the lines bears a constant proportion to the product of the other two.

It was known in antiquity that the locus in each case is a conic section passing through the intersections of the lines, but no general procedure for solving the problem was developed. Descartes' treatment of the question is algebraic and completely general, allowing us to express relations between the lines using only two variables. His approach is to show how the problem, explicitly solved for four lines but in a way which is theoretically generalizable to n lines, can, like all geometrical problems, be reduced to one in which all we need to know are the lengths of certain lines. These lines are the coordinate axes, and the lengths give us the abscissae and ordinates of points. The four-line problem is presented as follows (AT VI 382–7):

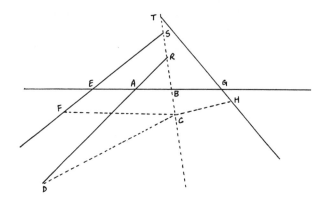

Here the full lines are the given lines and the broken lines those sought. Descartes takes AB and BC as the principal lines and proceeds to relate all the others to these. Their lengths are x and y respectively, and in fact AB is the x axis, and BC the y axis, a point obscured in Descartes' diagram by the fact that AB and BC are not drawn perpendicular to one another (since to do so would obscure the proportions). Now the angles of the triangle ABR are given, so the ratio AB:BR is known. If we let this ratio be $\frac{z}{b}$ then BR $= \frac{bx}{z}$, and CR $= y + \frac{bx}{z}$ (where B lies between C and R). The angles of the triangle DRC are also known, and if we represent the ratio CR:CD as $\frac{z}{c}$ then CR $= y + \frac{bx}{z}$ and CD $= \frac{cy}{z} + \frac{bcx}{z^2}$. Moreover, since the positions of AB, AD, and EF are fixed, the length k of AE is thereby given; therefore EB $= k + x$ (where A lies between E and B). The angles of the triangle ESB are also given, and hence so is the ratio BE:BS. If we let this ratio be $\frac{z}{d}$, then we get BS $= \frac{dk + dx}{z}$ and CS $= \frac{zy + dk + dx}{z}$ (where B is between S and C). The angles of the triangle FSC are given, therefore the ratio CS:CF is known. If we let this ratio be $\frac{z}{e}$ then we obtain CF $= \frac{ezy + dek + dex}{z^2}$. Letting l denote the given length of AB, we have BG $= l - x$; and if we let the known ratio BG:BT in the triangle BGT be $\frac{z}{f}$, then BT $= \frac{fl - fx}{z}$ and CT $= \frac{zy + fl - x}{z}$, and if we let CT:CH in the triangle TCH be $\frac{z}{g}$ then CH $= \frac{gzy + fgl - fgx}{z^2}$.

No matter how many lines of given position we are dealing with, the length of a line through C making a given angle with these lines can always be expressed in three terms of the form $ax + by + c$. For three or four fixed lines, the equation will be a quadratic equation, and this means that, for any known value of y, the values of x can then be found using only ruler and compass, and a sufficiently large number of values will enable us to trace the curve on which C must lie. For five or six lines the equation is a cubic, for seven or eight a quartic, for nine or ten a quintic, and so on, rising one degree with the introduction of every two lines.

Descartes' advance beyond ancient mathematics

In solving Pappus's problem Descartes has solved one of the most difficult problems bequeathed by ancient mathematics, and he has solved it in a simple, elegant, and generalizable way. In doing so, he has developed a technique that goes well beyond those employed in antiquity.

In the second book of the *Geometry*, Descartes extends his treatment of the Pappus loci for three or four lines by distinguishing the curves corresponding to equations of the second degree, namely the ellipse, hyperbola and parabola. This treatment is fairly exhaustive, but he considers very few cases corresponding to cubics, maintaining (somewhat optimistically as it turns out)[3] that his method shows how these are to be dealt with. His general classification of curves, and in particular his dismissal of transcendental curves, has provoked much discussion,[4] but will not concern us here. It is perhaps worth mentioning, however, that his method of drawing a tangent to curves took on a new importance with the development of calculus (to which Descartes made no direct contribution) as it is effectively equivalent to finding the slope of a curve at any point, which is a form of differentiation. Finally, in the third book, solid and super-solid problems are examined. This marks an important advance be-yond the Alexandrian mathematicians, who only recognized con-structions making use of curves other than straight lines and circles with reluctance, and the category of solid problems was never sys-tematically thought through. Here Descartes extends his algebraic analysis far beyond the concerns of mathematicians of antiquity. The most striking feature of his approach is that, in order to preserve the generality of his structural analysis of the equation, he is pre-pared to allow not only negative roots but also imaginary roots, despite the otherwise completely counterintuitive nature of these. To grasp just how radical this is, we need first to say a bit more about the nature of algebra and Descartes' place in its development.

3.2 THE ORIGINALITY OF DESCARTES' APPROACH

Geometrical algebra

The characteristic feature of algebra is its abstractness. It comprises mathematical structures defined purely in operational and relational terms, without any constraint on the nature of the *relata*. Strictly speaking, it has no content of its own, but acquires content only through interpretation. This is how we think of algebra now, but it has not always been seen in such abstract terms, and we can distin-guish two crucial stages in its development: the freeing of number from spatial intuitions, and the freeing of algebra itself from an exclusively numerical interpretation. The first of these we owe largely to Descartes. It is not always appreciated, however, just how novel Descartes' algebraic approach is. Until relatively recently it has been thought that the Greeks possessed a "geometrical algebra," i.e. a procedure for dealing with genuinely algebraic problems which, because of the crisis brought about by the Pythagorean dis-covery of linear incommensurability, resulted in the geometrical formulation and resolution of these problems. This geometrical alge-bra, it was argued, was subsequently rediscovered, stripped of its geometrical language, and hence made more general, in the work of Descartes and others. What is at issue here is whether the geometrical formulation and resolution of certain classes of mathematical problems by the Greeks can be construed as algebra in geometrical dress. It cannot be denied that there are many propositions in Euclid, for example, for which we can easily find algebraic results to which they are equivalent. Moreover, many of the propositions of the second book of Euclid's *Elements* can be given a very straightforward algebraic interpretation, whereas there has often been perceived to be problems in providing purely geometrical interpretations for these. Finally, it seems that geometrical algebra was exactly what was required as a response to the crisis in mathematics occasioned by the discovery of linear incommensurability, a discovery with which the available arithmetical procedures were unable to cope.

Challenges to this kind of interpretation have in fact existed since the 1930s, but it is only more recently that it has been widely appreciated that there is something wrong with the geometrical algebra view. Jacob Klein, in his pioneering work on the early development of algebra, for example, showed that very radical changes in the concept of number were required before algebra became possible, and that these were not effected until the work of Vieta at the end of the sixteenth century.[5] Secondly, it is now clear that the Pythagorean geometry of areas, far from being a geometrical algebra designed to solve the problem of incommensurability, was in fact designed to eliminate what was effectively regarded as an insoluble problem.[6] Third, all the propositions of Euclid's *Elements* do in fact have geometrical interpretations[7] and in a number of cases their algebraic presentation simply trivializes them.[8] The conclusion that we must draw from this is, I believe, that there is simply no evidence to support the traditional contention that Greek mathematicians operated with any genuinely algebraic ideas, consciously or otherwise.

However, to say that the Greeks did not operate with a geometrical algebra is not to say that geometry did not play a significant role in Greek arithmetic. It in fact played a very significant role indeed, but one quite contrary to the traditional interpretation, for it diminished rather than increased the abstractness of arithmetic. An understanding of this role is important if we are to appreciate fully the novelty of Descartes' algebra, and his approach is best contrasted with the very influential account of number that Aristotle had offered in his *Metaphysics*.[9]

The Aristotelian conception: number, matter, and space

For Aristotle, mathematical objects have matter and this matter is what he calls "noetic matter." Now mathematics is distinguished for Aristotle by the fact that its objects do not change and do not have independent existence. These objects are noetic, as opposed to sensible, and we come by them through abstraction from "sensible" numbers and shapes, i.e. the numbers and shapes of sensible objects. Sensible objects are made up of sensible matter, and Aristotle thinks that mathematical objects must be made up of noetic matter. He adopts this doctrine because he believes that numbers and shapes are properties, and that properties must always be instantiated in something. Sensible numbers and shapes are instantiated in sensible matter, but noetic numbers and shapes cannot be for these are only objects of thought; since they are properties, however, they must be instantiated in something, so Aristotle invents a new kind of purely abstract matter for them to be instantiated in.

In the case of geometry, Aristotle employs two different kinds of abstraction. The first involves disregarding the matter of sensible objects so that we are left with properties like "being triangular" and "being round." Geometry investigates "being round" in very general terms as the form of whatever, most generally speaking, is round. And whatever, most generally speaking, is round is something we arrive at by a complementary kind of abstraction, in which we disregard the properties of sensible objects so that what has these properties becomes the object of investigation. What we are left with is a substratum of indeterminate extension characterized solely in terms of its spatial dimensions: length, breadth, and depth. This abstraction can then be carried further yielding planes, and finally lines and points, each of these substrata having different dimensions. Now these substrata can neither be sensible, since they have been deprived of the properties that would render them sensible, nor can they have an independent existence, since they are merely abstractions, and they are what Aristotle calls noetic matter.

Aristotle makes the same claim about numbers, however, and this is more problematic. We can imagine geometrical noetic matter as spaces of one, two, and three dimensions, but how are we to imagine the noetic matter of number? The answer is: in much the same way – provided we bear in mind that, in Greek mathematics, whereas geometry operates with lines, arithmetic operates with line *lengths* (or areas or volumes). The distinction is of the upmost importance, as Aristotle is well aware. A line length, insofar as it is a determinate length, can be seen to be potentially divisible into discontinuous parts, i.e. into a determinate plurality of unit lengths. It is by treating the foot length as being indivisible, for example, that we can treat it as being a unit length, as being the measure of other lengths (cf. Book I of Aristotle's *Metaphysics*). And in this case the line length becomes effectively the same as number, which Aristotle defines as a plurality measured by a unit or a "one." The central distinction between arithmetic and geometry lies in the fact that the former deals with discontinuous and the latter with continuous magnitudes. The line considered simply as a line comes within the subject matter of geometry because it is infinitely divisible and hence a continuous magnitude, but considered either as a unit length or as a sum of unit lengths it comes within the subject matter of arithmetic.

In terms of this distinction, we can grasp clearly what arithmetic amounts to on Aristotle's conception: it is metrical geometry. Although he never explicitly mentions metrical geometry, his arithmetical terminology – *linear, plane,* and *solid* numbers, numbers being *measured,* factors *measuring* products in multiplication – consistently suggests that this is the conception of arithmetic that he is taking for granted. Indeed, metrical geometry is an essentially arithmetical discipline, common to the whole of ancient mathematics from the old-Babylonian period to the Alexandrians.[10] In the present context, its importance lies in the fact that, although it deals with lines, planes, etc., it deals with them not *qua* lines and planes but *qua* unit lengths and unit areas, or sums or products of such unit lengths and areas. Aristotle talks throughout his work of numbers in one dimension, plane numbers, and solid numbers and he never introduces the idea of the geometrical *representation* of numbers. Nor, indeed, does any Greek or Alexandrian author talk of numbers being represented geometrically. It is instructive here that the arithmetical propositions of Euclid's *Elements*, those taking up books VII to IX, are explicitly stated in terms of line lengths, as if numbers were line lengths: And this is exactly what they are.

Aristotle was not an innovator in mathematics. He was not attempting to develop a new form of mathematics but to provide a proper philosophical basis for the mathematics of his day. What he is providing a basis for in the case of arithmetic is not a form of arithmetic which, because of its grounding in geometrical algebra, is particularly abstract and general, but rather a form of arithmetic that, being construed in terms of metrical geometry, is dependent on spatial intuitions and as a result is severely limited. Consider, for example, the arithmetical operation of multiplication and, in particular, the dimensional change involved in this operation, which results in the product always being of a higher dimension. This is not a notational constraint, it is inherently connected with the idea that numbers, for Greek mathematicians, are always numbers *of* something. A consequence of this is that when we multiply, we must multiply numbers of something: we cannot multiply two by three, for example, we must always multiply two somethings by three somethings. It is in this sense that Klein has called numbers "determinate" for the Greeks. They do not symbolize general magnitudes, but always a determinate plurality of objects.[11] Moreover, not only are the dimensional aspects of geometry retained in arithmetical operations, so too is the physical and intuitive nature of these dimensions, so that, for example, no more than three line lengths can be multiplied together since the product here is a solid, which exhausts the number of available dimensions.[12]

Cartesian algebra and abstraction

Descartes explicitly opposes this spatial conception. At the beginning of the *Geometry*, after having shown us the geometrical procedures for multiplication and finding square roots, he introduces single letters to designate line lengths. But his interpretation of these letters is significantly different from the traditional interpretation. On the traditional interpretation, if a is a line length, a^2 is a square having sides of length a, ab is a rectangle having sides of length a and b, and a^3 is a cube having sides of length a. On Descartes' interpretation, however, these quantities are all dimensionally homogeneous:

It should be noted that all the parts of a single line should always be expressed by the same number of dimensions as one another, provided that the unit is not determined in the condition of the problem. Thus, a^3 contains as many dimensions as ab^2 or b^3, these being the component parts of the line that I have called $\sqrt[3]{a^3 - b^3 + ab^2}$ (AT VI 371).

Here the shift between arithmetic and geometry is something that furthers the abstraction of the operations, not something that constrains their abstraction, as on ancient conceptions. The question of level of abstraction is crucial. For mathematicians of antiquity, it was only if a determinate figure or number could be constructed or computed that one could be said to have solved a mathematical problem. Moreover, the only numbers allowable as solutions were natural numbers: negative numbers in particular were "impossible" numbers. It is true that toward the end of the Alexandrian period, most notably in Diophantus's *Arithmetica*, we begin to find the search for problems and solutions concerned with general magnitudes, but these procedures never make up anything more than auxiliary techniques forming a stage preliminary to the final one, where a determinate number is computed. Descartes is explicitly opposed to this, and in Rule XVI of the *Rules for the Direction of Our Native Intelligence* he spells out the contrast between his approach and the traditional one in very clear terms:

It must be pointed out that while arithmeticians have usually designated each magnitude by several units, i.e. by a number, we on the contrary abstract from numbers themselves here just as we did above [Rule XIV] from geometrical figures, or from anything else. Our reason for doing this is partly to avoid the tedium of a long and unnecessary calculation, but mainly to see that those parts of the problem which are the essential ones always remain distinct and are not obscured by useless numbers. If for example we are trying to find the hypotenuse of a right-angled triangle whose given sides are 9 and 12, the arithmetician will say that it is $\sqrt{225}$, i.e. 15. We on the other hand will write a and b for 9 and 12, and find that the hypotenuse is $\sqrt{a^2 + b^2}$ leaving the two parts of the expression a^2 and b^2 distinct, whereas in the number they are run together ... We who seek to develop a clear and distinct knowledge of these things insist on these distinctions. Arithmeticians, on the other hand, are satisfied if the required result turns up, even if they do not see how it depends on what has been given, but in fact it is in knowledge of this kind alone that science consists.

(AT X 455–6, 458: CSM I 67–8, 69)

For Descartes, concern with general magnitudes is constitutive of the mathematical enterprise. He recognizes no numbers or figures to be "impossible" on intuitive grounds. Indeed, he readily accedes to purely algebraic constraints requiring that "number" be extended to include not just integers, but fractions and irrationals as well. And his structural analysis of the equation leads him to accept negative and imaginary roots. Here our intuitions about what numbers are are effectively sacrificed to the structural definition of number provided by algebra.

In this respect, Descartes inaugurates a development in which the range of items coming under the category of "number" is expanded and consolidated as the generality of algebra is increased and its rules of operation define new kinds of entity as numbers. As Kneale has pointed out,[13] up to and including the introduction of complex numbers, mathematicians took an unreflective attitude to their extension of the idea of number. Retaining the general rules of algebra required them to introduce novel kinds of entities which they were forced to adopt to solve problems posed at an earlier stage, but they raised no general questions about this procedure. The situation changed in the late 1830s and early 1840s. In the first place, Peacocke, Gregory, and de Morgan began to conceive of algebra in such abstract mathematical terms that it was no longer necessary to construe the *relata* of its operations as numbers at all. Secondly, Hamilton began work on an algebra of hypercomplex numbers, which, while they are defined by algebraic operations, do not satisfy all the rules that hold up to complex numbers. These two developments suggested that algebra may be more general than had been thought. It was in this context that George Boole, regarded by many as the founder of modern formal logic, was able to devise an abstract calculus for logic. Showing how the laws of algebra can be formally stated without interpretation, and how the laws governing numbers up to complex numbers need not all hold together in every algebraic system, he was able to go on to develop a limited algebra which represented the operations of traditional syllogistic.

Freed of its exclusively numerical interpretation, algebra becomes a much more powerful apparatus and its application to logic takes it directly to the most fundamental issues. Such a development is a continuation of Descartes' work on algebra, but it is a continuation completely alien to Descartes' own approach. To understand why this is the case, we must consider what Descartes thinks is methodologically distinctive about algebra.

Algebra, deduction, and Cartesian "analysis" [14]

As we have seen, Descartes maintains that whereas earlier mathematicians were exclusively concerned with computing particular numerical solutions to equations, he abstracts from numbers because he is concerned with structural features of the equations themselves. Now it is possible to draw a direct analogy with logic here. If we are to think of logic in algebraic terms, in the same way that Descartes thinks of arithmetic algebraically, what we must do is to abstract from particular *truths* (just as Descartes abstracts from particular *numbers*) and explore the relations between truths, independently of their content, in abstract structural terms. But this move to a higher level of abstraction, which Leibniz glimpsed and which is constitutive of modern logic and the philosophy of mathematics, was utterly alien to Descartes. Descartes was blind to the possibility of logic being construed in terms of an extension of his algebraic techniques because he conceived of logic (which for him was Aristotelian syllogistic) as being a redundant method of presentation of already achieved results, whereas algebra, he thought, was something completely different, namely a method of discovery of new results. The question of method has been dealt with elsewhere in this volume, but a few words on how it specifically relates to algebra would not be out of place here.

When, in Rule IV of the *Rules for the Direction of Our Native Intelligence*, Descartes discusses the need for 'a method of finding out the truth', he turns his attention to mathematics. When he first studied mathematics, he tells us, he found it unsatisfactory. Although the results that mathematicians obtained were true, they did not make it clear how they had come by their results, and in many cases it seemed that it was a matter of luck rather than skill. Consequently, many had quite understandably rejected mathematics as empty and childish. But the founders of philosophy in antiquity had made mathematics a prerequisite for the study of wisdom. This indicates to Descartes that they must have had a "species of mathematics different from ours" (AT X 376: CSM I 18), and he claims to find traces of this "true mathematics" in the writings of Pappus and Diophantus. But these authors feared "that their method [of discovery], being so easy and simple, would become cheapened if it were divulged, and so, in order to gain our admiration, they put in its place sterile truths which, with some ingenuity, they demonstrated deductively" (AT X 376–7: CSM I 19).

The art of discovery that Descartes believes he had rediscovered is what he calls "analysis." In antiquity, analysis and synthesis were complementary procedures, and Pappus distinguished two kinds of analysis: "theoretical analysis," in which we attempt to establish the truth of a theorem, and "problematical analysis," in which we attempt to discover something unknown. If these procedures are successfully completed, we must then prove our result by synthetic means, whereby we start from definitions, axioms, and rules and deduce our result solely from these. The mathematical texts of antiquity, concerned as they were with rigorous demonstration, presented only synthetic proofs. Descartes does two things: he effectively restricts "analysis" to problematical analysis, and he completely rejects the need for synthesis. The latter is evident as soon as one glances at the *Geometry*. The traditional lists of definitions, postulates, etc. are completely absent, and we are immediately introduced to problem-solving techniques. For Descartes, the aim of the exercise, an aim he believes only algebra can enable one to achieve in a systematic way, is to solve problems. Once one has solved the problem, the presentation of the result in synthetic terms is, for Descartes, completely redundant. In more general terms, what this amounts to is a rejection of the value of deductive inference in mathematics.

This is one of the most problematic parts of Descartes' conception of algebra, and he parts company on this issue not only with modern mathematicians but also with his contemporaries. The source of the problem lies in his view that deductive inference can never have any epistemic value, and can never play any role in furthering knowledge. Leibniz was the first philosopher to respond fully to this view, and he pointed out that whereas analysis may be valuable as a way of solving particular problems, in the synthetic or deductive presentation of results in mathematics we set in train a systematic structuring of and extension of knowledge which enables gaps, difficulties, flaws, etc. to be recognized, precisely identified and solved.

The problem is a deep one, however, and many philosophers have questioned the standing of deduction. Sextus Empiricus, one of the most important of the ancient skeptics, offered the following ingenious argument against deductive inference.[15] Compare the following arguments:

	A	B
(1)	If it is day, it is light	It is day
(2)	It is day	It is light
(3)	It is light	

A is a deductive argument, B a nondeductive one. Sextus' argument is that deductive arguments are always, by their own criteria, flawed. In the present case, for example, either (3) follows from (2) or it does not. If it does, then B is a perfectly acceptable argument for in B we simply infer (3) from (2). But if this is the case then (1) is clearly redundant. On the other hand, if (3) does not follow from (2) then (1) is false, since (1) clearly asserts that it does. So deductive proof is impossible: what A tells us over and above B is either redundant or false. Not many philosophers have been prepared to go quite so far as Sextus, but many have raised general worries about the point of deduction. Some, such as J. S. Mill, have held that the premises contain the same assertion as the conclusion in deductive arguments, and that this is in effect what makes them valid.[16] Here, a question must be raised about the point of deductive arguments. Others, such as the logical positivists, have held that logical truths are analytically true and hence we can never learn anything new from them.

This surely cannot be right, for we do sometimes learn something new from deductive proofs. Consider, for example, Hobbes's first encounter with Euclid's *Elements*, as reported by Aubrey in his *Brief Lives:*

Being in a Gentelman's Library, Euclid's Elements lay open, and 'twas the 47 El. libri I. He read the proposition. By G – , sayd he (he would now and then sweare an emphatical oath by way of emphasis), this is impossible! So he reads the Demonstration of it, which referred him back to another, which he also read. [And so on] that at last he was demonstratively convinced of that trueth. This made him in love with Geometry.[17]

Here Hobbes begins not only by not believing something, but by not even believing it to be possible, and a chain of deductive reasonings convinces him otherwise. This is a clear case of epistemic advance, i.e. Hobbes ends up with a belief he would not otherwise have had, and it is a purely deductive argument that is responsible for his having this new belief. Now it is true that not all deductive arguments bring with them epistemic advance: the argument "if p, then p" clearly involves no epistemic advance, although it is a formally valid deductive argument. Where Descartes goes wrong is to deny that *any* deductive argument involves epistemic advance. This is simply not plausible, as the Hobbes case shows.

Moreover, even if deductive arguments *could* never bring about epistemic advance, we would still have good reason to be interested in the systematic relations between truths, e.g. the truths of geometry or the truths of arithmetic, since it is of some importance that we know in what way some follow from others and what precisely this "following from" consists in. But Descartes assumes that epistemic advance is the only criterion of worth, and this leads him to dismiss anything he does not believe to be a method of discovery. Algebra he sees as a method of discovery *par excellence,* and it is precisely because he sees it in this way that the possibility of thinking about deduction in algebraic terms is closed off to him.

3.3 THE APPLICATION OF MATHEMATICS TO REALITY

The abstract nature of algebra, as Descartes realizes, is the source of its power. But it is also a potential source of difficulties, for if mathematics is as abstract as Descartes maintains, its relation to the material world may become a problem. This is an especially important question for Descartes since he is concerned to develop a mathematical physics, an account of the material world that is completely mathematical. Descartes deals with the question of a mathematical physics in the *Rules for the Direction of Our Native Intelligence,* in a way that ties together mathematics, epistemology and natural science, and his account here is useful not just in helping us understand in what way he thinks something as abstract as algebra can relate to the natural world, but also in throwing some light on what he thinks this abstraction consists in.

Simple natures

Throughout the *Rules,* Descartes insists that knowledge must begin with what he calls "simple natures," which are those things that are not further analyzable and which we can grasp in a direct and intuitive way. Such simple natures can only be grasped by the intellect, although "while it is the intellect alone that is capable of knowledge, it can be helped or hindered by three other faculties; namely, the imagination, sense-perception and memory." (AT X 398: CSM I 32) In Rule XIV the connection between the intellect and the imagination is elaborated upon in a rather interesting way:

> By 'extension' we mean whatever has length, breadth and depth, leaving to one side whether it is a real body or merely a space. This notion does not, I think, need further elucidation, for there is nothing more easily perceived by our imagination. . . . For even though someone may convince himself, if we suppose every object in the universe annihilated, that this would not prevent extension *per se* existing, his conception would not use any corporeal image, but would be merely a false judgement of the intellect working alone. He will admit this himself if he reflects attentively on this image of extension which he tries to form in his imagination. For he will notice that he does not perceive it in isolation from every subject, and that his imagination of it and his judgement of it are quite different. Consequently, whatever our intellect may believe as to the truth of the matter, these abstract entities are never formed in the imagination in isolation from subjects.
>
> (AT X 442–3: CSM I 59)

Descartes goes on to argue that, whereas "extension" and "body" are represented by one and the same idea in the imagination, this is not true of the intellect. When we say that "number is not the thing counted" or "extension or shape is not body," the meanings of "number" and "extension" here are such that there are no special ideas corresponding to them in the imagination. These two statements are "the work of the pure intellect, which alone has the ability to separate out abstract entities of this type" (AT X 444: CSM I 60). Descartes insists that we must distinguish statements of this kind, in which the meanings of the terms are separated from the content of the ideas in the imagination, from statements in which the terms, albeit "employed in abstraction from their subjects, do not exclude or deny anything which is not really distinct from what they denote" (AT X 445: CSM I 61).

The intellect and the imagination

This distinction between the two kinds of proposition is perhaps most clearly expressed in the distinction between their proper objects, i.e. the objects of the intellect and the objects of the imagination, respectively. The proper objects of the intellect are completely abstract entities and are free of images or "bodily representations." Indeed, while engaging in its proper activity, the intellect "turns itself toward itself" (AT VII 73: CSM II 51) and beholds those things that are purely intellectual such as thought and doubt, as well as those "simple natures" which are common to both mind and body, such as existence, unity, and duration. But the intellect can also apply itself to "ideas" in the imagination. In doing so it also carries out an operation which is proper to it, but which the imagination cannot carry out, namely, that of separating out components of these ideas by abstraction.

It is here that the necessity for the imagination arises, because the intellect by itself has no relation at all to the world. Entities conceived in the intellect are indeterminate. The imagination is required to render them determinate. When we speak of numbers, for example, the imagination must be employed to represent to ourselves something that can be measured by a multitude of objects. The intellect understands "fiveness" as something separate from five objects (or line segments, or points, or whatever), and hence the imagination is required if this "fiveness" is to correspond to something in the world. What we are effectively dealing with here, as far as the intellect is concerned, is algebra. It is insofar as the objects of algebra, the indeterminate content of which has been separated out by the intellect, can be represented and conceived symbolically as lines and planes that they can be identified with the real world. Algebra deals with completely abstract entities, conceived in the intellect, but these abstract entities must be represented symbolically, and thus rendered determinate, which requires the aid of the imagination. The imagination thereby represents *general* magnitudes (abstract entities) as *specific* magnitudes (which are not distinct from what they are the magnitudes of).

However, not any kind of specific magnitude will do here. The privileged specific magnitude that Descartes wishes to single out is spatial extension. There are two reasons for this. First, algebraic entities can be represented geometrically, i.e. purely in terms of spatial extension. Secondly, Descartes argues (e.g. in Rule 12) that when we consider the physiological, physical and optical aspects of perception it is clear that what we see in no way resembles bodies in the world. The world itself contains no colors, odors etc. (no secondary qualities) but only spatially extended body. The secondary qualities that we perceive are simply a feature of the interaction of our sense organs, cognitive apparatuses, etc., with the external world. They are psychic additions of a perceiving mind. So the world is simply spatially extended body, and what is registered in the imagination is no less simply spatially extended magnitudes.

In sum, then, the corporeal world and the abstract entities of algebra are represented in the imagination as extended magnitudes and measures of extended magnitudes respectively, the former then being mapped onto the latter:

Intellect   abstract entities (algebra)
                              ↓

                  ⎧ lines, line lengths, etc.
Imagination   ⎨ (geometry and arithmetic)
                  ⎩ extended magnitudes
                              ↑

Corporeal world   material objects (material
                     extension)

In this schema, the pure thought characteristic of algebra which the intellect engages in does not map directly onto the corporeal world. Rather, a representation of it in the form of arithmetic and geometry maps onto a representation of the corporeal world, a representation consisting exclusively of two-dimensional shapes. This conception is subject to many problems, as might be expected from an account which deals with such fundamental questions, but it does provide us with the first explicit epistemological and metaphysical basis for a mathematical physics in the history of philosophy, and in many ways its role in Descartes' thought is more central than even the "Cogito."

CONCLUSION

What is remarkable about Descartes' work in algebra is its level of abstraction. This achievement has often been obscured, either by Descartes' own statement that all he was doing was rediscovering a secret method of discovery known to the mathematicians of antiquity, or by the widely held modern view that these mathematicians had a 'geometrical algebra', i.e. an algebraic interpretation of arithmetic that employed geometrical notation. I have given some reasons why I believe these, and especially the latter, to be wrong. In fact what the mathematicians of antiquity had was not an especially abstract algebraic interpretation of arithmetic but an especially concrete geometrical interpretation of it. The abstract interpretation comes only when the resources of arithmetic and geometry are combined to produce something far more powerful and abstract than either of them, and this is Descartes' achievement. He inaugurates (with Vieta and others) what I have identified as the first stage in the development of algebra, namely the freeing of number from spatial intuitions. This opened the way to the second stage, the freeing of algebra itself from an exclusively numerical interpretation. The move to this second stage was, however, one that went completely against the whole tenor of Descartes' approach. This was not so much because it takes one to a level of abstraction that even he was not prepared to countenance, for his early idea of a "universal mathematics" involves an extremely abstract (but unworkable) conception of mathematics that transcends any specific content, dealing only with whatever has order and magnitude (AT X 378: CSM I 19). It is rather because of his requirement that it be a method of discovery, which in turn means it must be epistemically informative. Deductive inference, he thinks (wrongly), can never be epistemically informative, so he rejects any connection between algebra and logic. Yet the second stage in the development of algebra comes about largely as a result of its application to systems of deductive reasoning.

Descartes was, then, not at all worried by the very abstract nature of his algebra in a mathematical context. But in many ways it is even more remarkable that he was not worried by it in a physical context either. His chief aim was to develop a mathematical physics and mathematics is, ultimately, algebra for Descartes. Well aware, at least after his early "universal mathematics" phase, that it could not just be a matter of applying a system as abstract as algebra to something as concrete and specific as the real world, he tried to establish that they do have one crucial thing in common: geometry. The only real properties of matter are those that can be understood wholly in geometrical terms, and algebra is represented in the imagination in purely geometrical terms. It is therefore geometry that ties the two together. This may not be the most fruitful way of establishing a basis for a mathematical physics,[18] but the sheer daring and ingenuity of the conception is breathtaking, and indeed it is the first explicit philosophical attempt to come to terms in any detail with how a mathematical physics might be possible.

In sum, Descartes' work in algebra is something whose interest extends far beyond mathematics. This work made him one of the greatest mathematicians of the seventeenth century. But in following through its consequences for the development of a quantitative mechanical understanding of the corporeal world, he became one of the greatest natural scientists of the seventeenth century; and in following through its consequences for the question of method, he became its greatest philosopher.

NOTES

1 For a full account of the *Geometry* see Scott, *The Scientific Work of René Descartes*, chs. 6–9.
2 Readers who find the mathematics in what follows difficult may wish to omit this section.
3 See Grosholz, "Descartes' Unification of Algebra and Geometry," in Gaukroger (ed.), *Descartes, Philosophy, Mathematics, and Physics*, pp. 156–68.
4 See in particular Vuillemin, *Mathématiques et métaphysique chez Descartes*.
5 Klein, *Greek Mathematical Thought and the Origin of Algebra*.
6 Szabó, *The Beginnings of Greek Mathematics*, especially the Appendix.
7 See especially the discussion of Proposition 5 of Book II of the *Elements*, ibid., pp. 332–53.
8 Unguru, "On the need to rewrite the history of Greek mathematics."
9 What follows is derived from Gaukroger, "Aristotle on intelligible matter," where a much fuller account can be found.
10 On the early development of metrical geometry, see Knorr, *The Evolution of the Euclidean Elements*, pp. 170ff.
11 Klein, *Greek Mathematical Thought*, pp. 133ff.
12 The only exception to this constraint on multiplication occurs in a relatively late Alexandrian work, Heron's *Metrica* I 8, where two squares, i.e., areas, are multiplied together.
13 Kneale and Kneale, *The Development of Logic*, pp. 390ff.
14 For a full discussion of the issues raised in this section, see Gaukroger, *Cartesian Logic*.

15 Sextus Empiricus, *Outlines of Pyrrhonism*, II, 159 (Loeb edition: Vol 1, pp.253–5).

16 See Book II of Mill, *A System of Logic* [1843] (London: Longmans, 1967).

17 *Aubrey's Brief Lives*, ed. Oliver Lawson Dick (London: Secker and Warburg, 1960), p. 150.

18 See Gaukroger, "Descartes' project for a mathematical physics," in Gaukroger (ed.), *Descartes*, pp. 97–140.

4 Cartesian metaphysics and the role of the simple natures

In the *Regulae,* in first part of Rule XII, Descartes characterizes "ideas" in terms of "figures" or "shapes" formed in the imagination (AT X 414: CSM I 41), thus reworking in a fairly precise, if critical, fashion the doctrines of Aristotle's *De Anima.* But in the second part of Rule XII, he abandons this seemingly cautious use of the traditional framework, and introduces an utterly new concept, that of the "simple nature" (*natura simplicissima; res simplex*). This is not only, or primarily, a terminological innovation; what is involved is an epistemological revolution.[1]

A simple nature has two characteristic features: it is neither simple, nor a nature. It is, first of all, opposed to "nature," since in place of the thing considered in itself, according to its *ousia* (essence), or *physis* (nature), it denotes the thing considered in respect of our knowledge: "when we consider things in the order that corresponds to our knowledge of them (*in ordine ad cognitionem nostram*) our view of them must be different from what it would be if it were speaking of them in accordance with how they exist in reality" (AT X 418: CSM I 44). Our knowledge, then does not apprehend things as they "really" (*re vera*) are, or "in their own categories," and "in some class of being" (AT X 381: CSM I 21); instead, leaving aside the truth of a thing's *ousia,* we apprehend the first knowable object, whatever it may be, provided it can be known "easily" and hence with certainty. Thus, so far from antecedently determining or regulating our knowledge, the "natures" are simply the end products of our knowledge. The "nature" is a "knowable object" in the sense of "object simply in so far as it can be know by us"; it thus deposes traditional *ousia* or essence, and banishes it once and for all from modern metaphysics (despite Leibniz's attempts to bring it back).

115

In the second place, a simple nature is not "simple" in the standard sense of the term. We are not dealing with the intrinsic simplicity of an atom or element or primary form; instead, the "simplicity" is purely relative, referring to whatever appears most simple to the mind. Each body, for example, is reducible to three simple natures – extension, shape, and movement. Yet it is no objection to say that shape could be reduced to the still simpler concepts of "extension" and "limit"; for even if the concept of limit is in itself more abstract then that of shape, this very abstractness allows it to be applied to a larger number of terms (not just extension for example, but duration and movement), thus making it complex from the point of view of our knowledge. The simple nature remains the simplest term, but the simplicity is an epistemological, not an ontological one: it does not relate to essence or *ousia*. "Hence we are concerned with things only in so far as they are perceived by the intellect, and so we term 'simple' only those things which we know so clearly and distinctly that they cannot be divided by the mind into others which are more distinctly known" (AT X 418: CSM I 44). The result is a concept of "idea" that is distinctly and originally Cartesian: "idea" defined as an object that is primary in respect of our knowledge and not in respect of its *ousia* or essence – primary in so far as it is "easy" to know, and not in respect of some indivisible form or *eidos*.

Given this definition of an idea as a "simple nature," our next task is to look at Descartes' use of the latter expression. Rule XII provides a detailed list of simple natures, grouped under three headings: (A) those that are "purely intellectual" and whose knowledge requires only "some degree of rationality" (*nos rationis esse participes*); (B) those that are "purely material" and require some contribution from the imagination; and (C) common simple natures or "common notions" (*communes notiones*). This last group is subdivided into two types. First, there are those that belong to simple natures irrespective of whether they are intellectual or material, such as existence, unity, etc; such natures are accordingly designated as "real." Second, there are those that allow other simple natures to be linked together – are "as it were links" (*veluti vincula quaedam*) – in virtue of being "common notions" in the Aristotelian sense; these include the fact that two terms that are themselves equal must be equal to a third term (hence the label for these natures is "logical"). Identified in this way, these simple natures, in the *Regulae*, allow us to specify the conditions of operation for *mathesis universalis* (Rule IV), given the addition of a theory of order (Rules V–VII) and, to complete the account, a theory of measurement (Rule XIV).[2]

But this uniform list conceals an outcome that is in fact very far from being homogeneous. In the development of the *Regulae* (as indeed will also be the case in the later *Essays* published with the *Discourse*), the simple natures are used only in tackling strictly scientific or epistemological issues: the theory of equations, the theory of curves (in optics), the theories of "analytic geometry," of reflection and refraction, of magnetism and so on. Descartes' actual program of work would thus appear to make use only of those simple natures that are purely material, linked together by the "common" simple natures. The intellectual simple natures, by contrast, though they are identified and listed, are not put to use at all at this stage; for their employment would, in effect, require reasoning of a purely intellectual kind, conducted in abstraction from the world of the senses – reasoning devoted to theoretical objects which cannot be perceived by the senses, and are in the strict sense of the term, metaphysical. The program of the sciences, and its method of procedure, is quite different: science deals with simple natures of the material kind – objects which can be apprehended only through the senses and the imagination. And even though the common notions or principles of logic apply to both the intellectual and the material domains, the mind nonetheless has to proceed quite differently depending on whether its knowledge depends on the "pure intellect" (*ab intellectu puro*) or on the intellect "as it intuits the images of corporeal things" (*ab eodem imagines rerum materialium intuente*, AT X 419: CSM I 45). The distinction between simple natures that are intellectual and those that are material corresponds to the distinction between metaphysics and physics, and hence also to that between understanding and imagination. This contrast, which Descartes articulated explicitly only after 1630,[3] is central to his work throughout the subsequent years, and is a recurring theme that runs through the *Meditations* and *Principles*: "the part of the mind which is of most help in mathematics, namely the imagination, does more harm than good in metaphysical speculations"; or again, "it generally happens with almost everyone . . . that if they are accomplished in metaphysics they hate geometry, while if they have mastered geometry they do not grasp what I have written on first philosophy."⁴ In short, the appearance of homogeneity which the simple natures present is specious: in reality they belong to faculties and sciences that are radically distinct – the material simple natures, grasped by the imagination, belonging to physics and mathematics, while the intellectual simple natures, apprehended by the understanding, belong to metaphysics. What is more, the mind must make a choice between these two areas of inquiry, since metaphysics transcends and is external to physics and mathematics, providing the foundations for these sciences; that indeed is its essential and defining function.

This last point could lead us to accept the following straightforward claim: "The *Regulae* does not therefore . . . contain any trace of metaphysics. On the contrary, the uncertainty which remains in that work about the nature of the mind, and its tendency to assume all truths under the same program, shows plainly that, when he wrote the *Regulae*, Descartes' thought was still operating at a purely scientific level."⁵ On this view, the function of the *Regulae* would be limited to that of constructing a theory of science, realized in mathematical and physical terms, without crossing the border into metaphysics at any point. But this thesis is immediately open to a decisive counter-example: The *Regulae* does refer to the purely intellectual simple natures, albeit not making any use of them, and thus already acknowledges the domain of thought that will later be revealed as the province of metaphysics: "the idea which represents for us what knowledge or doubt or ignorance is, or the action of the will which may be called 'volition,' and the like" (AT X 419: CSM I 44). At the very least we have to admit that, if the *Regulae* does not actually unfold a Cartesian metaphysics, it nonetheless articulates its fundamental concepts and assigns them a primary importance. The question this in turn raises is the following: why does Descartes not undertake to provide at least a sketch of his metaphysics in the *Regulae*, given that he has already got the requisite conceptual materials at his disposal?

This question is doubly pressing when we observe that the *Regulae* takes us right up to the very brink of metaphysics. It does not merely identify the intellectual simple natures (Rule XII), but, even as early as Rule III, attempts to link one of them with a (real) common simple nature, thus hinting, even at this early stage, at propositions that are strictly metaphysical. Among the examples he

gives of knowledge by intuition (*intuitus*), Descartes mentions –
even before geometrical knowledge (the definitions of the triangle
and the sphere) – the elements of the future Cogito of 1637 and
1641: "every one can mentally intuit that he exists, that he is thinking" (*uniusquisque animo potest intueri, se existere, se cogitare* . . . , AT X 368: CSM I 14). This clause juxtaposes an intellectual
simple nature (*cogitare*) and a common simple nature (*existere*). So
what more do we need here to enable us to reach the first principle of
metaphysics? Nothing, except for the necessary link between these
two simple natures – nothing, in other words, but the act of putting
them in the right order. The failure to take this final step is all the
more astonishing, given that Rule XII procedes to link together intellectual simple natures ("if Socrates says that he doubts everything, it
necessarily follows that he understands at least that he is doubting . . ." AT X 421: CSM 46), and also links two instances of the
common simple nature, existence ("I am, therefore God exists":
sum, ergo Deus est) (ibid.).[6] What is more, each of these two necessary linkings of simple natures relates to the components of the
Cogito (doubt – thought; finite existence – infinite existence); all
that is lacking is the final linking of the elements together in a single
chain (doubt – thought, finite existence – infinite existence). So if
the *Regulae* does not succeed, there and then, in articulating the
metaphysical pronouncement that is the Cogito, it is not due to any
incompatibility between metaphysical pronouncements and the simple natures, nor to any ignorance of the intellectual and common
simple natures, nor to any general inability to link them together;
what is missing is simply the capacity to establish a necessary order
between the simple natures that make up the Cogito. With the doctrine of the simple natures, the *Regulae* is already equipped with all
the elements required for articulating the first proposition of metaphysics; the transition to metaphysics depends not on any new elements or concepts, but merely on the necessity which links them
together – and this necessity depends in turn on *order*.

The hypothesis that I am putting forward – that the *Regulae* contains the elements of metaphysics (the intellectual simple natures)
but not their ordering (their necessary lining with the common simple natures) – allows us to take a fresh look at the verdict of Ferdinand Alquié and the much discussed problem he attempted to resolve. Instead of marking out an uncrossable frontier between the

Regulae (and *Discourse*) and the *Meditations*, a frontier designed to preserve the gap between method and metaphysics, we should recognize that metaphysics is itself embedded in the theory of method, in the *Regulae*; but it is present as a possibility which the *Regulae* does not grasp or unfold.[7] This hypothesis can only be confirmed after a further investigation, which will aim to establish that the simple natures do indeed have a metaphysical status and function in Descartes' later works.

The simple natures play a metaphysical role in at least two texts apart from the *Meditations*. The very letter that introduces the term "metaphysical" for the first time (AT I 144: CSMK 120), also claims, as if throwing down a challenge to the prevailing view, that "the mathematical truths which you call 'eternal' were established by God and depend entirely on him, no less than all other created things" (AT I 145). Mathematical truths are thus *created*; they are, in other words, subordinate to the transcendent demands of metaphysics. What is meant by mathematical truths in this context? Descartes makes this clear by providing an example: God was "as free to bring it about that it was not true that all the radii of a circle were equal as he was free not to create the world" (AT I 152). Now this example echoes the one given in Rule III, among other instances of simple natures: "that a triangle is formed by just three lines, and a sphere by a single surface, and the like" (AT X 368: CSM I 14). One could also cite the common simple nature of equality: "things that are the same as a third thing are the same as each other" (AT X 419: CSM I 45). The upshot is that the created mathematical truths consist of combinations of material simple natures (extension, shape) linked together by common, logical simple natures; and conversely that the material and common simple natures are created, and hence transcended by metaphysical authority. This in turn entails two conclusions. First, we must, yet again, distinguish those simple natures that are material (mathematical) and common from those that are intellectual; it is the first two types alone that are referred to when subordination to the creative power of God is being discussed. Second, this creative power corresponds to the involvement of "metaphysical questions" in physics (AT I 145, line 6), and the gap that marks out the intellectual simple natures from all the others is equivalent to the divide that separates metaphysics from mathematics, and hence from physics. Should our conclusion not therefore be that the frontier between the theory of science and metaphysics is much more subtle than is suggested by a crude chronological contrast between the earlier *Regulae* and the later *Meditations*, and that it cuts across the domain of the simple natures themselves?[8]

A second test confirms as much. Part I of the *Principles of Philosophy* is expressly concerned with metaphysics. Nonetheless, after unfolding the theory of truth and error developed in the Fourth Meditation, it proceeds to deal with the simple natures, or at least their equivalents. Having examined clear and distinct perceptions (articles 45–6), Descartes goes on in article 47 to look at "all the simple notions (*simplices notiones*) which are the basic components of our thoughts" (AT VIIIA 22: CSM I 208). He then distinguishes (in article 48) three types of "simple notions." (A) The first comprises the *maxima generalia* or "most general items . . . which extend to all classes of things," namely substance (which is here equivalent to existence in Rule XII), duration, order, and number; it is easy to recognize here what were earlier called the "common" simple natures. (B) The second type comprises extended substance, which is explained in terms of the "notions" (simple natures) of size, extension, shape, and position (*situs*); this corresponds, when expanded, to the list of material simple natures. (C) Thirdly, we have thinking substance, explained in terms of the "notions" (simple natures) of perception and will; this corresponds to the list of intellectual simple natures. Over and above these lists of simple natures, the *Principles* adds a fourth type – the "eternal truths" (*aeternae veritates*, article 49, title). Each eternal truth is a purely mental notion, not a concept of a thing, and consists of a "common notion" in the sense of "axiom." The examples given (the principle of noncontradiction, etc.) clearly enable us to recognize one of the two types of common simple natures presented in Rule XII, namely logical and mathematical axioms; but we may also discern here some of the "created" truths (logical as well as mathematical). In short, the *Principles* preserves the doctrine of the simple natures found in the *Regulae*, but develops the doctrine – as indeed it develops the entire system of science – from a metaphysical standpoint, and working from a metaphysical starting point.

But now the difficulty arises, as to whether there may not be an inconsistency in the evidence just provided to establish a metaphysical function for the simple natures. Are the simple natures meta-physical by default, as is implied by the *Regulae,* or are they meta-physical by subordination, as the letters of 1630 suggest, or finally, and in contrast to either of those, are they metaphysical in virtue of being integrated into the very foundations of the system, as the evidence of the *Principles* would have us suppose?

Whether the simple natures really do fulfill a metaphysical function, and whether the above evidence can be welded into a coherent argu-ment to support this view, must ultimately depend on an analysis of the *Meditations.* Can we find the simple natures (in the sense in which they are used in the *Regulae*) playing a role in the *Medita-tions?* And in this case, should we downgrade the *Meditations* to the level of a treatise on method, or, conversely, should we regard method as having a positive and integral function to perform in the development of metaphysics?

I propose to argue for a paradoxical but essentially simple thesis: we both can and should read all the *Meditations* as a figure com-posed of different types of simple natures that overlap, interrupt, and succeed each other. Understood in this way, the metaphysics of 1641 does not so much reject the elements forged by the 1627 theory of science as employ them in a radically new fashion and bring them to a perfection hitherto undreamed of. I shall try to establish this thesis by successively uncovering the interplay of the simple natures in the First Mediation, then in the Fifth Meditation, and finally, the most tricky case of all, in the Third Meditation.

The First Meditation does not precisely, or primarily, call into doubt the truths of mathematics, which only appear almost as an afterthought in the eighth paragraph; rather the attention is directed in the first instance to what are called the "simpler and more univer-sal things" (*magis simplicia et universalia*), or again the "simplest and most general things" (*simplicissimae et maxime generales res,* AT VII 20, lines 11 and 24: CSM II 14). What are referred to here are, of course, the simple natures, as is shown by at least three consider-ations.[9] First, the items introduced here owe their logical primacy to their simplicity; this simplicity rests not on an ontic but merely on an epistemic foundation, and arises solely in virtue of their containing "something certain and indubitable" (*aliquid certi et indubitati,* AT VII 20, line 27). These items thus possess the essential characteristic of the simple natures – simplicity as far as our knowledge is concerned, and simplicity defined by that knowledge. Secondly, the terms in question allow us to know the truth of what is perceived by the senses, while in no way admitting the slightest similarity between the idea perceived and the corresponding thing. Those ordinary "familiar events" (*usitata ista*, AT VII 19, line 11: CSM II 13), like wearing clothes and sitting in front of the fire, are cast into doubt, but they nonetheless presuppose more elementary notions (*particularia ista*, ibid., 29) such as stretching out one's hands, moving one's head, and so on; and these particulars in their turn, whether true or false, can only be conceived of by presupposing concepts that are absolutely "simple and universal" (*simplicia et universalia vera*, AT VII 20, line 11). This relationship, which arbitrarily links the pure object of sensation to the realm of perfect intelligibility, in effect reinforces the "coding" established in Rule XII whereby simple natures are encoded as sensations.[10] The terms which figure in the conclusion of the First Meditation thus perform the function of the simple natures of Rule XII. Thirdly, and most importantly, the First Meditation provides a list of "simple and universal things" (*simplicia et universalia*) that reproduces what Rule XII had termed "material simple natures." This is true despite a certain difference in the way the terms are grouped together: in 1627 the list reads "shape, extension, movement, etc." (AT X 419: CSM I 45), while in 1641, "corporeal nature in general" is explicated as "extension, the shape of extended things, the quantity or size and number of these extended things, the place in which they may exist, the time through which they may endure, and so on" (AT VII 20: CSM II 14). The first three concepts enumerated here exactly match the first three simple natures that are listed, while the later items also correlate closely enough, since they correspond with some of the common simple natures (unity, duration: AT X 419, line 22: CSM I 45).

Once we have grasped this parallelism between the *Regulae* and the *Meditations* we can go on to explore its consequences. It seems, first of all, that the starting point of the *Meditations* – the project of establishing science by means of hyperbolical doubt – is nothing else than the point reached by the end of the *Regulae*, namely science operating on the simple natures, both material and common. The second phase of the Cartesian enterprise does not begin out of nothing, but builds on secure achievements gained in the first phase;

accordingly, the interpretation of the idea as a simple nature remains operative in the *Meditations*, at least in part. A further piece of evidence comes to mind here: it is only the material simple natures that make their appearance at this point in the *Meditations*; there is no mention of the intellectual simple natures. Moreover, these material natures enter the game only to be disqualified by means of the hyperbolical doubt: "he may have brought it about that there is no extended thing, no shape, no size, no place." (AT VII 21, lines 4–6: CSM II 14). It is thus that the simple natures enter the realm of metaphysics; but since they are merely material (and common) simple natures, they make their entrance only to find themselves disqualified from participating. In one way there is nothing remarkable about this situation; yet in another way it is surprising enough. What we encounter is the outcome of the doctrine of the creation of the eternal truths (found in the letters to Mersenne of April and May 1630): when the authority of metaphysics in the strict sense is invoked, the laws of mathematics which regulate physics (via an encoding process) find themselves transcended and hence disqualified. All that the system of doubt developed in 1641 does is to give a negative interpretation to the incommensurability of the sciences,[11] based on the idea of the "incomprehensible," which had been interpreted in a positive way in the 1630 discussion of the foundations of science. The sciences that are based on the material (and common) simple natures are thus always subordinate to metaphysics. To confirm this hypothesis we shall first attempt to uncover further textual evidence in its favor in the *Meditations*.

The Fifth Meditation supports the essential point in the analysis just offered: hyperbolical doubt initially disqualifies only the material simple natures; once this doubt is removed (Third Meditation) and the rules of truth and falsity are reestablished (Fourth Meditation), it is the material simple natures that are rehabilitated first. In fact what is in question here (as earlier) is not the mathematical truths, but what makes them possible and thinkable at a logically prior level, namely the "true and immutable natures" (*verae et immutabiles naturae*, AT VII 64: CSM II 45); it is these that are reinstated first, constituting as they do the only true object of "ideas as far as they exist in my thought" (*quatenus sunt in mea cogitatione*, AT VII 63: CSM II 45). I suggest that we are dealing here with the self-same material simple natures that have already occupied our attention throughout the First Meditation. There are three reasons for this conclusion. First, the natures, while remaining immutable, eternal and general (AT VII 64, lines 11 and 16; AT VII 63, line 22: CSM II 44), still allow knowledge of countless particulars (*innumerae ideae, innumerae figurae,* 63, line 23; 64 lines 7 and 28). These "particular things" plainly hark back to the things, whether "particular" or "general," of which those "simple universals" are said to be composed in the First Meditation. (AT VII 19–20: CSM II 13–14). In short, what is going on here is the reinstatement of the code that was invalidated by the process of hyperbolical doubt. Second, the list of general terms matches the list of material simple natures (including one common simple nature): "I distinctly imagine quantity . . . or the extension of the quantity . . . in length, breadth and depth . . . sizes, shapes, positions and local motions . . . durations . . . countless particular features regarding shape number and motion. . . ." (AT VII 63: CSM II 44). As in the First Meditation and in the *Regulae,* the mathematical notions (in the Fifth Meditation, the essence of a triangle and its properties) enter the scene only subsequently, merely as examples rather than primary elements in their own right. Third, and following from the last point, the Fifth Meditation enables us to rediscover the validity of universal science, in which the material simple natures will be deployed as they were in the *Regulae:* the latter's *mathesis universalis* corresponds exactly with the *pura atque abstracta mathesis* of the Fifth Meditation, which has as its object "corporeal nature."[12]

The upshot of these arguments is not just that the simple natures are still playing a role in 1641; more than that, their destruction and subsequent reinstatement are the principal targets at which hyperbolical doubt and metaphysical certainty are aimed. It is their status, in effect, which determines the status of *mathesis,* and consequently of mathematics, and then in turn the functioning of physics (through the encoding process). It is this central thread and this alone – the role of the material simple natures – which enables us to understand why the *Meditations* puts to the test only and precisely that science whose certainty, in principle, has already been established in the *Regulae.* But this conclusion in turn gives rise to a new question. What is the role played by the other simple natures during this testing process? What, in particular, is the role of the intellectual simple natures?[13] That these do play a role in the Fifth Meditation is apparent from the fact that at the very moment when *pura mathesis* and its object are reinstated, we find a reference to "achieving knowledge of countless other matters both concerning God himself and other things whose nature is intellectual" (AT VII 71: CSM II 49). The function of these intellectual simple natures remains to be explained.

To throw a full light on the metaphysical function of all the simple natures we need to go back to the Second Meditation. This Meditation can in effect be read as a systematic and exhaustive examination of the four types of simple nature uncovered in Rule XII: intellectual, material, common in the real sense, and common in the logical sense. An analysis of the use of these four terms will enable us to compare the metaphysical role each of them plays.

The intellectual simple natures comprise cognition, doubt, ignorance, the action of the will, and so on (*cognitio, dubium, ignorantia, voluntatis actio,* AT X 419: CSM I 44). But the items presented in Rule XII as a list of concepts, without any internal organization or ontological implications, will reappear in the Second Meditation as an unfolding of the properties of *cogitatio* (thought) precisely because from this point onward thought has the status of a *thing* or *res:* "What then am I? A thing that thinks (*res cogitans*). What is that? A thing that doubts, understands, affirms, denies, is willing, is unwilling and also imagines and has sensory perceptions" (*res dubitans, intelligens, affirmans, negans, volens, nolens, imaginans quoque et sentiens,* AT VII 28: CSM II 19).[14] The parallelism here is quite obvious ("cognitio") in the *Regulae* becomes *cogitatio* ("thought") in the Second Meditation, with a further echo later in the list in the term *intelligens* ("thing . . . that understands"). *Dubium* ("doubt") becomes *dubitans* ("that doubts"); *ignorantia* ("ignorance") probably corresponds to *affirmans/negans* ("which affirms and denies"); *voluntatis actio* ("the action of the will") appears as the two modes of such action, *volens/nolens* ("is willing, is unwilling"). Here for the first time, in the Second Meditation, we follow the "order of reasons",[15] and the *res cogitans* takes certain concepts, the intellectual simple natures, which had hitherto been left without any job to do, and gives them a metaphysical function. What is involved is no mere recitation of the concepts as if they were abstract objects; rather, the *res cogitans* lays them out as modes of its own activity. The *res cogitans* can do its thinking only insofar as it deploys the intellectual simple natures as its own modes of functioning. Now the *Regulae*, while exploiting the material simple natures extensively, had not put the intellectual simple natures to work (though it did explicitly refer to them). We can now see why: only once the material simple natures are called into doubt (First Meditation) and hence removed from the scene, can the intellectual simple natures open the door to the operation of pure reason. And pure reason, operating metaphysically, and as it were beyond itself, must now acknowledge them. Our first conclusion, then, is this: The essence of the *res cogitans* is defined in terms identical to the list of intellectual simple natures.

Among the "common" simple natures ("common" in the sense that they apply equally to intellectual and to material realities), Rule XII lists "existence, unity, duration, and the like" (*existentia unitas, duratio*, AT X 419: CSM I 45). Now the performance of what we call "the Cogito" consists merely in picking up this list. The elements of it appear in both the formulations of the dictum in the Second Meditation: "so I must finally conclude that this proposition, *I am, I exist* is necessarily true whenever it is put forward by me or conceived in my mind"; "I am, I exist, that is certain. But for how long? For as long as I am thinking."[16] The Cogito consists in a single fact: the *ego* puts to work, by a performance of thinking, the common simple nature of existence. And because this performance takes place in time ("whenever" "for as long as"), it also puts to work the common simple nature of duration. It is thus that the *ego* manages to identify itself as a thinking thing: "Thinking . . . this alone is inseparable from me. . . . Were I totally to cease from thinking I should totally cease to exist" (AT VII 27: CSM II 18). The passage from essence to existence is strictly equivalent, as far as the *ego* is concerned, to following up the employment of the intellectual simple natures with the employment of the common simple natures. Our second conclusion is this: the existence of the *res cogitans* is manifested with the help of these common simple natures.

But by the "common" simple natures is also meant the common notions or principles of logic. The *Regulae* provides some examples – the fact that two equal terms are equal to a third term, the link between geometrical figures and their properties, and so on. These principles, in conformity with the basic thrust of the *Regulae*, depend on the limited self-evidence that applies to the purely material simple natures. But the list can be extended. The *Principles of Philosophy*, recapitulate – this time from a metaphysical standpoint – the common simple natures (described as "common notions or axioms"), and add to the *Regulae* list a new axiom, whose special task is to link intellectual simple natures to a real simple nature: "he who is thinking cannot but exist so long as he is thinking."[17] It was precisely the absence of this common simple nature, in Rule III, that blocked the move from a listing of evident simple natures ("that he is existing, that he is thinking" AT X 368: CSM I 14) to the articulation of the first principle of metaphysics. Equally, the necessary link established in Rule XII between Socrates's doubt and the assertion of truth and falsity (AT X 421: CSM I 46) fails to include the essential further step – that existence follows immediately from the very doubt; what is missing is the principle of a necessary link between intellectual simple natures and real common simple natures (in particular, existence). In the Second Meditation, by contrast, use is made of the common notion that can forge a necessary link between existence and thought, though the link is expressed the other way round: "It could be that were I totally to cease from thinking I should totally cease to exist" (AT VII 27: CSM II 18). Our third conclusion, then, is this: the link between the essence of the *ego* and its existence consists simply in the fact that a common simple nature or common notion is used to make the necessary link between an intellectual simple nature and a real common simple nature.

The material simple natures do, of course, also appear in the Second Meditation. But to establish the priority of the *res cogitans* over every other existing thing, the analysis of the piece of wax takes not just the sensible qualities of the wax but also its determinable aspect ("something extended, flexible, and changeable") and subordinates them to the primacy of "purely mental scrutiny" (*pura mentis inspectio*, AT VII 31: CSM II 21). The three characteristics, "extended; flexible" and "changeable" reintroduce the three chief material simple natures (extension, shape, and movement); and hence the analysis of the piece of wax ends up by subordinating the material to the intellectual simple natures. We thus have a reversal of the trend in the *Regulae*, which passed over the intellectual natures in silence and made use only of the material natures. A further conclusion follows from this: the goal and the result, of the Second Meditation is to reverse the hierarchy of the simple natures, and place the intellectual simple natures on top.

The Second Meditation is thus revealed as a marvelously coherent exercise in utilizing and ordering the simple natures. They are utilized since for the first time *all* the simple natures, including the intellectual ones, are systematically deployed and organized, whereas the *Regulae* totally neglected the latter type. And they are ordered, firstly because the intellectual natures take precedence over the material ones in certainty and self-evidence, and secondly and most importantly because they survive the hyperbolical doubt which disqualifies the material natures. It must be stressed that the First Meditation *never* deals with the simple natures in general, irrespective of their type; its target is *exclusively* the material simple natures. There is, to my knowledge, no text that brings doubt to bear on the intellectual simple natures;[18] and as a result the fact that I am thinking (and hence exist), am ignorant, doubting, willing and so on, is never threatened by doubt. This distinction certainly provides a radical answer to the supposed difficulty of the "Cartesian circle": this bogus problem simply does not arise unless one jumbles up simple natures, which are in fact of distinct types, as well as being ordered in a definite hierarchy.

This rereading of the *Meditations* has so far left out any reference to one crucial text – the Third Meditation – and has not yet tackled the question of whether the reinstatement of the simple natures is additionally guaranteed by God. The difficulties here are more complex than those we have so far encountered, and so we shall have to proceed more cautiously; the solutions to be offered will be correspondingly less cut and dried.

An initial observation will at least point us in the right direction; the Third Meditation confirms the results of the Second, insofar as it subordinates the material simple natures to the *ego* (and hence to the intellectual simple natures). To begin with, it reproduces, under the heading of "corporeal things" the list of material simple natures: "...size or extension...shape...position...and motion or change" (*magnitudinem sive extensionem...figuram...situm... et motum sive mutationem*). But in addition, without any reference to the difference of type involved, we have two real common simple natures that have already been encountered, "duration and number" (*duratio et numerus*). Most crucial of all, there is in addition a notion that has hitherto gone unrecognized, or even been rejected – that of *substance* (AT VII 43: CSM II 30).[19] The next step is establishing whether the *ego* can construct these notions simply from its own resources. The reply comes in two parts. Firstly, the real common simple natures "substance, duration, number and anything else of this kind" can be subsumed under the *ego*, principally because the latter is a substance and hence is acquainted with the classification "substance" (with the *ratio substantiae*), even in its extended form (AT VII 44, line 28 to AT VII 45, line 2). As for duration and number, the *ego* can construct these notions thanks to the variations in its own thinking, and hence can subsequently transfer them to corporeal things (ibid.). Secondly, the material simple natures are, as a result, themselves reducible to the *ego* – though via an argument that is admittedly more forced than convincing: extension, shape, position, and movement are, albeit material simple natures, nonetheless modes of a material substance and hence various modes of substance in general (*modi quidam substantiae*); now since I, the *ego*, am also a substance (*ego autem substantia*), the modes of a substance different from mine may therefore be contained in me eminently. Such at any rate is the supposition that Descartes blandly asks us to accept (AT VII 45, lines 5–8: CSM II 31). And hence the *ego*, and all the simple natures it comprises, contain "eminently" (*eminenter*) all the other simple natures, whether material or common.

This confirmation of a hierarchy in the simple natures is thus supposed to entail a more radical result: the fact that the simple natures can be reduced to, or deduced from the *ego*. Whatever "objective" or representative reality is contained in any of the simple natures, as objects of thought, is generated by the formal reality of the *ego*. Yet this result gives rise to a serious problem. The a posteriori proof of God's existence requires the uncovering of an idea which the *ego* must be incapable of generating – an idea not derived from the simple natures. But if nothing can be an object of thought except through the medium of the simple natures, and if the idea of God transcends all the simple natures, what the proof of God requires is an idea that both represents God and is at the same time an object of rational thought; yet no idea that meets both these conditions could possibly be available. To overcome this formidable problem Descartes is obliged to introduce – somewhat artificially – several new ingredients.

To begin with, as we have seen, the Third Meditation introduces *substance* as one of the real common simple natures. This innovation, besides appearing very late in the day, contradicts the radical critique of the notion of substance mounted in the *Regulae;* but the dubious move is unavoidable if Descartes is to apply to God a term which is both common (a stone or a mind are substances just as God is a substance) and yet proper to him alone: God is *substantia infinita,* infinite substance (AT VII 45, line 11: CSM II 31). This bringing together of the common and the special notions of substance is an attempt to do justice to two opposing requirements: (1) that of keeping the notion of God within the bounds of ordinary rationality, – hence the inclusion of God among the simple notions via the (doubtful) supposition that substance is such a nature – and (2) that of maintaining the transcendency of God vis-à-vis the *ego,* which is the sole source from which all the simple natures are deduced. It is this last point that underpins the adjective "infinite," for if substance can provide rigorous support for the simple natures, the infinite is debarred from doing the same, for one very powerful reason: every simple nature must by definition be comprehensible, whereas the infinite remains by definition incomprehensible (though it is intelligible). "The idea of the infinite, if it is to be a true idea, cannot be grasped (*comprehendi*) at all, since the impossibility of being grasped is contained in the formal definition of the infinite" (*incomprehensibilitas in ratione formali infiniti continetur,* Fifth Replies, AT VII 368: CSM II 253). An identical qualification also appears when the power of God is referred to: the impossibility of grasping the notion is immediately stressed as a corrective to the view that our access to the divine essence is too easy ("his immense and incomprehensible power"; *immensa et incomprehensibilis potentia,* First Replies, AT VII 100, lines 26–7: CSM 79). If he is thought of from the point of view of the infinite, God remains "unthinkable and inconceivable" (*incogitabilis et inconceptibilis,* Second Replies, AT VII 140, Line 2: CSM II 100, and AT VII 189, line 10: CSM II 133). From this perspective, God thus lies at the extreme limit of the simple natures; indeed, if one reflects on the extremely fragile and ambiguous status of the term "substance," he is outside their domain altogether.

We thus arrive at the following relatively straightforward schema: the material simple natures, which alone are subjected to hyperbolical doubt (First Meditation), are reinstated immediately after that doubt has been removed (Fifth Meditation). The intellectual simple natures are equivalent to the *res cogitans* and its modes, and hence, as the *ego*, take precedence over the material simple natures (Second Meditation). And as for God, he transcends both types of simple natures (Third Meditation). According to this schema, the First and Fifth Meditations (and hence the Sixth) precisely mark out the horizons of *mathesis universalis* (the "universal science" of the *Regulae*). The *ego*, by contrast, makes use for the first time of the potentiality of the intellectual simple natures which the *Regulae* had referred to without developing, and achieves a new dimension of *mathesis universalis*. Lastly, God transcends absolutely all the simple natures, completely escaping the bounds of *mathesis universalis* and revealing a horizon which is absolutely metaphysical in nature.

Nevertheless, the above schema should not be adhered to over-rigidly. The very fact that it is so neat and schematic prevents its doing justice to several pieces of textual evidence that point in the opposite direction – toward a close link between God and the simple natures, and hence toward a more subtle relationship between *mathesis universalis* and metaphysics. To begin with, God exists; indeed, the sole ambition of the *Meditations* ("in which the existence of God . . . is demonstrated," AT VII 17: CSM II 12) is to prove as much: "we must conclude that God necessarily exists" (AT VII 45: CSM II 31). Now existence belongs to the (real) common simple natures; moreover, in the Fifth Meditation, we find existence linked to essence by what the *Regulae* called a "necessary conjunction" (*conjunctio necessaria*) between simple natures. The comparison between the relation between a triangle and its properties, on the one hand, and the essence of God and his existence, on the other, only serves to reinforce our interpretation of existence as a simple nature. Other properties of God could undoubtedly also be expressed in terms of common real simple natures – in particular eternity (by comparison with duration) and unity. What is more, the debate on the boundary between the possible and the impossible for divine omnipotence would have had no sense if Descartes and his critics had not been prepared to accept implicitly that logical principles and common notions could relate, at least in principle, to God; what is at issue here is common logical simple natures. Accordingly, all the common simple natures remain relevant to inquiries about God.

In the second place, God thinks; that is, he assumes the most important simple nature, that of thought (*cogitatio*). This assertion, though absent from the *Meditations*, appears several times in subsidiary texts: "the most perfect power of thought which we understand to be in God . . ."; ". . . the clear and distinct idea of uncreated and independent thinking substance . . ." "divine thought."[20] We must not underestimate the importance of this, especially since it attributes to God the most crucial of the intellectual simple natures, despite the fact that the Third Meditation had reduced all such natures to the *ego* alone, and made them incommensurable with the idea of God. Consequently, along with the Cogito which subsumes them all, the intellectual simple natures relate to God as well. And hence all the simple natures (except the material ones)[21] can be attributed to God, subject to the standard caveat that operates when we are dealing with the infinite.

The upshot is that the frontier between method (*mathesis universalis*) and metaphysics cannot merely be analyzed in terms of a distinction between two types of simple natures. The primary object of metaphysics, the human mind (*mens humana*) is defined entirely in terms of the intellectual simple natures. It thus relates to universal *mathesis*, by focusing on at least one of its remaining possible objects of inquiry, and by dealing with the common simple natures and the most important of the intellectual simple natures. Should we not, therefore, conclude that metaphysics too belongs to *mathesis universalis*, and is simply one among the many objects of the method of inquiry described in the *Regulae*? I believe that there is one final criterion that absolutely rules out such a conclusion, and in so doing allows us to mark out in a quite emphatic way the true frontier between method and metaphysics. The criterion in question is hinted at in the definition of *mathesis universalis* employed during the discussion of "some order or measurement" (*aliquis ordo vel mensura*).[22] The essential point to grasp is the meaning of the contrast between order and measurement, and the best way to do this is to consider first of all the simplest and most frequent examples provided in the *Regulae* and the *Essays* (excluding the *Meteorology*). In these examples, the ordering process is accompanied by a measurement, e.g. in the theory of equations and the theory of curves. But it can also perfectly well happen that ordering (defined earlier in Rules V through VII) may provide us with a result that is rationally self-evident without our having recourse to measurement, or before we

engage in measurement (which is defined only as late as Rule XIV).
This is what happens in the case of many theories in physics (vortices, elementary particles, etc.), and in physiology (theories of perception via geometrical figuring, animal spirits, and so on). These scientific attempts, to be sure, met with unequal success: in ordering
without measuring Cartesian science sometimes fell into a chaotic
disorder. But in metaphysics, things are quite different; here the
renouncing of measurement is in no sense a defect, since all purely
intellectual objects lack extension, and so cannot, and hence must
not, be subjected to measurement. What is more, the most exalted
object of metaphysics, God, is defined precisely in terms of his infinity, in terms of his absolute incapability of being measured, his
nonmeasurable immensity. (Note that the adjective *immensus* derives from the negative prefix *in*, plus *metiri*, to measure; cf.
essentia immensa, AT VII 241, line 2–3: CSM II 168.)[23] God thus
resists all measurement, not by default, like extended objects which
we cannot manage to measure, but by excess, by being absolutely
beyond the realm of extension. This "immensity" by excess does
not, however, mean that metaphysics is totally divorced from
mathesis universalis. It only resists the second characteristic feature
of universal method, namely measurement, while perfectly conform-
ing to the first, namely order.

In fact the *Meditations* can be understood as a paradigmatic array
of ordered groups of simple natures necessarily linked together. And
this, indeed, is how they are presented: "the proper order of my
arguments and the connection between them" (*rationum mearum
series et nexus*, AT VII 9, line 29: CSM II 8); "considerations of order
appear to dictate" (*ordo videtur exigere*, AT VII 36, line 30: CSM II
25); "pay sufficient attention to the way in which what I wrote fits
altogether" (*ad cohaerentiam eorum quae scripsi attendere*, AT VI
379: CSM II 261). As an exercise in making conclusions evident by
the process of ordering, without recourse at any point to any measuring of extension, the *Meditations* with their supremely metaphysical character can even claim to fulfill the essential definition of
mathesis universalis: metaphysics and method alike are revealed as
uniquely grafted onto a single root – the order of rational self-
evidence. And since this order operates by deploying the simple
natures, the *Meditations* are able, with perfect legitimacy, to fulfill
their metaphysical aim with the help of the simple natures. One

may go further: the project of the *Meditations* is accomplished entirely in terms of the simple natures, since all that happens is that the material simple natures are left behind, so that the value of the intellectual simple natures can be realized. And this in turn is done by uncovering the necessary link between the intellectual simple natures and the real common simple natures (existence, etc.), by utilizing the common logical simple natures (principles and common notions).

Far from constituting an exception to the Cartesian method (or its principle component, that of order), and far from ignoring the objects of that method (the simple natures), the metaphysics of the *Meditations* brings them to fruition. But this special achievement of the *Meditations* in turn overturns the method, by revealing that metaphysics alone can reach its foundations, foundations that, from the very beginning, have belonged to the domain of metaphysics, and metaphysics alone.[24]

Translated by John Cottingham.

NOTES

1 Cf. Marion, *Sur l'ontologie grise de Descartes*, sect. 22, pp. 132ff; and Descartes, *Règles utiles et claires pour la direction de l'esprit*, trans. and ed. Marion, pp. 239f. See also Hamelin, *Le Système de Descartes*, pp. 85f; and O'Neil "Cartesian simple natures".

2 Should we add to these lists the recapitulation, or rather the brutal transformation, of the Aristotelian categories outlined in Rule VI (AT X 381, lines 22ff: CSM I 21–2)? The answer is yes, in so far as the procedure here conforms only to epistemological requirements; but a negative answer is suggested in so far as the categories in question are for Descartes contaminated by the source from which they are derived, and will shortly diasppear completely from the Cartesian system, taking on a wholly new significance.

3 The letter to Mersenne of 15 April 1630 introduces both the term "metaphysics" (and its associated philosophical issues) and the doctrine of the creation of the (mathematical) truths regarded as "eternal" (AT I 144, lines 4 and 15, and AT I 145, lines 7ff).

4 See, respectively, letter to Mersenne of 13 November 1639 (AT II 622, lines 13–16), and *Principles of Philosophy* (Dedicatory letter: AT VIIIA 4, lines 3–6: CSM I 192). See also the same distinction, in an extremely truncated form, in the letter to Elizabeth of 28 June 1643: "Metaphysical

thoughts, which exercise the pure intellect, help to familiarize us with the notion of the soul; and the study of mathematics, which exercises mainly the imagination in the consideration of shapes and movements, accustoms us to form very distinct notions of body" (AT III 692, lines 10–16). For this distinction, and other references, cf. Marion, *Sur le prisme métaphysique de Descartes*, pp. 14–33.

5 Alquié, *La Découverte métaphysique de l'homme chez Descartes*, p. 78. For an analysis of the strengths and weaknesses of Alquié's interpretation of the *Discourse* see Marion, "Le statut métaphysique de Discourse de la méthode" in Grimaldi and Marion (eds.) *Le Discours et sa méthode*.

6 See also Rule XII and Rule XIII (AT X 422, lines 2–6, and AT X 432, lines 24–7: CSM I 46, 53).

7 Cf. letter of end May 1637: "to show that this method can be applied to everything, I have included some brief remarks on metaphysics, physics and medicine in the opening discourse" (AT I 370, lines 25–7: CSMK 58).

8 Cf. letter to Mersenne of 27 May 1638 (AT II 138, lines 1–15).

9 Of course, the role of the simple natures in the First Meditation remains invisible unless we read it in the light of Descartes' earlier theory of sense perception (Rule XII, *Optics*, sects. 1 and 4; and *The World*, ch. 1). In his *Demons, Dreamers and Madmen*, ch. 6, Frankfurt denies that the simple natures are involved here, and his French translator S. Luquet (*Démons, rêveurs et fous* [Paris: Presses Universitaires de France, 1989]) goes further astray by construing this position in an even more radical way (p. 78 n.) [Frankfurt is, however, correct in pointing out a misunderstanding in Gueroult's interpretation of AT VII 19, lines 31ff in *Descartes selon l'ordre des raisons*, vol. I, pp. 34–5, and vol. II, p. 101). See further Marion, *Sur la théologie blanche de Descartes*, sect. 14, pp. 320f.] The only textual evidence for Frankfurt's claim is that the First Meditation employs the neuter adjective *simplicia* (AT VII 20, line 11: CSM II 14, or the noun *res* (line 25). But this proves nothing, since in the *Regulae* too we find the term *res* as well as *natura* (see references in Marion, *Sur l'ontologie grise*, p. 132). Moreover, the Fifth Meditation reintroduces the same concepts as the First, under the label "true and immutable natures" (*verae et immutabiles naturae*: AT VII 64, line 11: CSM II 45). A full discussion of the issue would require a detailed account of the concept of *la figuration codée*; cf. Marion, *Sur le prisme*. For a contrasting view cf. Laporte, *Le Rationalisme de Descartes*, pp. 13–44; and Curley, *Descartes against the Sceptics*.

10 The term "encoded" is used to underline the correspondence without resemblance that obtains between particular sensibilia and geometrical figures – a correspondence that unites, yet at the same time separates,

the two sets of related items. For this notion, see further Marion, *Sur la théologie blanche*, ch. 12, pp. 231ff.

11 The term "incommensurable" signifies irreducibility to a common standard of measurement (*immensus* Lat., negative of *mensus*, from *mensus*, from *metior*, to measure); the goal of *mathesis universalis* in the *Regulae* had been just such a reduction to a common order and measure (AT X 378). See further Marion, *Sur le prisme*, ch. 17, pp. 142ff.

12 "natura corporea quae est purae Matheseos objectum" (Fifth Meditation: AT VII 71, line 8: CSM II 49). CSM translates *pura mathesis* as "pure mathematics," a rendering which is debatable and, in my view, too restrictive: see the Sixth Meditation (AT VII 71, line 15; AT VII 74, line 2; and AT VII 80, line 10: CSM II 50, 51, 55). There is an unavoidable connection here with the *mathesis universalis* of Rule IV, but it does not follow that the two notions are identical. The *mathesis* of the 1641 meditations (which is *not* characterized as "universal") is explicitly restricted to the material (and common) simple natures, and involves the use of imagination, whereas the *mathesis* of the 1627 *Regulae*, explicitly described as *universalis*, extended in principle (if not de facto) to all the simple natures, including the intellectual ones. The restricted scope of this science or *mathesis* in the meditations nevertheless goes hand in hand with an enlarging of the effective use made of the simple natures. For *mathesis universalis* in the *Regulae*, see McRae, "Descartes: the project of a universal science"; Crapulli, *Mathesis universalis, genesi di una idea nel XVI secolo;* Marion, *Sur l'ontologie grise* sect. 11; and Marion (ed.), *Règles utiles*, pp. 144–64, 302–9; Perini *Il problema della fondazione nelle Regulae di Descartes;* Lachterman, "Objectum purae matheseos: mathematical construction and passage from essence to existence," in A. O. Rorty (ed.), *Essays on Descartes' Meditations*.

13 As for the material simple natures, they are necessarily limited to existence, and hence to the real common simple natures, when the Sixth Meditation attempts the move from possible existence (*posse existere*) to actual existence (*res corporeae existunt*) (AT VII 71, line 15; 80, line 4: CSM II 50, 55). Even the Fourth Meditation can be reduced to a variation on the simple natures in the discussion of *cognitio, dubitatio,* and *ignoratia.* For *cognitio* (knowledge) and *ignorantia* (ignorance) see AT VII 56, line 22; 57, line 17; 58, line 9; 59, lines 17ff. For *dubitatio* (doubt), see AT VII 59, line 26. The intellectual simple nature *voluntatis actio* (act of will) or *volitio* (volition), which appeared in the *Regulae* (AT X 419, lines 14–15), returns in that Fourth Meditation at AT VII 56, lines 28ff; 57, line 12; 58, line 21; 59, line 2; 60, line 5.

14 For other formulations, see AT VII 27, lines 20–3 (a list of things I am

not); 34, lines 18–21 (where the French translation adds "that loves, that hates" [*qui aime et qui hait*]); *Principles of Philosophy* Part I, arts. 9, 65. (CSM II 18, 24; CSM I 195, 216). These latter formulations allow us to get a clearer idea of what the passion of love consists of; cf. Marion, "L'unique Ego et l'altération de l'autre" in *Archivio di filosofia* LIV, 1–3 (1988): 607–24.

15 The allusion is of course to the title of Gueroult's *Descartes selon l'ordre des raisons*. Gueroult stresses a contrast that is fundamental (though seldom formulated explicitly in Descartes' writings) between the order of the subject matter (*l'ordre des matières*) and the "order of reasons" (*celui des raisions*) (letter to Mersenne, 24 December 1640: AT III 266). Without contesting Gueroult's basic thesis, I would want to claim that even the "order of reasons" is worked out in terms of certain fixed structures.

16 AT VII 25, lines 11–13, and 27, lines 9–10 (CSM II 17–18). For an interpretation of these phrases, which are absolutely unique in Descartes' work, see my analysis, Marion, *Sur la théologie blanche*, sect. 16 and *Sur le prisme*, sect. 11–12.

17 *Principles* Part I, art. 49. Cf. Book I, art. 10, where the *ego cogito ergo sum* is explicitly classified among the very simple natures (*notiones simplicissimae*), following the order of knowledge ("to anyone who philosophises in an orderly way"; *cuilibet ordine philosophandi*); the passage goes on to invoke intellectual simple natures (thought, certainty) and common simple natures both real (existence) and logical (the impossibility of something's thinking without existing). The famous, but sterile, debate over the status of the presupposition *pour penser il faut être* is surely due to a misunderstanding: what is at stake here is not the formal or syllogistic premises for the Cogito, but the simple natures that the Cogito utilizes and, in this sense, presupposes. Cf. the evidence cited in *Sur la théologie blanche*, sect. 16, pp. 372ff.

18 Note in particular that the famous highest level of doubt in the First Meditation (the deceiving God, AT VII 21, lines 1–16: CSM II 14) refers only to *material* simple natures (extension, shape, size, place, and arithmetical and geometrical notions); there is never any mention of intellectual simple natures (knowledge, thought, etc.).

19 The term "substance" (*substantia*) appears only in the second part of the Third Meditation (AT VII 43, line 20: CSM II 30); throughout the first two Meditations it has remained unknown. Leaving aside the *Discourse* (AT VI 33, line 4; 43, line 26: CSM I 127, 133), it is really only in the *Principles of Philosophy* that *substantia* is finally reintegrated among the *simplicies notiones*, duration, number, order, etc. (Part I, arts. 48, 49: CSM I 208–9). On this crucial point see Becco, "Première apparition du

terme de substance dans la Meditation III de Descartes," and idem, "Remarques sur le 'Traite de la substance' de Descartes." See also Marion, *Sur la théologie blanche*, sect. 16, pp. 395ff; and idem, *Sur le prisme*, sect. 10, pp. 131ff and sect. 13, pp. 161ff.

20 See, respectively (i) AT VII 373, lines 5–6: CSM II 257; (ii) *Principles* Part I, art 54: CSM I 211; and (iii) letter to Arnauld of 4 June 1648, AT V 193, line 17 CSMK 355. There are similar expressions elsewhere: *souveraine intelligence* (letter to Chanut 1 February 1647, AT IV 608: CSMK 309); *idea intellectionis divinae* (AT VII 188, line 19: CSM II 132); *nature intelligente . . . qui est Dieu* (letter to Mersenne, 15 November 1638, AT II 435: CSMK 129).

21 Hence the importance of refusing to attribute any kind of extension to God; contrast Henry More in his letter to Descartes of 11 December 1648: *Deus suo modo extenditur* (AT V 238–9). Such an attribution, by confusing material and intellectual simple natures, would, for Descartes, abolish the distinction between metaphysics and physics.

22 AT X 378, lines 1, 6: CSM I 19. CSM omits the "some" (*aliquis*) that Crapulli restored to the text in his critical edition of the *Regulae*, p. 15. See also my commentary on *Sur l'ontologie grise*, sect. 12, pp. 72ff, and the references to other formulations in my own edition, Marion, *Règles utiles*, pp. 159–60.

23 For other instances, see AT VII 55, lines 20ff; 56, line 4; 57, line 11; 110, lines 26–7; 119, lines 13; 188, line 23; 231, lines 26ff; 143, line 20 (CSM I 38–40, 79, 85, 152, 162, 299). For further discussion of these passages see my "The essential incoherence of Descartes' definition of Divinity," in Rorty, *Essays on Descartes' Medidations*, pp. 309ff.

24 I should like to record my thanks to John Cottingham for his helpful comments and suggestions for improvement, and for his limpid translation of the original French version of this chapter.

5 The Cogito and its importance

The basic story is well-known. Descartes goes looking for something absolutely certain, beyond even the slightest, most unreasonable doubt, to serve as the permanent foundation for his knowledge. He dismisses the propositions evidenced by his senses. The traditional skeptical worries about hallucinations, madness, dreams and deceiving gods convince him that there is no certainty there. He lands on a bedrock certainty capable of withstanding even his worries about a deceptive god: He exists.

> But I have convinced myself that there is absolutely nothing in the world, no sky, no earth, no minds, no bodies. Does it now follow that I too do not exist? No: if I convinced myself of something then I certainly existed. But there is a deceiver of supreme power and cunning who is deliberately and constantly deceiving me; and let him deceive me as much as he can, he will never bring it about that I am nothing so long as I think that I am something. So after considering everything very thoroughly, I must finally conclude that this proposition, *I am, I exist*, is necessarily true whenever it is put forward by me or conceived in my mind.
> (Second Meditation: AT VII 25: CSM II 16–17)

Descartes quickly includes claims about his mental state in his list of certainties. He is certain that he thinks, doubts, imagines, wills and the like: "But what then am I? A thing that thinks. What is that? A thing that doubts, understands, affirms, denies, is willing, is unwilling, and also imagines and has sensory experiences" (AT VII 28: CSM II 19). He is also certain of what he *seems* to perceive: "For example, I am now seeing light, hearing a noise, feeling heat. But I am asleep, so all this is false. Yet I certainly seem to see, to hear, and to be warmed. This cannot be false; what is called 'having a sensory perception' is strictly just this, and in this restricted sense of the term it is simply thinking" (AT VII 29: CSM II 19)

Descartes goes on to define the central problem of epistemology for the next three hundred years. How can we move from our certain knowledge of the content of our experience to a knowledge of its cause? How can we know whether our experience is caused by an external world that is basically the way the content of our experience represents it as being or by an external world that is radically different, say one that contains a deceptive god who manipulates our mind? Descartes solves the problem by appeal to an omnipotent, omnibenevolent God. Subsequent philosophers have made more plausible, but generally less elegant, moves.

I want to concentrate on Descartes' initial claim to certainty about his thought and existence. On the surface, the dictum generally used to sum up his position – "I am thinking, therefore I am" – seems as obvious and as uninteresting as the claim that fish do not need bicycles. The dictum is not even new with Descartes, since Augustine anticipates him.[1] Descartes admits that his position is obvious, telling us his dictum is "so simple and natural that it might have occurred to any writer" (letter of November 1640, AT II 24: CSMK 159).[2] Yet, Descartes' claim to certainty about his thought and existence is extremely important for both his epistemology and his metaphysics, and, once we get beyond a superficial reading of the text, his account of how he gains this certainty turns out to be one of the most confusing aspects of his philosophy. I shall briefly discuss the importance of Descartes' claim to certainty, and then I shall develop an interpretation of his position that clears away the main points of confusion. Finally, I shall consider some general philosophical problems that are raised by Descartes' position.

I. THE IMPORTANCE OF DESCARTES' POSITION

Descartes' claim to certainty about his thought and existence is central to his general program in epistemology. He wants to answer skepticism, and he wants to do so within foundationalism, the view that all our knowledge begins with some self-evident beliefs which are not evidenced by any others but yet provide our justification for all the rest we know. To succeed in this program, Descartes must define the set of self-evident beliefs and show that its membership is both certain and extensive enough to support the rest of our knowledge about the world. His claim to certainty about his thought and existence is the initial move in his attempt to do so.

Descartes also thinks that his claim to certainty of his thought and existence plays an important role in his metaphysics. In the letter where he says that the dictum, "I think, therefore I am," is so obvious that it might have come from anyone's pen, he observes that its real value is that it can be used to "establish that this I which is thinking is an immaterial substance with no bodily element" (loc. cit.). The idea that he can use his initial certainty about his thought and existence, and his initial uncertainty about his body, to establish that he is an immaterial substance distinct from his body is a continuing theme in Descartes' philosophy. He hints at it in the *Rules:* "Again there are many instances of things which are necessarily conjoined, even though most people count them as contingent, failing to notice the relation between them: for example the proposition, 'I am, therefore God exists', or 'I understand, therefore I have a mind distinct from my body'." (Rule XII: AT X 421–2: CSM I 46). Just as we can derive God's existence from our own, we can somehow derive the distinctness of our mind and body from the fact that we understand. Descartes' comments become more informative as his philosophy develops. In *The Search for Truth,* he sketches an argument from premises about his knowledge of himself and his ignorance of his body to the conclusion that he is distinct from his body:

Indeed, I do not even know whether I have a body; you have shown me that it is possible to doubt it. I might add that I cannot deny absolutely that I have a body. Yet even if we keep all these suppositions intact, this will not prevent me from being certain that I exist. On the contrary, these suppositions simply strengthen the certainty of my conviction that I exist and am not a body. Otherwise, if I had doubts about my body, I would also have doubts about myself, and I cannot have doubts about that. I am absolutely convinced that I exist, so convinced that it is totally impossible for me to doubt it.   (AT X 518: CSM II 412)

In the *Discourse on the Method,* Descartes begins with the premise that he is certain of his thought and existence but uncertain of his body:

Next I examined attentively what I was. I saw that while I could pretend that I had no body and that there was no world and no place for me to be in, I could not for all that pretend that I did not exist. I saw on the contrary that from the mere fact that I thought of doubting the truth of other things, it followed quite evidently and certainly that I existed; whereas if I had merely ceased thinking, even if everything else I had ever imagined had been true, I should have had no reason to believe that I existed.

and he infers that he is distinct from his body:

From this I knew I was a substance whose whole essence or nature is simply to think, and which does not require any place, or depend on any material thing, in order to exist. Accordingly this 'I' – that is, the soul by which I am what I am – is entirely distinct from the body, and indeed is easier to know than the body, and would not fail to be whatever it is, even if the body did not exist.   (AT VI 32–33: CSM I 127)

In the *Meditations*, Descartes says that thought is the only thing he knows to be part of his essence prior to proving God's existence, and that, "it follows from the fact that I am aware of nothing else belonging to my essence, that nothing else does in fact belong to it" (AT VII 8: CSM II 7). In the *Principles*, he reports his certainty of his thought and existence and his uncertainty of his body and then says that "this is the best way to discover the nature of the mind and the distinction between the mind and the body"(Part I, art. 8: AT VIIIA 7: CSM I 195).

The importance of Descartes' claim to certainty of his thought and existence extends beyond the role it plays in his programs in epistemology and metaphysics. Understanding and evaluating what he has to say requires us to come to grips with some basic philosophical issues that he himself ignores or treats only in passing, e.g. issues about how we think of ourselves and distinguish ourselves from other objects in the world. Descartes' position, thus, provides us with the occasion for more philosophic work and discovery.

It is time to gain a better appreciation of Descartes' position. I shall begin with an interpretation that captures many, but not all, of his statements.

2. THE SELF-EVIDENT INTUITION/IMMEDIATE INFERENCE INTERPRETATION

Descartes presents intuition and deduction as his only sources of certainty in the *Regulae*:

But in case we in turn should slip into the same error, let us now review all the actions of the intellect by means of which we are able to arrive at a knowledge of things with no fear of being mistaken. We recognize only two: intuition and deduction.   (Rule III: AT X 386: CSM I 14)

Deduction is "the inference of something as following necessarily from some other propositions which are known with certainty" (AT X 369: CSM I 15). Intuition is the faculty by which we gain the initial certainties that make deduction possible:

By 'intuition' I do not mean the fluctuating testimony of the senses or the deceptive judgement of the imagination as it botches things together, but the conception of a clear and attentive mind, which is so easy and distinct that there can be no room for doubt about what we are understanding. Alternatively, and this comes to the same thing, intuition is the indubitable conception of a clear and attentive mind which proceeds solely from the light of reason.   (AT X 368: CSM I 14)

Intuition is distinguished from deduction by the fact that it does not involve a movement of thought through a series of inferences and by its immediate self-evidence: "Hence we are distinguishing mental intuition from certain deduction on the grounds that we are aware of a movement or a sort of sequence in the latter but not in the former, and also because immediate self-evidence is not required for deduction, as it is for intuition" (AT X 370: CSM 15). Descartes decides that while self-evident propositions are known only by intuition and conclusions derived from them in several intuited steps are known only by deduction, propositions immediately inferred from self-evident intuitions may be described as known either by intuition or deduction, depending on our perspective: "It follows that those propositions which are immediately inferred from first principles can be said to be known in one respect through intuition, and in another respect through deduction. But the first principles them-selves are known only through intuition, and the remote conclu-sions only through deduction" (AT X 370: CSM I 15).

When we immediately infer a conclusion from an intuited self-evident premise, we are not aware of any movement of thought through a series of premises, so we may describe our knowledge of the conclusion as intuitive. No extended series of intuitions leads us to the conclusion; there is just one mental act in which the self-evident premise is intuited and the immediate conclusion is drawn.

Yet, we are also inferring a conclusion from a premise, so we may also describe our knowledge as deductive.

Descartes says that we gain knowledge of our thought and existence by intuition: "Thus everyone can mentally intuit that he exists, that he is a thinking thing, that a triangle is bounded by just three lines, and a sphere by a single surface, and the like. Perceptions such as these are more numerous than most people realize, disdaining as they do to turn their minds to such simple matters" (AT X 368: CSM I 14).

Descartes would presumably extend his appeal to intuition to account for his certainty about his particular mental states; e.g., that he doubts, wills, imagines, seems to see light, hear noise, feel heat.

Descartes' appeal to intuition is unclear. The set of intuited propositions includes both self-evident propositions not inferred from any others and propositions immediately inferred from self-evident premises. On which side of this distinction does Descartes place the propositions about his mental state and the proposition that he exists? Descartes seems to regard the propositions about his mental state as self-evident ones that are not inferred and the proposition that he exists as one that is immediately inferred from premises about his mental state. His knowledge of his mental state is intuitive in the primary sense that it is self-evident and not inferred. His knowledge of his existence is intuitive in the extended sense that he immediately infers his existence from intuited premises about his mental state.

Descartes tells the Marquis of Newcastle:

You will surely admit that you are less certain of the presence of the objects you see than of the truth of the proposition: I am thinking, therefore I exist? Now this knowledge is not the work of your reasoning, or information passed on to you by your teachers; it is something that your mind sees, feels and handles; and although your imagination insistently mixes itself up with your thoughts and lessens the clarity of this knowledge, it is, nevertheless, a proof of our soul's capacity for receiving from God an intuitive kind of knowledge.   (AT V 137: CSMK 331)

Descartes presents the inference that he thinks and therefore exists, and he says that his knowledge is intuitive and not a product of his reasoning. How can his knowledge both involve the inference "I think, therefore I am," and be intuitive? The answer is that Descartes intuits the self-evident proposition that he thinks and simultaneously immediately infers that he exists. His knowledge that he thinks is intuitive in the primary sense of being self-evident and entirely noninferential; his knowledge that he exists is intuitive in the extended sense of being immediately inferred from the simultaneously intuited premise that he thinks. He makes the same point to Mersenne:

And when we become aware that we are thinking beings, this is a primary notion that is not derived by means of any syllogism. When someone says, 'I am thinking, therefore I am, or exist,' he does not deduce existence from thought by a syllogism, but, recognizes it as something self-evident by a simple intuition of the mind. This is clear from the fact that if he were deducing it by means of a syllogism, he would have to have had previous knowledge of the major premise 'Everything which thinks is, or exists'; yet in fact he learns it from experiencing in his own case that it is impossible that he should think without existing.

(Second Replies: AT VII 140: CSM II 100)

Descartes again presents the immediate inference from his thought to his existence, and he says that his knowledge is not deductive but a simple intuition of the mind. His point again seems to be that his knowledge of his thought is intuitive since it involves his grasping a self-evident, noninferred premise, and his knowledge of his existence is intuitive since it involves his immediately inferring that he exists from the simultaneously intuited premise that he thinks. Descartes' remarks in the *Discourse* and *Principles* further support this interpretation:

And observing that this truth 'I am thinking, therefore I exist' was so firm and sure that all the most extravagant suppositions of the sceptics were incapable of shaking it, I decided that I could accept it without scruple as the first principle of the philosophy I was seeking.

(*Discourse:* AT VI 32: CSM I 127)

For it is a contradiction to suppose that what thinks does not, at the very time when it is thinking, exist. Accordingly, this piece of knowledge – *I am thinking, therefore I exist* – is the first and most certain of all to occur to anyone who philosophizes in an orderly way.

(*Principles* Part I, art. 7: AT VIIIA 7: CSM I 195)

In each passage, Descartes presents his immediate inference from his thought to his existence as a single piece of knowledge; it is the first principle of his philosophy. His point seems to be that in one act of intuition, he grasps the premise and immediately infers the conclusion.

It is important to note two other points. First, Descartes says that the initial premise that he thinks can be replaced by other claims about his mental state, e.g. that he seems to see:

For if I say 'I am seeing, or I am walking, therefore I exist', and take this as applying to vision or walking as bodily activities, then the conclusion is not absolutely certain. This is because, as often happens during sleep, it is possible for me to think I am seeing or walking, though my eyes are closed and I am not moving about; such thoughts might even be possible if I had no body at all. But if I take 'seeing' or 'walking' to apply to the actual sense or awareness of seeing or walking, then the conclusion is quite certain, since it relates to the mind, which alone has the sensation or thought that it is seeing or walking.   (*Principles* Part I, art. 9: AT VIIIA 8: CSM I 195)

Second, Descartes' talk of intuition and deduction from intuitions as our two sources of knowledge in the *Rules* gives way to talk of clear and distinct perception in the *Discourse, Meditations,* and *Principles.* He never announces that the faculties are the same, but their equivalence is strongly suggested by the fact that he designates them by similar descriptions: "the light of reason" and "the light of nature." We are told in the *Rules* that: "intuition is the indubitable conception of a clear and attentive mind which proceeds solely from the light of reason [*rationis luce*]" (Rule III: AT X 368: CSM I 14) and in the *Principles* that: "the light of nature [*lumen naturæ*] or faculty of knowledge which God gave us can never encompass any object which is not true in so far as it is indeed encompassed by this faculty, that is, in so far as it is clearly and distinctly perceived" (Part I, art. 30: AT VIIIA 16: CSM I 203; consider too *Meditations:* AT VII 38–9: CSM II 26–7)[3]

We may, then, state Descartes's explanation of his certainty of his thought and existence in terms of clear and distinct perception: all his clear and distinct perceptions are certain, he directly, non-inferentially, clearly and distinctly perceives the propositions about his thought, and he clearly and distinctly perceives that he exists by immediately deriving that claim from a clearly and distinctly perceived premise about his thought. As he puts it when he reflects on his knowledge that he is a thinking thing at the start of the Third Meditation: "In this first item of knowledge there is simply a clear and distinct perception of what I am asserting" (AT VII 35: CSM II 24).

I shall call this interpretation "The Self-Evident Intuition/Immediate Inference Interpretation." I now want to present some passages that cause problems for it. Then we can see how the problems can be solved.

3. OUR PRIOR KNOWLEDGE OF THE GENERAL PRINCIPLE THAT WHAT THINKS MUST EXIST

One problematic passage is in the *Principles*.

And when I said that the proposition I am thinking, therefore I exist is the first and most certain of all to occur to anyone who philosophizes in an orderly way, I did not in saying that deny that one must first know what thought, existence and certainty are, and that it is impossible that that which thinks should not exist, and so forth. But because these are very simple notions, and ones which on their own provide us with no knowledge of anything that exists, I did not think they needed to be listed.

(Part I, art. 10: AT VIIIA 8: CSM I 196)

Descartes says that prior to knowing that he thinks and therefore exists, he must know, not only what thought, existence and certainty are, but also the general proposition that it is impossible for what thinks not to exist. His point seems to be that his inference from his thought to his existence uses the general proposition as a suppressed premise. It is not, "I am thinking, therefore I exist"; it is, "I am thinking and whatever is thinking must exist, therefore I exist."

We might try to accommodate this passage by modifying our interpretation of Descartes' inference. His explanation of his certainty would then be that he clearly and distinctly perceives the self-evident proposition that he thinks and the self-evident proposition that whatever is thinking must exist, and he deduces that he therefore exists. His clear and distinct perception of the premises and the conclusion is enough to make them certain. We cannot get out of trouble this easily. Recall Descartes' comment to Mersenne:

And when we become aware that we are thinking beings, this is a primary notion that is not derived by means of any syllogism. When someone says, 'I am thinking, therefore I am, or exist,' he does not deduce existence from thought by a syllogism, but, recognizes it as something self-evident by a simple intuition of the mind. This is clear from the fact that if he were deducing it by means of a syllogism, he would have to have had previous knowledge of the major premise 'Everything which thinks is, or exists'; yet

in fact he learns it from experiencing in his own case that it is impossible
that he should think without existing.

> (Second Replies: AT VII 140: CSM II 100)

Descartes explicitly denies that his inference from his thought to his
existence is a syllogism using the general premise that whatever
thinks must exist. He also says that we learn that we think and
therefore exist *prior to* learning that whatever thinks must exist. He
repeats the point in response to one of Gassendi's objections:

> The author of the *Counter-Objections* claims that when I say 'I am think-
> ing, therefore I exist' I presuppose the major premise 'Whatever thinks ex-
> ists', and hence I have already adopted a preconceived opinion. . . . the most
> important mistake our critic makes here is the supposition that knowledge
> of particular propositions must always be deduced from universal ones,
> following the same order as that of a syllogism in Dialectic. Here he shows
> how little he knows of the way in which we discover the truth. It is certain
> that if we are to discover the truth we must always begin with particular
> notions in order to arrive at general ones later on (though we may reverse
> the order and deduce other particular truths once we have discovered gen-
> eral ones).
>
> (Appendix to the Fifth Objections and Replies: AT IX 205–6: CSM II 271)

If we modify our interpretation so that Descartes' inference uses the
general premise that whatever thinks must exist, we shall be in
conflict with his replies to Mersenne and Gassendi, but if we do not
modify out interpretation in this way, how are we to account for his
claim in the *Principles* that prior to knowing that we think and
therefore exist, we must know that whatever thinks must exist?[4]

Our Awareness of Substances

The *Principles* and Third Objections and Replies contain other problematic passages:

> However, we cannot initially become aware of a substance merely through
> its being an existing thing, since this alone does not have any effect on us.
> We can, however, easily come to know a substance by one of its attributes,
> in virtue of the common notion that nothingness possesses no attributes,
> that is to say, no properties or qualities. Thus, if we perceive the presence of
> some attribute, we can infer that there must also be present an existing
> thing or substance to which it may be attributed.
>
> (*Principles* Part I, art. 52: AT VIIIA 25: CSM I 210)

If I may briefly explain the point at issue: it is certain that a thought cannot exist without a thing that is thinking; and in general no act or accident can exist without a substance for it to belong to. But we do not come to know a substance immediately, through being aware of the substance itself; we come to know it only through its being the subject of certain acts.

(Third Objections and Replies: AT VII 175–6: CSM II 124)

Descartes seems to be saying the following. Each object consists of qualities and an underlying substance in which the attributes inhere. All we immediately observe when we are aware of an object is some of its attributes, and from the existence of the observed qualities and the general principle that every observed quality is in some substance, we infer the existence of the underlying subject.

This general position implies an account of self-knowledge that is at odds with the one we have attributed to Descartes. When we turn our attention inward and reflect on ourselves, all we are immediately aware of is our thoughts. Our initial knowledge is not correctly reported by the statement, "I am thinking," but by the statement, "Thought is taking place." We cannot immediately infer our existence from this knowledge. The best we can infer is that, since every observed quality is in some substance, some substance thinks. We can reason, "Thought exists and whenever any observed quality exists there is a substance that has it, so there is a thinking substance." Our knowledge is inferential, but the inference is syllogistic rather than immediate, and it has a different beginning and end than the inference "I am thinking, therefore I exist."

We cannot, of course, solve our problem by deciding that Descartes adopts the syllogistic inference just considered and offers it as his account of how he gains certain self-knowledge through clear and distinct perception. What would we then make of his explicit denials that his inference from thought to existence is a syllogism? What would we make of the fact that he states his inference from thought to existence so it includes an explicit reference to himself in particular: It is "I am thinking, therefore I exist"; not, "Thought is taking place, every observed quality is in some substance, therefore some thinking substance exists."[5]

The Uncertainty of Clear and Distinct Perception

The Self-Evident Intuition/Immediate Inference Interpretation attributes to Descartes the principle that clear and distinct perception always produces certainty, even in the face of reasons for doubt like the Deceptive God Hypothesis. Descartes is certain that he thinks and therefore exists, because he clearly and distinctly perceives that fact. Yet, while Descartes seems to make clear and distinct perception a sufficient condition for certainty in the *Rules*, he seems to change his mind when he subjects his faculties to a more critical examination in the *Meditations* and *Replies*.

In the beginning of the Third Meditation, he writes:

But what about when I was considering something very simple and straight-forward in arithmetic or geometry, for example that two and three added together make five, and so on? Did I not see at least these things clearly enough to affirm their truth? Indeed, the only reason for my later judgment that they were open to doubt was that it occurred to me that perhaps some God could have given me a nature such that I was deceived even in matters which seemed most evident. And whenever my preconceived belief in the power of God comes to mind, I cannot but admit that it would be easy for him, if he so desired, to bring it about that I go wrong even in those matters which I think I see clearly with my mind's eye.   (AT VII 36: CSM II 25)

Descartes' claims that a version of the Deceptive God Hypothesis gives him a reason to doubt simple truths, even when he sees them with his "mind's eye." His reference to his mind's eye sure seems to be one to clear and distinct perception.

Descartes' replies to his critics contain further indications that he does not take clear and distinct perception to be a sufficient condition for certainty. When Mersenne observes that: "an atheist is clearly and distinctly aware that the three angles of a triangle are equal to two right angles, but so far is he from supposing the existence of God that he completely denies it" (Second Objections: AT VII 125; CSM II 89). Descartes replies:

The fact that an atheist can be 'clearly aware that the three angles of a triangle are equal to two right angles' is something I do not dispute. But I maintain that this awareness of his is not true knowledge, since no act of awareness that can be rendered doubtful seems fit to be called knowledge. Now since we are supposing that this individual is an atheist, he cannot be certain that he is not being deceived on matters which seem to him to be very evident (as I fully explained).

(Second Replies: AT VII 141: CSM II 101)

Descartes denies that the atheist has "true knowledge" on the grounds that the atheist is uncertain of whether he is deceived by some god. Prior to proving God's existence and nondeceptive nature, Descartes is just as uncertain as the atheist about the existence of a deceptive god. His clear and distinct perceptions should not produce certainty for him either.[6]

It is difficult to see how the Self-Evident Intuition/Immediate Inference Interpretation can be modified to take these passages into account. We might try basing the interpretation on a weaker claim about clear and distinct perception: not all clear and distinct perceptions produce certainty, only a proper subset of them do, and Descartes' immediate inference that he thinks and therefore exists falls in that subset. What, then, is this proper subset? In the passages above from the Third Meditation, Descartes subjects even very simple propositions perceived utterly clearly by the mind's eye to the doubt raised by the hypothesis of a deceptive god.

The Irrelevance of Clear and Distinct Perception

A final problem for the Self-Evident Intuition/Immediate Inference Interpretation is raised by Descartes' Second Meditation discussion of his certainty of his existence:

But I have convinced myself that there is absolutely nothing in the world, no sky, no earth, no minds, no bodies. Does it now follow that I too do not exist? No: if I convinced myself of something then I certainly existed. But there is a deceiver of supreme power and cunning who is deliberately and constantly deceiving me; and let him deceive me as much as he can, he will never bring it about that I am nothing so long as I think that I am something. So after considering everything very thoroughly, I must finally conclude that this proposition, *I am, I exist,* is necessarily true whenever it is put forward by me or conceived in my mind.   (AT VII 25: CSM II 16–17)

Descartes claims certainty of his existence, but he does not once mention clear and distinct perception or an immediate inference from thought to existence. His explanation instead seems to be that he is certain he exists because he has no reason to doubt that belief, and he has no reason to doubt it, because every hypothesis that might give him a reason to doubt it, such as the hypothesis that some god deceives him, simply entails, and so affirms, it. Descartes' point about his belief in his existence can be extended to his belief that he thinks. Reasons for doubt like the Deceptive God Hypothesis simply entail that his belief is true.

Yet, if this is all there is to Descartes' position, what are we to make of his other claims to certainty about his mental state; e.g., his claim to be certain that he seems to see light? Reasons for doubt, like the Deceptive God Hypothesis, do not entail that he seems to see light. He must exist and think to be deceived; he does not need to seem to see light. What are we to make of Descartes' references to clear and distinct perception (intuition) as the source of his certainty and to his immediate inference, "I am thinking, hence I exist"? It has been suggested that the point of Descartes' inference is just that every reason for doubt entails his existence by entailing that he thinks. The problem with this suggestion is that Descartes says the premise in his inference can be any claim about his mental state; he may just as well reason, "I seem to see; hence I exist." The point of this inference surely is not that every reason for doubt entails Descartes' existence by entailing that he seems to see.[7]

We need to account for Descartes' point that his certainty of his thought and existence results from the fact that every potential reason for doubt affirms that he thinks and exists, but we need to do so in a way that still lets us account for his claim to certainty about his other mental states, his reference to clear and distinct perception, and his immediate inference from his mental state to his existence.

4. TOWARD AN IMPROVED INTERPRETATION

We have found several passages that conflict with the Self-Evident Intuition/Immediate Inference Interpretation, even though we initially developed that interpretation on the basis of strong textual evidence. Should we just decide that Descartes is wildly inconsistent, or, more charitably, that his brilliance causes him to see several ways to explain his certainty of his thought and existence, his open-mindedness keeps him from being able to choose between them, and his charity makes him leave the choice to us? I think not. We can modify the Self-Evident Intuition/Immediate Inference Interpretation to account for some, though not all, of the problematic passages. The rest have alternative readings consistent with the modified interpretation. To develop this new interpretation, I must first examine two basic concepts of Descartes' epistemology, his concept of certainty and his concept of a reasonable belief.

Descartes' epistemology contains *two degrees of epistemic appraisal;* that is to say, two degrees of justification relative to which beliefs are assessed. One is the top standard of certainty. The other is a lesser degree of justification, which Descartes describes as highly probable or very reasonable belief. In the First Meditation, after he decides that his sensory evidenced beliefs about the external world are not certain, he notes that they are nonetheless very reasonable:

My habitual opinions keep coming back, and, despite my wishes, they capture my belief, which is as it were bound over to them as a result of long occupation and the law of custom. I shall never get out of the habit of confidently assenting to these opinions, so long as I suppose them to be what they are, namely highly probable opinions – opinions, which, despite the fact that they are in a sense doubtful, as has just been shown, it is still much more reasonable to believe than to deny.   (AT VII, 22: CSM II 15)[8]

It is plausible to think Descartes would accept a few basic principles about these two grades of epitstemic appraisal. First, all the beliefs that meet the demands of certainty for him, such as his beliefs about his thought and existence in the Second Meditation, are also very reasonable, but some of his very reasonable beliefs, such as his sensory evidenced beliefs about the external world in the First Meditation, are not certain for him.

Second, which degree of epistemic appraisal a belief meets is determined by his evidence for the belief. The sensory evidence Descartes has for his external world beliefs in the First Meditation makes those beliefs very reasonable but not certain. The evidence Descartes has for his belief in his existence in the Second Meditation makes that belief both very reasonable and certain. When a belief is self-evident, Descartes' evidence for it consists of his act of clearly and distinctly perceiving it. When a belief is not self-evident, Descartes' evidence for it consists of those beliefs that constitute his reason for believing it.

Third, the difference between what is *merely* very reasonable and what is certain is that Descartes has a slight reason to doubt the former. Descartes' reason for doubt must be slight, since the beliefs are very reasonable – as he puts it, his reason for doubt is "metaphysical and exaggerated" (AT VII 460: CSM II 308) – but, even a slight

reason for doubt keeps a belief from being certain. A hypothesis gives
Descartes a reason to doubt one of his beliefs just when it is a possibility he has not ruled out and it indicates how his belief might be false
despite his evidence. The hypotheses that he is dreaming and that
some god deceives him are possibilities he has not ruled out in the
First Meditation, and they indicate how his very reasonable beliefs
about the external world might be false despite his sensory evidence
for them. Commentators have offered competing accounts of how a
reason for doubt is a possibility that Descartes has not ruled out. The
one most in keeping with Descartes' remarks is that a reason for
doubt is a possibility he has not ruled out in the sense that he is not
certain it is false. In the First Meditation, Descartes is not certain he is
not dreaming and not being deceived. Once he decides he is certain of
these points – at the end of the Sixth and Third Meditations,
respectively – he rejects the Dream and Deceptive God Hypotheses
as reasons for doubt. The fact that any hypothesis that has not been
ruled out with certainty is capable of serving as a reason for doubt is
just what makes Descartes' doubt "exaggerated," as he puts it. It is
also what makes his reasons for doubt so difficult to rule out.[9]

Relative to these points, we can better understand Descartes'
claim to certainty about his thought and existence. Descartes' claim
has two parts: (1) He has evidence for these beliefs that makes them
very reasonable, and (2) that evidence resists even the slightest, most
exaggerated reasons for doubt, so that his beliefs are certainties; no
hypothesis he has yet to rule out with certainty indicates how his
beliefs might be false despite his evidence for them. Since Descartes'
claim to certainty is complex, his explanation of it must be equally
complex. He must explain what makes his beliefs very reasonable
for him, and why no hypothesis he has yet to rule out with certainty
indicates how they might be false. Now that we better understand
the form Descartes' explanation must take, let us return to the Self-
Evident Intuition/Immediate Inference Interpretation and see how it
can best be modified.

The Modified Self-Evident Intuition/Immediate
Inference Interpretation

The first thing Descartes must do is explain what makes his beliefs
in his thought and existence very reasonable. This is where his fre-

quent appeals to clear and distinct perception and an immediate inference from his thought to his existence come into play. Descartes takes his belief in his thought to be very reasonable because the proposition that he thinks is a self-evident one he clearly and distinctly perceives to be true. His act of clear and distinct perception is the "evidence" that makes his belief that he thinks very reasonable. The same may be said of his other beliefs about his mental state. His belief in his existence is very reasonable, because he immediately infers it from a very reasonable belief about his mental state.

Yet, what makes these beliefs so reasonable as to be certain? Descartes' answer is that he has no reason to doubt them. Now his observation about how reasons for doubt just affirm his thought and existence comes into play. Consider once again how he puts the point: "But there is a deceiver of supreme power and cunning who is deliberately and constantly deceiving me; and let him deceive me as much as he can, he will never bring it about that I am nothing so long as I think that I am something" (Second Meditation: AT VII 25: CSM II 16–17). The Deceptive God Hypothesis does not give him a reason to doubt his beliefs that he thinks and exists; for it entails them and so fails to indicate how they might be false despite his clear and distinct perception. The same is true of the Dream Hypothesis.

Two aspects of this part of Descartes' position need development. First, the Deceptive God Hypothesis and the Dream Hypothesis clearly fail to cast doubt on his beliefs that he thinks and exists, but why it is that no other hypothesis can do so? Second, why do not these or other hypotheses cast doubt on such beliefs as that he seems to see light, which are sometimes used as premises for the Cogito? The Deceptive God Hypothesis does not entail that he seems to see light; could not a god deceive him about what he seems to see?

Descartes might deal with the first issue by adopting three plausible principles about reasons for doubt. First, no hypothesis casts doubt on a contingent belief it entails.[10] Second, an hypothesis indicates to Descartes how one of his beliefs might be false only if it entails the proposition he would express by "I exist." The idea is that Descartes must relate an hypothesis to himself before it gives him a reason to doubt, and he does that by making his first-person belief in his existence part of the hypothesis. The hypothesis that Descartes would express by "Some god deceives the greatest seventeenth-century philosopher" does not give him a reason to doubt his beliefs, but the one he would express by "Some god deceives the greatest seventeenth-century philosopher and I am that philosopher" does. Thid, an hypothesis indicates how one of Descartes' beliefs might be false only if it entails the proposition he would express by "I think." The idea is that each reason for doubt must indicate how Descartes' intellectual abilities are leading him astray, due to their own intrinsic limitations or to his mishandling of them, and any hypothesis to that effect will include the information that he thinks. These three principles entail that no hypothesis casts doubt on Descartes' reasonable beliefs in his thought and existence. The first principle requires that a reason to doubt those beliefs must not entail them; the second and third principles require that a reason to doubt must entail them. No hypothesis meets all three requirements.

It is more difficult to fill the gap in Descartes' account of why no hypothesis casts doubt on such mental state beliefs as that he seems to see light. Could not a deceptive god make him think he seems to see light when he really does not, or, perhaps, more plausibly, make him think he seems to see red when he really seems to see orange or has a pain when he really has an itch? The best way to fill this gap in Descartes' explanation may be a fourth principle: An hypothesis indicates how one of his contingent beliefs might be false only if it is possible for Descartes to have the belief while the hypothesis is true and the belief is false. The idea is that an hypothesis only indicates to Descartes how one of his contingent beliefs might be false if it shows how he could actually have the belief and be mistaken.[11] Relative to this principle, Descartes might argue that he has no reason to doubt his beliefs about the contents of his mental states since it is impossible for him to have those beliefs and for them to be false. They are all incorrigible for him. It is impossible for him to believe falsely that he seems to see red or that he is in pain. To believe that one seems to see red is, in part, to seem to see red. To believe that one is in pain is, in part, to be in pain.[12]

It is important to appreciate how we have modified the Self-Evident Intuition/Immediate Inference Interpretation. We have retained the view that, according to Descartes, he clearly and distinctly perceives the self-evident proposition that he thinks and immediately infers that he exists. Yet, we have retained this as Descartes' explanation of why his beliefs in his thought and existence are *very reasonable* for him. We have appealed to Descartes' statements about how reasons for doubt affirm his thought and existence to develop an explanation of why his beliefs are so reasonable as to be *certain*. It is now time to see how this modified interpretation deals with the passages that cause problems for the initial one. Some of the passages fit under the modified interpretation quite nicely; the rest can be reinterpreted so they do not conflict with it.

Evaluation of the Modified Self-Evident Intuition/ Immediate Inference Interpretation

Our modified interpretation easily avoids one of the problems we have examined. Our initial interpretation is inconsistent with Descartes' claim, in the *Meditations* and *Replies*, that some clear and distinct perceptions, specifically ones of very simple mathematical truths, are made doubtful by the Deceptive God Hypothesis. Our modified interpretation is consistent with Descartes' claim. It says all clear and distinct perceptions are very reasonable, and only those that concern our thought and our existence are certain. The difference between the certain clear and distinct perceptions and the merely very reasonable ones is that the former resist reasons for doubt like the Deceptive God Hypothesis. Such reasons for doubt do not indicate how our beliefs in our thought and existence might be false despite the clear and distinct perceptions that support them.[13]

A second problem is our initial interpretation's inability to account for Descartes' comments about how potential reasons for doubt entail that he thinks and exists. The interpretation makes these comments irrelevant, by reducing Descartes' position to just two claims: all clear and distinct perceptions are certain, and he clearly and distinctly perceives his thought and existence. Our modified interpretation avoids the problem. Descartes' references to clear and distinct perception explain the reasonableness of his beliefs about his thought and existence. His comments about how potential reasons for doubt entail his thought and existence help explain why those reasonable beliefs are certain. Both sets of comments are essential to Descartes' explanation.

A third problem concerns whether Descartes' inference from his thought to his existence is immediate or a syllogism. Recall the passage from the *Principles*, quoted above under Section 3, which insists on the importance of a prior knowledge of the general principle that whatever thinks must exist. The way to account for this passage is to pay close attention to what Descartes says he must know prior to knowing his thought and existence. He must know that what thinks must exist, and he must also know what knowledge, thought, existence and certainty are. His point surely is not that all this information must be added to his inference from thought to existence to bridge the gap between his initial premise and his conclusion. He does not need to add definitions of thought, existence and certainty to his argument to get from "I think" to "I exist." His point is this: he must have some of this information to understand the propositions that he thinks and that he exists and the rest to understand his account of why they are certain for him. He cannot understand the propositions, unless he knnows what thought and existence are. He cannot understand his account of why they are certain for him unless he knows what certainty is. He cannot understand his account of why they are certain unless he knows that what thinks must exist; for part of his account is that his belief that he thinks immediately entails, and so makes reasonable, his belief that he exists. Descartes does not offer the general principle that what thinks must exist as a suppressed premise in his inference from his thought to his existence. He offers it as something he must know to understand why his thought and existence are certain for him. Moreover, it is sufficient that this general principle is reasonable for Descartes; it need not be certain. When Descartes claims to be certain of his thought and existence in the Second Meditation, he does not offer that claim to certainty – "I am certain about my thoughts and existence" – as a certainty. He presents it and his explanation of why it is true as reasonable beliefs about his epistemic state.[14]

The last problem with our initial interpretation concerns Descartes' account of our awareness of substances. The trouble comes from the passages in the *Principles* and the Third Objections and Replies, quoted above on pp. 149–50, where Descartes seems to say that all we immediately observe when we are aware of an object is some of its qualities, and from the existence of the observed qualities and the general principle that every observed quality is in some substance, we can infer the existence of the underlying subject.

When we reflect on ourselves, then, all we immediately observe is our thought. Our initial knowledge is correctly given by the statement, "Thought is taking place," and from this we can at best reason, "Thought exists and whenever any observed quality exists there is a substance that has it, so there is a thinking substance." We do not gain initial knowledge of ourselves by an immediate inference from the self-evident premise, "I am thinking," to the conclusion "I exist."

There is a better interpretation of these passages, one that makes them irrelevant to the logic of Descartes' *Cogito* inference. Take the *Principles* passage first. Descartes is not concerned to make a general point about the content of our thought when we try to gain knowledge about substances. He is concerned with how we can know that a particular thing is a substance. His point is that we do not just intuit or observe the fact that a particular thing is a substance; as he puts it, the mere fact that something is a substance, "does not of itself have any effect on us." We learn that a particular thing is a substance by first observing that it has some qualities and then inferring that it is a substance, by the premise that whatever has observed qualities is a substance: "if we perceive the presence of some attribute, we can infer that there must also be present an existing thing or substance to which it may be attributed." Descartes may be interpreted as making the same point in the passage from the Third Objection and Replies. When he says that "we do not come to know a substance immediately, through being aware of the substance itself; we come to know it only through its being the subject of certain acts," his point is that we do not just directly observe or intuit that a particular thing is a substance; we infer that fact from the information that it has some observed qualities and that everything with observed qualities is a substance. In Descartes' own case, then, he does not intuit the proposition he would express by "I am a substance," and he does not immediately infer that proposition from any of the self-evident ones about his mental state. He learns that he is a substance by reasoning, "I think, whatever has an observed quality is a substance; therefore, I am a substance." This position is consistent with Descartes' claim to know that he thinks and exists by intuiting that he thinks and immediately inferring that he exists.[15]

The modified version of the Self-Evident Intuition/Immediate Inference Interpretation thus avoids the textual problems with the initial version.[16] It is time to consider some objections to Descartes' position. They will help us appreciate some of the underlying philosophical issues that Descartes leaves as exercises for his readers.

5. PROBLEMS FOR DESCARTES

If we grant that Descartes can transfer his reasonable belief from the proposition that he thinks to the proposition that he exists by an immediate inference, we still should object to his account of how he gains the very reasonable belief that he thinks to begin with.[17] He says he clearly and distinctly perceives that he thinks. His concept of clear and distinct perception is the least clear and distinct concept in his philosophy. He never adequately explains what this mental vision is or why apprehending a proposition by it is sufficient to make belief in the proposition very reasonable.[18] An especially perplexing point is that Descartes appeals to acts of clear and distinct perception to account for both his knowledge of contingent claims about his mental state and his knowledge of simple necessary truths: "Thus everyone can mentally intuit that he exists, that he is a thinking thing, that a triangle is bounded by just three lines, and a sphere by a single surface, and the like. Perceptions such as these are more numerous than most people realize, disdaining as they do to turn their minds to such simple matters" (*Rules*, III: AT X 368: CSM I 14). Our knowledge of our mental states is hardly the same as our knowledge of simple necessary truths. It is plausible to say that we learn that every sphere is bounded by a single surface in a mental vision in which we just grasp that the idea of the sphere includes the idea of being bounded by a single surface. Yet, this is not how we learn that we think. We do not learn that we think by perceiving a relation of containment, identity, diversity or the like between some ideas.[19] Descartes leaves us wondering exactly how our beliefs about our mental state and existence become reasonable.

Note that we will not improve matters by simply cutting Descartes' appeal to clear and distinct perception out of his explanation of his certainty of his thought and existence. We will then be left with only the second part of his explanation of his certainty and, in effect, with the observation that each potential reason for doubt entails that he thinks and exists. Descartes will be open to a criticism nicely stated by A. J. Ayer:

What Descartes thought that he had shown was that the statements that he was conscious, and that he existed, were somehow privileged, that, for him at least, they were evidently true in a way which distinguished them from any other statements of fact. But this by no means follows from his argument. His argument does not prove that he, or anyone, knows anything. It simply makes the logical point that the one sort of statement follows from another.[20]

Descartes needs both parts of his explanation of his certainty. He needs an account of what makes his beliefs in his thought and existence very reasonable and an account of why those reasonable beliefs resist every reason for doubt. Unfortunately, the first part of his position is basically uninformative.

Descartes also says very little about the content of his beliefs about his mental state and existence. He takes the content of his mental state beliefs to be the propositions he would express by "I am thinking" and "I am in pain," rather than those he would express by "Thought is taking place" or "Pain is occurring." The former propositions are about him in particular; they entail his existence. Yet, what exactly is the content of these propositions by virtue of which they are about him? To put the point another way, what is it about Descartes' self-awareness when he clearly and distinctly perceives that he thinks that makes his awareness an awareness *of him*? Is he directly acquainted with himself in the same way that he is directly acquainted with an idea, like a pain sensation? Is he aware of himself by virtue of conceiving a particular concept of himself? If so, what concept?

Descartes seems committed to the view that he is not directly acquainted with himself. He thinks of himself by conceiving an idea of himself. In the *Meditations*, he writes that:

Undoubtedly, the ideas which represent substances to me amount to something more and, so to speak, contain within themselves more objective reality than the ideas which merely represent modes or accidents. Again, the idea that gives me my understanding of a supreme God, eternal, infinite, <immutable> omniscient, omnipotent and the creator of all things that exist apart from him, certainly has in it more objective reality than the ideas that represent finite substances.   (AT VII 40: CSM II 28)

He writes in the *Second Replies* that: "Existence is contained in the idea or concept of every single thing, since we cannot conceive of anything except as existing. Possible or contingent existence is contained in the concept of a limited thing, whereas necessary and perfect existence is contained in the concept of a supremely perfect being" (AT VII 166: CSM II 117).

His general position seems to be that we think of substances by grasping ideas of them, and he never indicates that his thoughts about himself are an exception. What then is the idea by which Descartes thinks of himself, when he knows for certain that he thinks and exists? It cannot be a concept in which he conceives of himself relative to some of his nonmental traits, for he doubts whether he has any such traits in the Second Meditation. It might be a concept in which he conceives of himself relative to some of his mental traits. Descartes sometimes writes as though he conceives of himself in this way.

But immediately I noticed that while I was trying thus to think everything false, it was necessary that *I, who was thinking this*, was something.

(*Discourse:* AT VI 32: CSM I 127; my emphasis)

[I]t is easy for us to suppose that there is no God and no heaven, and that there are no bodies, and even that we ourselves have no hands or feet, or indeed any body at all. But we cannot for all that suppose that *we, who are having such thoughts*, are nothing.

(*Principles* Part I, art. 7: AT VIIIA 7: CSM I 194–5)

Descartes describes himself relative to his thoughts, but his point is unclear. He may be saying that his concept of himself is the concept of a thing with these thoughts. He may be giving us another version of the dictum, "I am thinking, therefore I am," by telling us that he has some thoughts and the fact that he has them entails that he exists.

Descartes is in trouble if he believes that he individuates himself relative to his thoughts. To begin with, his explanation of why he is certain of his thought and existence will need to be revised. He does not just "intuit" that he thinks and immediately infer that he exists. He first discovers a mental attribute, determines that it is a thought, decides that one and only one thing has it, and then concludes, "I think", or more properly, "The thing with this thinks," where "this" refers to the thought. Only then does he immediately infer, "I exist," or more properly, "The thing with this exists."[21]

The view that Descartes individuates himself relative to his thoughts is open to serious objections. Suppose that he considers one of his ideas, does not yet know whether he has produced it or whether God has produced it in him, and decides that whatever has produced it is perfect. Suppose too that he is the source of the idea. Clearly, the thought that Descartes would express by "The thing that produced this is perfect," where "this" refers to the idea, is not the same as the one he would express by "I am perfect." He believes the former but he may not believe the latter. The difference between the thoughts is that, although Descartes thinks of himself in each thought – he is the referent of both "the thing that produced this" and of "I" – in the first thought he only thinks of himself and in the second he thinks of himself *as himself*. This difference between the two thoughts is lost, if we analyze the thought Descartes would express by "I am perfect" as the one he would express by "The thing that has this is perfect," where "this" again refers to the idea. The difference between Descartes' thinking of himself and his thinking of himself as himself is surely not that between his thinking of himself as the cause of an idea, "The thing that caused this is perfect," and his thinking of himself as the thing that has the idea, "The thing that has this is perfect".[22]

A second objection is contained in Elizabeth Anscombe's question, "How do I know that I am not ten thinkers thinking in unison?"[23] Suppose Descartes observes his pain and says to himself, "I am in pain." He also observes his sadness and says to himself, "I am sad." He then takes note of both beliefs and infers, "I am in pain and sad." His third belief is justified by the first two, but it is hard to see how that can be, if each belief involves his individuating himself relative to his ideas. His inference becomes, "The thing with this[a] is in pain, and the thing with this[b] is sad, so the thing with this[c] is in pain and sad." The demonstratives refer to his pain ([a]), sadness ([b]) and the combination of his pain and sadness ([c]), respectively. He is justified in believing his conclusion on the basis of his two premises only if he is justified in believing the additional premise: The thing with this[a] is identical to the thing with this[b]. The additional premise is not justified for him. He has no reason to believe that the subject of the one sensation is identical with the subject of the other, given that all he is aware of is the sensations themselves.

In all, then, Descartes leaves us wondering how he thinks of himself when he forms his certain beliefs about his thought and existence. He seems committed to the view that he thinks of himself by conceiving some concept of himself. Yet, no adequate concept of him seems to be available. He does not think of himself through a concept that identifies him by his physical traits. He does not think of himself by one that identifies him relative to his mental traits. What is left?[24]

Another problematic aspect of Descartes' claim to certainty of his thought and existence is raised by the question of just how far his certainty about his thought extends. Descartes tells us that he is certain of such claims about his mental activities as that he doubts, and imagines; he tells us that he is certain about such claims about his particular mental contents as that he seems to see light, hear noise and feel heat. Yet, exactly how far can he go? Can he be certain whether or not he is angry, depressed, jealous, or in love? He does not say.

One way to fill this gap in Descartes' position is to return to a suggestion we considered earlier about why the Deceptive God Hypothesis fails to cast doubt on such beliefs as that he seems to see light. The hypothesis fails to indicate how these beliefs might be false, because it is impossible for him to have the beliefs, for the hypothesis to be true and for the beliefs to be false. The beliefs are incorrigible. Descartes cannot believe that he seems to see light unless he actually seems to see light; having the belief in the experience includes having the experience. Descartes might take a similar approach to explaining the extent of his certainty: he is certain of those beliefs about his mental state that are incorrigible. If his beliefs about whether he is angry, depressed, jealous, in love, and so on are not incorrigible for him, then they are not certain for him.

If Descartes' position is developed in this way, it is open to arguments that have been offered against the incorrigibility of even such mental state beliefs as his beliefs that he seems to see light and feel pain. In part, the issue concerns how we form our beliefs about our mental state. Do we always form them by an act of self-evident intuition, or can we also form them on the basis of an inductive inference from some other beliefs, just as our external world beliefs are formed? If they can be formed inductively, there is room for error, as critics of the incorrigible, such as Keith Lehrer, are quick to point out.

One might believe one is having a sensation S, a pain for example, because one is having a different sensation, S*, an itch for example, and one has mistaken S* for S, that is one has mistaken an itch for a pain. How could this happen? It might happen either because of some general belief, to wit, that itches are pains, which one has been led to believe by some authority, or one may simply be misled on this occasion because one has been told by some authority that one will experience a pain. In short, one might have some false belief which together with the sensation of an itch produces the belief that one is in pain. Beliefs about sensations can be inferential, and one can infer that one is in a conscious state that one is not in by inferring from some false belief that this is so.[25]

The issue of the incorrigibility and certainty of mental state beliefs also takes us back to the question of the content of those beliefs. According to some critics of Descartes' position, these beliefs are corrigible and uncertain, because they involve the classification of an experience and the act of classification can be mistaken. A. J. Ayer puts the point in this way.

The fact is that one cannot in language point to an object without describing it. If a sentence is to express a proposition, it cannot merely name a situation; it must say something about it. And in describing a situation, one is not merely 'registering' a sense-content; one is classifying it in some way or other, and this means going beyond what is immediately given.[26]

Ayer applies this observation about language even to beliefs about what we seem to experience. The content of our belief that we seem to see white is the proposition that we are having an experience similar in color to others we, and perhaps others, have called "white." This classification of our present experience relative to others can be mistaken and, hence, is uncertain.

[E]ven if we exclude all reference to other people, it is still possible to think of a situation which would lead me to suppose that my classification of a sense-content was mistaken. I might, for example, have discovered that whenever I sensed a sense-content of a certain quality, I made some distinctive overt bodily movement; and I might on one occasion be presented with a sense-content which I asserted to be of that quality, and then fail to make the bodily reaction which I had come to associate with it. In such a case I should probably abandon the hypothesis that sense-contents of that quality always called out in me the bodily reaction in question. But I should not, logically, be obliged to abandon it. If I found it more convenient, I could save this hypothesis by assuming that I really did make the reaction, although I did not notice it, or, alternatively, that the sense-content did not have the quality I asserted it to have. The fact that this course is a possible one, that it involves no logical contradiction, proves that a proposition which describes the quality of a presented sense-content may as legitimately be doubted as any other empirical proposition.[27]

It is unclear how Descartes would respond to these arguments. He might avoid Lehrer's by limiting his claim to certainty to those mental state beliefs that are intuited rather than inductively inferred from some evidence. To meet Ayer's, he might reject the initial claim that each mental state belief involves classifying an experience; he will then have to give an alternative account of the content of those beliefs.

In all, then, Descartes' account of his certainty about his thought and existence leaves a number of important questions unanswered. We are left wondering what clear and distinct perception is, how he conceives of himself, which of his beliefs about particular mental states resist every reason for doubt, what he takes the content of those beliefs to be, and how he would defend their incorrigibility, assuming that that is a partial source of their certainty. Descartes says just enough to raise these important philosophical issues; that he raises them is part of what makes his position interesting and important.

In conclusion, we have examined the role that Descartes's claim to certainty of his thought and existence plays in his philosophy and the interpretative and philosophical issues that are raised by his claim. We have settled the main interpretative issues. The philosophical issues remain as part of Descartes' legacy to us.[28]

NOTES

1 See Augustine, *De Trinitate*, Book X, ch. 10. Descartes claims that he moves beyond Augustine's point by seeing that his certainty of his thought and existence and his uncertainty about his body provide the basis for a defense of the distinction between himself and his body: AT III 247: CSMK 159. For more on the relation between Descartes' position and Augustine's, see Anscombe, "The first person," Curley, *Descartes against the Skeptics*, and Noonan, "Identity and the first person."

2 The addressee of this letter is a matter of debate; cf. AT V 660 n.

3 Descartes uses "natural reason" (*ratio naturalis*) and "the natural light"

(*lumen naturale*) interchangeably in *Comments on a Certain Broadsheet* (AT VIIIB 353: CSM I 300).

4 Williams, *Descartes*, pp. 91–2 suggests that Descartes' position should be understood relative to two ways of interpreting the claim, "Whatever thinks must exist." We can read the claim so it presupposes that there are things that think, or we can read it so it does not. When Descartes says he must know the general claim in order to know that he exists, he is thinking of the nonexistential version. His inference from his thought to his existence is, "I think, whatever thinks must exist; therefore, I exist," where the general premise is read so it does not presuppose the existence of thinking things. When Descartes says that his knowledge of the general claim is based on his knowledge of the particular claims that he thinks and he exists, and when he says that he does not use a syllogism in which the general claim is a premise to learn that he exists, he has the existential version of the claim in mind. Yet this suggestion still runs up against Descartes' assertion that his knowledge of his thought and existence does not involve reasoning and is intuitive; for we have seen that he applies the term "intuition" only to what is either self-evident or *immediately* inferred from the self-evident.

5 Descartes sometimes goes out of his way to stress the first-person element in his claim to certainty of his thought and existence by adding the pronoun "ego," which is superfluous in Latin. Twice in the *Principles* and once in the Second Objections and Replies, he writes: *ego cogito, ergo sum* (AT VIIIA 7: CSM I 195; AT VIIIA 8: CSM I 196; AT VII 140: CSM II 100).

6 Of course, in replying to Mersenne, Descartes only refers explicitly to clarity and not to both clarity and distinctness. Yet while he only mentions clarity, he does not go on to deny Mersenne's claim that an atheist can have both a clear and a distinct perception. Instead he goes on to deny that an atheist can have the certainty required for scientific knowledge. It hardly seems likely that he would do this if his argument with Mersenne was over whether an atheist could have both a clear and a distinct perception.

7 See Curley, *Descartes against the Skeptics*, for the suggestion of how to capture Descartes' inference. See Hintikka, "Cogito ergo sum: Inference or performance," and "Cogito ergo sum as an inference or a performance," for an interpretation of Descartes' position that relies heavily on the Second Meditation passage at hand, to the point of paying inadequate attention to Descartes' references to clear and distinct perception and to an immediate inference from his mental state to his existence. For discussions of Hintikka's interpretation, see Feldman "On the per-

formatory interpretation of the Cogito"; Frankfurt, *Demons, Dreamers and Madmen*, Kenny, *Descartes*; and M. D. Wilson, *Descartes.*

8 The certain and the very reasonable are not the only grades of epistemic appraisal in Descartes' epistemology. For example, early in the Sixth Meditation, he takes the claim that the body exists to be probable on the grounds that it provides the best explanation of some data about the imagination (AT VII 73: CSM II 51). The degree of appraisal involved here is lower than either the certain or the very reasonable (the *highly probable*). The data about his imagination does not support the existence of body to the point of making it either certain or very reasonable.

9 Descartes sometimes uses the terms "metaphysical certainty" and "moral certainty," for example, in the *Discourse:* AT VI 37–8: CSM I 129–30, and the Seventh Objections and Replies: AT VII 471: CSM II 317. As I understand him, "metaphysical certainty" refers to what I have been calling "certainty," and "moral certainty" refers to what I have been calling "reasonableness" and "high probability." Descartes also writes of a form of certainty that is best termed, "psychological certainty," since it has to do, not with the strength of our evidence for a proposition, but with our inability to doubt it. See his remarks in the *Meditations:* AT VII 65: CSM II 45; AT VII 69–70: CSM II, 48. Note that the points I make in the text are somewhat independent of these issues, e.g., one can accept the points I make in the text without also accepting my view that morally certain beliefs are to be equated with very reasonable or highly probable ones. For more on all three forms of certainty, see Feldman, "On the performatory interpretation;" Gewirth, "The Cartesian Circle"; Curley, *Descartes against the Skeptics*; and Markie, "The Cogito puzzle" and *Descartes's Gambit.*

10 The principle is restricted to logically contingent propositions to avoid problems caused by the fact that, as logical entailment is strictly defined, every hypothesis entails every proposition that is a logically necessary truth. A proposition p entails a proposition q, just when it is logically impossible that p be true and q be false. Some may prefer a more vague principle that is not formulated in terms of the logical relation of entailment between the hypothesis and the belief and so does not have to be restricted to contingent propositions: No hypothesis h casts doubt on a believed proposition p, if h "contains" p. The notion of containment is undefined. The next two principles may be modified accordingly.

11 Note that this principle is also restricted to beliefs in logically contingent propositions; that is, to ones that might have been false. Beliefs in propositions that are necessarily true cannot satisfy the principle, since it is impossible for them to be false. Again, some may prefer a more vague principle that does not use logical entailment: A hypothesis indi-

cates how one of Descartes' beliefs might be false only if the state of affairs of the hypothesis being true and Descartes having the belief does not "contain" the state of affairs of the belief being true.

12 Some commentators have noted the Descartes' beliefs about his particular mental activities are not immune to reasons for doubt in exactly the same way as his beliefs that he thinks and exists are. They have taken this to indicate that either Descartes is not serious in claiming certainty of his particular mental states or he is not to be taken literally in his claim that the premise that he thinks may be replaced by such claims as that he seems to see. See Cottingham, *Descartes*, pp. 38–42. If I am on the right track, there is no need for such interpretive gymnastics.

13 Some commentators think we should deal with the problematic passages by interpreting them so they do not contain the claim that some clear and distinct perceptions are uncertain. Discussion of this issue is mainly found in debates on the "Cartesian Circle." See, Cottingham, *Descartes*; Curley, *Descartes against the Skeptics*; Doney, "The Cartesian Circle" and "Descartes's conception of perfect knowledge"; Feldman, "Epistemic appraisal and the Cartesian Circle"; Frankfurt, *Demons, Dreamers and Madmen*; Gewirth, "The Cartesian Circle," "The Cartesian Circle reconsidered," and "Descartes: Two disputed questions"; Kenny, *Descartes* and "The Cartesian Circle and the eternal truths"; Van Cleve, "Foundationalism, epistemic appraisal and the Cartesian Circle"; and Markie *Descartes's Gambit*.

14 For more on this point see my work in *Descartes's Gambit*, esp. chs. 2 and 5. It is also worth taking note of a passage from the *Conversation with Burman* that relates to the *Principles* passage. Burman reports (AT V 147: CSMK 333) that Descartes explains the relation between the *Principles* passage and his insistence that his knowledge of his thought and existence is intuitive by drawing a distinction between explicit and implicit knowledge. In the Second Meditation, he explicitly knows that he thinks and therefore exists, but he only implicitly knows that whatever thinks must exist. The difference between explicit and implicit knowledge escapes me; it may or may not be related to the solution I have offered. For more on these issues see, Curley, *Descartes against the Skeptics*; Frankfurt, "Descartes' discussion of his existence"; Williams, *Descartes*; and M. D. Wilson, *Descartes*.

Some commentators seem to think that Descartes claims to be certain that he is certain of his thought and existence, which would require him to be certain of his explanation. See Gueroult, *Descartes selon l'ordre des raisons*, p. 51, and perhaps Cottingham, *Descartes*, pp. 41–2, 69–70. I know of no textual support for this position. Descartes does not claim to be certain of his certainty about himself, and nothing he says commits him to such a view.

15 There is another way to interpret the passages so they are consistent with our modified interpretation. Instead of being concerned with our knowledge *that* something is a substance, Descartes may be concerned with our knowledge *of* those things that are substances. His point may be that we never just know a substance per se. We only know a substance by knowing propositions about it to the effect that it has some attributes. This may be what he has in mind when he writes in the Third Replies that "we do not come to know a substance immediately, through being aware of the substance itself; we come to know it only through its being the subject of certain acts." In his own case, Descartes does not just know himself per se; he knows himself by knowing propositions that attribute qualities to him. He is never just aware of himself; he is always aware of himself as having some attribute. This reading again makes the passages consistent with our modified interpretation. It has also been suggested by M. D. Wilson, *Descartes*, pp. 66–7, though she seems to have more reservations about it than I do. Two other passages may also be read in the same way; see *Principles* Part I, art. 11: AT VIIIA 8: CSM I 196; and Fourth Objections and Replies: AT VII 222: CSM II 156. For a treatment of Descartes' position that assumes that he does reason, "Thought is taking place, every attribute is in a substance, therefore, some substance exists," see Sievert, "Descartes's self-doubt" and "Sellars and Descartes . . ."; and Kenny, *Descartes*; see also my discussion of Sievert and Kenny in "The Cogito puzzle" and *Descartes's Gambit*.

16 I have not discussed a Third Meditation passage that might still be regarded as problematic for even the modified version of the Self-Evident Intuition/Immediate Inference Interpretation. Descartes writes: "And since I have no cause to think that there is a God at all, any reason for doubt which depends simply on this supposition is a very slight, and, so to speak, metaphysical one. But in order to remove even this slight reason for doubt, as soon as the opportunity arises I must examine whether there is a God, and, if there is, whether he can be a deceiver. *For if I do not know this, it seems that I can never be quite certain about anything else*" (AT VII 25: CSM II 25; my emphasis). Descartes' remark implies that until he knows that God exists and is not a deceiver, he cannot be certain of even his own thought and existence. He thus rejects by implication the very claim to certain self-knowledge that we have been trying to understand. Descartes later modifies his position so it does not contain this implication. Mersenne points the implication out to him: "It follows from this that you do not yet clearly and distinctly

know that you are a thinking thing, since, on your own admission, that knowledge depends on the clear knowledge of an existing God; and this you have not yet proved in the passage where you draw the conclusion that you clearly know what you are" (Second Objections: AT VII 125: CSM II 89). Descartes relplies: "When I said that we can know nothing for certain until we are aware that God exists, I expressly declared that I was speaking only of knowledge of those conclusions which can be recalled when we are no longer attending to the arguments by means of which we deduced them. Now awareness of first principles is not normally called 'knowledge' by dialecticians" (Second Replies: AT VII 100: CSM II 100). Descartes is mistaken about what he "expressly declared" in the Third Meditation, but the important point is that, upon consideration, he rejects the view that he must know God to be certain of his own thought and existence.

17 Some commentators object to Descartes' attempt to infer his existence immediately from the premise that he thinks. M. D. Wilson, *Descartes*, p. 55; and Kenny, *Descartes*, pp. 169–70, object that the immediate inference is not valid in first-order quantification theories without existential presuppositions. Hintikka, "Cogito ergo sum: Inference or performance" pp. 114–15, objects that it is question-begging. See my "The Cogito puzzle" and *Descartes's Gambit* for replies to both objections; see M. D. Wilson, *Descartes*, for a reply to Hintikka. To some extent, the criticisms of Descartes' inference are encouraged by his own criticisms of syllogistic reasoning. See Curley, *Descartes against the Skeptics*; and Markie, *Descartes's Gambit*, for discussions of Descartes' criticisms.

18 Descartes gives his most formal definition of clear and distinct perception in *Principles* Part I, art. 45: AT VIIIA 21–2: CSM I 207–8. The issue is complicated by the fact that Descartes writes of his clear and distinct perception of propositions (e.g., *Discourse*: AT VI 33: CSM I 127), but also of his clear and distinct perception of ideas (e.g., *Principles* Part I, arts. 45–6: AT VIIIA, 21–2: CSM I 207–8), of clear and distinct propositions (e.g., *Principles* Part I, art. 30: AT VIIIA 17: CSM I 203), and of clear and distinct ideas (e.g., *Meditations*: AT VII 46: CSM II 31). For further discussion of this topic see Frankfurt, *Demons, Dreamers and Madmen*; Gewirth, "Clearness and distinctness"; Kenny, *Descartes*; and Markie, *Descartes's Gambit*.

19 I assume that Descartes' assertion, "I am thinking" does not have the same content as, "Thought is taking place."

20 Ayer "I think, therefore I am," p. 82. Feldman ("On the performatory interpretation") makes a similar objection to Hintikka's interpretation, which, as we have noted, stresses the logical relations between particular claims and downplays the role of clear and distinct perception.

21 Note the difference between this account of the process by which Descartes gains certainty of his existence and the position considered earlier according to which Descartes reasons, "Thought is taking place, every observed quality exists in some substance; therefore, some substance thinks." Descartes would express different propositions by "Thought is taking place," and "The thing that has this thinks," where "this" refers to a thought of which he is immediately aware; the former proposition is not about him in particular, while the latter is. See Van Cleve, "Conceivability and the Cartesian argument for dualism," for an interpretation according to which Descartes individuates himself relative to his thoughts. Zemach, "*De Se* and Descartes," also attributes that position to Descartes and then revises it to address some contemporary issues about self-reference.

22 For more on this point, see Markie, *Descartes's Gambit*, esp. ch. 3.

23 Anscombe, "The first person," p. 58.

24 Descartes might say that the concept by which he thinks of himself is just the concept of being him. For a contemporary statement of this approach to self-reference, see Chisholm, *Person and Object*; see, too, my discussion in *Descartes's Gambit*.

25 See Lehrer, "Why not scepticism," pp. 351–2 and also Parsons, "Mistaking sensations."

26 Ayer, *Language Truth and Logic*, p. 91.

27 Ibid., pp. 92–3.

28 I am indebted to John Cottingham and Margaret Wilson for their written comments on an earlier draft of this chapter. A version of this chapter was presented to the philosophy department at St. Mary's College, Maryland; participants in the discussion, especially Reg Savage, made several helpful comments.

6 The idea of God and the proofs of his existence

THE ROLE OF GOD IN DESCARTES' SYSTEM

There is a paradox at the heart of Cartesian metaphysics. On the one hand, Descartes' whole system of scientific knowledge depends on our assured knowledge of God;[1] but on the other hand, the idea of God is explicitly stated by Descartes to be beyond our comprehension.[2] This paradox emerges in Descartes' proofs of God's existence, and hinges on the relationship between the affirmation of God's existence and the elucidation of the idea of God, which is the basis for that affirmation. The relationship is difficult to explicate precisely: is the idea of God prior to the demonstration of his existence?

All the proofs Descartes offers of God's existence, whether a priori or a posteriori, make use of the idea of God. And we are told that "according to the laws of true logic, one must never ask if something exists [an sit] without knowing beforehand what it is [quid sit]" (AT VII 107–8: CSM II 78); in the absence of such prior knowledge, we could not identify as God the being whose existence we are demonstrating. The idea of God would thus appear to be a necessary premise for all the proofs of his existence, and this clearly implies that we must possess within us the relevant idea in order to be able to infer that its object or ideatum really exists outside our minds. But in spite of this, Descartes maintains that the same reasoning that enables us to infer the existence of God also enables us at the same time to know what he is (Principles Part I, art. 22). It thus appears that the idea of God is made manifest only in the actual unfolding of the proof of his existence, and, more curious still, that its content is made explicit only at the end of the proof, after the affirmation of

God's existence. There seems to be a serious inconsistency here, which talk of the 'incomprehensibility' of the idea of God might seem designed to conceal from view.

There are two lines of thought that may help us to get to grips with this difficulty. One concerns the different structure of the various proofs of God's existence, and the exact role the idea of God plays in each of them. The second has to do with the relationship, in the realm of metaphysical inquiry, between the affirmation of something's existence and the determination of its essence: the relationship between the 'that' (quod) which corresponds to the question 'is it?' and the 'that which' (quid) which corresponds to the question "what kind of thing is it?" By bringing these two lines of thought together, we shall be able to see more precisely the connection between, on the one hand, the various attributes that make up the idea of God (considered as an idea that is constructed by us), and, on the other hand, the principle whereby these attributes are conjoined (in virtue of which the idea is innate in us). In articulating this connection, we are brought face to face with exactly what Descartes calls "incomprehensibility" in the positive sense – that incomprehensibility which is the hallmark of the infinite (Fifth Replies: AT VII 368, lines 2–4: CSM II 253).

THE VARIOUS PROOFS OF GOD'S EXISTENCE

If we examine the definitive presentation of Cartesian first philosophy, the *Meditations*, the various different proofs of the existence of God all involve, as one of their premises, an explicit reference to the idea of God.

The proofs which proceed from effect to cause "are incomplete unless we add to them the idea which we have of God" (letter to Mesland of 2 May 1644: AT IV 112: CSMK 232). And in the Third Meditation Descartes does indeed begin by defining what he understands by God. In fact he provides such a definition twice. The first occasion is when he discusses the disparity which applies to different ideas in respect of their objective reality: "the idea which gives me my understanding of (per quam intelligo) a supreme God, eternal, infinite, [immutable,] omniscient, omnipotent and the creator of all things that exist apart from him" (AT VII 40: CSM II 28). The second occasion is when he succeeds in finding the only idea of which I could not be the author: "by the term 'God' I understand (*intelligo*) a substance that is infinite, [eternal, immutable,] independent, supremely intelligent, supremely powerful, and which created both myself and everything else (if anything else there be) which exists" (AT VII 45: CSM II 31). There is a perfect identity here between the idea whereby I conceive of God (in the first passage) and the meaning of the term 'God' (in the second passage); the proof cannot succeed, or even get off the ground, "if one has no idea, i.e. no perception, which corresponds to the meaning of the word 'God' " (AT IXA 210, lines 2–4: CSM II 273). In the structure of the causal, or a posteriori, proofs, God plays the role of a predicate in the conclusion reached: there necessarily exists outside of me a cause *which is God*. The idea of God is thus required in a double sense. To begin with, it constitutes, within the effect which is the point of departure for the proof, a starting point for the argument: either this is the effect in its entirety in the first version of the proof, (where I am looking for the cause of my idea of God), or else it is an indispensable aspect of this effect in the second, and more 'straightforward' version of the proof[3] (where I am looking for the cause of my existence as a being who possesses this idea of God). And in addition, with respect to the conclusion finally reached, the idea of God is what defines the nature of the cause whose existence is inferred. It is what gives a determinate nature to what would otherwise be indeterminate; without it, it would be as if we were saying that we believed in the existence of a *nothing* (AT IXA 210, lines 5–6: CSM II 273).

When we pass to the a priori argument in the Fifth Meditation, called, since Kant, the ontological argument, the role of the idea of God undergoes a crucial change: God is no longer the predicate but the subject, and existence is the predicate attributed to him. Here the idea is no longer the meaning of a word, but a "true and immutable nature". The initial definition of a supremely perfect being leads us to recognize the existence of that being as one of its perfections.

We can thus understand how Descartes was able, when he came to write the *Principles of Philosophy*, to bring together all his proofs, both a priori and a posteriori, as constituting one single way of proving the existence of God, "namely by means of the idea of God" (*per ejus scilicet ideam: Principles* Part I, art. 22). But how far does this rapprochement reflect a genuine similarity of structure in Descartes' proofs of God's existence?

To answer the question just posed, we need to look at an earlier passage from the *Discourse on the Method* whose importance has been recognized by Willis Doney.[4] The relevant text comes in Part IV of the *Discourse*, in between the two versions of the a posteriori proof and the presentation of the a priori proof. After showing that I cannot be the author of my own existence, Descartes adds: "For, acording to the arguments I have just advanced, in order to know the nature of God, as far as my own nature was capable of knowing, I had only to consider, for each thing of which I found in myself some idea, whether or not it was a perfection to possess it" (AT VI 35: CSM II 128). It is immediately clear from this passage that the elucidation of the divine nature, or, to put it more precisely, the elaboration of an idea of God, so far from preceding the a posteriori proof, follows it, or at least is parallel to it. As Ferdinand Alquié has pointed out,[5] "it is always in the course of reasoning about his own nature that Descartes raises himself up to contemplate God" – to contemplate the divine existence, to be sure, but also, along with this, the divine nature.

This text has no parallel in the *Meditations*, but if we look at Descartes' later presentation, in the *Principles of Philosophy*, we at once find a corresponding passage. Book I, art. 22 talks of the "great advantage" of the Cartesian method of proving the existence of God by means of the idea of God; namely, that "the method allows us at the same time to come to know the nature of God (*simul quisnam sit . . . agnoscamus*), in so far as the weakness of our nature allows (*quantum naturae nostrae fert infirmitas*)" (AT VIIIA 13: CSM I 200). Coming back to the argument in the *Discourse*, we are now struck by the contrast between the a priori proof, which indeed starts (as in the Fifth Meditation) from an idea of God ("the idea which I had of a perfect being"), and the a posteriori proofs, which (in contrast to the Third Meditation) presuppose no such idea. All that the a posteriori proofs in the *Discourse* require is an "inquiry into the source of my ability to think of something more perfect than I was" (AT VI 33: CSM I 128). In both versions of the causal proof in the *Discourse*, Descartes simply moves from "a nature which was truly more perfect that my own" to the existence of "some other more perfect being." There thus remains a considerable gap, almost a gulf, between two conclusions which (following Doney) we may call "A" and "B": a "more perfect being" [A] falls far short of "the most perfect thing which we are capable of conceiving" [B]. The transition which remains to be made between A and B is underlined in the following passage in the *Discourse:* "So there remained only the possibility that the idea had been put into me by a nature truly more perfect than I was, *and even (et même)* possessing in itself all the perfections of which I could have any idea, that is – to explain myself in one word – by God" (AT VI 34: CSM I 128).[6]

Now, we could try to plug this gap by supposing that the argument in the *Discourse* is not fully developed, and that it should be interpreted as implicitly presupposing the idea or definition of God which is explicitly laid out in the Thid Meditation. But it may be more instructive to see Descartes as looking for a way to *generate* the idea of God by means of a construction that operates in parallel with the proof of his existence. On this view, it is only once that construction is complete that we can move on to the a priori proof which will start out from the (by now fully realized) idea of a supremely perfect being.

THE IDEA OF GOD AND THE GOAL AT WHICH I AIM

The a priori proof of God starts from the supposed fact, which is taken for granted, that all perfections are united in a single nature which is called "God." All that remains to be done is to analyze this unity, and isolate one of the perfections in question, namely existence. By contrast, the two a posteriori proofs start by noticing a gap between myself, or my nature, and the thought or idea of something more perfect than myself. The starting point in the argument is this gap or inequality, which may, for the purposes of the argument, be thought of as either small (I think of a being who may be a little bit wiser than myself) or enormous (a being of infinitely greater perfection in every dimension of being or of perfection). Beginning from the comparative ('*more* perfect *than*'), we end up with the absolute term which transcends comparison – the incomparable nature which is infinite and beyond comprehension.

Should we conclude from this that in following Descartes' a posteriori proofs of God's existence we witness the *construction* of an idea of God – and that the relevant idea is one which is put together or made up by the human mind?[7]

In one sense the answer to this question is a clear yes; and the second of the a posteriori proofs is the more illuminating here. It is in noting the fact that my nature is not such as I would ideally wish it to be, that I come to infer that the being on whom I depend possesses all the perfections which I lack and which I desire. The inference has two parts. (1) In each class of perfection, for example, knowledge, power, duration, constancy and so on, I have a conception of a more perfect being, and eventually I come to conceive of this perfection as infinite (or, which amounts to the same, as indefinite[8]). (2) Next, I pass in a lateral manner, as it were, from one class of perfection to another, and thus construct the idea of an absolutely infinite, or supremely perfect, being. One could perhaps sum up the point by saying that God is (in this sense) both constructed and defined as the goal towards which I strive, as that which I aspire to be. We should not confuse ideas and thoughts here: certain of my thoughts, such as desire or doubt, are not ideas; an idea is that which represents an object. Nonetheless, it is, in this context, my entire being as a thinking thing that is considered for the purposes of setting up the idea of God. The idea of God – the "mark of the craftsman stamped on his work" – is in fact not something separate from the work itself (AT VII 51: CSM II 35); my desire, doubt and will are not ideas as such, but with respect to God they serve as marks or traces – signatures which are the starting point for the eventual construction of the idea of God. The construction here is in reality a kind of rediscovery: "how could I understand that I doubted or desired – that is, lacked something, unless there were in me some idea of a more perfect being (entis perfectioris) which enabled me to recognize my own defects by comparison?" (AT VII 45–6: CSM II 31). "If I was independent of any other being, and was myself the author of my existence, I should certainly not be subject to any kind of doubt, and would not have anything left to desire" (AT IXA 38: CSM II 33).[9]

In short, there is an assimilation here between the concept of the deity and the status which I would ideally wish to have. Forming the idea of God amounts, in effect, to determining the goal at which I aim.

CONSTRUCTING VERSUS MAKING EXPLICIT

Let us now turn from the way in which the idea of God is generated to the way in which it is, to use Doney's apt terminology, elicited or *made explicit*. The argument, as we have seen, works first by expanding or amplifying the perfections found within me, and second by unifying or putting together the various infinite (or indefinite) perfections. But these processes do not generate the idea of God; if they did, the idea would be invented or constructed by the human mind. Instead, they make the idea explicit: it is the prior presence of the idea which makes the thought processes possible. And it is only and precisely because the idea of the infinite is primary and incomprehensible that it can comprise or encompass these thought processes without being reduced to them.

Descartes stresses on each occasion that the idea which I thereby form, or which is made explicit in this fashion, is one which is adapted to the finite nature of my mind, or which takes account of the disparity between the infinite and my finite mind. The idea allows me to have genuine knowledge of the infinite, as it really is, but only "in so far as my own nature is capable of so doing" (*Discourse* Part IV: AT VI 35, line 8f: CSM I 128), "in so far as the eye of my darkened intellect allows" (Third Meditation: AT VII 52: CSM II 36), or "so far as the weakness of our nature permits" (*Principles* Part I, art. 22). In short, the infinite which is so represented is indeed represented as incomprehensible: For the true way for a finite mind to open itself to the infinite, and to know it in a methodical and rational way, is for it to make use of an idea which represents the infinite faithfully, and as a true object, but without presuming to encompass it, and without hiding the distance which separates us from it. Only at this respectful distance, as subjects approach their king, can the finite mind approach the infinite.

If we look at the passage from the *Principles* mentioned earlier, which parallels the discussion in the *Discourse*, we find an express reference to the innateness of the idea of God, and to the fact that it precedes the whole process of mental construction. "When we reflect on (*respicientes*) the idea of God which we were born with (*ejus ideam nobis ingenitam*) . . ." (Part I, art. 22): the various predicates ('eternal', 'omniscient' etc.) which Descartes goes on to specify are all attached to the innate idea of God – something which has led

Alquié to talk of a reasoning process which is analogous to the ontological proof.[10] The reasoning is indeed analogous, though of course by no means identical, since the argument depends not so much on analyzing the linkage between the various predicates included in an already given idea, as on developing that idea by adding a determinate content to the unitary form of infinity or perfection (the two notions are here interchangeable, since the argument refers to "infinite perfections" or to "absolute immensity, simplicity and unity" (AT VII 137, line 15f: CSM II 98).

Throughout the proof, nevertheless, the idea of God precedes, at any rate in terms of its status in the argument, the aspiration of the human mind to perfection. It is not human aspiration which defines the idea of the infinite; rather, the idea of the infinite is what arouses that aspiration. When I start with the finite perfections I possess, or observe in external things, and move to the greater perfections I aspire to and imagine, it is the idea of the infinite that dominates the process of amplification whereby those finite perfections are raised up to the infinite:

I had only to consider, for each of the things *of which I found some idea within me*, whether it was or was not a perfection to possess the item in question, in order to be certain that none of the items which involved some imperfection were present in him, while all the others were indeed present in him.   (*Discourse*, Part IV: AT VI 35: CSM I 128)

The desire which each of us has to possess all the perfections *which we can conceive*, and hence all those which we believe to be present in God, comes from the fact that God has given us a will which has no limits. And it is above all this infinite will that is in us which enables us to say that God has created us in his image.

            (Letter to Mersenne of 25 December 1639: AT II 628: CSMK 141–2)

When we reflect on the idea of God which we were born with, we see ... finally that he possesses within him everything *in which we can clearly recognize* some perfection that is infinite or unlimited by any imperfection.

                                        (AT VIIIA 13: CSM I 200)

The idea of perfection is thus found, conceived and recognized prior to, and independently of, any human aspiration. And the idea of the unity between all the perfections, which is the basis of the truly infinite nature of each of them, and of the 'positive incomprehensibility' of the whole, is prior to any other idea. It is innate, and, like

every innate idea, is not so much an actually present idea as a power
or faculty for producing the idea.[11]

The fact that this faculty is a positive power explains why it is
appropriate to say that it is we who construct the idea of God. Nevertheless, the ability to construct the idea is ultimately rooted in something passive: that sense of 'wonder and adoration' which comes
over the intellect when it turns its gaze towards, and submits itself
to, the infinite.[12]

GOD AND INFINITY

Let us now return to the rather low-key passage in the *Discourse*
where the argument starts merely from the notion of something
"more perfect than I," and proceeds in the first instance only to the
modest conclusion that "there exists a being more perfect than I."
As we have seen, this modest opening leads on to a more ambitious
undertaking, which could be termed a *making explicit* (of an innate
idea which is like a form whose content is yet to be filled in), or a
process of construction (of an idea which is built up as the mind
assembles its various contents). What we have here is exactly compa-
rable to the way in which the concept of the infinite is generated in
mathematics, whether in geometry or arithmetic.

The ability of the mind to develop a progression, for example in
counting by numbers, is exercised to begin with at the level of finite
numbers – for example by starting with a small number and adding
one to it. But the mind very quickly perceives that it has an indefinite power of repeating the process: one could say that in the process
of constructing larger and larger numbers we generate the idea of
infinity. Another way of putting it would be to say that from the
start the mind exercises its natural power only within the horizon of
an infinite number, or in virtue of what could be termed the idea of
arithmetical infinity. Descartes observes that this power we have of
starting from a given number and adding to it indefinitely provides
us with a proof that we are not the causes of ourselves, but depend
on a being who surpasses us (Second Replies: AT VII 139: CSM II
100). But of course this power alone (the power of arithmetical addition) does not allow us to know the nature of the being in question.
Once we have established that God exists, it will be possible to refer
to him (as its cause) this power which we experience within the

realm of numbers; the power which exists formally in us will be found to exist eminently in God.[13] But even at the stage where we do not yet know whether or nor God exists, we can recognize that there is some external cause, outside the mind, of the power of indefinite addition we possess: if this cause is not a true God, then it may be, for example, a genuine infinite number that exists outside of us. In the technical terminology Descartes employs, we would say that in this number there exists 'formally' all the numerical perfection that exists 'objectively' in our idea, when we think of it (whereas, if God does indeed exist, then the perfection exists 'eminently' in him).[14]

It should be clear from this how the idea of God is related to the idea or concept of an infinite number; the comparison is a valid one, but must not be pushed to far. In the first place, the infinite number belongs to a single domain, that of number, and is should therefore be regarded as merely indefinite, whereas God is truly infinite, since he comprises the complete set of perfections (and their absolute unity constitutes his true essence) (AT VII 50, lines 16ff; 137, lines 15ff; 163, lines, 8ff: CSM II 34; 98; 115). And secondly, existence cannot be derived from the idea of an infinite number (because it may or may not exist), whereas existence arises necessarily from the idea of God, since existence is one of his perfections.

ESSENCE AND EXISTENCE

We are now in a position to draw some conclusions on the relation between the affirmation of existence (the *quod*) and the determination of essence (the *quid*). Cartesian metaphysics generates three existential claims: I am, I exist (the Cogito); God exists (divine veracity); corporeal things exist (the foundations of physics). Now if the laws of true logic dictate that the determination of essence (the *quid*) must always precede the positing of existence (the *quod*), this is going to be a difficult rule to apply when it comes to metaphysics.

It is only in the case of the last of the three affirmations, that of the existence of corporeal things, that the rule is strictly followed, and here we are dealing with an area that is almost outside the realm of metaphysics proper, since it has to do with the transition from first philosophy to physics. The essence of corporeal things ("the whole of that corporeal nature which is the subject matter of pure mathematics" – AT VII 71: CSM II 49) is elucidated in the Fifth

Meditation, before the meditator has established whether or not they exist. And the proof of their existence, in the central portion of the Sixth Meditation, will therefore take the meaning of the term 'body' (*corpus*) as already determined: the corporeal things whose existence is established are not the objects perceived by the senses, but simply material things – those that have extension.

In the case of the first truth of the Cartesian system, by contrast, it is the affirmation of existence ("I am, I exist") which precedes, and calls forth, the inquiry into essence ("what is this 'I' that exists?") AT VI 25: CSM II 17). But nevertheless, the general "rule of true logic" cannot be violated: to establish my existence, it is necessary for me to know already, at least implicitly, what I am. The task that remains is to make this knowledge precise and explicit. But the precise specification that follows in the Second Meditation ('I am therefore in the strict sense only a thing that thinks' – *sum igitur praecise tantum res cogitans*; AT VII 27: CSM II 18) is both a restriction ("only a thing that thinks"), and also, within this restricted domain of thought, an enumeration ("a thing that thinks, that is to say which doubts, understands, affirms, denies . . ." (AT VII 28: CSM II 19). In effect, the two questions of existence (*quod*) and essence (*quid*) are resolved together and in parallel, and this parallelism has two consequences. The first affects the *quod*: if I should happen to make a mistake about the *quid*, about my essence, then the *quod* – the "I" that exists – would be thrown into doubt (AT VII 25, line 17: CSM II 17). The second consequence affects the *quid*: there is ultimately no preexisting meaning for the terms which the meditator is about to use to define his essence, such as 'mind' or 'intelligence' or 'reason'; these are "words of whose meaning I have hitherto been ignorant" (AT VII 27, line 15: CSM II 18). These terms draw their sense only from the very operation whereby I establish both my existence and my essence. The idea of myself, the notions of *thought* or of a finite thinking substance, are to be sure innate ideas; but their precise content is made determinate and actualized only in and through the operation which, through a process of systematic doubt, separates me from all other objects and establishes my existence.

The movement of thought is clearly the same when we come to the proof of God, and there is again a clear contrast with the proof of corporeal objects. In the case of God, it is one and the same process which both establishes the *quod*, the existence of God, and also elucidates the *quid*, his nature. Of course we have to possess an implicit knowledge of what God is if we are to be sure of identifying correctly the being whose existence we are proving. But the task remains of making precise the innate idea of God, which is the idea of a unity that is beyond our comprehension. The process of making this precise will involve both a restriction (by excluding everything whose addition would transform the true God into a false God and make it possible to deny his existence) and also an enumeration (the cataloguing of the divine predicates). In going on to use the term 'God,' does the meditator arrive (as he did in using the term 'mind' or 'understanding') at a "word of whose meaning he has hitherto been ignorant"? Descartes does not, of course put the matter this way – to do so would have seemed grotesque to a seventeenth-century thinker; but it remains true that it is in and through the process of metaphysical reflection that both the content of the idea of God is determined, and also, at the same time, his existence is proved. The union of the infinite and the perfect which Descartes unfolds via the notion of the "positive incomprehensibility" of God is so essential to the idea of God that it is in effect required even for the ontological proof. This proof starts from the idea of God which is already established, and proceeds by analyzing it and drawing out existence as a necessary consequence. But if I were to comprehend God, I could not prove his existence, for "my thought does not impose any necessity on things" (AT VII 66: CSM II 46). It is, rather, "the necessity of the thing itself which imposes itself on my thought," and this depends precisely on the incomprehensibility of God. Descartes expressly tells us that there are "only two places" in the *Meditations* where we must simultaneously reflect both on the incomprehensibility and on the perfect clarity and distinctness which are to be found in the idea of God. The first passage he mentions comes after the proof of God from his effects, when we have to assure ourselves by reflection that we have not based our reasoning on an idea which might be materially false; the second passage referred to is from the a priori proof, at the very moment when the demonstration unfolds.[15]

THE CONSISTENCY PROBLEM

The various definitions of God, as we have seen, play a vital role in the structure of Cartesian metaphysics, and these definitions emerge as lists of attributes, or names applied to God. But is the connection between the items on the list properly established? More important still, is their union even logically possible? Talk of the 'incomprehensibility' of the divine nature might, as we noted at the start of this paper, be taken as a kind of pretext to hide the inconsistencies and contradictions which threaten to emerge in the list of divine attributes. Leibniz's celebrated critique of the ontological proof comes to mind here: before the proof can get off the ground, the internal consistency of the idea of God needs to be established.[16] In our own day, the same theme has been taken up with a number of variations. Edwin Curley has argued that the divine attributes may be ultimately incompatible (or "incompossible"), and has pointed out Descartes' failure to provide any principle enabling us to determine how each individual attribute contributes to "supreme perfection".[17] He has also underlined the desperately indefinite character of the idea of God: "when we replace the idea of a being possessing all perfections with the idea of a being possessing all compossible perfections . . . we introduce a fatal weakness into the argument. The idea of a being possessing all compossible perfections is hopelessly indefinite."[18] From another standpoint, Jean-Luc Marion has pointed out the clash between various theological traditions which are partially assimilated in Descartes in a haphazard and unregulated way, and which generate in his system "irremediable tensions" and "irreducible inconsistencies," amounting to nothing less than a "system of contradictions."[19]

I am not entirely confident that the Cartesian system can satisfactorily be defended against objections of this kind. What I am sure of is that any plausible reply must be sought via an explication of Descartes' notion of the "positive incomprehensibility" of God. For it is this that is the key to the union between the two essential divine attributes *infinite* and *perfect*; and it is also what enables us to pass from the notion of substance or being in general to the "clear and distinct idea of uncreated and independent thinking substance, that is to say, of God" (*Principles* I 54).

The first point to be made is that the Cartesian list of divine predicates never leads to a unitary definition which could be the basis of a rigorous deduction of all the divine attributes. In this connection, it is instructive to compare Spinoza's procedure in the *Ethics*, and Descartes' attempt at a "synthetic" presentation at the end of the Second Replies – the "arguments presented in geometrical fashion" (AT VII 160ff: CSM II 113ff). In Spinoza's Definition 6, God is defined as "an absolutely infinite being, that is, a substance consisting of an infinity of attributes each of which expresses an eternal and infinite essence."[20] This appears to be a generative definition which provides us with a principle for bringing together the infinity of divine attributes, each one of which is infinite in its own kind. Descartes' Definition 8, by contrast, defines God as "the substance which we understand to be supremely perfect, and in which we conceive absolutely nothing that implies any defect or limitation in that perfection" (AT VII 162: CSM II 114). This does not allow the human understanding to construct the idea of God; it is not a matrix which generates an infinite set of possible definitions of the divine nature, each starting from a given perfection which is augmented or raised up to the infinite. Instead, it is a kind of sieve or filter which lets through anything which belongs to our understanding (*intelligere*) of supreme perfection, and eliminates anything which is conceived (*concipere*) as a defect or limitation in that perfection.

What this definition makes clear is the gap between *understanding* something and *conceiving* something. The inability to be *conceived* is exactly what Descartes means by incomprehensibility, and it is the hallmark of the infinite. If we could start from the unity of the divine essence, and arrive at a principle of deduction for each of his attributes, then God would be comprehensible – in which case he would no longer be God. In the expression 'supremely perfect' (*summe perfectum*), the adverb "supremely" (*summe*) does not merely connote the superlative, but refers to the incomprehensible infinite (just as, when Descartes opposes the "infinite in the positive sense" to the "indefinite," it is the totality of all perfections that he has in mind).[21] In every passage where Descartes discusses the divine nature, the two adjectives "infinite" and "perfect" are both to be found.

But in the various proofs of God's existence we never find one single predicate emerging as the dominant one. It is true, as Curley points out, that there is a gradual transition in the Third Meditation, from "explicating the idea of God by an enumeration of his perfections to explicating it by a more general formula";[22] but no reduction to a single predicate is possible. Neither omnipotence nor perfection can play this role. God has no "principal attribute,"[23] precisely because the absolute unity of his attributes entails that each attribute, through its relation to every other attribute, is identically infinite, in its own way.

If there was a genuine deduction of the divine attributes, it would involve our grasping, in the intuition of a simple nature, the logical connection between each of the predicates. But in that case the incomprehensible distance between the finite and the infinite would disappear, and the resulting idea would be a negation of God. The definition Descartes in fact offers in his 'geometrical' presentation proceeds in a completely different manner. It starts from each particular predicate which we meet in our finite experience, and allows it to be amplified to the point where it becomes infinite and incomprehensible, and united with all the other predicates. And each time we encounter a limitation, an imperfection or contradiction, we exclude, or filter out, that which we conceive to be incompatible with God.

CARTESIAN "INDUCTION" AND LATERAL THINKING

If we look at the procedure just discussed and ask how it avoids the ultimate incoherence summed up in Curley's charge that the idea of God is "hopelessly indefinite," the answer lies in what we may call a 'lateral' piece of reasoning in which there is a movement from one divine attribute to another.

Descartes makes a careful distinction between intuitive knowledge of God (something we never possess) and the movement of thought from one attribute to another. When he came to describe the latter process in 1648, he resurrected a term which he had used earlier in the *Regulae*, namely 'induction' (letter to Newcastle or Silhon of March or April 1648: AT V 138, line 28: CSMK 332). In the *Regulae*, he had made a distinction between two kinds of deductive process. One involves a linear series of inferences beginning with a simple nature that is accessible to us, where each link in the chain is intuited. But there is a second type where no reduction to a series of intuitions is possible, because the process ranges over a class of objects that are irreducible heterogeneous; this process is called 'induction' or 'enumeration' (Rule VII: AT X 388f: CSM I 25f).

Now the self-same methodology and terminology applies, without any qualification, to Descartes' later metaphysics and, in particular, his account of our knowledge of God. In the deduction of the divine attributes, incomprehensibility prevents us from mastering a simple nature, or reducing the deduction to an intuition. There is no question of the kind of adequate concept which would enable us to grasp a divine essence whose principle of composition one had fully mastered:

You see clearly that knowing God through himself, that is to say by an immediate illuminating power of the divine nature on our mind, which is what is meant by intuitive knowledge, is quite different from making use of God himself to make an *induction* from one attribute to another, or to put the matter more aptly, making use of our natural . . . knowledge of one of God's attributes so as to construct an argument which will enable us to infer another of his attributes

(letter to Newcastle or Silhon of March or April 1648: AT V 138: CSMK 332).

To clarify this 'induction' from one attribute to another, let us start from the particular attribute of God which relates to knowledge. To develop the notion of God's omniscience, we heighten or increase the attribute of knowledge until it becomes a supreme *cogitatio* or thought, which equals his supreme power, since God is not only the highest object of thought ("the clearest and most distinct of all our ideas," AT VII 46, lines 8, 27–8: CSM II 31–2), but also the supreme thinker – *substantia cogitans*, in the full and primary sense which implies something uncreated and independent (AT VIIIA 26, lines 2–3: CSM I 211). As noted earlier, there is a double movement of thought whereby the idea of God is generated from our own experience. Firstly, there is the movement in one category (in this case, knowledge or *intellectus*) from the finite to the infinite or indefinite (*cognitio indefinita sive infinita*: AT VII 137, lines 24–5: CSM II 99); and then there is a further movement from this category to others. It is the second of these developments that is our present concern.

We experience this latter process at our own human level, at the level of the finite. The second proof of God by his effects leads us to the core of the matter: not, to be sure, to the inner nature of God himself, whose majestic unity is incomprehensible to us, but to the structure of the idea of God, which is a true idea, in so far as the disproportion between the infinite and the finite allows. Descartes' position, from the *Discourse* onward, is that the acquisition of knowledge allows us to acquire "by the same means" all other goods (AT VI 28, lines 3–13: CSM I 125). Our human way of acquiring all other goods by means of knowledge gives us, (allowing for the irreducible disproportion between the finite and the infinite) a faithful image of what it is for God to possess all of them together. "For I am now experiencing a gradual increase in my knowledge, and I see nothing to prevent its increasing more and more . . . Further, I see no reason why I should not be able to use this increased knowledge to acquire (*adipisci*) all the other perfections of God" (AT VII 47: CSM II 32). The exact phrasing here is important. Descartes insisted on keeping it despite the objections of Mersenne, who wanted to substitute 'understand' (*intelligere*) for 'acquire' (*adipisci*) (AT III 329: CSMK 174). And he also defended it when challenged by Burman to explain why knowledge contributed to the acquisition of the other perfections: it supplies the "means for their attainment" (*medias ad eas conquirendas:* AT V 154: CSMK 339). What we have here is a model of induction, in Descartes' technical sense of that term.

In short, human beings cannot reach the essential nature of God, but we glimpse this absent unity when we discover, in a lateral movement of thought, the causal link between terms which remain distinct (albeit connected) in our ordinary human experience.

DIVINE UNITY AND THE UNITY OF THE SELF

The foregoing remarks show us right away how to answer the problem raised by Curley about the compossibility of the divine attributes. If every category of being was of equal status, it would be impossible to be sure that some further perfection might not turn up which was incompatible with those so far discovered, thus undermining the logical stability of the ensemble. But the various categories of being are not of equivalent status. Extension is excluded from the divine nature because of its divisibility (AT VI 35, lines 24–6: CSM I 128. Cf. *Principles* Part I, art. 23); it is only the category of thought which is a fitting dwelling place for positive infinity or supreme perfection. Being or substance in the full primary sense is an intellectual nature – the "uncreated and independent thinking substance that is God."

To say that God is a mind or spirit is in no way to cancel out the distance between the incomprehensible infinite and myself; it is simply to recognize that thinking substance, *substantia cogitans*, is not originally something created and dependent, even though the meditator begins by encountering, in the Cogito, one such substance which is indeed an incomplete and dependent thing. It should be no surprise to find these issues developed in the long letter on the subject of love which Descartes wrote to Chanut in 1647. Love is here given a privileged status, since "the true object of love is perfection,"[24] and it can bridge even the vast gulf that separates, for example, subjects and their Queen, transcending the courtly sentiments of "respect, veneration and admiration" (AT IV 611, line 10: CSMK 310). The issue of incomprehensibility is resolved, not beyond the realm of thought, but within it, through the relationship between two thinking substances (created and uncreated): "We must consider that God is a mind, or a thing that thinks, and that our soul's nature resembles his sufficiently for us to believe that it is an emanation of his supreme intelligence" (AT IV 608: CSMK 309). But what if we consider the infinity of God's power? In that case we must avoid the metaphysical error of taking a predicate as univocal when applied to God and to man (AT VII 433, lines 5–6: CSM II 292), and the moral failing of pride – the "extravagance of wanting to be Gods" (AT IV 608, lines 20–1: CSMK 309).

The consistency and coherent unity of the divine attributes is thus never revealed in the intuition of a simple nature, but is confirmed by the experience of our finite nature as thinking things. The infinite perfection of God is in fact an 'end point' toward which our indefinite striving toward perfection dimly aspires (AT IV 608, line 19, CSMK 309). Because there is an infinite gap between us and God, the unity which we experience within us is limited and fragile,[25] whereas the unity which we glimpse in God, and in the idea of God, is absolute and beyond our comprehension. But just as there is a resemblance between our mind and the divine mind, so when we experience within ourselves a unity among various different faculties, this provides us with a representation of what is, in God, the absolute simplicity of a unique act,[26] and in this way we are assured of the complete consistency of our idea of God. Illustrative examples of this kind of experienced unity are the unity between intellect and will when we necessarily but freely affirm a self-evident truth,[27] and the unity between science or true philosophy and the technical mastery of nature.[28] The unity of the divine predicates is warranted by, though not logically demonstrable from, the unity of the self.

UNDERSTANDING GOD: THOUGHT VERSUS POWER

In Spinoza, thought becomes one of the two attributes of God that is known (along with extension, which of course Descartes denies of God). And in the light of the previous section it may be seen that it is indeed the attribute of thought, even more than independence (or, which comes to the same thing, the infinite power manifested in a being who is *causa sui*, his own cause) which establishes that God can be understood, despite our inability to comprehend him.

But could a non-thinking thing be independent? It may be that Descartes vacillated on this point. On the 15 November 1638 he wrote to Mersenne "if an intellectual nature is independent, it is God, but if we said that a purely material nature was independent, it would not follow that it was God" (AT II 435, lines 10–18: CSMK 129). Not long afterward, however, on 30 September 1640, he wrote; "we cannot conceive distinctly that the sun, or any finite thing, is independent; for independence, if it is distinctly conceived, entails infinity" (AT III 191: CSMK 154). The two passages are nevertheless reconcilable if we realize that in reality no purely material thing can be truly independent, that is, cause of itself in the positive sense.[29]

The central point is that once we arrive at this thinking (or intellectual) uncreated independent substance, our inability to comprehend (*comprehendere*) it does not threaten our ability to understand (*intelligere*) it. It is admittedly true that incomprehensibility makes the distance between my finite mind and the infinite (or God) unbridgeable, and prevents us mastering or constructing the idea of God; for we are obliged to recognize an infinite number of *other* unknown perfections in addition to those we do know (AT VII 46, lines 19–21: CSM II 32). Indeed, we are prevented from *fully* comprehending even those perfections which we do conceive (AT VII 52, lines 4–6: CSM II 35). In short, incomprehensibility eliminates any possibility of predicates being applied *univocally* to God and to humans (AT VII 137, line 22: CSM II 98). Nevertheless, thanks to the resemblance between man and God which is assured by the fact that both are thinking beings, the lack of univocity is not tantamount to mere equivocity. The idea of the infinite enables me to know not a part of the infinite but the whole of it, though in a manner that is appropriate for a finite mind (AT VII 367–8: CSM II 253–4).

It is possible, therefore, for me to acquire further knowledge of

God which will make my idea of him more explicit or more distinct. But just as the coherence of the idea of a triangle cannot be impugned by the reliable discovery of fresh properties, so the coherence of the idea of God is guaranteed as soon as I have realized how the perfections which I extend to infinity are all combined in the unity of the divine mind. If God were not an "intellectual nature" (1637: AT I 353, line 23: CSMK 55), a 'thinking substance' (1644: AT VIIIA 26 line 2: CSM I 211) or a 'thinking thing' (1647: AT IV 608, line 12: CSMK 309), the concept of a supremely perfect being would indeed be 'hopelessly indefinite.' But once God's nature as a thinking being is recognised, the problem of 'incomprehensibility' loses some of its force. If God is considered as 'lacking all limits,' then the knowledge we have of him cannot perhaps be 'intuitive' (1637); the divine substance, being uncreated and independent, is not a substance in the same sense as created substances (1644); and since God is 'infinite' he retains 'his own place' and leaves us in ours (1647). In short, we know God by analogy – but the analogy is a rigorous one, maintaining a balance between the respects in which we resemble God (albeit without univocity) and those respects in which (without equivocity) we differ.

SUMMARY AND CONCLUSIONS

It may be useful to end this chapter by summarizing a number of the issues we have examined.

(1) The theological traditions which influenced Descartes included on the one hand a conception of God as *perfect*, linked to a positive way of understanding the deity by attributing comprehensible predicates to him, and on the other hand, a tradition which conceived of God as *infinite*, and took a negative stance on our understanding of God, regarding him as transcending the limits of intelligibility. Now whether or not there is in fact a contradiction between these two traditions, it would, in my view, be fallacious to infer that this contradiction infects the Cartesian idea of God.[30] Descartes' God is *both* perfect *and* infinite. Infinity acts on perfection, making it incomprehensible: no infinite perfection is within our comprehension. But perfection also acts on infinity, making it intelligible: the infinity of God is positive and perfectly understood. Descartes' views on these matters are consistent, probably from

1628–9 onward, and certainly from the letters of 1630 onward.[31] We encounter one and the same idea of God in the major texts (*Discourse, Meditations* and *Principles*) and in the various proofs of God (the two versions of the a posteriori proof, and the a priori proof).

(2) The idea of God is often presented in Descartes as a catalogue of properties whose validity is left unjustified ("By 'God' I understand a being who is infinite and perfect, and who has the properties a, b, c, . . . etc."). And this at first gives the impression of what is often thought of as the 'Cartesian sophism': in proving God's existence, Descartes starts from the idea of God, but if an idea is simply the meaning of a word, and if we put into the meaning of the term "God," or the infinite and perfect being, any properties we choose, then we can hardly congratulate ourselves on our achievement at having demonstrated that these properties apply to an infinite and perfect being.[32] The appearance of a sophism dissolves, however, if we see how the idea of God acquires its content at the same time as the existence of the *ideatum* is proved, and also how it is constructed by amplifying the perfections encountered in our experience of the finite, but in accordance with an internal principle (the innate idea) which imposes certain logical constraints on the process of construction.

(3) The innate idea of God is not a generative rule for constructing the concept, but a filter. If it was a generative rule, the idea of God would not merely be clear and distinct, it would be complete – we would have a concept that was fully adequate to its object.[33] The incomprehensibility of God excludes this kind of mastery by the human intellect, which would involve intuitive knowledge. Instead, what we have is a filtering principle which retains certain properties and excludes others in a coherent fashion. Without this coherence, the incomprehensible would indeed become unintelligible, and we would be left with an idea which was indeed, in Curley's phrase, "hopelessly indefinite."

(4) The second version of the proof of God from his effects makes Descartes' strategy clear. Reflecting on what I would have made of myself if I were independent both shows me what perfections should be conceived as belonging to God, and also shows me their coherence. The gap or distance between myself and God, i.e. his incomprehensibility, is established when I acknowledge that I am not, and will never be, *that*. What is revealed to me is thus the infinite itself,

entire and as it really is; but it is revealed to me as something which
I am not, and which I cannot comprehend. And this is the appropriate way for an infinite being to manifest itself to a finite mind.

(5) Because I can never penetrate into the essence of God by
possessing an internal principle which links his properties, I cannot
fully establish his nature, or deduce each of his properties, starting
from an actual intuition of his essence. No systematic or archi-
tectonic deduction of the divine predicates is possible. What is
available instead, is induction: I pass in a lateral fashion from one
attribute to another. This inductive process operates within me
when I pass from one finite perfection to another (for example, the
greater my knowledge the greater my power); and it operates analo-
gously in God, in the move from one infinite perfection to another.
When Descartes draws up his catalogue of divine perfections it
might look at first like mere rhapsodizing; but in fact the procedure
finds a secure place in the terminology of his method as 'induction'
or 'enumeration.'

(6) There is no principal attribute in God, since in God there are
no modes; everything in God is an attribute, and all attributes have
identical status. But in my case there is a principal attribute –
thought (*cogitatio*), which is the essence of the self, the soul or mind
(contrasted with body or extension). It is because thought, in contrast to extension, is a fit dwelling place for infinity and perfection
that it may be attributed to God. And it is because it is attributable
to God (as one of his attributes) and also to me (as my principal
attribute) that the mechanism of induction can function, in myself,
in God, and in the movement of thought from myself to God. Because of this resemblance, the incomprehensible can be understood
in a positive way, and thus, given a sufficiently ordered and careful
induction, it escapes the danger of vagueness and inconsistency.
When the induction has been accomplished, have we reached the
end of knowledge? Not at all: induction in no way involves cognitive mastery or determination of every point; it can always be re-
sumed and continued, or its material tackled in a different order. "I
have never dealt with the infinite," Descartes wrote, "except in
order to submit myself to it, and never to determine what it is or
what it is not" (letter to Mersenne, 28 January 1641: AT III 293:
CSMK 172). But although our knowledge is never complete, we do
indeed have knowledge which is secure and unshakeable, a stable

foundation for the construction of the sciences, a fixed point of certainty. The incomprehensibility of God thus conforms perfectly to the demands of the Cartesian method, and opens the door to the long chain of scientific truths, and to progress in our indefinitely long journey of comprehension.[34]

Translated by John Cottingham

NOTES

1 "The certainty and truth of all knowledge depends uniquely on my awareness of the true God, to such an extent that I was incapable of perfect knowledge about anything else until I became aware of him" (Fifth Meditation: AT VII 71: CSM II 49).

2 "We cannot comprehend [or 'grasp', *comprendre*] the greatness of God, even though we know it [*connaissons*]" (letter to Mersenne, 15 April 1630: AT I 145: CSMK 23); "Since God is a cause whose power exceeds the bounds of human understanding, and since the necessity of these truths [the eternal truths of mathematics] does not exceed our knowledge, these truths are therefore something less than, and subject to the incomprehensible power of God" (letter to Mersenne, 6 May 1630: AT I 150: CSMK 25); "I say that I know it, not that I conceive or comprehend it, because it is possible to know that God is infinite an all-powerful even though our soul, being finite, cannot comprehend or conceive him" (letter to Mersenne, 27 May 1630: AT I 152: CSMK 25).

3 "Palpabilius adhuc idem demonstravi, ex eo quod mens, quae habet istam ideam, a se ipsa esse non possit" (Second Replies: AT VII 136, line 7: CSM II 98). For the term *palpabilius*, see Gouhier, *La Pensée métaphysique de Descartes*, chap. V, § 3.

4 See Doney, "Les preuves de l'existence de Dieu dans la quatrième partie du Discours," in Grimaldi and Marion (eds.), *Le Discours et sa méthode*, pp. 323ff.

5 See Alquié, *Descartes, Œuvres philosophiques*, vol. I, p. 607, note 1.

6 Emphasis supplied. Cf. the Latin translation of the *Discourse*, where the corresponding phrase *imo etiam* is used (AT VI 559, line 34)

7 Making it one of the ideas described as *"a me ipso factae"* (AT VII 38, line 1: CSM II 26)

8 Cf. Second Replies: AT VII 137, lines 24–5: CSM II 99. See also *Descartes' Conversation with Burman*, AT V 154: CSMK 339.

9 Following the French version, which adds the phrase "independent of any other being." Cf. the Latin at AT VI 48, lines 7–8, and cf. CSM II 33, note 1.

10 Alquié, *Descartes, Œuvres philosophiques*, vol. III, p. 104, note 2.

11 Cf. Third Replies: *facultas illa eliciendi* (AT VII 189, lines 1–4: CSM II 132); and *Comments on a Certain Broadsheet*, AT VIIIB 366, lines 15–28: CSM I 309 (*potentia*, line 18; *facultas*, line 20).

12 The phrase "wonder and adoration" (*admirari, adorare*) comes at the end of the Third Meditation (AT VII 52: CSM II 36). Cf. the First Replies, where it is said that we should try "not so much to take hold of the perfections of God as to surrender to them" (*perfectiones . . . non tam capere quam ab ipsis capi*: AT VII 114, line 6: CSM II 82).

13 For the terms "formally" and "eminently," cf. Second Replies: AT VII 137, lines 25–7: CSM II 99. Who can give three coins to a beggar? Either a poor man who has (*formally*) the coins in his purse, or a rich banker who has (*eminently*) far greater assets in his account. Sometimes there is a problem for the rich banker: how to get the cash (cf. Definition IV at AT VII 161: CSM II 114).

14 See preceding note. If I dream of the three coins, they have only an "objective" reality (in my mind); if I wake up and either find them in my purse or their equivalent in my bank account, they also have "formal" reality (outside of my mind); the three coins that existed "objectively" in my mind will now also exist "formally" (in my purse) or "eminently" (in my account).

15 "When I said that God can be clearly and distinctly known, I was referring merely to knowledge of the finite kind just described, which corresponds to the small capacity of our mind . . . I made the statement about clear and distinct knowledge of God in only two places. The first was where the question arose as to whether the idea we form of God contains something real . . . and the second was where I asserted that existence belongs to the concept of a supremely perfect being." (First Replies: AT VII 114–5: CSM II 82). The two passages referred to are from the Third Meditation (AT VI 46: CSM II 32), and the Fifth Meditation (AT VII 65: CSM II 45).

16 Cf. Leibniz, *Discours de métaphysique*, §23

17 "How are we to compare a being possessing much knowledge and a little power with one possessing much power and little knowledge?" Curley, *Descartes against the Skeptics*, chap. 6, p. 130.

18. Ibid., p. 168.

19 See Jean-Luc Marion, *Sur le prisme métaphysique de Descartes*, ch. IV, § 19; translated by Van de Pitte, "The essential incoherence of Descartes' definition of divinity," in Rorty (ed.), *Essays on Descartes' Meditations*, pp. 297ff.

20 *Ethics*, Part I, Definition 6.

21 Cf. First Replies, AT VII 113, lines 7–8: CSM II 81; *Principles* Part I, art.

18 (AT VIIIA 11, lines 27–8: CSM I 199) and art. 27 (AT VIIIA 15, lines 22–3: CSM I 202); *Comments on a Certain Broadsheet*: AT VIIIB 362, line 12: CSM I 306.

22 Curley also notes that this is one of the ways in which the Third Meditation lays the groundwork for the Fifth; (*Descartes against the Skeptics* p. 167).

23 In contrast to finite substances, see *Principles* Part I, art. 53

24 Descartes had asserted this earlier, in the letter to Elizabeth of 15 September 1645: AT IV 291: CSMK 265

25 Although, as internally experienced, even our own freedom, though supposedly infinite, is perfectly comprehended; cf. *Principles* Part I, art. 41: AT VIIIA 20, lines 25, 28: CSM I 206.

26 Cf. *Principles*, Part I, art. 23, and *Descartes' Conversation with Burman*, AT V 165: CSMK 346.

27 On the experience of enlightened freedom, cf. Fourth Meditation, AT VII 59, lines 1–4: CSM II 41; see also Axiom VII of the "geometrical presentation" (AT VII 166: CSM II 117).

28 Cf. *Discourse* Part VI: AT VI 61–2: CSM I 142–3.

29 On the notion of *causa sui* in the positive sense, cf. First Replies: AT VII 109–111: CSM II 79–80, and Fourth Replies: AT VII 235–45: CSM II 164–71.

30 Compare Marion's claim about a "system of contradictions" (above, note 19). The fallacy of analyzing problems from outside the Cartesian texts and using them to cast doubt on the coherence of Descartes' own position might be called "Gilson's sophism," in the light of Gilson's claim that Descartes' views on liberty are inconsistent. To establish this, Gilson carefully explored the links between Descartes' position and Gibieuf's views on the one hand and Petau's on the other (the former, a critic of the notion of indifference; the latter, a defender). The fact that Gibieuf's and Petau's doctrines were inconsistent led Gilson to see in Descartes a juxtaposition of incoherent doctrines; in reality, however, Descartes finds within his system a perfectly logical place for two different aspects of freedom – freedom of choice and freedom of enlightenment. See further Gilson, *La Doctrine cartésienne de la liberté et la théologie*.

31 We have evidence that Descartes wrote a first draft of a treatise on metaphysics during a winter retreat in Holland in 1628–9; cf. AT I 17: CSMK 5. The first explicit summary of its contents is given in a letter to Mersenne of 15 April 1630 (AT I 144ff: CSMK 22ff).

32 Though Descartes does sometimes slip into such self-congratulation; cf. letter to Mersenne of 28 January 1641: "j'ai prouvé bien expressément que Dieu était créateur de toutes choses, et ensemble tous ses autres

attributs: car j'ai démontré son existence par l'idée que nous avons de lui" (AT III 297: CSMK 172).

33 A clear and distinct idea (as defined for example in *Principles* Part I, arts. 45, 46) need not yet be adequate (as defined in *Principles* Part I, art. 54: AT VIIIA 26, lines 3–5: CSM I 211). To qualify as adequate, an idea must represent everything that is to be found in its object; cf. AT VII 140, lines 2–5; 189, lines 17–18; 220, lines 8–10; 365, lines 3–5 (CSM II 100, 133, 155, 252). It is impossible for a finite mind to *have* an adequate idea of an infinite being; nor can it *know that it has* an adequate idea even of a finite being, even though it is perhaps possible for a finite mind to *have* an adequate idea of a finite being. See further, Fourth Replies: AT VII 220: CSM II 155, and *Descartes' Conversation with Burman*, AT V 151–2: translated in Cottingham (ed.), p. 10 (and see commentary on pp. 65–7).

34 I am deeply indebted to John Cottingham for his perspicacious translation of the original French text of this essay and for his many suggestions for improvements.

7   The Cartesian circle

THE TRUTH RULE AND THE PROBLEM OF THE CARTESIAN CIRCLE

Descartes writes in the second paragraph of the Third Meditation: "So I now seem to be able to lay it down as a general rule that whatever I perceive very clearly and distinctly is true" (AT VII 35: CSM II 24).[1] I call this principle *the truth rule.* In the third paragraph, Descartes decides that it is premature to take the truth rule to be established. He writes of "very simple and straightforward" propositions in arithmetic and geometry: "the . . . reason for my . . . judgment that they were open to doubt was that it occurred to me that perhaps some God could have given me a nature such that I was deceived even in matters which seemed most evident" (AT VII 36: CSM II 25). The matters that seem most evident, in the context of paragraph two, are beliefs based on clear and distinct perception, so that these beliefs (together with any that seem less evident) are themselves open to doubt. Descartes writes: "in order to remove . . . this . . . reason for doubt, . . . I must examine whether there is a God, and, if there is, whether he can be a deceiver" (AT VII 36: CSM II 25). In the Third Meditation, Descartes offers an argument for the existence of a nondeceiving God. The truth rule is finally proved in the Fourth Meditation. Descartes concludes, on the ground that God is no deceiver, that "if . . . I restrain my will so that it extends to what the intellect clearly and distinctly reveals, and no further, then it is quite impossible for me to go wrong" (AT VII 62: CSM II 43).

Descartes' procedure has been thought to suffer from an obvious difficulty. The truth rule is proved after even the most evident beliefs have been placed in doubt. The premises of the argument for

200

the truth rule in the Third and Fourth Meditations can at best be matters that seem most evident, matters that are themselves open to doubt in light of the supposition of a deceiving God. Even if the premises for the demonstration of the truth rule are confined to beliefs based on clear and distinct perception, Descartes' argument relies on premises whose truth has been called into question in order to show that he is not deceived in these very matters. The problem of "the Cartesian circle" is the problem of acquitting Descartes of the charge that his procedure is question-begging.

An enormous literature offers a bewildering variety of solutions to this problem. I believe that two broad lines of interpretation now vie for each other as solutions.[2] We can highlight the difference between them with reference to Descartes' claim that he must consider whether there exists a deceiving God in order to "remove" (*tollere*) the reason for doubt. According to the first interpretation, Descartes holds that the argument for the truth rule removes the reason for doubt in that it provides a *good reason* not to doubt beliefs based on clear and distinct perception, or at least shows that there is no *good reason* to doubt them. I call this the *epistemic* interpretation. Proponents of this interpretation include Curley, Doney, Frankfurt, and Gewirth.[3] According to the second interpretation, Descartes holds that the argument for the truth rule removes the reason for doubt in that it renders it *psychologically impossible* to doubt beliefs based on clear and distinct perception, or at least enables one to attain a state in which it is *psychologically impossible* to doubt them. I call this the *psychological* interpretation. Larmore and Rubin are most clearly proponents of this interpretation.[4] Bennett is a proponent of a guarded version of the interpretation.[5] I believe the psychological interpretation merits a more sustained development than it has received. This interpretation has not crystallized in the literature, even though a good deal of recent work on the problem of the circle points in its direction. In this paper, I explore the textual merit of what I take to be the most promising version of the psychological interpretation.

A PSYCHOLOGICAL INTERPRETATION OF UNSHAKABILITY AND SCIENTIFIC KNOWLEDGE

In a 1640 letter to Regius, Descartes writes of a "conviction based on an argument so strong that it can never be shaken by any stronger argument" (AT III 65: *cf.* CSMK 147). A belief could be shakable before one comes to possess a particular argument, and unshakable thereafter (cf. AT VII 460: CSM II 309). A person's belief is unshakable precisely when the person possesses arguments that prevent the belief from being shaken by argument. How is this condition to be understood? Descartes frequently writes of beliefs that are firm or solid (AT VI 31; VII 17, 145, 146: CSM I 126; II 12, 103, 104). Firmness is explicitly associated with unshakability in the Second Replies, where Descartes writes of "a conviction so firm that it is quite incapable of being destroyed (*tollere*)" (AT VII 145: CSM II 103). The metaphor is also associated with unshakability in *The Search After Truth*, a work that contains persistent references to the notion of a firm or solid basis for knowledge (AT X 496, 506, 509, 513: CSM II 400, 405, 407, 408). Beliefs are not firm if arguments can "overturn" (*renverser*) them (AT X 512, 513: CSM II 408). These passages suggest that a belief is unshakable just in case the person possesses arguments that prevent the belief from being dislodged by argument.[6] I say for brevity that an unshakable belief cannot be dislodged by argument, or cannot be dislodged.

Descartes' characterization of unshakability, in the passages cited from the letter to *Regius* and the *Search*, is not epistemic. These passages do not say that an unshakable belief is one that it would be *unreasonable,* or *unjustified,* or *unwarranted* to disturb or relinquish in the face of argument.[7] More generally, these passages do not provide a normative characterization of "unshakability." They do not say that an unshakable belief is one that *one ought not* disturb or relinquish in the face of argument. An unshakable belief is one that cannot de dislodged by argument. Whether or not a belief is unshakable is a question of descriptive psychology. This is not to deny that we can locate discussions of unshakability that seem more epistemic or normative in character. The important point is that a psychological account of unshakability is available for our use.[8]

Although unshakability is not itself a normative notion, Descartes regards unshakability or firmness as a doxastic objective – a goal which our beliefs ought to attain. This is implicit in the discussion in the *Search* of how to achieve firmness (cf. AT X 509–13: CSM II 406–9). It is explicit in the first paragraph of the First Meditation, where Descartes writes of "the necessity to start again right from the foundations to establish anything at all in the sciences that was stable (*firmum*)" (AT VII 17: CSM II 12), and in the first paragraph of the *Search*, where he formulates the objective of laying "the foundations for a solid science" (AT X 496: CSM II 400). The metaphor of a firm foundation also appears in Parts II and IV of the *Discourse on the Method* (AT VI 12–14, 31: CSM I 117–18, 126), and is developed at length in the Seventh Replies (AT VII 536–56: CSM II 365–80).[9] Descartes writes in the Second Replies:

First of all, as soon as we think that we correctly perceive something, we are spontaneously convinced that it is true. Now if this conviction is so firm that it is impossible for us ever to have any reason for doubting what we are convinced of, then there are no further questions for us to ask: we have everything that we could reasonably want. . . . For the supposition which we are making here is of a conviction so firm that it is quite incapable of being destroyed; and such a conviction is clearly the same as the most perfect certainty. (AT VII 144–5: CSM II 103)

This is perhaps Descartes' most developed statement of unshakability as an objective of inquiry.[10]

The Second Replies identifies unshakable belief with "perfect certainty." The letter to Regius identifies unshakable belief with *scientia*, "scientific knowledge" (AT III 65). There is related terminology elsewhere: "certain science" (AT VIIIA 10: CSM I 197), "true knowledge" (AT VII 141: CSM II 101), "true and certain knowledge" (AT VII 69: CSM II 48), "perfect knowledge" (AT VII 71: CSM II 49), and a proposition's being "perfectly known" (AT VII 69: CSM II 48). Such expressions appear to be terminological variants of the notion of scientific knowledge.[11] Knowledge, in the strict sense of scientific knowledge, is identified with unshakable belief, and hence itself has a psychological characterization.[12]

THE SKEPTICAL SUPPOSITION, SHAKABILITY, AND DOUBT

In explaining the reason for doubt in the Third Meditation, Descartes does not claim that he has any reason to believe that a deceiving God exists; rather, "it occurred to me that perhaps" God is a deceiver. He points out that he has "no cause to think that there is a deceiving God" and that he does "not yet even know for sure whether there is a God at all" (AT VII 36: CSM II 25). Descartes appeals to these features of his situation in observing that "any reason for doubt which depends simply on this supposition [of a deceiving God] is a very slight and, so to speak, metaphysical one" (AT VII 36: CSM II 25). To *suppose* that God is a deceiver need not be to believe that God is a deceiver. I suggest that we understand the notion of supposing broadly; to suppose that *p* is to believe, assume, hypothesize, conjecture, suspect, conceive, or imagine, that *p*. To suppose that *p* is to be in the psychological state of holding one of these propositional attitudes toward *p*.

The supposition that there exists a deceiving God is not, strictly speaking, the only supposition that renders even the most evident beliefs doubtful:

As for the kind of knowledge possessed by the atheist, it is easy to demonstrate that it is not . . . certain. As I have stated previously, the less power the atheist attributes to the author of his being, the more reason he will have to suspect that his nature may be so imperfect as to allow him to be deceived even in matters which seem utterly evident to him.

(AT VII 428: CSM II 289)

The supposition that one is caused by something less powerful than God is itself a cause for doubt. The supposition, in its most general form, that renders beliefs based on clear and distinct perception doubtful is *that one's faculty of clear and distinct perception is defective* – whether as the result of a deceiving God, a powerful demon, some other chain of events, or chance (cf. AT VII 21: CSM II 14). I refer to the propositional content indicated in italics as *the skeptical hypothesis*. If the truth rule is true – if whatever one clearly and distinctly perceives is true – then the skeptical hypothesis is false. I refer to the supposition that the skeptical hypothesis is true as *the skeptical supposition*.

Descartes claims in paragraph fourteen of the Fifth Meditation that beliefs based on clear and distinct perception are shakable insofar as they are held by someone who lacks knowledge of (the existence of a nondeceiving) God and of the truth rule:

And so other arguments can now occur to me which might easily undermine my opinion, if I did not possess knowledge of God; and I should thus never have true and certain knowledge about anything, but only shifting and changeable opinions . . . I can easily fall into doubt . . . , if I am without knowledge of God. For I can convince myself that I have a natural disposition to go wrong from time to time in matters which I think I perceive as evidently as can be.   (AT VII 69–70: CSM II 48)

Knowledge of the truth rule is a necessary condition for scientific knowledge. (I defer the question of what constitutes knowledge of the truth rule in this context.) The psychological account of unshakability is operative here. A person who lacks knowledge of the truth rule can suppose that clear and distinct perception is defective. Descartes does not state that, in light of this supposition, one ought to disturb or relinquish beliefs based on clear and distinct perception; rather, the supposition can "undermine (*deicere*)" or dislodge those beliefs.

Furthermore, someone who supposes that the skeptical hypothesis is true thereby falls in doubt. This point, which occurs in a number of additional passages (cf. AT VIIIA 9–10; VII 141, 428: CSM I 197; II, 101, 289), establishes a connection between a belief's being doubtful and a belief's being shakable. The fact that someone who lacks knowledge of the truth rule can suppose that the skeptical hypothesis is true, and thereby fall into doubt, would not show that the person's beliefs are shakable, unless doubt is a state that has the psychological property of being able to dislodge belief. This connection is confirmed in the Second Replies. Descartes writes: "I maintain that this awareness of his is not true knowledge, since no act of awareness that can be rendered doubtful seems fit to be called knowledge" (AT VII 141: CSM II 101). Four (Adam and Tannery) pages later, he identifies "perfect certainty" with "a conviction so firm that it is quite incapable of being destroyed" (AT VII 145: CSM II 103). Belief that is doubtful is not scientific knowledge. Doubt must therefore be a state that has the psychological property of being able to dislodge belief.

I suggest that doubt is able to dislodge belief in virtue of its unsettling or destabilizing belief. A belief that is unstable is liable to be dislodged, though it might remain in place. This model generates a coherent picture of relevant texts. When a belief is "shaken" (*concutere*), as in the letter to Regius, it is destabilized.[13] The persistent metaphors of firm and solid belief (*firmus* in Latin and *firme* or *solide* in French) are to be understood in terms of stability.[14] Unshakable or firm belief is belief that cannot be destabilized by argument. The reference to shifting or inconstant (*vagas*) belief in the Fifth Meditation passage also suggests that doubt is destabilizing.[15] Descartes does not hold that doubt is sufficient to dislodge belief; he holds that doubt (until such time as it is removed) is sufficient to destabilize belief.[16] The fact that a belief is destabilized explains how it can be dislodged. It remains the case that a belief is unshakable just in case it cannot be dislodged by argument; an unshakable belief cannot be dislodged by argument because it cannot be destabilized by argument.

THE UNSHAKABILITY OF CURRENT VERSUS RECOLLECTED CLEAR AND DISTINCT PERCEPTIONS

The claim that beliefs based on clear and distinct perception are shakable by the skeptical supposition requires qualification. Clear and distinct perception is psychologically compelling in that the belief that p is irresistible at any time p is clearly and distinctly perceived: "my nature is such that so long as I perceive something very clearly and distinctly I cannot but believe it to be true" (AT VII 69: CSM II 48). The textual basis for this doctrine is overwhelming (cf. AT VIIIA, 21; VII 38, 144, 460; III 64; IV 115–16; V 148: CSM I 207; II 27, 103, 309; CSMK 147, 233, 334). Clear and distinct perception divides into intuition, the apprehension of the truth of a proposition all at once or in a moment, and demonstration, a connected sequence of intuitions (cf. *Rules for the Direction of our Native Intelligence*, III, VII, XI). Descartes writes, again in paragraph fourteen of the Fifth Meditation: "when I consider the nature of a triangle, it appears most evident to me . . . that its three angles are equal to two right angles; and so long as I attend to the proof, I cannot but believe this to be true" (AT VII 69–70: CSM II 48). The *Principles* and the *Conversation with Burman* reiterate the point that the doctrine of the irresistibility of clear and distinct perception applies to demonstration as well as to intuition (cf. AT VIIIA 9; 30–1; V 148: CSM I 197, CSMK 334–5). The belief that p is psychologically irresistible at any time that one intuits p or attends to a demonstration of p.[17]

I call the belief that p, at any time one clearly and distinctly perceives p, a *current* clear and distinct perception. Consider a time at which one is not having a current clear and distinct perception that p, but recollects that one previously clearly and distinctly perceived that p. I call the belief that p, at the time of the recollection, a *recollected* clear and distinct perception. (Recollected clear and distinct perceptions, as I have characterized them, are *merely* recollected in the sense that they are not also clearly and distinctly perceived at the time of the recollection.) Beliefs *based on* clear and distinct perception are either current or recollected clear and distinct perceptions. I call a proposition that a person has intuited an *axiom* for that person, and a proposition that a person has demonstrated (but not intuited) a *theorem*. Current clear and distinct perceptions include current axioms and current theorems; recollected clear and distinct perceptions include recollected axioms and recollected theorems.[18]

Descartes persistently invokes the distinction between current and recollected theorems in passages germane to the circle (see AT VIIIA 9–10; VII, 69–70, 140, 145–6, 246; III 64–5: CSM I 197; II 48, 100, 104–5, 171; CSMK 147). In all but two of these passages (AT VII 140, 246: CSM II 100, 171), he explicitly maintains that although the belief that p is irresistible so long as it is a current theorem, the belief that p is not irresistible at times it is a recollected theorem. Here is a more extensive quotation from paragraph fourteen of the Fifth Meditation:

Admittedly my nature is such that so long as I perceive something very clearly and distinctly I cannot but believe it to be true. But ... often the memory of a previously made judgement may come back, when I am no longer attending to the arguments which led me to make it. And so other arguments can now occur to me which might easily undermine my opinion, if I did not possess knowledge of God; and I should thus never have true and certain knowledge about anything, but only shifting and changeable opinions. For example, when I consider the nature of a triangle, it appears most evident to me ... that its three angles are equal to two right angles; and so long as I attend to the proof, I cannot but believe this to be true. But as soon as I turn my mind's eye away from the proof, then in spite of still remembering that I perceived it very clearly, I can easily fall into doubt about its truth, if I am without knowledge of God. For I can convince myself that I have a natural disposition to go wrong from time to time in matters which I think I perceive as evidently as can be.   (AT VII 69–70: CSM II 48)

The skeptical supposition cannot dislodge a current theorem, since current theorems are irresistible; it can dislodge recollected theorems (cf. AT VIIIA 9–10: CSM I 197). Recollected theorems, evidently, are not psychologically irresistible. More generally, recollected clear and distinct perceptions can be dislodged by the skeptical supposition (cf. AT VII, 460: CSM II 309).[19] Recollected clear and distinct perceptions, unlike current clear and distinct perceptions, are not psychologically irresistible (cf. AT V 178: CSMK 353).[20]

The psychological doctrine that recollected clear and distinct perceptions can be dislodged by the skeptical supposition will seem more plausible against the background of my suggestion that doubt is a state that destabilizes belief. If this suggestion is correct, we should expect that the skeptical supposition destabilizes belief, since someone who supposes that the skeptical hypothesis is true falls into doubt. The psychological irresistibility of current clear and distinct perceptions is caused by their *being* clearly and distinctly perceived, not by one's *believing* that they are clearly and distinctly perceived. By contrast, one believes a recollected clear and distinct perception, at least in part, on the ground that one previously clearly and distinctly perceived the proposition. Let the belief that p be a recollected clear and distinct perception. Consider the following psychological states: the belief, on the ground that p was clearly and distinctly perceived, that p; and the supposition that the faculty of clear and distinct perception is defective. It seems plausible that these states, taken together, are unstable – especially if the supposition that clear and distinct perception is "defective" is taken to mean that it is unreliable, that it produces false beliefs more often than true beliefs.[21] The skeptical supposition therefore destabilizes the belief that p. This explains how the skeptical supposition can dislodge recollected clear and distinct perceptions.

Unshakability could in principle be achieved by avoiding recollected clear and distinct perceptions in favor of current clear and distinct perceptions. A person who followed this policy would reintuit any axiom, and redemonstrate any theorem, at every time he believed the axiom or theorem in question. Because his beliefs based on clear and distinct perception would be confined to current clear and distinct perceptions, and hence be irresistible, they would be unshakable by the skeptical supposition. I believe Descartes would reject this technique for achieveing unshakability simply on the ground that humans do not have sufficient conscious cognitive capacity at any time to intuit every axiom, and demonstrate every theorem, that they believe at that time – "the mind cannot think of a large number of things at the same time" (AT V 148: CSMK 335).[22]

How can unshakability be achieved? Descartes writes in paragraph fifteen of the Fifth Meditation:

> Now, however, I have perceived that God exists, . . . and I have drawn the conclusion that everything which I clearly and distinctly perceive is of necessity true. Accordingly, . . . there are no counter-arguments which can be adduced to make me doubt it, but on the contrary I have true and certain knowledge of it. And I have knowledge not just of this matter, but of all matters which I remember ever having demonstrated, in geometry and so on.   (AT VII 70: CSM II 48)

Knowledge of the truth rule is a sufficient condition, as well as a necessary condition, for the unshakability specifically of recollected clear and distinct perceptions.[23] This claim is repeated in the Second Replies (AT VII 146: CSM II 104–5) and the letter to Regius (AT III 65: CSMK 147).[24] Consider a proposition that one previously clearly and distinctly perceived, and such that one retains belief in the proposition, without either clearly and distinctly perceiving the proposition, or remembering that one clearly and distinctly perceived the proposition. The retained belief is neither a current nor a recollected clear and distinct perception in my sense of these terms; it (merely) lingers in memory. Such beliefs originate in clear and distinct perception, but they are not *based on* clear and distinct perception in my stipulated sense. One cannot in general apply the truth rule to a lingering belief in a proposition, because one need not believe that the proposition was clearly and distinctly perceived.[25] One can only apply the truth rule to a proposition that one takes to have been clearly and distinctly perceived. This is why Descartes claims that knowledge of the truth rule is sufficient for the unshakability specifically of propositions that one remembers having clearly and distinctly perceived.[26] Since current clear and distinct perceptions are unshakable in any case, knowledge of the truth rule is sufficient for the unshakability of beliefs *based on* clear and distinct perception. In the context of the problem of the Cartesian circle, we may confine our attention to a more limited claim: that knowledge of the truth rule is a sufficient condition for the unshakability *of* beliefs based on clear and distinct perception, *by* the supposition that the skeptical hypothesis is true. This is what I have in mind when I write of "unshakability" below.

KNOWLEDGE OF THE TRUTH RULE AS SECURING UNSHAKABILITY: A CONFLICT

The passages from the Fifth Meditation, the Second Replies, and the letter to Regius do not explain how knowledge of the truth secures unshakability. The material developed to this point permits a relevant inference. An unshakable belief has the psychological property that it cannot be dislodged by argument. If the skeptical supposition can dislodge recollected clear and distinct perceptions, and if knowledge of the truth rule results in the unshakability of recollected clear and distinct perceptions, then *knowledge of the truth rule must be psychologically incompatible with the supposition that the skeptical hypothesis is true.*[27] Descartes writes in the Second Replies:

> Hence you see that once we have become aware that God exists it is necessary for us to imagine that he is a deceiver if we wish to cast doubt on what we clearly and distinctly perceive. And since it is impossible to imagine that he is a deceiver, whatever we clearly and distinctly perceive must be completely accepted as true or certain.　　　(AT VII 144: CSM II 103)

Knowledge that an all-perfect God exists (and that deception is an imperfection), is psychologically incompatible with the supposition that God is a deceiver. Because Descartes claims that if God exists, clear and distinct perception could be defective only if God is a deceiver, he presumably holds that knowledge that an all-perfect God exists is psychologically incompatible with the supposition that clear and distinct perception is defective. The Second Replies therefore confirms the present interpretation.[28]

It remains to refine the thesis that "knowledge" of the truth rule is sufficient for unshakability. Current clear and distinct perceptions are psychologically irresistible. Belief in the truth rule is psychologically irresistible whenever it is a current clear and distinct perception. At times when the belief that whatever one clearly and distinctly perceives is true is psychologically irresistible, it is psychologically impossible to suppose that clear and distinct perception is defective. At least Descartes would take this to be psychologically impossible provided he assumes that the presence of an irresistible belief that p is psychologically incompatible with a concurrent supposition that $-p$. Descartes relies on this assumption in the passage from the Second Replies quoted in the preceding paragraph. A current clear and distinct perception of the truth rule is psychologically incompatible with the supposition that the skeptical hypothesis is true, so that recollected clear and distinct perceptions are unshakable at any time the truth rule is a current clear and distinct perception. (Because the irresistibility of current clear and distinct perception applies to both intuition and demonstration, this result holds for any time one intuits the truth rule or attends to its demonstration – for any time the truth rule is a current axiom or a current theorem.[29] It is for this reason that Descartes does not maintain, either in paragraph fifteen of the Fifth Meditation, or in the letter to Regius, that an intuition of the truth rule is required to secure unshakability. For expository purposes, I often assume that the truth rule is a theorem, not an axiom – demonstrated, not intuited.)

The explanation of why a current clear and distinct perception of the truth rule is psychologically incompatible with the skeptical supposition does not generalize to recollected clear and distinct perceptions. Because recollected clear and distinct perceptions are not psychologically irresistible, the recollection that one previously demonstrated the truth rule is not psychologically incompatible with the skeptical supposition. It is psychologically possible for the skeptical supposition to arise, and to dislodge recollected clear and distinct perceptions, at times when the truth rule is a recollected theorem.[30] Recollected clear and distinct perceptions, unlike current clear and distinct perceptions, do not constitute "knowledge" of the truth rule for the purposes of securing unshakability.

Recollected clear and distinct perceptions would be unshakable *at all times* for someone who always or continually attends to the demonstration of the truth rule.[31] I believe Descartes would reject this technique for achieving unshakability at all times simply on the ground that it is not humanly possible to sustain such perpetual attention: "my nature is . . . such that I cannot fix my mental vision continually on the same thing, so as to keep perceiving it clearly" (AT VII 69: CSM II 48 cf. AT VII 62; VIIIA 9: CSM II 43; I 197). Descartes claims in the Fifth Meditation that the recollection that one demonstrated the truth rule is sufficient for unshakability, even if one is no longer attending to the demonstration (cf. AT VII 70: CSM II 48).[32] There is a similar passage in the letter to Regius (cf. AT III 65: CSMK 147).[33] Descartes' claim that a demonstration of the truth rule is sufficient for unshakability means that unshakability is secured if the truth rule is either a current theorem, or (subject to a qualification to be discussed) a recollected theorem. As we have seen, however, the recollection that one demonstrated the truth rule does not secure unshakability.[34] Our task is to reconcile this conflict.

A FIRST STEP IN RESOLVING THE CONFLICT: TWO SENSES OF "UNSHAKABILITY"

The first step in the explanation is to locate a weakened notion of unshakability. I have characterized an unshakable belief as one that cannot be dislodged by argument. I now call this *unshakability in the strong sense*. A weaker sense of unshakability emerges in the Fifth Meditation. In paragraph fourteen, Descartes has explained that, if he lacks knowledge of the truth rule, he can entertain the skeptical supposition, a supposition that can undermine recollected clear and distinct perceptions. He writes in paragraph fifteen:

Now, however, I have perceived that God exists, . . . and I have drawn the conclusion that everything which I clearly and distinctly perceive is of necessity true. Accordingly, even if I am no longer attending to the arguments which led me to judge that this is true, as long as I remember that I clearly and distinctly perceived it, there are no counter-arguments which can be adduced to make me doubt it, but on the contrary I have true and certain knowledge of it. And I have knowledge not just of this matter, but of all matters which I remember ever having demonstrated, in geometry and so on. For what objections can now be raised?   (AT VII 69–70: CSM II 48)

Subsequent to demonstrating the truth rule, "there are no counter-arguments which can be adduced to make [*impellere*] me doubt" either the truth rule itself, or other recollected theorems. The Latin '*impellere*' can mean either 'force', 'make', 'constrain', or 'compel', on the one hand, or 'cause', 'lead', 'bring', or 'induce', on the other. These readings differ, though either yields a psychological account of unshakability. Doubt is a state that is able to dislodge belief. To claim that no counter-arguments can be adduced to *cause* one to doubt recollected theorems is to claim that recollected theorems cannot be dislodged – that they are unshakable in the strong sense. *Causing* one to lose a belief differs from *forcing* one to lose a belief. Someone might cause a self-defense expert to relinquish some money, without forcing him to relinquish the money, if the self-defense expert does not avail himself of his means of preventing the loss. Similarly, an argument could cause one to lose a belief, without forcing one to lose the belief, if one possessed the means to prevent loss of the belief, but failed to avail oneself of those means. The belief would nevertheless be unshakable, in the sense that one is able to prevent its being dislodged. I call this *unshakability in the weak sense.* Somewhat more precisely, a person's belief is unshakable, in the weak sense, just in case the person possesses arguments that enable him to prevent the belief's being dislodged by argument. A belief that is unshakable in the strong sense is unshakable in the weak sense, but not *vice versa.*[35] To claim that no counter-arguments can be adduced to *force* one to doubt recollected theorems is to claim that one can prevent recollected theorems from being dislodged – that they are unshakable in the weak sense.

In the French edition of the *Meditations,* Descartes adds, following "For what objections can now be raised . . .", "to oblige me to call these matters into doubt" (AT IXA 56: CSM II 48).[36] Once one has demonstrated the truth rule, there are no arguments that can *oblige* (*obliger*) one to doubt recollected clear and distinct perceptions. Descartes' point is that recollected clear and distinct perceptions are unshakable because there are no objections that can *force* one to doubt them, and hence that one can prevent their being dislodged. This evidence that Descartes is concerned to achieve unshakability in the weak sense occurs in one of the two passages where Descartes claims that the recollection that one demonstrated the truth rule is sufficient for scientific knowledge.[37] Apart from such textual details, the verb *'impellere'* permits us to read Descartes as concerned with the weakened sense of unshakability. We should adopt that reading, if it enables us to find in Descartes an explanation of how recollecting that one demonstrated the truth rule secures unshakability.

A SECOND STEP IN RESOLVING THE CONFLICT:
REPRODUCIBILITY

The second step in the explanation is to observe that recollecting that one demonstrated the truth rule does secure unshakability in the weak sense, *provided one retains the ability to reproduce the demonstration.* Recollecting that one demonstrated the truth rule, though psychologically compatible with the supposition that the skeptical hypothesis is true, enables one to attain a state that is psychologically incompatible with that supposition, provided one retains the ability to reproduce the demonstration. The (attentive) exercise of the ability to reproduce the demonstration generates an irresistible belief in the truth rule, thereby preventing one from supposing that the skeptical hypothesis is true, and thus preventing one's recollected clear and distinct perceptions from being dislodged. Someone who retains the ability to reproduce the demonstration of the truth rule possesses arguments – arguments that include the demonstration of the truth rule – that enable him to prevent recollected clear and distinct perceptions being dislodged; these beliefs are unshakable in the weak sense. I am now in a position to add the required qualification to Descartes' claim that recollecting that one demonstrated the truth rule is a sufficient condition for unshakability. It is sufficient for someone who retains the ability to reproduce the demonstration.[38] I call the position sketched in this paragraph *the reproducibility account* of how recollecting that one demonstrated the truth rule secures scientific knowledge.

The reproducibility account commits Descartes to an asymmetry between two kinds of recollected clear and disinct perceptions. I call propositions that are essential to the demonstration of the truth rule *basic propositions.* The basic propositions include, among others, the principles about causation invoked in the Third Meditation in the course of the demonstration that God exists, and the propositions that God exists, that deception is an imperfection, and that God is no deceiver. We can think of any proposition as essential to its own demonstration, so that the truth rule is itself a basic proposition. Nonbasic propositions are not essential to the demonstration of the truth rule – a theorem in geometry would be an example. According to the reproducibility account, all recollected clear and distinct perceptions – whether they are beliefs in basic or nonbasic propositions – are rendered unshakable by the ability to reproduce the demonstration of the truth rule. The reproducibility account imposes no general requirement that one retain the ability to reproduce the demonstrations of propositions that one recollects having demonstrated. The ability to reproduce the demonstration of the truth rule, however, presupposes the ability to reproduce clear and distinct perceptions of each of the basic propositions – one cannot reproduce the demonstration of the truth rule without clearly and distinctly perceiving that God exists, that God is no deceiver, etc. Recollected clear and distinct perceptions of basic propositions constitute a special case; they cannot be rendered unshakable unless one retains the ability to reproduce their own demonstrations.[39]

The reproducibility account goes beyond anything Descartes directly says insofar as it requires that achieving unshakability in the weak sense depends upon retaining the ability to reproduce the demonstration of the truth rule. We need to inquire whether it is plausible to attribute this view to Descartes. There is no obstacle in principle to a person's retaining the ability to reproduce a particular demonstration. It is no objection that particular persons might lack this ability. Any account of Descartes' attempt to remove the doubt about clear and distinct perception will assign a role to the demonstration of the truth rule. It is no objection that some persons are not capable of comprehending this demonstration. Descartes is trying to show how knowledge is possible for humans with ordinary cognitive endowments (cf. AT VI 1–3: CSM I 111–12), not that any human – even one with subnormal cognitive abilities – can achieve knowledge. The present version of the psychological interpretation takes "knowledge," that is, scientific knowledge, to require unshakable belief. Descartes' claim is that unshakable belief is possible for someone who does retain the ability to reproduce the demonstration of the truth rule. If some persons do not retain this ability, this at most shows that such persons do not have unshakable beliefs.

PASSAGES THAT BEAR DIRECTLY ON THE
REPRODUCIBILITY ACCOUNT

I turn to textual obstacles to the reproducibility account. Of the many passages in which Descartes claims that unshakability depends upon "knowledge" of the truth rule, only two mention that the recollection that one demonstrated the truth rule secures unshakability. The issue is whether recollecting that one demonstrated the truth rule constitutes knowledge of the truth rule (for the purpose of securing unshakability) even if one is no longer able to reproduce the demonstration. In the Fifth Meditation passage, Descartes claims that various beliefs are unshakable "even if I am no longer attending to the arguments which led me to judge that this is true, so long as I remember that I clearly and distinctly perceived it." The letter to Regius contains similar language. We can distinguish two situations in which one remembers having demonstrated a proposition, without at the same time attending to the demonstration. In the first, (i) one is not attending to the demonstration because one has forgotten it; one has not retained the ability to reproduce the demonstration. In the second situation, (ii) one is not attending to the demonstration even though one has not forgotten it; one remembers the demonstration in the sense that one retains the ability to reproduce it, but is not exercising that ability at the time of the recollection. It would be an obstacle to the reproducibility account if Descartes held that recollecting, in situation (i), that one demonstrated the truth rule secures unshakability. Descartes' language, however, is compatible with (ii).

In the two passages under consideration, Descartes states the conditions for securing the unshakability specifically of basic propositions, and generalizes the result to nonbasic propositions. Descartes writes in paragraph fifteen of the Fifth Meditation: "I have drawn the conclusion that everything which I clearly and distinctly perceive is of necessity true. Accordingly, even if I am no longer attending to the arguments which led me to judge that this is true, as long as I remember that I clearly and distinctly perceived it, there are no counter-arguments which can be adduced to make me doubt it." Once one has demonstrated the truth rule, belief in the truth rule, a basic proposition, is unshakable. Descartes extends this result: "And I have knowledge not just of this matter [the truth rule], but of all matters which I remember ever having demonstrated, in geometry and so on." Nonbasic propositions are also unshakable, once one has demonstrated the truth rule. In the letter to Regius, Descartes also distinguishes between basic and nonbasic propositions, and holds that the unshakability of both is secured by remembering that one demonstrated basic propositions, even if one no longer attends to *their* demonstration (cf. AT III 65: CSMK 147). In the two passages in which Descartes directly addresses the question of what qualifies as "knowledge" of the truth rule for the purpose of securing unshakability, Descartes applies language compatible with situation (ii) specifically to basic propositions.

There are seven passages in which Descartes claims that the

unshakability of recollected clear and distinct perceptions depends upon knowledge of the truth rule, without distinguishing between the unshakability of basic and nonbasic propositions. Six of these passages contain the language, or a modest variant of the language, of remembering having clearly and distinctly perceived a proposition without at the same time attending to the clear and distinct perception (cf. AT V 178; VIIIA 9–10; VII 69–70, 140, 245–6, 460: CSMK 353; CSM I 197; II, 48, 100, 171, 309). These six passages are compatible with situation (ii). Some of these passages use supplementary language strongly suggestive of situation (ii) rather than situation (i). Descartes writes: "as soon as I turn my mind's eye away from the proof, then in spite of still remembering that I perceived it very clearly, I can easily fall into doubt about its truth, if I am without knowledge of God" (AT VII 70: CSM II 48).

Only one passage is *prima facie* incompatible with the reproducibility account. Descartes writes in the Second Replies:

> There are other truths which are perceived very clearly by our intellect so long as we attend to the arguments on which our knowledge of them depends; and we are therefore incapable of doubting them during this time. But we may forget the arguments in question and later remember simply the conclusions which were deduced from them. The question will now arise as to whether we possess the same firm and immutable conviction concerning these conclusions, when we simply recollect that they were previously deduced from quite evident principles ... My reply is that the required certainty is indeed possessed by those whose knowledge of God enables them to understand that the intellectual faculty which he gave them cannot but tend towards the truth ... This point was explained so clearly at the end of the Fifth Meditation that it does not seem necessary to add anything further here.   (AT VII 146: CSM II 104–5)

The language of remembering a conclusion though we have forgotten the arguments for it suggests that Descartes is envisioning situation (i). I do not think this is strong evidence against the reproducibility account. First, if the reproducibility account is correct, Descartes' position has the complexity of involving the asymmetry noted above – recollected clear and distinct perceptions of nonbasic propositions, unlike basic propositions, can be rendered unshakable even if one does not retain the ability to reproduce their demonstrations. The Second Replies passage is not incompatible with this interpretation, if Descartes is focusing on nonbasic propositions. Second, the final sentence of the passage refers the reader to the close of the Fifth Meditation for a fuller statement of Descartes' position. We have seen that in the Fifth Meditation Descartes' discussion of the unshakability specifically of basic propositions is compatible with situation (ii). Finally, the Second Replies is an exception insofar as it seems to envision (i). The eight other discussions of securing unshakability – the six cited in the preceding paragraph, together with the two passages in which Descartes claims that the recollection that one demonstrated the truth rule is sufficient for unshakability – are all compatible with (ii).[40] Indeed, in light of these eight passages, it seems permissible to understand the Latin 'oblivisci' (AT VII 146) and the French 'oublier' (AT IXA 115) less literally as "lose sight of" or "be unmindful of." This reading of the Second Replies is compatible with (ii). The overall textual evidence strongly suggests that Descartes did not hold that recollected clear and distinct perceptions are unshakable once one has demonstrated the truth rule, even if one is no longer able to reproduce the demonstration.[41]

IMMUTABILITY AND PERMANENCE

There remain textual obstacles to the reproducibility account from another quarter. Descartes' notion of unshakability – or firmness or solidity – is one of a cluster of interconnected concepts. Descartes writes of beliefs that are both firm and immutable (or unchangeable) (AT VII 145, 146: CSM II 103, 104), and of beliefs that are immutable (AT VII 428: CSM II 289) – in contrast to beliefs that are mutable (AT VII 69: CSM II 48). He also writes of beliefs that are both firm and lasting (or permanent) (AT VII 17: CSM II 12) – in contrast to beliefs that are fluctuating (AT X 368: CSM I 14). It seems clear that immutable belief and permanent belief are themselves objectives of inquiry. Permanence is *prima facie* distinct from immutability, understood literally. Whereas a belief that is literally immutable must be permanent, a belief could be permanent without being immutable. A belief, once one holds it, could be mut*able*, even though it does not in fact change. Although Descartes places more weight on immutability, permanence is prominent in the first paragraph of the *Meditations*. The reproducibility account owes us an explanation of the interconnections between unshakability, immutability, and permanence. In particular, it needs to be shown that securing unshakability is compatible with securing immutability and permanence.

I begin with immutability. (In what follows, I construe 'immutable' to mean "immutable specifically by argument.") A belief that is unshakable in the strong sense that it cannot be dislodged could be immutable.[42] A belief that is unshakable in the weak sense can be dislodged, if one does not exercise the ability to prevent its being dislodged. A belief that can be dislodged, even if it is not dislodged, is not literally immutable. Unshakability in the strong sense is compatible with literal immutability, but cannot itself be achieved; unshakability in the weak sense can be achieved, but is not compatible with literal immutability.

The only escape from this dilemma is to locate some nonliteral, technical sense of the term 'immutable' that is compatible with mere unshakability in the weak sense. Although there are a number of passages that provide discursive treatments of "unshakability," "immutability" (as it applies to human belief or knowledge) does not receive equal treatment. The closest approximation to a gloss occurs in the Second Replies:

> For the supposition which we are making here is of a conviction so firm that it is quite incapable of being destroyed; and such a conviction is clearly the same as the most perfect certainty.
>
> But it may be doubted whether any such certainty, or firm and immutable conviction, is in fact to be had.   (AT VII 145: CSM II 103)

Descartes identifies firm conviction with perfect certainty, and perfect certainty with conviction that is firm or unshakable *and immutable*. What is the force of this additional condition in the account of scientific knowledge?[43]

Suppose that, at time t, one believes that p, remembers clearly and distinctly perceiving that p, and retains the ability to reproduce a demonstration of the truth rule; suppose, in other words, that the belief that p is unshakable at t. The unshakability of a belief at a time t does not guarantee its unshakability at a subsequent time t'. There are various possibilities: (a) one might have forgotten the belief by t'; (b) one might retain the belief at t', but have forgotten that it was clearly and distinctly perceived; or (c) one might, at t', retain the belief and remember that it was clearly and distinctly perceived, but have forgotten the demonstration of the truth rule. In case (a), one no longer has a belief, much less an unshakable belief, in the proposition at t'. In case (b), one could not apply the truth rule to the belief at t'. In case (c), one does not, at t', satisfy a necessary condition for the unshakabilitty of any recollected clear and distinct perception. Unshakable beliefs can withstand being dislodged by argument. In cases (a–c), belief is not dislodged by argument; rather, unshakable belief is lost due to forgetfulness. Possession of an unshakable belief that p at t does not guarantee continued possession of an unshakable belief that p. (This conclusion applies to unshakability both in the strong and weak senses.) Immutability, by contrast, carries the connotation of a continuing property of a belief. Because the unshakability of a belief is relative to a specific time, unshakability does not entail immutability.

I suggest that the immutability requirement represents Descartes' recognition of a gap between unshakability at a time and continuing unshakability. We can think of the requirement as imposing such further conditions as are necessary for the possession of an unshakable belief in a proposition to guarantee the continued possession of an unshakable belief in that proposition. This requirement adds to the concept of scientific knowledge, without requiring that a belief be literally immutable. We can explain why Descartes does not emphasize the distinction between unshakability and immutability. In each of cases (a–c), unshakability is insufficient for continuing unshakability due to the possibility of forgetfulness.[44] Forgetfulness is a matter of individual variation in cognitive ability or performance, it is not intrinsic to human nature. Individual limitations in forgetfulness do not preclude the possibility of human knowledge, even if such knowledge requires *continuing* unshakability (in the weak sense).[45]

I turn to permanence. Even continuing unshakability in the weak sense is compatible with impermanence; a belief with continuing unshakability in the weak sense can be lost if one fails to avail oneself of one's means of preventing the belief's being dislodged. The issue is whether continuing unshakability in the weak sense is also compatible with permanence. Insofar as recollected clear and distinct peceptions are dislodged by the skeptical supposition, permanence requires that one never suppose that the skeptical hypothesis is true. It is tempting to think that securing the *permanence* of recollected clear and distinct perceptions – much as securing their unshakability *in the strong sense* – would therefore require continual attention to the demonstration of the truth rule. This overlooks Descartes' claim that it is not humanly possible continually to attend to any one matter so as to perceive it clearly. Just as one's own nature prevents one from continually attending to the demonstration of the truth rule, one's own nature prevents one from continually attending to the skeptical hypothesis. The ability to reproduce the demonstration of the truth rule need not be continuously exercised, even to achieve permanence in belief, because the supposition that the skeptical hypothesis is true will not itself continually recur.[46]

What about those occasions when the skeptical supposition does recur? Some commentators have observed that the supposition can then be dislodged by exercising one's ability to reproduce the demonstration of the truth rule.[47] This is a technique for restoring beliefs dislodged by the skeptical supposition by dislodging the skeptical supposition itself. Restoring a dislodged belief, however, does not achieve permanence in belief; it minimizes the loss or the impermanence – much as a self-defense expert might exercise his ability to recover his money after relinquishing it. Permanence in belief requires the *preventative* or *preemptive* exercise of the ability to reproduce the demonstration of the truth rule. A self-defense expert's ability to prevent relinquishing his money depends upon his ability both to recognize that the loss of his money is impending, and to react defensively, on a timely basis. Similarly, the preemptive exercise of the ability to reproduce the demonstration of the truth rule depends upon the ability both to recognize that the supposition that the skeptical hypothesis is true is impending, and to reproduce the demonstration of the truth rule, on a timely basis. Impermanence due to the skeptical supposition can be avoided by such preemptive exercise of one's ability to reproduce the demonstration of truth rule. Although this does not show that permanence can be achieved, it does show that there is nothing intrinsic to the reproducibility account to preclude achieving permanence.

In sum, I see no significant textual obstacle to an interpretation on which Descartes holds that achieving unshakability depends upon retaining the ability to reproduce the demonstration of the truth rule. This completes my exposition of the textual basis for a version of the psychological interpretation that incorporates the reproducibility account. Before closing, I offer some brief remarks concerning philosophical objections that might be raised to Descartes' position as characterized by the psychological interpretation.

PHILOSOPHICAL OBJECTIONS TO THE PSYCHOLOGICAL INTERPRETATION

The demonstration of the truth rule begs the question against the skeptical supposition. That it does beg the question will be apparent, even to persons who have demonstrated the truth rule and recollect having done so, if they review their prior argumentative procedure. Such a person would also know that a current clear and distinct perception of the truth rule has the result that one irresistibly believes the truth rule, even though it is the conclusion of a question-begging argument. To proceed, under these conditions, to reproduce the demonstration of the truth rule seems akin to knowingly taking a pill, or knowingly submitting to a hypnotic spell, that induces an irresistible belief for which one lacks good evidence.[48] This is knowingly to enter an epistemological illusion.

The present version of the psychological interpretation does not succumb to this objection. Descartes is trying to show how scientific knowledge can be achieved. Although one cannot avoid believing the truth rule when one does reproduce its demonstration, one can avoid reproducing its demonstration. Someone who has the continuing ability to reproduce the demonstration of the truth rule can decline to exercise that ability. Such a person has nevertheless achieved continuing unshakability in the weak sense, and hence scientific knowledge, any scruples about the illusion notwithstanding. The objection can be put in a slightly different form. Would not someone who, under the conditions outlined, proceeded to reproduce the demonstration of the truth rule in order to restore a dislodged belief, or to preempt impermanence, be a party to the illusion? Or consider someone who supposes that the skeptical hypothesis is true. It comes to his attention that there is an argument, such that if he attends to the argument, he will irresistibly believe that the skeptical hypothesis is false. He wonders whether it is not in the nature of the case that the argument, whatever its details, will beg the question against the skeptical supposition. He satisfies himself that, inevitably, it will beg the question. This person's beliefs are not yet unshakable. Would he not be a party to the illuson if he proceeded to attend to the argument for the truth rule for the first time?

I speculate that Descartes would respond with reference to the costs of not entering the illusion. The illusion consists in the irresistible belief in the truth of a proposition for which one lacks good evidence. Any clear and distinct perception is implicated in the illusion. There is no clear and distinct perception for which one has good evidence, if good evidence requires a non-question-begging argument against the skeptical supposition. Avoiding the illusion requires that one decline to exercise one's faculty of clear and distinct perception altogether. Descartes holds that whereas clear and distinct perception is internally coherent, sense perception is internally incoherent – sense perception on its own generates conflicting beliefs. Clear and distinct perception resolves these conflicts by sustaining one of the conflicting beliefs, and correcting the other. The resolution is effected in virtue of an asymmetry in the psychological properties of the faculties: whereas clear and distinct perception is psychologically irresistible, sense perception generates suppressible inclinations to hold beliefs.[49] In declining to exercise the faculty of clear and distinct perception, one deprives oneself of the means for resolving the conflicts that arise within sense perception. The resulting doxastic system would be inherently, and ineliminably, unstable.[50] This instability could be avoided only by declining to exercise the faculty of sense perception as well as that of clear and distinct perception. The cost of entering the illusion must be weighed against the cost of not doing so – ineliminable instability, or declining to use one's cognitive faculties.

It might be felt that these observations are not responsive to the underlying point of the objection – that the psychological response to the problem of the circle is of mere psychological, and no epistemic, significance.[51] This objection is likely to be offered by those who think that an adequate solution to the problem of the circle must be epistemic in character. A complete reply would require a detailed comparision of the strengths and weaknesses of the epistemic and psychological interpretations. In my view, all known versions of the epistemic interpretation either fail to acquit Descartes of begging the question, or acquit him of that charge only by misconstruing the question at issue, or collapse (under scrutiny) into versions of the psychological intepretation. Space does not permit me to defend this view. I can nevertheless state a partial reply: Descartes' interest is in scientific knowledge as *he* conceives it; he does offer purely psychological characterizations of this and related notions that provide the materials for the psychological response to the problem of the circle.[52] The texts provide an alternative to the epistemic account.

I do take note of a strategy for accommodating passages that seem to require the epistemic interpretation. Much as one can irresistibly believe that whatever one clearly and distinctly perceives is true, one can irresistibly believe that the truth rule provides a good (or even conclusive) *reason* not to doubt beliefs based on clear and distinct perception. One can irresistibly believe this if one also clearly and distinctly perceives, and hence irresistibly believes, relevant epistemic principles about the relationship between good reasons for a belief and the likelihood that the belief is true. More generally, from the perspective of the psychological interpretation, we can think of passages suggestive of the epistemic interpretation as implicitly embedded within the propositional attitude "I irresistibly believe that . . ," or as reports of what can be irresistibly believed.[53] The details require development.

THE SIGNIFICANCE OF THE PSYCHOLOGICAL INTERPRETATION

The psychological interpretation, and the replies I have sketched to the philosophical objections to the position it attributes to Descartes, rely on Cartesian doctrines about the psychological properties of the cognitive faculties. Some might conclude that the psychological interpretation should be dismissed, on the ground that it makes Descartes' position depend upon an accidental or contingent fact of human psychology – that current clear and distinct perception is psychologically irresistible. This might be a reason for rejecting the psychological response to the problem of the circle. It is not a reason for rejecting the *psychological interpretation*, the attribution of the psychological response to Descartes. To the contrary, the considerable textual merit of this interpretation suggests that Descartes' rationalism cannot be understood apart from the doctrine that clear and distinct perception, unlike sense perception, is psychologically irresistible.[54] (The interesting historical question is why

Descartes insisted on this psychological doctrine.[55]) Indeed, I argue elsewhere that, for Descartes, the superiority or priority of reason or clear and distinct perception to sense perception ultimately rests on the greater irresistibility of reason.[56]

I am inclined to think that the psychological properties of the cognitive faculties play a more essential role in seventeenth- and eighteenth-century epistemology than is generally understood.[57] I believe that both Descartes and Hume adopt doxastic objectives characterized in psychological terms – objectives that relate to such properties as the permanence, unshakability, and stability of belief. In this sense, Descartes and Hume are engaged in a common epistemological project. An account of how to achieve such psychologically defined objectives is inextricably linked to a conception of the psychological properties of the cognitive faculties. It is in their conceptions of these properties that Descartes and Hume diverge: for Descartes, only reason generates psychologically irresistible beliefs; for Hume, irresistible beliefs result from sense-perception, memory, and causal inference, as well as from reason, or intuition and demonstration.[58] This contrast is crucial to the difference between Descartes' rationalism and Hume's empiricism.[59]

NOTES

1 References to specific paragraphs of the *Meditations* follow the paragraph divisions of the second Latin edition of 1642, as edited by Adam (AT VII); this is the edition translated by Cottingham in CSM.

2 Interpretations in which memory, not clear and distinct perception, is called into doubt have not been a live option in the aftermath of the critique of Frankfurt, "Memory and the Cartesian Circle" and *Demons, Dreamers, and Madmen*, ch. 14. For the obituaries, see Doney, "Descartes's conception of perfect knowledge," p. 671, n. 4; Prendergast, "Review of Frankfurt," p. 304; Sanford, "Review of Frankfurt," p. 122; Curley, *Descartes against the Skeptics*, p. 104; Williams, *Descartes*, p. 193, n. 7; and Van Cleve "Foundationalism, epistemic principles, and the Cartesian Circle," pp. 56–7. There was already substantial criticism of the memory interpretation in Merrylees, *Descartes*, ch. IV, § 3–4; Levett, "Note on the alleged Cartesian Circle"; Laporte, *Le rationalisme de Descartes*, pp. 162–3; and Wolz, "The double guarantee of Descartes' ideas," pp. 481–2. For additional criticism that is independent of Frankfurt, see Gouhier, *La pensée métaphysique de Descartes*, pp. 302–5;

Beck, *The Metaphysics of Descartes*, pp. 147–8; and Etchemendy, "The Cartesian Circle," §§ 2–3.

3 See Gewirth, "The Cartesian Circle," "The Cartesian Circle reconsidered," and "Descartes: Two disputed questions"; Frankfurt, "Descartes' validation of reason" and *Demons, Dreamers, and Madmen*, esp. ch. 15; Doney, "Descartes's conception of perfect knowledge"; and Curley, *Descartes against the Skeptics*, ch. 5. Doney, in "Descartes's conception of perfect knowledge," abandons the memory interpretation he had espoused in "The Cartesian Circle."

4 See Rubin, "Descartes's validation of clear and distinct apprehension"; and Larmore, "Descartes' psychologistic theory of assent." Indeed, Cottingham, in *Descartes*, pp. 69, 76–7, takes Frankfurt (*Demons, Dreamers, and Madmen*) to be an instance of the psychological interpretation, and Markie (*Descartes's Gambit*, pp. 43–4, to include n. 4) cites Curley, *Descartes against the Skeptics*, and Gewirth, "The Cartesian Circle," as providing a psychological account of how the reason for doubt is removed. The interpretation and classification of positions in the literature is itself a difficult matter.

5 Bennett takes the psychological response to the problem of the circle, and related doctrines, to represent a "lesser strand" that does not constitute Descartes' "principal, official account" of his procedure, though it is in Descartes' mind "at some level" ("Truth and stability in Descartes's *Meditations*," §§ 1, 10, 12, 14). My chapter for the present volume was nearing completion when Bennett's (then unpublished) manuscript came to my attention.

6 Bennett's "stability" is a generalized notion of unshakable belief, belief that cannot be dislodged by argument or otherwise (cf. "Truth and stability", § 4).

7 The fact that "unshakability" is characterized with reference to the notion of an "argument" or "reason" (*ratio*: AT III 65; cf. VII 69, 70) does not render the account "epistemic," rather than "psychological," in my senses of these terms. Suppose, for the sake of discussion, that the notion of an "argument" can only be characterized epistemically. The unshakability of a belief is relative to the arguments one possesses; unshakability is a relational property. We can formulate epistemic accounts of this relation, e.g., a person's belief is unshakable just in case the person possesses arguments *that constitute good reasons for not relinquishing* the belief in the face of argument. We can formulate psychological accounts of this relation, e.g., a person's belief is unshakable just in case the person possesses arguments *that, as a psychological matter of fact, prevent the dislodging* of the belief in the face of argument. Of the two italicized accounts of the relation, only the first in-

vokes epistemic notions. We can distinguish epistemic and psychological accounts of unshakability, even if Descartes provides an epistemic as well as a psychological account, and even if he holds that a belief is unshakable in some specified psychological sense just in case it is unshakable in some specified epistemic sense.

8 Tlumak provides a number of epistemic characterizations of unshakability – "irrevisability" in his terminology ("Certainty and Cartesian method," pp. 45, 46, 48). He explicates "metaphysical certainty" as irrevisability (pp. 44–5), and holds that metaphysical certainty "has normative force in the context of the Cartesian problem" (p. 43). I believe the normativity of the notion derives from Descartes' adoption of unshakability as an objective of inquiry (see below). We need not regard the normative characterization as fundamental. This point undermines the second of Tlumak's arguments against the psychological interpretation (p. 57).

9 Bennett details the way in which this material supports the psychological interpretation ("Truth and stability," § 1).

10 The reference to a "reason for doubting" suggests an epistemic reading of the operative notion of unshakability. As Bennett observes, however, the Latin causa can also mean "cause," a rendering that is more consistent with the remainder of the passage ("Truth and stability").

11 For discussions of one or both of the interrelated concepts of unshakability and scientific knowledge, see Doney, "The Cartesian Circle," p. 337; Kenny, Descartes, pp. 191–3; Doney, "Descartes's conception of perfect knowledge," esp. pp. 388–91; Frankfurt, Demons, Dreamers and Madmen, pp. 24, 124, 179–80; Curley, Descartes against the Skeptics, pp. 104–5; Tlumak, "Certainty and the Cartesian method," pp. 44–50, 57–60; Williams, Descartes, pp. 62, 200–4; Gombay, "Mental conflict: Descartes," pp. 491–4; Williams, "Descartes' use of skepticism," p. 345; Cottingham, Descartes, pp. 2–3, 25, 67, 70–1; Markie, Descartes's Gambit, pp. 59–72; Rodis-Lewis, "On the complimentarity of Meditations III and V," pp. 277–81; and Garns, "Descartes and indubitability," esp. §§ 1–11.

12 Although he holds that Descartes employs epistemic and psychological conceptions of certainty, Markie (Descartes's Gambit, pp. 34, 53–7) offers only an epistemic account of scientific knowledge (pp. 59–72). This leaves Markie, on his own admission, without a solution to the problem of the circle (cf. p. 162, n. 12).

13 Kenny's rendering concuti as "shaken" (CSMK 147) and Rodis-Lewis's ébranlée (Descartes, p. 266) are nearer the mark than Gewirth's "destroyed" ("The Cartesian Circle," p. 390) or Williams' "knocked out" (Descartes, p. 204).

14 They are sometimes so translated, for example at CSM II 12. See also Etchemendy's suggested translation of *firmanda* (AT VII 15) in terms of "stabilization" ("The Cartesian Circle," pp. 37–8).

15 Doney, who frequently invokes the terminology of "unsettled belief" ("Descartes's conception of perfect knowledge," pp. 390, 391, 401), renders *vagas* as "unstable" (p. 389).

16 The ontologically most economical reading of Descartes' position would *identify* doubt with unstable belief. On this reading, the claim that the skeptical supposition renders beliefs based on clear and distinct perception doubtful means that the supposition destabilizes these beliefs. This is a Peircian position: the end of inquiry is settled or firm belief – doubt is a stimulus to this state. See Charles S. Peirce, "The fixation of belief," *Popular Science Monthly*, 1877, §§ III–IV, reprinted in Tomas, ed., *Charles S. Peirce, Essays in the Philosophy of Science.*

17 I leave open the question of precisely what is involved in attending to a demonstration. Descartes seems to hold that attending to a demonstration requires that "we are able to grasp the proof . . . in its entirety" (AT V 149: CSMK 335).

18 It is possible for there to be recollected axioms if it is possible to recollect that one intuited a proposition without intuiting the proposition at the time of the recollection. No Cartesian doctrines preclude this possibility, though some axioms are such that we cannot think of them without clearly and distinctly perceiving them (cf. AT VII, 145: CSM II 104).

19 Axioms that cannot be thought of without being clearly and distinctly perceived are an exception (cf. note 18).

20 Since doubt is a state that is able to dislodge belief, we should expect Descartes to hold that current clear and distinct perceptions cannot be doubtful. This is Descartes' position at AT VII 146, 460, 477; V 178: CSM II 104, 309, 321; CSMK 353).

21 Descartes writes, however, of the supposition that clear and distinct perception "from time to time" leads to error (AT VII 70, 428: CSM II 48, 289), that "the way I am made makes me prone to frequent error" (AT VII 70: CSM II 48). In the First Meditation, by contrast, the skeptical supposition is explicitly that one is deceived "all the time" (AT VII 21: CSM II 14). (The Haldane and Ross translations of the first and third of these passages obscure the Latin; see E. S. Haldane and G. R. T. Ross, *The Philosophical Works of Descartes* (Cambridge University Press, 1911, repr. 1970), Vol I, pp. 184 and 147, respectively.). For previous discussion of the contrast, see Gouhier *La pensée métaphysique de Descartes* pp. 301–2. It is controversial whether the scope of the skeptical supposition in the First Meditation extends beyond sense-perception (cf. Frankfurt, *Demons*, esp. chs. 7–8). Even if it does not, we should expect

that if Descartes subjects sense-perception to the supposition that it is systematically defective, he is obliged to subject clear and distinct perception to the analogous supposition. It is surprisingly difficult to find explicit textual evidence that he does so. For additional disanalogies between the skeptical suppositions in the First and Second Meditations, see Loeb, "Is there radical dissimulation in Descartes' Meditations?", pp. 247–53.

22 Cf. Etchemendy, "The Cartesian Circle," p. 8; and Cottingham, *Descartes*, pp. 70, 77, n. 24. The technique would also sacrifice the objective of achieving a comprehensive system of beliefs (cf. AT X 371–2; IXB 2–3: CSM I 16, 179–80).

23 There is a related passage in the Third Meditation: "The only reason for my later judgement that they [simple propositions of mathematics] were open to doubt was that it occurred to me that perhaps some God could have given me a nature such that I was deceived even in matters which seemed most evident" (AT VII 35–6: CSM II 25). Beliefs based on clear and distinct perception are doubtful *only* insofar as they are held by someone who does not have knowledge of the truth rule; such knowledge is sufficient to remove doubt. If doubt is not only able to dislodge belief, but also necessary for belief to be dislodged, then this passage is equivalent to the claim that knowledge of the truth rule is sufficient for unshakability.

24 In the letter to Regius, Descartes claims that a demonstration *of the existence of a nondeceiving God* is sufficient to secure unshakability. This should be understood against the background of the passages from the Fifth Meditation and the Second Replies; such a demonstration is sufficient insofar as it enables one to demonstrate the truth rule.

25 One might believe on the basis of some inductive evidence that the proposition had been clearly and distinctly perceived.

26 Descartes is considering the unshakability of beliefs that one remembers having clearly and distinctly perceived, on the assumption that the memory is correct. Cf. Frankfurt, "Memory and the Cartesian Circle," pp. 510–11; *Demons*, pp. 160–1; and Bennett, "Truth and stability," §§ 7, 12. Descartes does not directly confront the question of whether the unshakability of the memory belief that one did clearly and distinctly perceive the proposition can itself be secured. I believe there are difficulties here for any interpretation of Descartes, irrespective of whether "scientific knowledge" is conceived psychologically or epistemically.

27 Alternatively, knowledge of the truth rule, though compatible with the skeptical supposition, defeats the ability of the skeptical supposition to dislodge recollected clear and distinct perceptions. It will become apparent that Descartes does not envision this alternative.

28 Rubin has noted that this passage confirms the psychological interpretation ("Descartes's validation," p. 205).

29 In requiring that "the truth rule must be gone through in a single intellectual sweep, all held before the mind at once" ("Truth and stability" § 9), Bennett overlooks Descartes' application of the doctrine of the irresistibility of clear and distinct perception to attending to a demonstration. It is the memory interpretation that exerts pressure in the direction of the requirement that a clear and distinct perception of the truth rule be compressed into a momentary intuition – a demonstration of the truth rule relies on memory of the earlier steps, and therefore apparently could not be invoked to validate memory. Cf. Stout, "The basis of knowledge in Descartes," esp. pp. 463–7; Doney, "The Cartesian Circle," pp. 328–9; Frankfurt, "Memory and the Cartesian Circle," pp. 508–9, and *Demons, Dreamers, and Madmen*, pp. 158–9.

30 Cf. Feldman and Levidson, "Anthony Kenny and the Cartesian Circle," p. 496. Rubin overlooks this point ("Descartes's validation of clear and distinct perception," pp. 206–8).

31 Cf. Parsons, "Review of Frankfurt," p. 40; and Garns, "Descartes and indubitability," p. 89. Van Cleve ("Foundationalism," n. 31) and Bennett ("Truth and stability," § 9) suggest that this represents Descartes' position. I do not see how this suggestion can accommodate the texts I proceed to cite.

32 For discussions of the bearing of this claim on the problem of the Cartesian Circle, see Doney, "Descartes's conception of perfect knowledge," esp. pp. 393–6; Frankfurt, *Demons, Dreamers, and Madmen*, pp. 159–60, 172–7; Parsons, "Review of Frankfurt," pp. 40–1, 43; Curley, *Descartes against the Skeptics*, pp. 104ff.; Gombay, "Mental conflict," pp. 495–7; Etchemendy, "The Cartesian Circle," pp. 11–12, 18–19, 34–5; and Garns, "Descartes and indubitability," pp. 88–9.

33 There is one apparent difference (apart from that discussed at note 24). Descartes claims in the Fifth Meditation that beliefs based on clear and distinct perception are unshakable, provided one recollects having clearly and distinctly perceived the truth rule; the proviso in the letter to Regius is that one recollect this "conclusion" (AT III 65: CSMK 147) – not that one recollect having clearly and distinctly perceived the truth rule. Descartes writes in the Second Replies: "The question will now arise as to whether we possess the same firm and immutable conviction concerning these conclusions, where we simply recollect that they were previously deduced from quite evident principles (our ability to call them 'conclusions' presupposes such a recollection)" (AT VII 146: CSM II 104). If we apply the parenthetical principle to the proviso in the letter to Regius, it is equivalent to the proviso in the Fifth Meditation.

34 Observing that "the skeptic . . . cannot doubt [the existence and benevo-
    lence of God] while he intuits the proofs of it," Williams addresses the
    possibility that "the skeptic, ceasing to intuit the proofs, then reverts to
    objecting merely because he is no longer intuiting": "[T]he use of propo-
    sitions one is not at that instant intuiting is a minimal structural condi-
    tion on getting on at all in the acquisition of systematic knowledge,
    and . . . it would be unreasonable to spend all one's time rehearsing the
    proofs of the general answer to skepticism" ("Descartes' use of skepti-
    cism", p. 349, and cf. p. 352, n. 13; cf. *Descartes*, p. 206). Unshakability
    plays no essential role in Williams' interpretation. It would be necessary
    to use previous clear and distinct perceptions for acquiring systematic
    knowledge whether unshakability is a goal of inquiry or not. Also, be-
    liefs that are "cumulative" ("Descartes' use of skepticism," p. 345; *Des-
    cartes*, p. 202) and systematic could be dislodged by the skeptical suppo-
    sition. Although Williams holds that scientific knowledge should be
    unshakable in the sense of "immune to being recalled into doubt" ("Des-
    cartes' use," p. 349, and cf. pp. 344, 345; cf. *Descartes*, pp. 202, 204), he
    does not explain how unshakability (as he has characterized it) can be
    achieved, or even how the "minimal structural condition" can be satis-
    fied in the case of the truth rule. According to Williams, the skeptic is
    enjoined to continue to use or accept (cf. *Descartes*, pp. 200–6) the truth
    rule when it is a recollected clear and distinct perception. Belief in the
    truth rule, as distinct from irresistible belief in the truth rule, is compati-
    ble with the skeptical supposition, a supposition that can dislodge recol-
    lected clear and distinct perceptions, to include the truth rule itself. For
    a useful exposition and critique of Williams, see Stubbs, "Bernard Wil-
    liams and the Cartesian Circle."

35 Of the commentators cited in note 11, only Gombay (p. 492) is sensitive
    to this distinction. Bennett's notion of "stability" is akin to unshakabil-
    ity in the strong sense: belief "that one won't later be forced to give up"
    ("Truth and Stability," § 1).

36 Haldane and Ross (see note 21 above), Vol. I, p. 184, do not translate the
    material from the French edition.

37 The second passage, in the letter to Regius, is susceptible to the same
    treatment: "There is conviction when there remains some reason which
    might lead [*impellere*] us to doubt, but scientific knowledge is convic-
    tion based on argument so strong that it can never be shaken by any
    stronger argument" (AT III 65: cf. CSMK 147). Here too, we can under-
    stand *impellere* in the sense of "to force."

38 Garns speculates ("Descartes and indubitability," p. 97) that Descartes
    intends that whenever a meditator who has demonstrated the existence
    of a nondeceiving God and internalized the rules of Cartesian method

considers the notion of God, or an omnipotent being, or the source of his being, he will automatically recall the proof that this being is a non-deceiver (pp. 98–9). (Garns does not embed this suggestion within the psychological interpretation. He endorses a nonpsychological solution to the problem of the circle–cf. pp. 87–8.) Garns takes this position to be unsuccessful because it ignores the hypothesis that there exists an evil demon (pp. 97–9) – the notion of an evil demon would not automatically trigger the proof of the existence of a nondeceiving God (p. 99). This consideration is not compelling. The demon hypothesis places clear and distinct perception in doubt only if one supposes that the demon is "evil" in the sense of causing one to have a defective faculty of clear and distinct perception. Why not say, in the spirit of Garns's speculation, that Descartes holds that *this* supposition automatically leads one to recall the proof that clear and distinct perception is not defective? A more serious difficulty is that Descartes nowhere maintains that there are circumstances in which the consideration of appropriately related propositions or notions automatically triggers reproduction of a given demonstration. Laporte, citing the penultimate paragraph of the Fourth Meditation, holds a weaker version of the position: by "attentive and repeated meditation" (AT VII 62: CSM II 43), a Cartesian meditator can habituate himself to remember the conclusion that God is no deceiver in order to check the skeptical supposition (*Le rationalisme de Descartes*, p. 161). If the truth rule is merely a recollected theorem, however, it will not be psychologically irresistible, and will not suffice to block the skeptical supposition.

39 Etchemendy considers a strengthened version of the reproducibility account, on which *our knowledge that* we have the ability to reproduce the demonstration of the truth rule (rather than our merely having the ability) protects us from metaphysical doubt. Etchemendy then rejects this position, appealing to an argument designed to show that such knowledge would be otiose (cf. "The Cartesian Circle", p. 19). An adaptation of his argument suggests that the ability to reproduce the demonstration of the truth rule would itself be otiose: if the ability to reproduce the demonstration of the truth rule secures unshakability, then the ability to reproduce the demonstration of any proposition that we recollect having clearly and distinctly perceived would equally secure that proposition's unshakability. This overlooks the point that Descartes seeks to secure, insofar as humanly possible, the (concurrent) unshakability of *all* recollected clear and distinct perceptions. In the absence of the ability to reproduce the demonstration of the truth rule, such unshakability can be achieved only if one has the ability (i) to reproduce the demonstrations of *every* recollected clear and distinct perception, and (ii) to do so *concurrently*. The human mind's finite capacity – as Etchemendy should grant (cf. p. 8) – is

incompatible with (ii). Also, for reasons just explained in the text, (i) is a much more burdensome condition than that required by the reproducibility account (See also pp. 219–20, above).

40 Haldane and Ross translate a portion of *Principles*, Part I, art. 13: "But since it cannot always devote this attention to them [when it remembers the conclusion and yet cannot *recollect* the order of its deduction], and conceives that it may have been created of such a nature that it has been deceived even in what is most evident, it sees clearly that it has great cause to doubt the truth of such conclusions" (op. cit. at note 21, above, Vol. I, p. 224; emphasis added). They translate a portion of the Fifth Meditation: "As I often recollect having formed a past judgment without at the same time properly *recollecting* the reasons that led me to make it, it may happen meanwhile that other reasons present themselves to me, which would easily cause me to change my opinion" (vol. I, p. 183; emphasis added). The language of remembering a conclusion without recollecting its demonstration suggests that the demonstration has been forgotten, that Descartes is envisioning situation (i). In the first passage, the bracketed material renders the French: "*sans prendre garde à l'ordre dont elle peut etre demontrée*" (AT IXB 30–1). In the seoncd passage, the Latin verb is *attendere* (AT VII 69). Neither text carries any suggestion that the demonstration has been forgotten. Tlumak is mistaken in his claim that "Descartes repeatedly insists that, once the existence of a good God . . . is acknowledged, we are certain of the conclusion of a proof we correctly remember having clearly and distinctly perceived, even though we cannot reproduce its premises" ("Certainty and Cartesian method," p. 49). Descartes says this at most once, in the Second Replies.

41 The reproducibility account can be generalized: if the ability to *re*produce the demonstration of the truth rule is sufficient for unshakability, the ability to *produce* a demonstration of the truth rule ought to be sufficient for unshakability. Descartes nowhere claims that a (current or previous) demonstration of the truth rule is *necessary* for unshakability. He does say that "firm and immutable conviction concerning" recollected clear and distinct perceptions "is indeed possessed by those whose knowledge of God enables them to understand that the intellectual faculty which he gave them cannot but tend towards the truth" (AT VII 146: CSM II 104–5: HR II 42–3). Unshakability requires the ability to demonstrate the truth rule, not that the truth rule has been demonstrated.

42 "Could" – rather than would – for reasons that emerge below: immutability, unlike unshakability, is a continuing property of a belief.

43 Gombay – the only commentator I know who attempts to distinguish firmness and immutability – identifies immutability, rather than firm-

ness, with unshakability (cf. "Mental conflict," pp. 492–4, 498–500). I do not see how this interpretation can accommodate the evidence from the Second Replies and the *Search* cited in my earlier discussion of the firmness metaphor.

44 Distinctions between basic and nonbasic propositions, between various objectives of inquiry, and between various kinds of forgetfulness are necessary in order to evaluate whether nonforgetfulness is, for Descartes, itself an objective of inquiry, or a requirement for scientific knowledge. There is an additional case: (d) one might have forgotten the demonstration of *p* by *t'*. Since this reduces to case (c) if *p* is a basic proposition, I restrict (d) to propositions that are not basic. In case (d), the memory loss does not preclude continuing unshakability through time *t'*. In cases (a–c), the memory loss does preclude continuing unshakability through time *t'*. In cases (a–d), the memory loss is compatible with the unshakability of the belief that *p* at the earlier time *t*. As far as I can see, only in case (a) is the memory losss automatically incompatible with the permanence of the belief that *p*. For previous discussions of forgetfulness, see Feldman and Levison, "Anthony Kenny and the Cartesian Circle," p. 496; Kenny, "A reply to Feldman and Levison," p. 498; Tlumak, "Certainty and Cartesian method," p. 49; and Markie, *Descartes's Gambit*, pp. 65–9.

45 Perhaps some forgetfulness of the sort in cases (a) or (b) *is* intrinsic to human nature. This does not show that continued unshakability *for the greater part of those beliefs that were once clearly and distinctly perceived* is an unrealistic goal; it is only unrealistic for individuals who have systematic failures of memory, a condition that is not intrinsic to human nature. Cases (a) and (b) are incompatible with the continued unshakability specifically of the proposition *p* in question. It is case (c) alone that is incompatible with the continued unshakability of *any* belief, but it is humanly possible to remember the demonstration of the truth rule. This point undermines an objection that Feldman and Levison ("Anthony Kenny and the Cartesian Circle," p. 496, third paragraph) direct at Kenny.

46 I assume that a mere disposition to suppose that the skeptical hypothesis is true would not be sufficient to dislodge occurent recollected clear and distinct perceptions; in order to do so, the supposition would have to be occurrent. Cf. Descartes' language at AT VII 25: CSM II 25.

47 Cf. Laporte, *Le rationalisme de Descartes*, p. 161; Larmore, "Descartes' psychologistic theory of assent," p. 71; Cottingham, *Descartes*, p. 72; and Garns, "Descartes and indubitability," pp. 98–9.

48 Cf. Rubin, "Descartes's validation," p. 208; Williams, *Descartes*, p.

207; Gombay, "Mental conflict," p. 495; and Bennett, "Truth and stability," § 13.

49 I defend the attribution to Descartes of these doctrines in "The priority of reason in Descartes," §§ 2–3.

50 It would also lack comprehensiveness (cf. n. 22).

51 Cf. Gewirth, "The Cartesian Circle," p. 379; Frankfurt, "Descartes' validation of reason," p. 153, and Demons, Dreamers, and Madmen, pp. 170–1; Wilson, Descartes, p. 133; and Markie, Descartes's Gambit, p. 44.

52 I do not see how Markie can claim that there is "no textual support" for "purely psychological accounts of how reasons for doubt are ruled out" (Descartes's Gambit, p. 44).

53 Cf. Rubin, "Descartes's validation," pp. 197–8; and Loeb, "The priority of reason," § 6. Some passages that, in translation, seem to require an epistemic intepretation, are susceptible to alternative translations that are more hospitable to the psychological interpretation. Such passages can be accommodated without recourse to the strategy I have outlined; on this point, cf. n. 10.

54 Cf. Larmore, "Descartes' psychologistic theory of assent," pp. 61–2.

55 For some attempted explanations, see Kenny, Descartes, p. 185; Doney, "Descartes's conception of perfect knowledge," pp. 399–400; Frankfurt, Demons, Dreamers, and Madmen, p. 164; and Loeb, "The priority of reason," § 4. An adequate explanation would play a rôle in a more complete assessment of the merit of the psychological interpretation of Descartes' position on the problem of the circle.

56 Cf. Loeb, "The priority of reason," esp. §§ 1–6.

57 For a more developed version of the themes in this paragraph, cf. Loeb, "The priority of reason," § 7.

58 Cf. Hume's Treatise, pp. 8, 31, 153, 225.

59 I thank Jonathan Bennett for access to a draft of his "Truth and stability" prior to its publication. I am grateful to Paul Boghossian, Richard Brandt, Stephen Darwall, Allan Gibbard, Gideon Rosen, Lawrence Sklar, William Taschek, David Velleman, Nichols White, and Stephen Yablo for helpful discussion. I am especially grateful to John Cottingham for detailed written comments and suggestions. Finally, it should be noted that although the editor of the present volume has, throughout, provided standardized references to CSM and CSMK, the actual wording in the quotations from the letter to Regius (pp. 202, 203, and 231, above) is taken from A. Kenny (ed.), Descartes, Philosophical Letters (Oxford: Clarendon, 1970), p. 74. Kenny's translation was incorporated in its entirety into CSMK, but with some modifications; CSMK had not appeared when the present chapter was completed.

8   Cartesian dualism: theology, metaphysics, and science

Throughout his life Descartes firmly believed that the mind, or soul, of man (he made no distinction between the two terms)[1] was essentially nonphysical. In his earliest major work, the *Regulae* (c.1628), he declared that "the power through which we know things in the strict sense is purely spiritual, and is no less distinct from the whole body than blood is distinct from bone, or the hand from the eye" (AT X 415: CSM I 42). In his last work, the *Passions de l'âme* (1649), he observed that the soul, although 'joined' or 'united' to the "whole assemblage of bodily organs" during life, is "of such a nature that it has no relation to extension, or to the dimensions or other properties of the matter of which the body is composed" (AT XI 351: CSM I 339). And between these chronological extremes we have the central claim of the *Meditations* (1641): there is a 'real' (*realis*) distinction between the mind and body; in other words, the mind is a distinct and independent 'thing' (*res*).[2] The thinking thing that is 'me' is "really distinct from the body and can exist without it" (AT VII 78: CSM II 54).

The message appears to be all of a piece. The thesis of the incorporeality of the mind seems, from first to last, a fixed point in Descartes' thinking. Indeed the now widespread adoption of the label 'Cartesian dualism' to refer to the incorporeality thesis has had the effect of making that thesis the very hallmark of Descartes' philosophy. Yet though it is undeniable that Descartes did repeatedly assert the incorporeality thesis, his reasons for subscribing to it were by no means homogeneous. This chapter will look at three quite distinct types of consideration that motivated Descartes 'dualism', namely the theological, the metaphysical and the scientific. It will be argued that there is a certain harmony between the first and second of these

236

strands, even though the relation between them is certainly not one of mutual entailment. Between the second and third strands, by contrast, it will be suggested that there is a certain kind of tension; for whereas Descartes' metaphysical arguments seem designed to rule out even the possibility that dualism might be false, in what may be called his 'scientific' discussions of the nature of the mind, the tone is far less dogmatic, and the outcome far more sensitive to empirical evidence, than the standard expositions of 'Cartesian dualism' normally allow.

THEOLOGY: FROM FAITH TO REASON

Informal soundings of people's views nowadays regarding the incorporeality thesis suggest a tendency to divide along religious lines: committed theists are more likely to be dualists. One important reason for this may have to do with the doctrine of the afterlife, which seems to many to require that that which survives death, the bearer of personality and consciousness, be some kind of incorporeal soul. Was this assumption part of the seventeenth-century background?

Certainly Descartes himself, in his published work, underlined the connection between religious belief and dualism. The Dedicatory letter to the Theology Faculty of the Sorbonne, which was prefixed to the first edition of the *Meditations*, notes that the faithful are obliged to accept that "the human soul does not die with the body" and suggests that a demonstration of this claim by 'natural reason' would serve the cause of religion and combat atheism (AT VII 3; CSM II 4). Although Descartes had a personal interest in promoting his book by obtaining the approbation of the theologians, it would be wrong to dismiss as a mere specious afterthought his professed religious motivation for writing on mind–body metaphysics. For the same motivation is expressed in private correspondence, as early as 1630, when Descartes had recently begun work on the so-called *Petit Traité* – a short treatise on metaphysics (now lost), which was designed amongst other things to combat those "audacious and impudent persons who would fight against God," by establishing the "existence of our souls when they are separate from the body" (letter to Mersenne, 25 November 1630: AT I 182: CSMK 29).

Clearly, in the seventeenth century, as now, any defender of orthodox Christianity is obliged to defend the doctrine of the immortality of the soul. What is not so clear, however, is that this doctrine in turn requires the truth of dualism. Despite Descartes' insistence on the links between his own metaphysics and the teachings of the Church, the mainstream of orthodox religious teaching certainly did not specify that the bearer of post-mortem consciousness should be an unextended, nonspatial *res cogitans* of the kind envisaged by Descartes; on the contrary, one influential strand in the Christian tradition saw the afterlife in terms of the existence of some kind of new, 'resurrection' body – not, to be sure, this earthly coil of flesh and blood but for all that something having some kind of materiality.[3] If we scrutinize it carefully, however, Descartes' claim is not that his brand of dualism is necessary for the immortality of the soul, but that it is *sufficient* to establish it: the aim of the *Petit Traité* was to establish 'the independence of our souls from our bodies, from which their immortality follows' (*d'où suit leur immortalité*; letter to Mersenne, loc. cit.).

The logic of this last clause evidently worried Father Mersenne, and he chose to voice his doubts in public some ten years later, when compiling the second set of Objections to the *Meditations*. To establish the incorporeality of the soul, he complained, is not *eo ipso* to establish its immortality; God might, for example, have endowed it with "just so much strength and existence as to ensure that it came to an end with the death of the body" (AT VII 128: CSM II 91). In his reply Descartes now admitted that he could not supply a cast iron proof of the soul's immortality. But he urged that we have "no convincing evidence or precedent" to suggest that the annihilation of a substance like the mind can result from "such a trivial cause" as bodily death, which is simply a matter of a "division or change of shape" in the parts of the body (AT VII 153: CSM II 109).

Underlying these cryptic comments we can glimpse something of the gulf that separates Descartes' metaphysics from the ideas of his scholastic predecessors. In the Aristotelian conception of the soul, which is never far beneath the surface of scholastic doctrine, there is an integral connection between soul and body. Soul is to body as form is to matter; and what this means, in effect, is that a given set of functions (locomotion, digestion, sensation) depends on the relevant parts of the body being 'informed' or organized in a certain fashion. One result of this Aristotelian picture is that there is a kind of continuity between all living things. Plants, animals and man, all

things which are alive or 'ensouled' (*empsychos*), belong on a contin-
uum, where matter is progressively organised in a hierarchy, with
each function higher up the chain presupposing those functions
which operate on a lower level.⁴ In a purely mechanical Cartesian
universe, by contrast, there is an important sense in which there is
no real difference between 'living' and 'dead' matter. "The matter
existing in the entire universe is one and the same," Descartes wrote
in the *Principles of Philosophy*, 'and it is always recognised as matter simply in virtue of its being extended (Part II, art. 23: AT VIIIA
52: CSM I 232). It is thus a serious error, on Descartes' view, to
suppose that bodily death is somehow caused by the absence of
'soul.' As he explained in the *Passions of the Soul*:

Death never occurs through the absence of soul, but only because one of the
the principal parts of the body decays . . . The difference between the body of
a living man and that of a dead man is just like the difference between, on
the one hand, a watch or other automaton (i.e. a self-moving machine) when
it is wound-up and contains within itself the corporeal principle of the
movements for which it is designed, together with everything else required
for its operation; and, on the other hand, the same watch or machine when
it is broken, and the principle of its movement ceases to be active.

(AT XI 331: CSM I 329)

When this purely mechanical view of biology is combined with
Descartes' thesis that the conscious mind is a separate incorporeal
substance, the upshot is that bodily death becomes, in a sense,
wholly irrelevant to the question of personal immortality. Descartes
makes the point quite explicitly in the Synopsis to the *Meditations*:

The human body, in so far as it differs from other bodies, is simply made up
of a certain configuration of limbs and other accidents of this sort; whereas
the human mind is not made up of any accidents in this way, but is a pure
substance. For even if all the accidents of the mind change, so that it has
different objects of the understanding and different desires and sensations, it
does not on that account become a different mind; whereas the human body
loses its identity merely as a result of a change in the shape of some of its
parts. And it follows from this that while the body can very easily perish,
the mind is immortal by its very nature.   (AT VII 14: CSM II 10)

The argument is still not quite watertight; it needs the additional
metaphysical premise that a substance, once created by God, is "by
its nature incorruptible and cannot ever cease to exist unless reduced

to nothingness by God's denying his concurrence to it" (ibid.).[5] Yet even when this additional premise is plugged in, the 'unless' clause at the end still leaves the argument a shade short of qualifying as a completely rigorous demonstration. There is, to be sure, a strong presumption that a substance, once created, will continue to exist; but this, Descartes reminds us, must ultimately depend on the efficacious will of God, and we cannot know for certain what he has planned for the soul after death.[6] This caveat – coupled with his enduring reluctance to tread on the toes of the theologians – explains why, when questioned on the soul's immortality, Descartes generally stepped back from any claim to provide a logically compelling proof of the matter.[7]

These qualifications notwithstanding, Descartes could still plausibly claim that his own metaphysical system stood on much firmer ground than scholastic metaphysics when it came to the problem of reconciling natural philosophy with the requirements of the Christian faith. The scholastics were faced with a *prima facie* problem about the immortality of the soul. If the Aristotelian 'hylemorphic' ('materio-formal') account of *psyche* is adhered to, then it is not easy to see how a given psychic function, such as thought, can possibly survive in the absence of a material substrate. Admittedly Aristotle himself had, in one notoriously obscure passage in the *De Anima*, introduced the concept of an 'active intellect' which, being defined in terms of pure activity, was supposed to be capable of some kind of 'separation' from the body; but as the Church's struggle with the heretical followers of Averroes later demonstrated, this strange notion hardly provided unambiguous support for anything like the concept of an individual personal consciousness capable of surviving death.[8] The fact remained that the Aristotelian system, on its most natural and plausible interpretation, no more allowed for souls apart from bodies than (to use Aristotle's own analogies) it allowed for sight apart from the eye, or an axe's function of chopping wood to exist apart from the materials that make up its blade. Faced with this difficulty, many theologians were tempted to assert that personal immortality was a doctrine that could not be defended by human reason, but had to be based on faith alone.[9] Against this background, Descartes – and there is no good reason to doubt his sincerity here – saw his own philosophy as breaking new ground.[10] The theologians could now be offered a metaphysic in which con-

sciousness was a *sui generis* phenomenon, wholly detached from
corporeal events of any kind, and therefore inherently immune to
the effects of bodily dissolution. In providing, as he thought he
could, a philosophical demonstration of the incorporeality of the
mind, Descartes thus explicitly saw himself as fulfilling the edict of
the Lateran council, that Christian philosophers should use all the
powers of human reason to establish the truth of the soul's immortality (AT VII 3: CSM II 4).

There is, however, one further twist to the story. What is 'pure'
and incorporeal, in Descartes' account of the mind, is intellection
and volition, not sensation or imagination. The latter faculties are
not part of our essence as thinking things (AT VII 73: CSM II 51);
they are, as Descartes frequently stresses, 'special' modes of consciousness which depend on the soul's union with the body.[11] But
what this seems to entail is something which Descartes himself
never discusses but which occupied the earnest attention of Cartesian disciples like Louis de la Forge later in the century: after bodily
death, when the soul is disunited, its cognition will be devoid of all
particularity. When sensible ideas and images fade, the soul will be
left to contemplate merely abstract and general ideas such as those
of mathematics. And this in turn makes it hard to see how any real
personality or individuality could be preserved. Just as the Thomists
had earlier wrestled with the problem of what differentiates one
angel from another, so the later Cartesians were in trouble explaining how one impersonal, disembodied *res cogitans* could be distinct
from another. In the end, the ghost of Averroës, which had plagued
the scholastics, returned to haunt the Cartesians.[12]

METAPHYSICS: THE RECURRING FALLACY

We cannot know what proofs of the incorporeality thesis Descartes
envisaged in his early 'Little Treatise' on metaphysics. In the *Regulae*
of 1628 he merely affirms the incorporeal nature of the power of
thought, observing that 'nothing like this power is to be found in
bodily things' (AT X 415: CSM I 42); and in his 'Treatise on Man'
composed during the years 1629–30 as part of his general exposition
of physics, *Le Monde*, he largely confines himself to a physiological
account of the mechanisms of the central nervous system, simply

asserting that God unites a rational soul (*une âme raisonable*) to the bodily machine, placing its principal seat (*son siège principal*) in the brain, and endowing it with such a nature that it is adapted to have a whole range of sensations corresponding, one for one, to the different ways in which the brain is stimulated via the nerves (AT XI 143: CSM I 102). It was not until his first published work that he ventured to offer a sketch of how the non-physical nature of the soul might be established. In a letter written to Jean de Silhon in May 1637, on the eve of the publication of the *Discours de la Méthode,* he sums up his approach as follows: "a man who doubts everything material cannot for all that doubt his own existence. From this it follows (*il suit*) that he, that is his soul, is a being or substance which is not at all corporeal (*point du tout corporelle*), but whose nature is solely to think (*sa nature n'est que de penser*), and that this is the first thing, one can know with certainty" (AT I 353: CSMK 55).[13]

The wording here closely matches the famous passage in Part IV of the *Discourse,* where, in what is, or ought to be, regarded as one of the most notorious nonsequiturs in the history of philosophy, Descartes moves from the proposition that he can doubt the existence of his body to the conclusion that he can exist without his body – that he is a being "which does not require any place, or depend on any material thing, in order to exist" (AT VI 33: CSM I 127). Even when writing to Silhon, Descartes admitted that his argument was not as accessible as it might be: to make it fully convincing, he says, he "would have had to explain at length the strongest arguments of the sceptics to show that there is no material thing of whose existence one can be certain" (loc. cit.).

But the difficulty in the argument is, of course, not just that the 'method of doubt' is not made vivid enough to carry the reader along. That defect Descartes was amply to make good later in the dramatic monologue of the First Meditation. What remains is the logical flaw which was immediately fastened on by an astute contemporary critic of the *Discourse:*

From the fact that the human mind, when directed towards itself, does not perceive itself to be anything other than a thinking thing, how does it follow that its nature or essence consists only in its being a thinking thing, where the word 'only' (*tantum*) excludes everything else that could be said to belong to the nature of the soul?   (AT VII 8: CSM II 7)

Quoting this objection in the Synopsis to the *Meditations*, Descartes admits that he needs to justify the move from 'I am not aware of anything belonging to my essence except thought' to 'nothing in fact belongs to my essence except thought'. Yet, almost perversely, he apparently proceeds to repeat the same unsatisfactory move in the Second Meditation: "What is this 'I' that I know?," asks the meditator; "I am in the strict sense only a thing that thinks, that is, I am a mind or intelligence or intellect or reason" (*sum precise tantum res cogitans, id est mens, sive animus, sive intellectus, sive ratio*, AT VII 27: CSM II 18).

When he was asked about this passage some years later, by Gassendi, Descartes insisted that the qualifier 'only' (*tantum*) was supposed to go with 'in the strict sense' (*praecise*), not with 'a thing that thinks' (*res cogitans*). In other words, he did not mean to assert that he was *only* a thinking thing, and nothing else; the claim was the more modest one that he was 'in the strict sense only' a thinking thing (AT IXA 215: CSM II 276).[14] But what does this 'strict sense' come down to? Descartes cannot avoid admitting that, for all the meditator in the Second Meditation knows, the 'thinking thing' he is aware of might well be a corporeal being of some kind; his ability to doubt the existence of corporeal objects is quite compatible with the possibility that what is *doing* the doubting is after all, something essentially embodied.

In his reply to Gassendi, Descartes angrily insisted that he had acknowledged just this possibility in the Second Meditation: "I showed that by the words 'in the strict sense only' I did not mean an entire exclusion or negation, but only an abstraction from material things; for I said that in spite of this we are not sure that there is nothing corporeal in the soul, even though we do not recognise anything corporeal in it" (AT IXA 215: CSM II 276). This seems at least partly disingenuous. Admittedly, Descartes had in the Second Meditation raised the possibility that the material things he had imagined not to exist might be identical with the 'thinking thing' of which he was aware: '*fortassis contingit ut haec ipsa, quae suppono nihil esse . . . in rei veritate non differant ab eo me quem novi*' (AT VII 27: CSM II 18, lines 29–31). But although this possibility is initially left hanging in the air, by the end of the paragraph Descartes seems effectively to have ruled it out: no corporeal object which the imagination can conceive is relevant to my awareness of myself, and hence 'the mind must be most carefully diverted from such things if it is to perceive its own nature as distinctly as possible' (AT VII 28: CSM II 19). Whatever Descartes later said to Gassendi, it is hard to avoid reading this passage as subtly insinuating that any attempt to identify the mind's nature with something material would be radically misconceived. If, however, we delete this insinuation, then all that Descartes' talk of a 'precise' or 'strict' way of speaking can logically boil down to is the unexciting assertion that the meditator can arrive at *some* kind of conception of himself as an isolated, disembodied doubter.

There seem to be two possible interpretations of what is going on here. On the uncharitable interpretation, Descartes initially just failed to see the flawed nature of the move from "I can doubt I have a body" to "the body is not essential to me," and, having boldly run this flag up the masthead in the *Discourse,* could not quite bring himself to haul it down and jettison it. On the more charitable interpretation, he is quite clear that his subjective awareness of himself as a disembodied doubter is no more than that – a piece of subjective awareness – and that all the work still remains to be done to establish that the conception so arrived at does indeed match the nature of reality. The more charitable version is hard to square with the passages in the Second Meditation already cited, and above all with the texts quoted above from the letter to Silhon and the *Discourse,* where no amount of varnish seems enough to cover the glaring paralogism. But the kinder view is supported by other passages, including one in as early a text as the *Regulae,* where Descartes makes a quite explicit distinction between subjective cognition and essential reality, and readily and frankly admits that "when we consider things in the order that corresponds to our awareness of them" (*in ordine ad cognitionem nostram*), our view of them may be different from what it would be if we were speaking of them "in accordance with how they exist in reality" (*prout re vera existunt,* AT X 418: CSM 1 44).[15] So a defender of Descartes has some case for accepting the protestation in the *Synopsis* that, when he excluded body from his essence, Descartes did not mean to make the exclusion "in an order corresponding to the actual truth of the matter" (*in ordine ad ipsam rei veritatem*), but only in an order corresponding to his own perception (*in ordine and meam perceptionem,* AT VII 8: CSM II 7).

But even to interpret Descartes charitably in this respect is of course very far from vindicating his metaphysical arguments for dualism. The gap between subjective cognition and objective reality, once acknowledged, is not easily closed; and though Descartes does at least attempt to close it – most notably in the argument from divinely guaranteed clear and distinct perceptions in the Sixth Meditation – it is familiar ground, and was so even in the seventeenth century, that his argument is highly vulnerable. The most notorious pitfall is Arnauld's circle: The gap between subjective cognition and essential reality is bridged by proving God's existence; yet the proof itself depends on the reliability of just that subjective cognition which needs to be validated. But even *granting* the divinely underwritten reliability of the intellect, there is a second trap (which again Arnauld was the first to highlight): my ability clearly to perceive X apart from Y (e.g. mind apart from body) cannot, since my intellect is limited, rule out the possibility that there is a chain of necessary connections, *unperceived* by me, which would reveal that Y is after all essential to X.[16]

That Descartes' metaphysical manoeuvres fail to provide a plausible defence of the incorporeality thesis is hardly a new complaint. What is interesting is that Descartes' confidence in that thesis was entirely unshaken by the telling criticisms to which his arguments were repeatedly subjected, by Arnauld and many others.[17] It is almost as if he felt that, irrespective of whether his metaphysical demonstrations could be shored up, there were still solid, and quite independent considerations for insisting on the incorporeal nature of the mind. These considerations are hinted at in his earlier work on physiology and articulated with considerable force in the scientific section of the *Discourse*. It is to this quite distinct 'scientific' strand in Cartesian dualism that we must now turn.

DESCARTES' SCIENCE OF THE MIND: THE DISAPPEARING SOUL

In Descartes' early work on the nature of man, what is striking is not the use made of the term 'soul' but the extent to which appeals to the soul are declared to be redundant. A radical mechanistic reductionism pervades the *Traité de l'homme* composed in the early 1630s, and a whole range of human activities are ascribed to the

operations of a self-moving machine which, like a "clock or an artificial fountain or mill" (*horlorge, fontaine artificielle, moulin*), has
the power (*la force*) to operate purely in accordance with its own
internal principles, depending solely on the disposition of the relevant organs (*la disposition des organes*) (AT XI 120: CSM I 99).
Descartes proudly, and provocatively, declares that it is not necessary to posit any "sensitive or vegetative soul" or other principle of
life apart from the internal fire of the heart – a fire which has the
same nature as the fires to be found elsewhere in inanimate objects:
*il ne faut point . . . concevoir en elle aucune autre âme végétative,
ni sensitive, ni aucun autre principe de mouvement et de vie
que . . . la chaleur du feu qui brûle continuellement dans son coeur,
et qui n'est point d'autre nature que tous les feux qui sont dans les
corps inanimés* (AT XI 202: CSM I 108).

The list of functions to be explained in this way, without any
reference to soul, is highly ambitious. It comprises:

digestion of food, the beating of the heart and arteries, the nourishment and
growth of the limbs, respiration, waking and sleeping, the reception by the
external sense organs of light, sounds, smells, tastes, heat and other such
qualities, the imprinting of ideas of these qualities in the organ of the 'common' sense and the imagination, the retention or stamping of these ideas in
the memory, the internal movements of the appetites and passions, and
finally the external movements of all the limbs which aptly follow (*suivrent
à propos*) both the actions and objects presented to the senses and also the
passions and impressions found in the memory.   (ibid.)

The remarkable thing about this list is how far it goes beyond what
we might think of as 'pure physiology'. What we declared to be
capable of mechanistic explanation are not just functions belonging
to the autonomic nervous system such as respiration and heartbeat,
but, on the face of it at least, 'psychological' functions like sense
perception and memory, internal sensations like fear and hunger,
and even, apparently, voluntary actions such as running. When a
sheep sees a wolf and runs away, Descartes was later incredulously
asked, are we really supposed to believe that this can occur in the
absence of any kind of "sensitive soul"? His answer was unequivo-
cal: yes. And he went on to insist that, *in the case of humans too,* a
mechanistic explanation was quite sufficient to explain even such
waking actions as walking and singing, when they occur 'without

the mind attending to them' (*animo non advertente*, AT VII 230: CSM II 161).[18]

The last qualification is, of course, crucial. Where mental attention is involved, Descartes is clear that we must posit a separate 'rational soul' (*âme raisonable*) which is, by a special act of the creator, 'united' to the complex machinery of the human body (AT XI 143: CSM I 102). But though the soul has not quite vanished, its functions are very severely reduced in comparison with the role played by the *psyche* of the Aristotelians. It does not, for example, even function as the initiator of the physical movements: the traditional 'locomotive soul' drops out of the picture, and all that is left is for the *âme raisonable* to do is act like a fountain keeper (*fontenier*), surveying the flow of the waters (the 'animal spirts' of the body) and diverting them into this or that channel, without affecting the quantity of motion in the system as a whole (AT XI 131: CSM I 101).[19] Descartes' mechanistic reductionism is starkly eliminative: *entia non sunt multiplicanda* – wherever we can possibly dispense with the soul, we should.[20] The Cartesian soul, in short, is rather like the "God of the Gaps" of some present-day physicists – invoked only as a last resort, when the experimenter comes up against a phenomenon that baffles the explanatory powers of the scientist. In Descartes' case, the reason why he saw his science of man as unable ultimately to dispense with the soul is not made clear in the *Treatise on Man*, but emerges with great vividness in the *Discourse* – not in the fourth, metaphysical, section of that work, but in the fifth section, devoted to the physical world and the unfolding of the "laws of nature."

The main scientific argument for dualism, as presented in *Discourse* Part V, hinges on the intellectual capacities of man – not on *la pensée* in the wide sense which Descartes sometimes uses to cover the whole spectrum of consciousness including feeling and sensation,[21] but on the power to form concepts, and to express them in language: *composer un discours pour faire entendre les pensées* (cf. AT VI 57: CSM I 140). The "Chomskian" argument, as we may anachronistically but appropriately term it,[22] starts from the observation that a machine, or a *bête machine*, is essentially a stimulus–response device. You may be able to train a magpie to utter "words," as Descartes later wrote to the Marquess of Newcastle, but each word will be a fixed response to an external stimulus causing a given change in the nervous system (AT IV 574: CSMK 303).[23] As Descartes put it in the *Discourse:*

> We can certainly conceive of a machine so constructed that it utters words
> (*paroles* . . . corresponding to . . . a change in its organs (e.g. if you touch it in
> one spot it asks what you want of it, and if you touch it in another spot it
> cries out that you are hurting it). But it is not conceivable that such a
> machine should produce arrangements of words so as to give an appropri-
> ately meaningful answer (*pour répondre au sens*) to whatever is said in its
> presence, as even the dullest of men can do.   (AT VI 56: CSM I 140)

In short, the human language-user has the capacity to respond appropriately to an indefinite range of situations, and this capacity seems
toto caelo different from anything that could be generated by a
"look-up tree" or finite table correlating inputs with outputs. What
is interesting about this celebrated Cartesian argument as it appears
in the *Discourse* is that the insistence on the radical *limitations* of a
mere machine immediately follows a paragraph which had invited
the reader to reflect on the *power* of mechanical explanations. Descartes has just claimed that the purely mechanized operations of the
brain and nervous system can, provided that they are sufficiently
complex, explain a whole range of actions which might, to the un-
prejudiced eye, seem entirely beyond the scope of a mere machine.
The purely physical processes of the animal spirits, and the mechanical processing of the *fantasie* or "corporeal imagination," can produce a rich array of behavior which is entirely "appropriate to the
objects of its senses and internal passions" (*à propos des objets qui
se presentent à ses sens et des passions qui sont en lui*). The skeptic
is invited to consider just how complex the responses of ingeniously
constructed man-made automata can be: if a physical artifact can
exhibit such complexity of response, then why not accept that a
purely physical body, 'made by the hand of God' can do even more?
"This will not seem at all strange to those who . . . are prepared to
regard the body as a machine (*consideront le corps comme une machine*) which, having been made by the hand of God (*ayant été faite
des mains de Dieu*), is incomparably better ordered, and contains in
itself far more remarkable movements than any machine that could
be invented by man" (*est incomparablement mieux ordonée, et a en
soi des movements plus admirables, qu'aucune de celles qui peu-
vent être inventées par les hommes*, AT VI 56: CSM I 139).

But now if this is right, if God has at his disposal minute physical mechanisms of such incomparable complexity, can we really know a priori that he could not construct, out of purely material structures, a thinking, talking machine – a human being? Descartes' answer – and here is the crux – is that we cannot absolutely rule this out. The appeal to the flexibility and scope of human linguistic capacity generates an argument whose conclusion has the status only of an overwhelming probability, not of an absolute certainty:

Since reason is a universal instrument (*instrument universel*) which can be used in all kinds of situations, whereas [physical] organs need some particular disposition for each particular action, it is *morally impossible* (*moralement impossible*) for a machine to have enough different organs to make it act in all the contingencies of life in the way in which our reason makes us act.   (AT VI 57: CSM I 140, emphasis supplied)

"Moral certainty" as Descartes later explained in the 1647 (French) edition of the *Principles of Philosophy*[24] is "certainty which is sufficient to regulate our behaviour, or which measures up to the certainty we have on matters relating to the conduct of life which we never normally doubt, though we know it is possible absolutely speaking that they may be false" (*bien que nous sachions qu'il se peut faire, absolument parlant, qu'elles soient fausses*) (Part IV, art. 205: AT IX 323: CSM I 290). Descartes' position is thus quite clear. His reflections on our uniquely human ability to respond to "all the contingencies of life" led him to believe that the 'universal instrument' of reason could not feasibly be realised in a purely physical set of structures; but the possibility of such a physical realization is one that, good scientist that he is, he is not prepared absolutely to rule out.

The sense in which Descartes' 'scientific' stance on the nature of the mind is open to empirical evidence now begins to emerge. What makes a physical realization of the 'instrument of reason' hard for him to envisage is, at least partly, a matter of *number and size* – of how many structures of the appropriate kind could be packed into a given part of the body. Descartes made no secret of his enthusiasm for anatomical dissection as the key to understanding the minute structures of the nervous system and other bodily organs.[25] But what such investigations established, so he believed, was the essential underlying *simplicity* of those structures. Everything that went on in heart and brain, nerves, muscles and 'animal spirits' manifested, at the level of observation that was available to him, nothing more than elementary "push and pull" operations – operations not in principle any different from the simple workings of cogs and levers and pumps and whirlpools that could be readily inspected in the ordinary macro world of "medium-sized hardware." Everything happened *selon les règles des méchaniques qui sont les mêmes que celles de la nature* (AT VI 54: CSM I 139).[26] And apparently Descartes could not envisage the brain or nervous system as being capable of accommodating enough mechanisms of the requisite simplicity to generate enough responses of the complexity needed to constitute genuine thought or linguistic behavior. Yet this in turn prompts the in one way absurdly hypothetical but in another way curiously illuminating question: would Descartes have maintained his stance on the incorporeality of the mind had he been alive today? The argument in the *Discourse* hinges on the practical impossibility of a physical mechanism possessing a sufficiently large number of different parts (*assez de divers organes*) to facilitate the indefinite range of human responses to "all the contingencies of life" (AT VI 57). Such an argument, it seems, could hardly survive the modern discovery of the staggering structural richness of the microstructure of cerebral cortex, comprised as we now know, of over ten billion neural connections. Indeed, at a simpler level, it is not even clear that it could survive an appeal to modern chess-playing machines, capable, though composed of nothing more than plastic and metal, of responding coherently and appropriately to an indefinite range of moves, in ways which are often new and surprizing, often capable of outwitting human opponents, and most crucial of all, incapable of being predicted in advance even by their programmers.

The purpose of these appeals to modern science is not pointlessly to berate Descartes for a failure to take account of evidence he could not possibly have dreamt of, but simply to underline the philosophical status of his scientific arguments for dualism. There is, however, a more apposite criticism that can be made against Descartes' arguments, namely that, even on his own terms, and within the limitations of his own scientific methodology, he seems to have been a trifle cavalier about the likely limitations of 'mere matter'. Sometimes he seems content to rest his case on a simple appeal to the difficulty of seeing how mere extended stuff could generate thought. "When I examine the nature of body" he wrote to one critic, "I just do not find anything in it which savours of thought" (*nihil prorsus in ea reperio quod redoleat cogitationem*, AT VII 227: CSM II 160). In taking this "swift and easy" line with his critics, Descartes seems to verge on inconsistency with his scientific procedure elsewhere; for he certainly would not have accepted any protestations of his scholastic opponents to the effect that when they examined the nature of matter they could find nothing in it which savored of fire, or of gravity, or of life. In all these three latter cases, Descartes' reply would have been brusque: what matters, he would surely have insisted, is not what anyone can easily see straight off as following from the definition of 'extended stuff' but what can ultimately be shown to arise out of complex configurations of that extended stuff, when it is divided into indefinitely small particles of various sizes and shapes, all moving at various speeds and in different directions (cf. *Principles*, Part II, art. 64 and Part IV, art. 187).

Descartes, in short, cannot have it both ways. His general reductionist program insists that apparently mysterious, seemingly *sui generis* phenomena like fire or gravity, or even life itself, can all be explained if we are prepared to go deeply enough into the purely physical mechanisms operating at the micro level. Yet having taken that stance, he is not in a very easy position to insist on the impotence of "mere" extended stuff to generate cognition and speech along similar lines. The point is reinforced when one remembers that many of the standard explanations of Descartes' physics posit (though we have to take their existence on trust) micro events of near inconceivable minuteness. Consider, for example, the 'subtle matter' (matter composed of very tiny fast moving particles) invoked to explain gravity (the subtle matter pushing terrestrial particles toward the center of the earth; cf. *Principles* Part IV, art. 23). When one of Descartes' correspondents ventured to identify this subtle matter with the "particles of dust we see flying in the air," Descartes scornfully retorted that this was a complete misunderstanding: the particles of subtle matter were utterly undetectable by the senses, smaller by a whole order of magnitude even than invisible particles of air, which are in turn far smaller than tiny dust particles (letter to Morin, 12 September 1638: AT II 373: CSMK 123). Yet again, this does not sit happily with the scientific claim that the size of the brain does not allow for enough microstructures to generate the richly varied responses of human behavior.

Despite these occasional overswift manoeuvres, the general thrust of Descartes' scientific work on the human nervous system points unmistakably in the direction of the *homme-machine* envisaged by Julian de la Mettrie in the following century, and beyond that to the "neurophilosophy" of the mind, which attracts wide support in our own day.[27] Once Descartes had taken the vital step of assigning so many of the traditional functions of the 'soul' to the minute physical mechanisms of the nervous system, it was only a matter of time before Western science would go all the way, and make even the residual *âme raisonable* redundant. Although it is too early to say whether the modern research program of neurophilosophy will succeed in all its aims, what can be said is that Descartes himself unequivocally and undogmatically allowed that the question of the limits of physics was sensitive to empirical evidence. Whether or not cognition was beyond the powers of a corporeal machine was a matter for scientific argument. The probabilities in favour of a specially created soul are, on the arguments given in *Discourse* Part V, overwhelmingly strong; but there is no logically watertight guarantee.

CONCLUSION

Of the triad of considerations, theological, metaphysical and scientific, which motivated Descartes' adherence to the thesis of the incorporeality of the mind, it would be difficult or impossible to single out any one as having the primacy in structuring his own personal convictions.[28] If his dying words *"ça mon âme; il faut partir"* are reported accurately[29] he ended his days without wavering in his devout belief that the essential part of him – *ce moi, c'est-à-dire l'âme par laquelle je suis ce que je suis* (AT VI 33) – would continue its existence in a future life, unimpeded by the confining prison house of the body. And though he vacillated on whether to advertize to the world his claim to demonstrate the theological doctrine of personal immortality, he undoubtedly saw his dualism as providing better support for that doctrine than did the Aristotelianism of his predecessors. On the metaphysical front, his attempts to demonstrate the distinctness of soul from body were widely rejected as invalid even in his own day, bedeviled as they were by the central flaw in his method – its failure to find a convincing route outward from the inner prison of subjective cognition to the reliable knowledge of objective reality. Lastly, when he approached the issue from the outside, from his investigations of animal and human behavior, he was driven by a unificatory and reductionist vision, which led him progressively to banish the soul from science; when it appears, the soul is "tacked on" at the end of the story[30] invoked to account for the phenomena of thought and language that appeared to Descartes, for empirical reasons, radically resistant to mechanistic explanation. Whether that resistance can be overcome by the theoretically more sophisticated and empirically far richer resources of modern neurophysiology remains to be seen. As for Descartes himself, he was no doubt able to take satisfaction from the thought that ultimately the demands of faith, of demonstrative reason and of scientific inquiry all seemed to pull in the same direction – toward the conclusion that the soul of man is entirely and truly distinct from his body: *mon âme est entièrement et véritablement distincte de mon corps.*[31]

NOTES

1 Cf. Synopsis to *Meditations:* "*l' esprit ou l'âme de l'homme (ce que je ne distingue point).*" (AT IX 10: CSM II 10n., emphasis supplied). This assertion of the interchangeability of the terms "mind" and "soul" in Cartesian metaphysics appears in the 1647 French version of the *Meditations.* The original 1641 Latin text refers simply to the mind (*mens,* AT VII 14). Cf. also the French and Latin versions of the title of Meditation Six.

2 The term "real" (*realis*) is much more precise in Descartes than is suggested by the looser and vaguer connotations of the modern English term "real": "strictly speaking a real distinction exists only between two or more substances" (*Principles* Part I, art. 60: AT VIIIA 28: CSM I 213).

3 This seems to be the predominant picture both in the Jewish and Christian scriptures. Cf. Job 19:25: "though worms destroy this body, yet *in the flesh* shall I see God": and I Corinthians 16:42–4: "So also is the resurrection of the dead. It is sown in corruption; it is raised in incorruption. . . . It is sown a biological body (*soma psychicon*) and it is raised a spiritual body (*soma pneumation*)". The Nicene Creed (A.D. 325) affirms the "resurrection of the body." However, the doctrine of purgatory that arose early in Christian thought apparently does imply an intermediate state in which wholly bodiless souls await the resurrection. Such a soul, however, could not, according to Aquinas, be a "complete substance" (*Summa Theologiae* Ia 75.4 and Ia 118.2. See also Suarez, *Metaphysical*

Disputations Disp. 33, Sect. 1, art. 11: "anima etiamsi sit separata ... est pars ... essentialis, habetque incompletam essentiam ... et ideo semper est substantia incompleta," cited in Gilson, *Index Scolastico-Cartésien*, p. 278. See also Swinburne, *The Evolution of the Soul*, p. 311.

4 Aristotle distinguished five functions – vegetative, sensory, appetitive, locomotive, and intellectual (*De Anima*, II 3); these were in turn incorporated into the Thomist system as the *quinque genera potentiarum animae*; cf. *Summa Theologiae* I 78.1, and Gilson, *Index Scolastico-Cartésien*, pp. 12–15.

5 "Concurrence" is the continuously exercised power of God the preserver, without which (on the orthodox doctrine of creation and preservation that Descartes followed) all things would collapse into nothingness. Cf. AT VII 49: CSM II 33.

6 "I do not take upon myself to try to use the power of human reason to settle any of these matters which depend on the free will of God" (AT VII 153: CSM II 109).

7 The claim in the subtitle of the first (1641) edition of the *Meditations* – "in qua ... animae immortalitas demonstratur" – was dropped in the second edition of 1642; cf. letter to Mersenne of 24 December 1640: AT III 266: CSMK 163. The most marked retreat from the demonstrability claim occurs in the letter to Elizabeth of 3 November 1645: "je confesse que, par la seule raison naturelle nous pouvons bien faire beaucoup de conjectures ... et avoir de belles espérances, mais non point aucune assurance" (AT IV 333: CSMK 277). For Descartes' disinclination to encroach on the province of the theologians, see esp. AT V 176, translated in Cottingham, (ed.), *Descartes' Conversation with Burman*, pp. 46 and 115f.

8 For Aristotle's "active intellect," see *De Anima* III 5. Averröes, the great Muslim commentator on Aristotle, took it that after the death of the body, human souls lost any individuality and were merged into a universal spirit. The Lateran council of 1513 condemned the Averröean heresy; cf. AT VII 3: CSM II 4.

9 In the "Coimbran" commentaries on the *De Anima* published by a group of Jesuit writers in 1598, there is a hostile reference to "certain recent philosophers who assert that since the rational soul is the form of the body, its immortality rests on faith alone, because, so they claim, no form of a body can be shown by philosophical principles to have the power to exist outside matter." (*Commentarii in tres libros de Anima Aristolelis* Bk. II, ch. 1, qu. 6, art. 2; cited in Gilson, *Index Scolastico-Cartésien*, p. 142.)

10 In the letter to Plempius for Fromondus of 3 October 1637, Descartes explicitly contrasts his views on the soul with those of the scholastics and suggests that he can avoid many of the theological difficulties that

beset the latter; see esp. AT I 414ff: CSMK 62f. See also the letter to Regius of January 1642 (AT III 503: CSMK 207–8). For the sincerity of Descartes' religious commitments, cf. letter to Mersenne of March 1642 (AT III 543: CSMK 210).

11 *Speciales modi cogitandi:* Sixth Meditation, AT VII 78: CSM II 54. See further, Cottingham, "Cartesian trialism," 226ff. Post-mortem consciousness, devoid of these "special modes" would, it seems, be a thin and meager affair – at least as far as personal individuality is concerned. Cf. the remarks on "decorporealised immortality" in C. Wilson *Leibniz's Metaphysics*, p. 197; Wilson suggests that Descartes' concern for the prolonging of corporeal life may have been motivated by an implicit realization of the meager quality of existence realizable by a pure incorporeal intellect. For Leibniz's own criticisms of Cartesian immortality, see Supplementary Texts, no. 16, in Martin and Brown (eds.), *Leibniz, Discourse on Metaphysics*, p. 127.

12 See Louis de la Forge, *Traité de l'âme humaine*, cited in Watson, "Descartes and Cartesianism," p. 593. For the problem of individuating angels, cf. Aquinas, *Summa Theologiae* I, 50.4. See also AT V 176, and Cottingham (ed.), *Descartes' Conversation with Burman*, 19 and 84.

13 That the addressee of this letter is Silhon is a conjecture of Adam, rendered plausible by the fact that Silhon had written two treatises on the immortality of the soul; cf. AT I 352.

14 Gassendi's criticisms of this passage from the Second Meditation were published in his *Disquisitio Metaphysica* in 1644; Descartes' reply occurs in the letter to Clerselier of 12 January 1646, which was reprinted in the French translation of the *Meditations with Objections and Replies*, published in 1647. See further CSM II 268 n.

15 "We are concerned here with things only in so far as they are perceived by the intellect" (*hic de rebus non agentes nisi quantum ab intellectu percipuntur*), loc. cit. For more on the significance of Descartes' arguments in this part of the *Regulae*, see above, Chapter 4.

16 For Arnauld's circle, see Fourth Objections: AT VII 214: CSM II 150. For his criticism of the argument from clear and distinct perception, see AT VII 201f: CSM II 141f. For an analysis of this critique, see Cottingham, *Descartes*, pp. 113ff.

17 Among the many arguments that Descartes seems to have been able blithely to ignore, see esp. Gassendi's arguments in the Fifth Objections: AT VII 334ff: CSM II 232ff; cf. also the comments of "Hyperaspistes" in the letter of August 1641: AT III 423f: CSMK 189f. The criticisms that did succeed in worrying Descartes concern not the incorporeality thesis itself, but the explanation of the soul's union and interaction with the body. See below, note 31.

18 For more on the relation between pyschology and physiology in Descartes' thought, see Chapter 11.

19 This, at any rate, is one possible reading of the (somewhat vague and schematic) fountain keeper passage. Cf. also *Passions of the Soul*, art. 12: there is a continuous flow of animal spirits from brain to muscles, but the activity of the soul may "cause more to flow into some muscles than others" (AT XI 337: CSM I 332). As far as I am aware, Descartes never *explicitly* asserts that the soul can change the direction, but not the overall quantity, of bodily motions, though later Cartesians certainly made such a claim on his behalf. The claim was keenly criticized by Leibniz, who aptly insisted that any change in direction must imply a change in overall momentum: to say that the soul can at least change the *direction* of the animal spirits is "no less inexplicable and contrary to the laws of nature" than asserting that it could directly increase the speed or force of flow (*Philosophischen Schriften*, ed. Gerhardt, vol. VI, p. 540; translated in Loemker, *Philosophical Papers and Letters*, p. 587).

20 For Descartes' "occamism," cf. *Meteorology*: "it seems to me that my arguments must be more acceptable in so far as I can make them depend on fewer things" (AT VI 239: CSM II 173 n).

21 For Descartes' use of *la pensée*, and the extent to which his "wide" employment of this term has been overstressed by commentators, see Cottingham, "Descartes on thought," 208ff.

22 Cf. Chomsky, *Language and Mind*.

23 Descartes does, however, add the curious comment that the word so produced will be the "expression of one of the bird's passions (e.g., the hope of eating)." For Descartes' not entirely consistent stance on whether animals have, if not thought, then at least sensation, see Cottingham, "A brute to the brutes? Descartes' treatment of animals," 551ff.

24 This comment is not to be found in the original 1644 Latin text; like many of the significant additions and clarifications that appear in the 1647 French translation of the *Principles*, it is almost certainly supplied by Descartes himself, not by the translator, Picot. See further CSM I 177f.

25 In a letter to Mersenne of 20 February 1639, Descartes' claims that his anatomical investigations had been a major interest for at least eleven years: "c'est un exercise où je me suis souvent occupé depuis onze ans, et je crois qu'il n'y a guère médecin qui ait regardé de si près que moi" (AT II 525: CSMK 134). For a general account of Descartes work in this area, see Lindeboom, *Descartes and Medicine*, ch. 3 (Lindeboom, perhaps rightly, suspects that, despite the boast to Mersenne, Descartes' empirical researches were in actual fact conducted at a fairly unsystematic, not to say amateurish, level.)

26 See further Descartes' comments in the *Description of the Human Body:* AT XI 224ff: CSM I 314ff. The "simplicist" assumption (or prejudice?) that informs so much of Descartes' scientific methodology is stated most explicitly in a letter to Huygens of 10 Octo r 1642: "la nature ne se sert que de moyens qui sont fort simples" (AT III 797: CSMK 215). See further Chapter 9, below.

27 La Mettrie's *L'Homme machine* appeared in 1747 or modern physicalist approaches to the mind, cf. Churchland, *Neurophilosophy*, pt. 2.

28 See, however, the celebrated study of Henri Gouhier, *La Pensée religieuse de Descartes*, which regards Descartes' religious faith as the mainspring of his metaphysics: "il partit d'un si bon pas parce qu' une foi profonde avait écarté de son âme toute inquiétude (p. 314).

29 There are various versions. The actual phrase, according to Clerselier's account, was rather more elaborate: "ça mon âme, il y a long temps que tu es captive; voici l'heure que tu dois sortir de prison et quitter l'embaras de ce cors" (AT V 482).

30 The *âme raisonable* is introduced right at the end, both in the order of exposition in the *Traité de l'homme* (AT XI 131: CSM I 101) and in the summary recapitulation presented in *Discourse* Part V (AT VI 59: CSM I 141).

31 Sixth Meditation: AT IX 62: CSM II 54. The Latin text, as often, avoids the word "soul" and refers instead simply to the "thinking thing" that is me: "quatenus sum tantum res cogitans . . . certum est me a corpore meo revera esse distinctum" (AT VII 78). In the later psychology of Descartes (especially in the letters to Elizabeth of 21 May and 28 June 1643), there is a subtle and important shift of focus away from the distinctness of soul and body and toward the notion of their "substantial union" (AT III 665ff and 691ff: CSMK 218 and 226). The upshot of these maneuvers (which are the subject for another paper) does not detract from the incorporeality of pure thought or the "rational soul" in which it resides. What Descartes does do, however, is systematically to develop hints in his earlier metaphysics that the phenomena of "feeling," "sensation," and "imagination" cannot straightforwardly be assigned to soul *simpliciter* but should be regarded as properties of that mysterious soul–body hybrid that is the human being. Some of the issues that arise here are examined in Cottingham, *Descartes* pp. 127ff. One important implication of assigning all sensory experience to the mind–body union is that the post-mortem consciousness of Descartes' immortal soul will, it seems, be confined to "pure," abstract thought; cf. above, pp. 240–1. I am grateful to Stuart Brown, Gary Hatfield, Pauline Phemister, David Scott, and Roger Woolhouse for helpful comments on an earlier draft of this chapter.

9 Descartes' philosophy of science and the scientific revolution

Descartes' concept of science can be understood only by paying careful attention to the historical context in which it was constructed. The scientific revolution of the seventeenth century involved two related developments: a change in scientific practice (or, more accurately, a whole series of such changes) which is reflected in the founding of new scientific societies such as the Royal Society and the *Académie royale des sciences*, and a complementary change in how natural philosophers described the kind of knowledge that resulted from the new scientific practices. Descartes contributed to both developments. He shared this distinction with such eminent figures as Galileo Galilei, Francis Bacon, William Harvey, Robert Boyle, Christian Huygens, and Isaac Newton, all of whom were concerned both with improving our knowledge of nature and with clarifying the status of that knowledge.

It would be an obvious oversimplification to classify all the natural philosophers of the seventeenth century as, in some fundamental sense, proposing the same scientific theories. It is equally unsatisfactory to suggest that they all accepted the same theory of science or the same model of scientific knowledge. Yet, despite the pitfalls involved, it may be helpful – at least prior to examining Descartes' texts – to think of many of the most famous natural philosophers of the scientific revolution as sharing a number of new insights about the nature of scientific knowledge and, more importantly, as repudiating certain features of the model of science that was generally accepted in colleges and universities at that time. In fact, there was more agreement about what was being rejected than about what was being proposed in its place. Descartes occupies a pivotal role in the history of this development, in the transition from a widely accepted

258

scholastic concept of science to its complete rejection by practising scientists and the endorsement of some kind of hypothetical, empirically based knowledge of nature. The historical context in which Descartes worked should lead us to expect, therefore, that he struggled with the epistemological and methodological issues involved in this transition. It should also lead us to expect that the transition was neither quick nor clear-cut. In other words, there is a strong likelihood that seventeenth-century natural philosophers continued to accept various features of precisely the model of science which they claimed explicitly to reject, while at the same time adopting elements of the newly developing concept of science that were incompatible with their traditional allegiance.

The traditional concept of science that was almost universally taught in colleges and universities included a number of key features; one was the certainty or necessity of genuine knowledge claims, and their universality. Aristotle says in the *Posterior Analytics:*

We suppose ourselves to possess unqualified scientific knowledge of a thing, as opposed to knowing it in the accidental way in which the sophist knows, when we think that we know the cause on which the fact depends, as the cause of that fact and of no other, and, further, that the fact could not be other than it is. . . . Since the object of pure scientific knowledge cannot be other than it is, the truth obtained by demonstrative knowledge will be necessary.[1]

The paradigm of this type of knowledge was pure mathematics. One begins with definitions or first principles which are known with absolute certainty, one proceeds "demonstratively" by deducing other propositions from those already known as certain, and the logical validity of our inferences guarantees the same degree of certainty for our conclusions as was available for the initial premises. The mathematical model of demonstrated knowledge inspired one of the dominant features of the scholastic concept of science that was widely accepted in the early seventeenth century.

Another feature of this concept of science was the claim that our knowledge of physical nature depends ultimately on the reliability of our everyday observations and judgments.[2] This involved two elements. One was the assumption that all our knowledge ultimately depends on sensory evidence and that it includes nothing that was not learned through sensory experience.[3] Secondly, the cognitive faculties with which God has equipped us are completely reliable as long as they are used within the scope of their Creator's design. Thus we know the way the world is, and we can know it with certainty, by consulting the ways in which the world appears to us in sensation.

A further element of the scholastic tradition was the assumption that, if we wish to explain the natural phenomena which appear to us in sensations, we must use the distinction between "matter" and "form."[4] This was a very widely used distinction which varied in meaning from one context to another. It was designed to reflect our common experience of the same type of thing being instantiated in a variety of different ways; for example, dogs may be small or large, their colors can vary, as may many other inessential features, without their ceasing to be dogs. The common, essential features of a dog could be described as the *form* of a dog, while the nonessential, variable features could be described (metaphysically) as the *matter*. What appears in sensation, therefore, is the appearance of an underlying reality (form) which, in turn, is the more fundamental dimension of any reality. This underlying reality, or form, is what explains whatever is necessary or essential in anything. Because the traditional concept of scientific knowledge was limited to knowledge of what is necessarily true, it follows that scholastic *scientia* was directed to acquiring knowledge of forms. Thus a scholastic explanation of a natural phenomenon is a discovery of the forms that underlie the appearances manifest to the human perceiver in reliable sensations.

This very brief summary is almost a caricature of what scholastics claimed about scientific understanding. However, many of Descartes' contemporaries argued that it was precisely this philosophy that obstructed the consideration of alternative ways of investigating nature. It was this simple-minded model of knowledge that was invoked by those who objected to the new sciences, and that was used as a foil by proponents of the new sciences to show in relief the distinctive features of their own philosophy of science.

HYPOTHESES

Descartes began his account of the natural world in *Le Monde* (c.1632) by discussing the *un*reliability of our sensations as a basis for scientific knowledge.

In proposing to treat here of light, the first thing I want to make clear to you is that there can be a difference between our sensation of light . . . and what is in the objects that produces that sensation in us . . . For, even though everyone is commonly persuaded that the ideas that are the objects of our thought are wholly like the objects from which they proceed, nevertheless I can see no reasoning that assures us that this is the case. . . . You well know that words bear no resemblance to the things they signify, and yet they do not cease for that reason to cause us to conceive of those things . . . Now if words, which signify nothing except by human convention, suffice to cause us to conceive of things to which they bear no resemblance, why could not nature also have established a certain sign that would cause us to have the sensation of light, even though that sign in itself bore no similarity to that sensation?   (AT XI 3–4)[5]

Descartes goes on to use the same example as Galileo, to argue that a tickling sensation caused by a feather does not resemble anything in the feather. "One passes a feather lightly over the lips of a child who is falling asleep, and he perceives that someone is tickling him. Do you think the idea of tickling that he conceives resembles anything in this feather?" (AT XI 6)[6] In a similar way, there is no reason to believe "that what is in the objects from which the sensation of light comes to us is any more like that sensation than the actions of a feather . . . are like tickling" (AT XI 6).[7] If we cannot argue validly from a description of our sensation of light to the claim that the light that causes this sensation resembles our experience, then we have a fundamental problem in attempting to base scientific knowledge on our sensations of the world around us. The distinction between our subjective experiences or sensations and their objective causes, between primary and secondary qualities, opens up an epistemic gap that can only be bridged by some other strategy apart from assumptions of resemblance. This strategy is hypothesis, or guesswork. Our guesses may turn out to be very secure, and there may eventually be many reasons for thinking that they are as certain as one can hope for in the circumstances; but that does not change the fact that we come to have these ideas, in the first place, by guesswork.

What should a natural philosopher assume about the physical causes of our perceptions? There are a few reasons why Descartes opts for one assumption rather than another at this crucial juncture, some of which rely on his concept of explanation (which is discussed below). Apart from those reasons, he also presupposes a radical distinction between matter and mind for which he argues in the *Medita-tions* and the *Principles*. It follows from this that the objective causes of our sensations are material, in some sense. In order to fill in some of the relevant detail, Descartes must engage in elementary physical theory.

The speculations about matter on which Descartes' theory of mat-ter and, subsequently, his concept of science depend include the as-sumption that the size, shape and motion of small particles of matter would be adequate to explain all their physical effects, including the physical effects on our sensory faculties which stimulate sensations. Some of the reasons for this degree of parsimony in theory construc-tion are mentioned below. In postulating three types of matter in *Le Monde*, Descartes is not very convincing about why he assumes three (rather than more or fewer); however, once they have been intro-duced, he is quick to take refuge in the construction of a hypothetical world which allows his imagination complete freedom, without hav-ing to explain the rationale for each hypothesis as it is made.

Many other things remain for me to explain here, and I would myself be happy to add here several arguments to make my opinions more plausible. In order, however, to make the length of this discourse less boring for you, I want to wrap part of it in the cloak of a fable, in the course of which I hope that the truth will not fail to come out sufficiently . . .   (AT XI 31)[8]

By the time Descartes wrote the *Principles* twelve years later, he had become more self-conscious about the hypothetical character of his assumptions concerning the size, shape, etc. of particles of matter.

From what has already been said we have established that all the bodies in the universe are composed of one and the same matter, which is divisible into indefinitely many parts, . . . However, we cannot determine by reason alone how big these pieces of matter are, or how fast they move, or what kinds of circle they describe. Since there are countless different configurations which God might have instituted here, experience alone must teach us which con-figurations he actually selected in preference to the rest. We are thus free to make any assumption on these matters with the sole proviso that all the consequences of our assumption must agree with our experience.

(AT VIIIA 100–1: CSM I 256–7)

Descartes does not claim that we are completely free to assume anything we wish about matter. He argues at great length about the fundamental properties of matter, i.e. their primary qualities, and discusses in detail the need to include or exclude certain primary qualities in a viable theory of nature. He also argues in some detail about the laws of motion or, as he calls them, the laws of nature, which determine the motions of material bodies and the ways in which they may transfer motion from one to another by contact action. However, the relevant point here is that, having decided which variables to attribute to matter, we cannot determine by similar arguments the values of these variables; we cannot decide a priori the number, size, or speed of the various small parts of matter which underpin the whole edifice of Cartesian physics. Nor could we hope to discover by observation which particles there are, what shapes they have or with what speed they move; they are much too small to be perceived directly, even with the use of a microscope. We can do no better than hypothesize answers to these questions, and then subsequently check the plausibility of our guesswork.

Thus the logic of Descartes' theory of sensation and the implications of his theory of matter both suggest that he would have to acknowledge a central place for hypotheses in any coherent account of physical phenomena. The extent to which he recognized this varied from his earlier reflections in the *Regulae* (c.1628), in which there was only a minimal recognition of the role of hypotheses in natural science, to his more mature considerations in the *Discourse* (1637), where the significance of hypotheses and experiments is explicitly acknowledged. The *Discourse* is of paramount importance in this context, because it was composed over a number of years while Descartes was preparing for publication the three major scientific essays for which it serves as a preface. In the "Discourse on the method of rightly conducting one's reason and seeking the truth in the sciences," Part VI, Descartes writes:

Should anyone be shocked at first by some of the statements I make at the beginning of the *Optics* and the *Meteorology* because I call them 'suppositions' and do not seem to care about proving them, let him have the patience to read the whole book attentively, and I trust that he will be satisfied. For I take my reasonings to be so closely interconnected that just as the last are proved by the first, which are their causes, so the first are proved by the last, which are their effects. . . . For as experience makes most of these effects quite certain, the causes from which I deduce them serve not so much to prove them as to explain them; indeed, quite to the contrary, it is the causes which are proved by the effects.   (AT VI 76: CSM I 150)

This passage raised a number of queries from readers, one of whom was Father Morin. Descartes replied to his concerns in 1638 and answered the objection that hypothetical essays should not be described as demonstrated: "there is a big difference between proving and explaining. To this I add that one can use the word 'demonstrate' to mean one or the other, at least if one understands it according to common usage and not according to the special meaning which philosophers give it" (13 July 1638: AT II 198: CSMK 106). This shows Descartes explicitly breaking with the scholastic tradition, for which the term "demonstrate" had special connotations of deducing a conclusion rigorously from first principles. Instead he invites his readers to understand "demonstration" in a less strict sense in which it can include the reasoning process by which one argues from effects to hypothetical causes or, in the opposite direction, from assumed causes to observed effects.

The relative novelty of this type of demonstration is underlined in a letter to Mersenne in 1638, in which Descartes explains that the types of demonstration available in physics are very different from those which one expects in mathematics:

You ask if I think that what I wrote about refraction is a demonstration; and I think it is, at least insofar as it is possible to give one in this matter, without having first demonstrated the principles of physics by means of metaphysics . . . and to the extent that any other question of mechanics, optics or astronomy, or any other matter which is not purely geometrical or arithmetical, has ever been demonstrated. But to demand that I give geometrical demonstrations in a matter which depends on physics is to demand the impossible. And if one wishes to call demonstrations only the proofs of geometers, one must then say that Archimedes never demonstrated anything in mechanics, nor Vitello in optics, nor Ptolemy in astronomy, and so on; this, however, is not what is said. For one is satisfied, in these matters, if the authors – having assumed certain things which are not manifestly contrary to experience – write consistently and without making logical mistakes, even if their assumptions are not exactly true. . . . But as regards those who wish to say that they do not believe what I wrote, because I deduced it from a number of assumptions which I did not prove, they do not know what they are asking for, nor what they ought to ask for.[9]

One implication is clear. We cannot expect the same kind of demonstrations in physics as in pure mathematics, and we will have to settle for something else. However, it is not yet clear what this alternative is. Whatever its precise structure and the kind of results which it can deliver, it involves making assumptions about the causes of physical phenomena and then "demonstrating" the plausibility of these assumptions by examining their explanatory role in some comprehensive natural philosophy, a project to which Descartes repeatedly refers in his claim that he could (at least in principle) demonstrate those assumptions from some kind of metaphysical foundation.

THE CONCEPT OF EXPLANATION

Descartes shared with many of his contemporaries the insight that the forms and qualities of the scholastic tradition were, in some fundamental sense, nonexplanatory. If we notice some natural phenomenon such as the effect of a magnet on small pieces of iron, the scholastic tradition tended to explain this by saying that the magnetic stone attracts (or repels) certain bodies because it has a "magnetic form" or a "magnetic quality." There is an obvious sense in which this is true. If any natural object does something, then it must have the capacity to do so! As long as we do not understand what that capacity is or what it consists in, we might name the inscrutable property in question in terms of the effect it produces. Then sleeping pills have a dormitive power, magnets have magnetic powers, and human beings have thinking powers. So far, there is nothing wrong with this; it merely labels what needs to be explained.

However, if one follows the natural tendency of scholastic philosophy and reifies these newly named powers as if they were properties distinct from the natural objects which have them, then two problems emerge. One is a metaphysical one; namely, the multiplication of entities beyond demonstrated necessity. By applying Occam's principle, one would stop short of introducing hundreds of new forms or qualities which overpopulate one's metaphysical space.[10] Descartes adverts to this question about the redundancy of forms in Chapter 2 of *Le Monde*, where he explains how a piece of wood burns and, as it burns, emits light and heat:

someone else may, if he wishes, imagine the form of 'fire', the quality of 'heat', and the action that 'burns' it to be completely different things in this wood. For my part, afraid of misleading myself if I suppose anything more than what I see must of necessity be there, I am content to conceive there the motion of its parts. . . . provided only that you grant me that there is some power that violently removes the subtler of its parts and separates them from the grosser, I find that that alone will be able to cause in the wood all the same changes that one experiences when it burns.

(AT XI 7–8)[11]

Secondly, the introduction of scholastic forms in this context gave the impression that one had made progress in explaining natural phenomena, and that little else remained to be done. However, the very forms which are assumed as explanatory entities are themselves in need of explanation: "If you find it strange that, in setting out these elements, I do not use the qualities called 'heat', 'cold', 'moistness', and 'dryness', as do the philosophers, I shall say to you that these qualities appear to me to be themselves in need of explanation" (AT XI 25–6).[12]

Thus, for Descartes, scholastic forms are both redundant and pseudo-explanatory. The alternative suggested was to find the material and efficient causes of natural phenomena. Descartes argued that these causes must be described mechanically; in fact, he notoriously argued in a reductionist way that most of the properties that natural phenomena exhibit can be explained ultimately in terms of the size, shape, and motions of the small parts of matter into which, he assumed, physical objects can be analyzed. Therefore to explain any natural phenomenon, in this sense, is equivalent to constructing a model of how small, imperceptible parts of matter can combine to form perceptible bodies, how the properties of bodies result from the properties of their constituent parts, and why we perceive them as we do as a result of the interaction of these bodies with our sensory organs.

It has already been indicated above that Cartesian scientific explanations must be hypothetical, and that one of the reasons for this admission was the unobservability of the particles of matter in terms of which the explanation of natural phenomena must be constructed. But how are we supposed to describe and measure the properties of unobservable particles of matter? Father Morin had this type of objection in mind when, having read the scientific essays of 1637, it seemed to him that Descartes might be attempting to explain what we can readily observe by reference to what we neither observe nor understand: "... problems in physics can rarely be resolved by analogies [*comparaisons*]; there is almost always some difference [between the model and reality], or some ambiguity, or some element of the obscure being explained by the more obscure (12 August 1638: AT II 291). Part of Descartes' reply to this objection includes the claim that there is no way of proceeding in physics except by constructing large-scale models of what is happening at the microscopic level. Thus, for example, we might think of imperceptible particles of light by analogy with wooden spheres the size of billiard balls.

> I claim that they [i.e. models and analogies] are the most appropriate way available to the human mind for explaining the truth about questions in physics; to such an extent that, if one assumes something about nature which cannot be explained by some analogy, I think that I have conclusively shown that it is false.   (12 September 1638: AT II 368: CSMK 122)

This point had already been made in correspondence with Plempius the previous year: "There is nothing more in keeping with reason than that we judge about those things which we do not perceive, because of their small size, by comparison and contrast with those which we see" (3 October 1637: AT I 421: CSMK 65). Descartes' reply to Father Morin also included the claim that the only relevant features of the model were the size and shape of the spheres, and the direction and speed of their motions, so that the disparity in size could be ignored in constructing an explanation.

> in the analogies I use, I only compare some movements with others, or some shapes with others, etc.; that is to say, I compare those things which because of their small size are not accessible to our senses with those which are, and which do not differ from the former more than a large circle differs from a small one.   (12 September 1638: AT II 367–8: CSMK 122)

Apart from the interesting assumptions about which features of a model are relevant to constructing an explanation, Descartes' comments also raise a question about the extent to which hypotheses must be true in order to be explanatory. In other words, would it help in explaining a physical phenomenon if one constructed a mechanical model of its efficient cause which, in fact, is not true to the reality? Descartes thought so, or at least he argued that a plausible though incorrect model is better than none at all. Besides, it may be the case that we can never discover the values of the variables with which we describe microscopic particles of matter, so that we will have to settle for something less than the ideal understanding which is available to God.

The first concession about false hypotheses is made in a number of places where Descartes wonders about the evolution of the universe from its initial chaos to the highly structured world we see today. Theologians commonly believed in his day, based on a nonmetaphorical reading of *Genesis*, that the world as we see it had been created by God. Descartes comments:

even if in the beginning God had given the world only the form of a chaos, provided that he established the laws of nature and then lent his concurrence to enable nature to operate as it normally does, we may believe without impugning the miracle of creation that by this means alone all purely material things could in the course of time have come to be just as we now see them. And their nature is much easier to conceive if we see them develop gradually in this way than if we consider them only in their completed form.   (AT VI 45: CSM I 133–4)

This suggests that an explanation of the natural world is better if we imagine the world as gradually evolving from an intial chaos under the control of the laws of nature, than if we concede to the theologians' belief that God simply made it as it is. The same idea is expressed in the *Principles:*

There is no doubt that all the world was created with all of its perfection from the very beginning... Nevertheless, to understand the nature of plants or of man, it is much better to consider how they can gradually develop from seeds, than to consider how they were created by God at the beginning of the Universe. Thus if we can think of a few very simple and easily known principles from which we can show that the stars and the earth, and everything else we can observe on earth, could have developed as if from seeds – although we know they did not in fact develop in this way – we could explain their nature much better in this way than if we simply described them as they are now, or how we believe they were created.
                                        (AT VIIIA 99–100: CSM I 256)

Thus, Descartes believed for theological reasons that his evolutionary account of the development of natural phenomena was false; he also claimed that, despite being false, it was explanatory.

The second reason for accepting hypotheses which are possibly false was Descartes' pessimism about the feasibility of identifying and accurately measuring relevant variables at the microlevel. There were a number of reasons for this which, in retrospect, would seem to have been well justified and would strike the modern reader as a realistic appraisal of the experimental techniques of the early seventeenth century. If one insisted on withholding hypotheses until all the complexity of the natural world is taken into account, one would make no progress whatsoever. Descartes argued along these lines in response to Mersenne's objections, in 1629, about the interference of the air in measuring the speed of falling bodies.

However, as regards the interference from the air which you wish me to take into consideration, I claim that it is impossible to cope with it and *it does not fall within the scope of science;* for if it is warm, or cold, or dry, or humid, or clear, or cloudy, or a thousand other circumstances, they can all change the air resistance.[13]

The same justification was offered, almost eighteen years later, for the apparent failure of the impact rules to coincide with our experience of colliding bodies. A number of correspondents objected that the rules proposed by Descartes in the *Principles* (Book II, arts. 46 ff) were contradicted by our experience. Descartes' response was:

Indeed, it often happens that experience can seem initially to be incompatible with the rules which I have just explained, but the reason for this is obvious. For the rules presuppose that the two bodies *B* and *C* are perfectly hard and are so separated from all other bodies that there is none other in their vicinity which could either help or hinder their movement. And we see no such situation in this world.   (AT IXB 93)

This was a standard reply to objections about a lack of fit between theory and reality. Cartesian explanations were constructed by analogy with the interactions of macroscopic physical bodies in motion. The underlying reality they purported to explain is microscopic, is inaccessible to human observation, and may involve so many interfering factors that our model is far short of adequately representing it.[14]

Thus a Cartesian explanation is a hypothesis that may be acknowledged to be either false or significantly inadequate to the reality it purports to explain. When we lack the evidence required to identify the actual cause of some phenomenon, "it suffices to imagine a cause which could produce the effect in question, even if it could have been produced by other causes and we do not know which is the true cause" (letter of 5 October 1646: AT IV 516). The suggestion that we settle for the best hypothesis available is reflected in the epistemic status claimed for various explanations in the *Principles*. For example, different astronomical hypotheses are examined, not to decide which one is true, but rather to find out which is more successful as an explanation: "Three different hypotheses, that is suggestions, have been discovered by astronomers, which are considered not as if they were true, but merely as suitable for explaining the phenomena" (AT VIIIA 85: CSM I 250). Descartes' preferred hypothesis is chosen "merely as a hypothesis and not as the truth of the matter" (AT VIIIA 86: CSM I 251).

Evidently it would be better if we could discover the true causes of natural phenomena; but if we cannot, it is still worth while to settle for a possible or plausible cause:

As far as particular effects are concerned, whenever we lack sufficient experiments to determine their true causes, we should be content to know some causes by which they could have been produced . . .

I believe that I have done enough if the causes which I have explained are such that all the effects which they could produce are found to be similar to those we see in the world, without inquiring whether they were in fact produced by those or by some other causes.   (AT IXB 185, 322)

The methodology suggested here, of constructing mechanical models as best we can, coincides with Cartesian scientific practice. Descartes and his followers in France in the seventeenth century were almost profligate in imagining hypothetical models to explain natural phenomena and, in some cases, to explain what could only be called alleged phenomena; they even constructed explanations of nonevents. It was this widespread and notorious dedication to unrestrained hypothesis construction that helps explain Newton's famous disclaimer: "I do not construct hypotheses."[15]

Yet, despite the fact that the logic of Descartes' philosophy implied that explanations of natural phenomena had to be hypothetical, there are equally clear intimations in his work of a very different methodology. Descartes often referred to the possibility of constructing a natural philosophy based on a metaphysical foundation that would realize the kind of certainty and unrevisability which is apparently at issue in the *Meditations*. This feature of his methodology needs some clarification before inquiring if it is compatible with the story told thus far.

In the Preface to the French edition of the *Principles*, Descartes introduces a metaphor that accurately expresses his views about the relationship of physics to metaphysics. "Thus the whole of philosophy is like a tree. The roots are metaphysics, the trunk is physics, and the branches emerging from the trunk are all the other sciences, which may be reduced to three principal ones, namely medicine, mechanics and morals" (AT IXB 14: CSM I 187). There was nothing unusual in this suggestion. Descartes had maintained for about twenty-five years prior to this that physics, as he understood it, is based on or depends on metaphysics and that any natural philosopher worth his salt had better get his metaphysics in order first, before tackling the explanation of specific natural phenomena. For example, he wrote to Mersenne in 1630 about a short essay on metaphysics he himself had begun to write: "It is there that I have tried to begin my studies; and I can tell you that I would not have been able to discover the foundations of physics if I had not looked for them in this direction" (15 April 1630: AT I 144). This helps explain why he objected to Galileo's methodology. According to Descartes, the Italian natural philosopher had ignored questions about foundations and had applied himself instead directly to explaining particular physical phenomena: "without having considered the first causes of nature, he [Galileo] has merely looked for the explanations of a few particular effects, and he has thereby built without foundations" (to Mersenne, 11 October 1638: AT II 380: CSMK 124). The question arises, therefore, about the kinds of foundations Descartes envisaged for physics, and the connection between those foundations and the various sciences that depend on them.

One way of focusing on this issue is to contrast Descartes' approach with what is standard practice in modern science. Physicists or physiologists of the twentieth century do not begin their research with a study of metaphysics, although they may well make metaphysical assumptions in the course of constructing their theories. Instead, they first develop scientific theories which are tested for viability, and the metaphysical implications of the theories are subsequently read off from the finished scientific product. In this approach there is no independent criterion for the acceptability of ontological commitments, apart from the success or otherwise of a given theory. Descartes held the opposite view. He assumed that we can, and ought, to construct our metaphysics first, and that we should subsequently consider physical theories which are consistent with our metaphysical foundation. Thus there must be available independent criteria for deciding which metaphysics to adopt.

On this issue Descartes is very close to scholastic philosophy. The epistemic foundation of Cartesian metaphysics is reflection on "common sense" or on our everyday experience of the natural world. Rule II of the method proposed in the *Discourse,* which reflects Rule IX of the *Regulae,* was "to begin with the simplest and most easily known objects in order to ascend little by little, . . . to knowledge of the most complex" (AT VI 19: CSM I 120).[16] Where metaphysics is concerned, we begin with such everyday experiences as the experience of thinking, of feeling, of moving, etc. Among these experiences, Descartes favors the most simple, accessible and widely available experiences because he hopes thereby to find indubitable foundations. This strategy was outlined in Part VI of the *Discourse:*

I also noticed, regarding observations, that the further we advance in our knowledge, the more necessary they become. At the beginning, rather than seeking those which are more unusual and highly contrived, it is better to resort only to those which, presenting themselves spontaneously to our senses, cannot be unknown to us if we reflect even a little. The reason for this is that the more unusual observations are apt to mislead us when we do not yet know the causes of the more common ones, and the factors on which they depend are almost always so special and so minute that it is very difficult to discern them.   (AT VI 63: CSM I 143)

The privileged position of everyday experience coincides with a complementary distrust of sophisticated experiments; the latter are likely to mislead us because they may be poorly executed, their results may be incorrectly interpreted, or they may be compromised by various interfering factors of which we are unaware.[17] Therefore, experimental evidence is too unreliable to provide metaphysical foundations for scientific theories; that can only be done by reflection on ordinary experience.

The central claims of Cartesian metaphysics are summarized in the *Meditations* and in Part I of the *Principles*. While they are discussed elsewhere in this volume, the relevant feature here is the extent to which Descartes relies on a scholastic set of concepts to interpret metaphysically the personal experiences for which he claims indubitability. For example, the distinction between a substance and its modes is central to the Cartesian argument in favor of a radical distinction between things that can think and those that cannot.[18] The same distinction is put to work in defining the essence of matter and in denuding matter of many of the primary qualities other natural philosophers were willing to attribute to it, such as gravity or elasticity. In summary, Descartes' metaphysics is a subtle combination of scholastic categories, metaphysical axioms (e.g., *ex nihilo nihil fit*), and apparently incontrovertible common experience.[19]

Once this foundation is in place, the second stage of theory construction is the formulation of the so-called "laws of nature." Despite the fact that these are said to be "deduced" from a metaphysical foundation, the evidence adduced in favor of the laws, both in *Le Monde* and the *Principles*, is a mixture of metaphysical axioms and everyday observation. For example the first law, to the effect that a material object continues in its condition of rest or motion unless some cause intervenes to change its condition, is partly justified by reference to the general axiom that every event or change requires a cause, and partly by reference to our everyday experience: "our everyday experience of projectiles completely confirms this first rule of ours" (AT VIIIA 63: CSM I 241).[20] The other two laws of nature are confirmed in the same manner, by appealing to metaphysical axioms and to our everyday experience of physical objects that move about in the world (AT VIIIA 64–5: CSM I 242).

Thus the metaphysical foundations Descartes claimed to establish for scientific knowledge included a number of related elements, which relied on the kind of the evidence just discussed: (a) a radical distinction between matter and spirit, and a preliminary identification of the primary qualities of matter. This included an equally confident dismissal of various properties which Descartes claimed matter does not have; (b) a rejection of the scholastic understanding of explanation and, in its place, the substitution of an uncompromising model of mechanical explanation; (c) a sketch of three fundamental laws of nature according to which material particles interact and exchange various quantities of motion.

Once these were in place, the question arose of how Descartes might make progress in constructing the type of mechanical models required by his method. What kind of inference was available to move from general principles to the explanation of specific natural phenomena?

Descartes' actual scientific practice coincided with his description of theory construction in Part VI of the *Discourse*. As he moved further away from general principles and closer to particular phenomena, he found he needed hypotheses and experimental tests:

First I tried to discover in general the principles or first causes of everything that exists or can exist in the world. . . . Next I examined the first and most ordinary effects deducible from these causes. In this way, it seems to me, I discovered the heavens, the stars, and an earth . . . and other such things which, being the most common of all and the simplest, are consequently the easiest to know. Then, when I sought to descend to more particular things, I encountered such a variety that I did not think the human mind could possibly distinguish the forms or species of bodies that are on the earth from an infinity of others that might be there if it had been God's will to put them there. Consequently I thought the only way . . . was to progress to the causes by way of the effects and to make use of many special observations. . . . I must also admit that the power of nature is so ample and so vast, and these principles so simple and so general, that I notice hardly any particular effect of which I do not know at once that it can be deduced from the principles in many different ways; and my greatest difficulty is usually to discover in which of these ways it depends on them. I know no other means to discover this than by seeking further observations whose outcomes vary according to which of these ways provides the correct explanation.

(AT VI 63–4: CSM I 143–4)

This text is clear in admitting that it is not possible to deduce, in an a priori manner, an explanation of particular natural phenomena from the very general laws of nature Descartes defended, because there is an almost infinite number of alternative paths – all consistent with the laws of nature – by which God might have caused particular natural phenomena. To discover which path he chose, i.e. to discover the mechanism by which natural phenomena are caused by the interaction of particles of matter, one has to have recourse to crucial experiments. And, as has been already acknowledged above, the results which can be gleaned by this method are still hypothetical.

However, Descartes is not consistent in acknowledging that hypothetical initiatives must remain hypothetical, and that they cannot be converted subsequently into something more like the purely formal deductions of mathematics. And, despite the need for experiments to help decide how a natural phenomenon occurs, he sometimes described the results of his scientific method in language which could almost have been taken directly from the section of Aristotle's *Posterior Analytics* quoted above: "As far as physics is concerned, I believed that I knew nothing at all if I could only say how things may be, without being able to prove that they could not be otherwise" (letter of 11 March 1640: AT III 39: CSMK 145). This raises a question about the kind of certainty Descartes claimed for the results of his scientific method when applied to natural phenomena.

CERTAINTY AND PROBABILITY

Descartes' claims about the relative certainty of scientific explanations are appropriately ambivalent. The ambivalence reflects the comparatively unsophisticated concepts of certainty and uncertainty available to the early seventeenth century. The scholastic tradition was committed to a sharp dichotomy between two kinds of knowledge-claim; one was certain and demonstrated, and the other was dialectical and uncertain. As far as scholastics were concerned, therefore, one had to choose between claiming to have demonstrated, certain knowledge – which was the only kind worth having – or the type of uncertain opinion which hardly deserved further discussion, since it was completely uncorroborated. Descartes' efforts to describe the degree of certainty that resulted from his scientific practice are best understood as a doomed attempt to classify the probability produced by the new scientific method in the language of the scholastics. Thus he sometimes claims that his explanations are certain; he cannot concede that they are uncertain without automatically excluding them as genuine alternatives to the established explanations of the schools. At the same time he recognizes that they are not absolutely certain, that they do not enjoy the type of certainty that can be realized in mathematics, that they are only morally certain or as certain as one could hope to be in this type of enterprise.[21] Another compromise, consistent with the claims about a metaphysical foundation, is the argument that the first principles are certain whereas the explanations of particular natural phenomena are more or less uncertain.

Descartes consistently claims that his first principles, or the more general claims about matter and the laws of nature, are very certain.

as regards the other things I assumed which cannot be perceived by any sense, they are all so simple and so familiar, and even so few in number, that if you compare them with the diversity and marvellous artifice which is apparent in the structure of visible organs, you will have far more reason to suspect that, rather than include some which are not genuine, I have omitted some which are in fact at work in us. And knowing that nature always operates in the most simple and easy way possible, you will perhaps agree that it is impossible to find more plausible explanations of how it operates than those which are proposed here.   (AT XI 201)

This point was reiterated on a number of occasions; the basic hypotheses of the Cartesian system were said to be simple and relatively few, and at the same time they explained a great variety of disparate natural phenomena. "Simple" had connotations of being easily understood, possibly by analogy with some natural phenomenon with which we are ordinarily familiar. It also implied that a hypothesis was consistent with the limited categories available in Cartesian natural philosophy, such as size, speed, and quantity of motion. In other words, it was possible to imagine or construct a mechanical model of a so-called "simple" hypothesis, whereas the kinds of explanations proposed by others were allegedly difficult to understand, not amenable to simple modeling, and probably expressed in the metaphysical language of the schools. Thus he wrote in Part III of the *Principles:* "I do not think that it is possible to think up any alternative principles for explaining the real world that are simpler, or easier to understand, or even more probable" (AT VIIIA 102: CSM I 257).

Descartes was aware of the objection that one could construct a hypothesis to explain any conceivable phenomenon and that, as a result, hypotheses could be accused of being ad hoc. His answer to this objection included a number of elements. One was that he used only a few hypotheses to explain many different phenomena: "it seems to me that my explanations should be all the more accepted, in proportion as I make them depend on fewer things" (AT VI 239).

Given the few principles from which he begins, the variety of phenomena which are explained provides an extra degree of confirmation.

In order to come to know the true nature of this visible world, it is not enough to find causes which provide an explanation of what we see far off in the heavens; the selfsame causes must also allow everything which we see right here on earth to be deduced from them. There is, however, no need for us to consider all these terrestrial phenomena in order to determine the causes of more general things. But we shall know that we have determined such causes correctly afterwards, when we notice that they serve to explain not only the effects which we were originally looking at, but all these other phenomena, which we were not thinking of beforehand.

(AT VIIIA 98–9: CSM I 255)

Apart from the points just mentioned, Descartes also argued that the new natural philosophy should be compared, not with some abstract criterion of what counts as a good theory, but with other theories available in the 1630s to explain the same range of phenomena. In that context, Cartesian science was claimed to be the best available. This is clear from a letter to Father Morin of 13 July 1638:

Finally, you say that there is nothing easier than to fit some cause to any given effect. But although there are indeed many effects to which it is easy to fit different causes, one to one, it is not so easy to fit a single cause to many different effects, unless it is the true cause which produces them. There are often effects where, in order to prove which is their true cause, it is enough to suggest a cause from which they can all be clearly deduced. And I claim that all the causes which I have discussed are of this type . . . If one compares the assumptions of others with my own, that is, all their real qualities, their substantial forms, their elements and similar things which are almost infinite in number, with this one assumption that all bodies are composed of parts – something which can be observed with the naked eye in some cases and can be proved by an unlimited number of reasons in others . . . and finally, if one compares what I have deduced about vision, salt, winds, clouds, snow, thunder, the rainbow, and so on from my assumptions, with what they have deduced from theirs . . . I hope that would suffice to convince those with an open mind that the effects which I explain have no other causes apart from those from which I deduce them.

(AT II 199–200: CSMK 107)

The conclusion of the *Principles* repeats the same claim; if a few assumptions can explain a wide variety of disparate phenomena, then that argurs well for their plausibility:

Now if people look at all the many properties relating to magnetism, fire and the fabric of the entire world, which I have deduced in this book from just a few principles, then, even if they think that my assumption of these principles was arbitrary and groundless, they will still perhaps acknowledge that it would hardly have been possible for so many items to fit into a coherent pattern if the original principles had been false.

(AT VIIIA 328: CSM I 290)

If we accept the point being made, that a few basic hypotheses are put to work in explaining all the natural phenomena mentioned, what degree of certainty should Descartes claim for his first principles? Not surprisingly, one finds two rather different claims in this context: one of them concedes that the confirmed principles are only more or less probable, whereas the other assumes that they are certain and demonstrated. The more modest claim is found in a letter to an unknown correspondent, written about 1646: "I would not dare claim that those [principles] are the true principles of nature. All I claim is that, by assuming them as principles, I have satisfied myself in all the many things which depend on them. And I see nothing which prevents me from making some progress in the knowledge of the truth" (AT IV 690). The more confident claim about moral and metaphysical certainty comes in the penultimate article of the *Principles:*

there are some matters, even in relation to the things in nature, which we regard as absolutely, and more than just morally, certain. . . . This certainty is based on a metaphysical foundation . . . Mathematical demonstrations have this kind of certainty, as does the knowledge that material things exist; and the same goes for all evident reasoning about material things. And perhaps even these results of mine will be allowed into the class of absolute certainties, if people consider how they have been deduced in an unbroken chain from the first and simplest principles of human knowledge. . . . it seems that all the other phenomena, or at least the general features of the universe and the earth which I have described, can hardly be intelligibly explained except in the way I have suggested.

(AT VIIIA 328–9: CSM I 290–1)

The French version of this text is even more explicit on the demonstrative character of the explanations found in Cartesian physics:

I think that one should also recognise that I proved, by a mathematical demonstration, all those things which I wrote, at least the more general

things concerning the structure of the heavens and the earth, and in the way
in which I wrote them. For I took care to propose as doubtful all those things
which I thought were such.   (AT IXB 325)

The problem of classifying the type of certainty Descartes might
reasonably have claimed for his principles and hypotheses is best
understood historically, by taking account of the lack of a concept of
probability in the early part of the seventeenth century and of the
assumption of the scholastic tradition that anything less than demonstrated truths was as unreliable as mere opinion or guesswork. In
this context, Descartes claimed that his natural philosophy was certain and demonstrated; at the same time, realizing that it could
hardly be as certain as the formal proofs of mathematics, he con-
ceded that only the more general assumptions of his system were
certain, whereas the explanations of particular natural phenomena
were more or less certain.

This point reopens the question about the kind of evidence Descartes thought was appropriate to supporting scientific claims, and
the relative importance of metaphysical arguments vis-à-vis experi-
ential evidence. There is no suggestion that Descartes ever reneged
on the conviction, so clear in the *Meditations*, that one can realize a
degree of certainty which is equivalent to indubitability by reasoning about concepts and axioms. This kind of metaphysical certainty
is appropriate to the foundations of our knowledge, whether that
knowledge is mathematical, physical, or otherwise.

However, if we wish to make judgments about the physical world,
then we cannot assume naively that our sensations reflect the way
the world is. Nor can we discover in any detail what kind of natural
phenomena occur, nor what mechanisms explain their occurrence,
by introspecting our ideas. There has to be some provision, therefore, for beginning with clear and distinct metaphysical concepts
and axioms and somehow making the crucial transition to describing and explaining the natural world around us. This can be done
only by consulting our experience of the natural world, and this
implies that we use our senses in order to gain scientific knowledge.

At the same time, Descartes can be correctly described as a critic
of the reliability of empirical evidence. His critique was carefully
developed to identify a number of ways in which we might draw
erroneous conclusions from our sensory experience. Two of these

have already been identified: (a) We might ignore the distinction between primary and secondary qualities and, as a result, assume that our sensations resemble the causes of our sensations; and (b) we might argue too hastily from an experiment to some conclusion without taking account of the many ways in which an experiment can mislead. In general, we are in danger of spontaneously making naive, uncritical judgments about the physical world without questioning the reliability of our sensations or the logic of conclusions drawn from reliable observations. Such spontaneous judgments should be distinguished from other judgments, equally based on sensation, which we make after due deliberation and reflection. Unfortunately for the modern reader, Descartes expressed this distinction in terms of a contrast between experience and reason; what he meant was a contrast between two types of judgment, both equally based on experience. This is made explicit in the following text:

> It is clear from this that when we say 'The reliability of the intellect is much greater than that of the senses,' this means merely that when we are grown up the judgments which we make as a result of various new observations are more reliable than those which we formed without any reflection in our early childhood; and this is undoubtedly true.
>
> (Sixth Replies: AT VII 438: CSM II 295)

For this reason, a true philosopher "should never rely on the senses, that is, on the ill-considered judgments of his childhood, in preference to his mature powers of reason" (AT VIIIA 39: CSM I 232).

It is obvious, then, that one cannot avoid the necessity of relying on experientially based evidence. Descartes acknowledges the need for this kind of evidence in natural philosophy and uses it extensively in the scientific experiments which he describes. He says openly, in Part VI of the *Discourse,* "regarding observations, that the further we advance in our knowledge, the more necessary they become" (AT VI 63: CSM I 143). On this point, his scientific practice corresponded with his methodological rule, for he spent much more time doing experiments or reading about those done by others than he ever spent in mere thinking. However, for reasons already mentioned, he had little confidence in experiments he had not checked himself.[22] Hence there were serious limits to the extent to which he could hope to complete a comprehensive explanation of nature; he was likely to be frustrated "by the brevity of life or the lack of observations" (AT VI 62: CSM I 143). For this reason, Descartes decided to devote his life to the pursuit of what he called a "practical philosophy which might replace the speculative philosophy taught in the schools" (AT VI 61: CSM I 142). "I will say only that I have resolved to devote the rest of my life to nothing other than trying to acquire some knowledge of nature from which we may derive rules in medicine which are more reliable than those we have had up till now" (AT VI 78: CSM I 151). This is equivalent to a commitment to doing experiments, the cost of which he often complained of. To attempt to gain this practical knowledge in any other way, apart from experimentally, would be to join those "philosophers who neglect experience and think that the truth will emerge from their own heads as Minerva did from that of Jupiter" (*Regulae* Rule V: AT X 380).

A full account of the contribution of Descartes to the history of philosophies of science would involve examining his work in the light of his successors in the seventeenth century. Without examining this supplementary evidence here – which would include the ways in which Descartes was understood by, for example, La Forge, Malebranche, Rohault, Poisson, Cordemoy and Régis – there is reason to believe that his successors shared a common interpretation of the main features of Descartes' philosophy of science.²³ These common features are best understood in contrast with the scholastic philosophy for which they were proposed as a substitute. For Descartes, the contrast was between the practical and the speculative, the explanatory and the nonexplanatory, the critical and the naively uncritical, the mechanistic and the formal, the mathematical and quantitative versus the qualitative. Despite the favorable contrast with the natural philosophy of the schools, however, Descartes continued to accept the scholastic assumption that we should construct our metaphysics first, on the epistemic basis of reflection on ordinary experience, and that any subsequent explanations of natural phenomena must be consistent with the foundational metaphysics.

Once the foundations were in place, it was accepted that we could never know the way the world is by consulting our sensations and inferring from them that the causes of our sensations must resemble our subjective experiences. Besides, if we assume that physical phenomena are constituted by the interactions of very small particles of matter, then the sheer size of such particles of infinitely divisible matter would put their observation beyond our reach. For these two reasons, we can only come to know how the physical world is by hypothesis.

For Descartes, to explain a natural phenomenon is not to redescribe it in the language of forms and qualities, as was done in the schools. To explain, in this context, is to construct a mechanical model of how the phenomenon in question is caused. This model construction is necessarily hypothetical. So, beginning with the basic laws of nature and the metaphysical foundations established in the *Meditations* or in Book I of the *Principles*, Descartes set out to construct the kind of models his concept of explanation demanded. Although he continued to claim absolute certainty for the foundations, it was clear that he could not be as confident about the more detailed explanations of natural phenomena. These explanations depended on observations, and on performing complex experiments the interpretation of which introduced new reasons for doubt. There was also another reason for caution which emerged at this stage, namely Descartes' skepticism about the possibility of ever identifying the multiplicity of variables involved in any complex natural phenomenon. What begins on "indubitable" foundations, therefore, quickly gets mired in the almost immeasurably complex detail of unobservable particles of matter interacting at unobservable speeds. The crucial experiments which we perform to help choose the most plausible explanation are open to various interpretations. Hence the birth of the well-known Cartesian tradition of simply imagining some mechanism by which small parts of matter in motion might have caused some natural phenomenon which we observe.

To those who objected: this does not result in the kind of demonstrated knowledge prized by the scholastic tradition, Descartes replied that those who demand such demonstrations do not know what they are looking for, nor what they ought to look for. It is not possible to realize the same kind of certainty in physics as in mathematics or metaphysics. We have to settle for less.

This suggests that Descartes' philosophy of science was very much a product of the time in which it was developed. The 1630s and 1640s were a time of transition from the science of forms and qualities to what we describe now as modern science. One finds features of both of these philosophies of science in Descartes. What was significantly new was the commitment to mechanical explanation rather than the "occult powers" of the scholastic tradition, and the recognition that this type of explanation must be hypothetical. But for Descartes, lacking a theory of probability, this seemed compatible with the continued claim that his natural philosophy was not only superior in explanatory power to that of the schools, but that it was just as certain; or at least, that its more fundamental principles were demonstrated.

NOTES

1 *Posterior Analytics*, 71b 8–12, 73a 21–2.
2 The extent to which scholastic philosophy influenced the curriculum of colleges and universities in France in the seventeenth century is comprehensively documented in Brockliss, *French Higher Education in the Seventeenth and Eighteenth Centuries*.
3 This was summarized in the axiom: "nihil est in intellectu quod prius non fuit in sensu." French Cartesians in the period immediately after Descartes understood his theory of innate ideas as, in part, a response to what they considered to be a generally accepted scholastic doctrine, that all ideas derive originally from sensation. See, for example, Poisson, *Commentaire ou remarques sur la méthode de M. Descartes*, unpaginated preface, which discusses the "famous principle on which depends some of the dogmas of scholasticism, that nothing enters the mind which does not pass first through the senses." The same doctrine is discussed at some length on pp. 124–38. Cf. Le Grand, *An Entire Body of Philosophy*, p. 4. Among scholastic defenders of the thesis, even after Descartes, see Huet, *Censura Philosophiae Cartesianae*, pp. 51–3.
4 Even dedicated Cartesians, such as Jacques Rohault, continued the tradition of explaining natural phenomena in terms of matter and form. See Rohault, *A System of Natural Philosophy*, translated by J. Clarke, pp. 21–2. The original French text was published in 1671.
5 Mahoney (trans.), *The World*, pp. 1–3.
6 Mahoney, *The World*, p. 5.
7 Mahoney, *The World*, p. 7.
8 Mahoney, *The World*, p. 49.
9 Letter to Mersenne, 27 May 1638 (AT II 141–2, 143–4:CSMK 103). The same use of the word "demonstration" is found in Descartes' letter to Plempius, 3 October 1637 (AT I 420:CSMK 64).
10 The principle of parsimony in metaphysics, that one should not postu-

late the existence of more distinct entities or types of entity than is necessary, is usually attributed to William of Occam (1280?–1349?). See for example his *Quodlibeta* V, Q.1

11 Mahoney, *The World*, p. 9.

12 Mahoney, *The World*, p. 39.

13 Although the letter was written in French, the italicized phrase was in Latin: *sub scientiam non cadit*. Descartes to Mersenne, 13 November 1629 (AT I 73). See also Descartes to Mersenne, 11 June 1640 (AT III 80); Descartes to Cavendish, 15 May 1646 (AT IV 416–17).

14 Cf. similar responses to Mersenne, 23 February 1643 (AT III 634) and 26 April 1643 (AT III 652).

15 In the original Latin text, "hypotheses non fingo." Isaac Newton, *Mathematical Principles of Natural Philosophy and His System of the World*, ed. Cajori, p. 547.

16 Cf. Rule Nine of the *Regulae:* AT X 400: CSM I 33.

17 Descartes frequently pointed to problems in interpreting experimental results, especially when they seemed to disconfirm his own theories. However, the objections he raised were, in principle, legitimate. See, for example, Descartes to Mersenne, 9 February 1639 (AT II 497–8), 29 January 1640 (AT III 7), 11 June 1640 (AT III 80), 4 January 1643 (AT III 609).

18 Cf. *Principles* Part I, arts. 51–7: AT VIIIA 24–7: CSM I 210–12.

19 In the Third Meditation, Descartes argues that "something cannot arise from nothing" (*nec posse aliquid a nihilo fieri*) (AT VII 40: CSM II 28). In the Second Replies to Objections, he says that the causal principle on which he relied in the Third Meditation was equivalent to "nothing comes from nothing" (*a nihilo nihil fit*) (AT VII 135: CSM II 97).

20 Cf. Mahoney, *The World* pp. 61–76: AT XI 38–47.

21 There was a tradition in scholastic philosophy and theology of distinguishing various degrees of certainty in terms of the kind of evidence required to achieve them and the relative importance of acting on our beliefs in different contexts. "Moral certainty" referred to the certainty required for important human actions, such as marrying one's partner or defending oneself against an aggressor. In this type of case, one does not usually have mathematical certainty about various relevant features of the context, but one is sufficiently certain to act and to be excused of responsibility if, despite taking normal precautions, one is mistaken. Cf. French version of *Principles*, Part IV, art. 205: "moral certainty is certainty which is sufficient to regulate our behaviour, or which measures up to the certainty we have on matters relating to the conduct of life which we never normally doubt, though we know that it is possible, absolutely speaking, that they may be false" (CSM I 289).

22 "I have little trust in experiments which I have not performed myself" (letter to Huygens of 1643: AT III 617).

23 For an analysis of how these authors understood Descartes' philosophy of science, see Clarke *Occult Powers and Hypotheses*.

10   Descartes' physics

Physics and its foundations were central to Descartes' thought. Although today he is probably best known for his metaphysics of mind and body, or for his epistemological program, in the seventeenth century Descartes was at very least equally well known for his mechanistic physics and the mechanist world of geometrical bodies in motion which he played a large role in making acceptable to his contemporaries. In this essay I shall outline Descartes' mechanical philosophy in its historical context. After some brief remarks on the immediate background to Descartes' program for physics, and a brief outline of the historical development of his physics, we shall discuss the foundations of Descartes' physics, including his concepts of body and motion and his views on the laws of motion.

I. BACKGROUND

Before we can appreciate the details of Descartes' physics, we must appreciate something of the historical context in which it emerged and grew.

Most important to the background was, of course, the Aristotelian natural philosophy that had dominated medieval thought.[1] Aristotelian natural philosophy had come under significant attack in what came to be known as the Renaissance.[2] But it is important to realize that well into the seventeenth century, throughout Descartes' life, the Aristotelian natural philosophy was very much alive, and relatively well; it was what Descartes himself studied at La Flèche, and what was still studied there (and in most other schools in Europe and Britain) in 1650 when Descartes met his death in Sweden.[3]

The Aristotelian natural philosophy was a matter of enormous complexity. But briefly, what concerned Descartes most directly in his own physics is the doctrine of substantial forms.[4] For the schoolmen, bodies were made up of prime matter and substantial form. Matter is what every body shares, while form is what differentiates bodies from one another. And so, it is form that explains why stones fall, and fire rises, why horses neigh and humans reason. There are, of course, numerous different ways of understanding what these forms were to the schoolmen.[5] Descartes was fond of thinking of them as little minds attached to bodies, causing the behavior characteristic of different sorts of substances. In the *Sixth Replies*, for example, he has the following remarks to make about the scholastic conception of heaviness which he was taught in his youth:

But what makes it especially clear that my idea of gravity was taken largely from the idea I had of the mind is the fact that I thought that gravity carried bodies towards the centre of the earth as if it had some knowledge [*cognitio*] of the centre within itself. For this surely could not happen without knowledge, and there can be no knowledge except in a mind.

(AT VII 442: CSM II 298) [6]

This natural philosophy will be one of Descartes' most important targets in his own writings on natural philosophy.

Descartes was by no means alone in opposing the philosophy of the schools. As I noted earlier, there had been numerous attacks on the Aristotelian natural philosophy by the time Descartes learned his physics at school, various varieties of Platonism, Hermeticism, the Chemical Philosophy of Paracelsus, among other movements.[7] But most important to understanding Descartes was the revival of ancient atomism. In opposition to the Aristotelian view of the world, the ancient atomists, Democritus, Epicurus, Lucretius, attempted to explain the characteristic behavior of bodies, not in terms of substantial forms, but in terms of the size, shape, and motion of the smaller bodies, atoms, that make up the grosser bodies of everyday experience, atoms which were taken to move in empty space, a void. Atomistic thought was widely discussed in the sixteenth century, and by the early seventeenth century it had a number of visible adherents, including Nicholas Hill, Sebastian Basso, Francis Bacon, and Galileo Galilei.[8] When all was said and done, Descartes' physics wound up retaining a number of crucial features of the physics he was taught in school, and differing from the world of the atomists; most notably, Descartes rejected the indivisible atoms and empty spaces that characterize atomistic physics. But Descartes' rejection of the forms and matter of the schools, and his adoption of the mechanist program for explaining everything in the physical world in terms of size, shape, and motion of the corpuscles that make up bodies, is hardly conceivable without the influence of atomist thought.

2. THE DEVELOPMENT OF DESCARTES' SYSTEM

Descartes attended the Jesuit college of La Flèche, where he received a full course in Aristotelian natural philosophy.[9] In addition to Aristotle, taught at La Flèche from a humanist perspective, Descartes received an education in mathematics quite unusual for the Aristotelian tradition.[10] But Descartes' career as a natural philosopher, properly speaking, begins with his meeting with Isaac Beeckman in November of 1618 in the town of Breda. Descartes, then twenty-two years old and out of school for only two years, had been leading the life of a soldier, apparently intending to be come a military engineer. Beeckman, eight years the young Descartes' senior, was a devoted scientific and mathematical amateur, and had been for some years; his journals, rediscovered only in this century, show an interest in a wide variety of scientific and mathematical subjects. The journals also give the record of the conversations between the two young men. It is clear from those records that Descartes was very much drawn into the new mechanistic and mathematical physics that Beeckman was enthusiastically (if unsystematically) developing. Beeckman set problems and questions for his younger colleague, and in his journal are the records of Descartes' struggles over a wide variety of questions in harmony and accoustics, physics, and mathematics, all approached in a decidedly non-Aristotelian way, attempting to apply mathematics to problems in natural philosophy.[11] There is little in these early writings that suggests Descartes' own later physics in any real detail, to be sure; indeed, there is every reason to belived that the young Mr. du Peron, as Descartes styled himself at that time, subscribed to the doctrines of atoms and the void that Beeckman held and he, Descartes, was later to reject.[12] But though the actual contact lasted only a few months (Beeckman left Breda on 2 January 1619), the effects were profound. As he wrote to Beeckman on 23 April 1619, a few months after parting: "You are truly the only one who roused my inactivity, who recalled from my memory knowledge that had almost slipped away, and who led my mind, wandering away from serious undertakings, back to something better" (AT X 162–3: CSMK 4).

The decade or so that followed the meeting with Beeckman was very productive for Descartes. There is every evidence that it was then that he worked out his celebrated method, his geometry, and important parts of his theory of light, in particular, his law of refraction.[13] From discussions in the *Rules for the Direction of the Mind*, there is also reason to believe that he was also concerned with other problems, like that of the nature of magnetism.[14] Furthermore, in the *Rules* there are also evidences of his interest in the foundations of the mechanical philosophy that now characterized his thought. In particular, in his doctrine of simple natures, he seems to have presented the seeds of an argument that everything in the physical world is explicable in terms of size, shape, and motion. In the later sections of the *Rules* we also have a strong suggestion of the doctrine of the identification of body and extension that characterizes his mature thought.[15]

But the mature natural philosophy only begins to emerge in the late 1620s, after Descartes sets aside the composition of the *Rules*, and turns to the construction of his full system of knowledge. Important here is, of course, the now lost metaphysics of the winter of 1629–30, which, for Descartes, was clearly connected with the foundations of his science.[16] But at the same time that he was worrying about the soul and God, he was also working on the sciences themselves. Letters from 1629 and 1930 show that he was working on the theory of motion, space, and body, on optics and light, on the mechanist explanation of the physical properties of bodies, on the explanation of the particular atmospheric and clestial phenomena, and anatomy.[17] This work culminated in 1633 with the completion of *The World*. *The World*, as it comes down to us, is composed of two principal parts, the *Treatise on Light*, and the *Treatise on Man*. The *Treatise on Light* deals with physics proper. After a few introductory chapters, Descartes envisions God creating a world of purely extended bodies in the "imaginary spaces" of the schoolmen. He then derives the laws those bodies would have to obey in motion, and argues that set in motion and left to themselves, they would form the cosmos as we know it, innumerable stars around which travel planets, and shows how features of our world like gravity and heaviness would emerge in that context. In this way he explains many features of our physical world without appeal to the substantial forms of the schoolmen. The *Treatise on Man*, on the other hand, deals with human biology. Imagining God to have made from this extended stuff a machine that resembles our bodies, Descartes shows how much explained by the schoolmen in terms of souls can be explained in terms of size, shape, and motion alone.

This sketch of a mechanical world was not to be published in Descartes' lifetime, though. When Descartes found out that Galileo had been condemned in Rome in 1633, he withdrew his *World* from publication, and, indeed, vowed not to publish his views at all.[18] However, his vow was short-lived. Though *The World* never did appear in Descartes' lifetime, by September or October of 1634, Descartes was at work on a new project, and by March 1636, a new work was finished.[19] The work in question was a collection of three scientific treatises in French, the *Geometry*, the *Optics*, and the *Meteorology*, gathered together and published in June of 1637 with an introduction, the *Discourse on the Method*. Much of the work that appears in these writings dates from much earlier. But what is distinctive about this work is the way in which it is presented. A central feature of the *Discourse* and *Essays* is the lack of the full framework of physics and metaphysics that, Descartes admitted, lay under the samples of work that he presented. The full system was sketched out, to be sure. In Part IV of the *Discourse* Descartes presented an outline of his metaphysics, and in Part V a sketch of the physics of *The World*. But, as Descartes explained in Part VI of the *Discourse*, the actual scientific treatises that follow give just the results of his investigations; the material in the *Optics* and *Meteorology* is presented hypothetically, using plausible but undefended assumptions and models, not because Descartes thought that this was the best way to present a body of material, but because in this way he could present his results without revealing the details of his physics that he knew would raise controversy.[20] The *Essays* contained much of interest, including the laws of refraction, a discussion of vision, and Descartes' important analysis of the rainbow. But conspicuously missing was any discussion of Copernicanism, or any account of Descartes' doctrine of body as essentially extended.

The reception given to the *Discourse* and *Essays* must have been sufficiently encouraging, for by the late 1630s, Descartes decided to embark on a proper publication of his system, set out in proper order, beginning with the metaphysics and the foundations of his physics. First to be completed was the *Meditations*, finished in the spring of 1640, and published in August of 1641. Although the *Meditations* are mainly concerned with metaphysical issues, they do contain elements of the foundations of Descartes' physics, including the existence of God (essential for grounding the laws of motion, as we shall see), and the existence and nature of body. In January 1641, on the eve of the publication of the *Meditations*, Descartes confided to Mersenne:

I may tell you, between ourselves, that these six *Meditations* contain all the foundations of my physics. But please do not tell people, for that might make it harder for supporters of Aristotle to approve them. I hope that readers will gradually get used to my principles, and recognize their truth, before they notice that they destroy the principles of Aristotle.

(AT III 297–8: CSMK 173)

But more directly important for the dissemination of Descartes' views on the natural world is the publication of the *Principles of Philosophy.*

Descartes began to contemplate the publication of his complete physics as early as the autumn of 1640, while the *Meditations* were circulating and he was awaiting the objections that he intended to publish together with his answers. Originally Descartes had planned to publish a textbook of his philosophy in Latin, unlike *The World* and the *Discourse*, together with an annotated version of the *Summa* of Eustachius a Sancto Paulo, a textbook widely used in the schools. In this way, Descartes thought, he could demonstrate the weakness of the standard Aristotelian physics, and the superiority of his own mechanical philosophy.[21] This plan was soon set aside in favor of a direct exposition of his own views.[22] The first parts of the incomplete work went to the printer in February 1643, and appeared in July of 1644.[23] The work proved popular enough to issue in a French version in 1647. Though Descartes himself did not do the translation, many of the significant changes between the Latin and French editions suggest that he took a real interest in the preparation of the new edition.

Descartes represents the project to his friend Constantijn Huygens as if the *Principles* were merely a translation of *The World*. Refering to some disputes he was involved with at the University of Utrecht, Descartes writes: "Perhaps these scholastic wars will result in my *World* being brought into the world. It would be out already, I think, were it not that I want to teach it to speak Latin first. I shall call it the *Summa Philosophiae* to make it more welcome to the scholastics" (AT III 523: CSMK 209–10). But the *Principles* is much more than a translation of *The World*. Leaving aside the numerous places in which Descartes has significantly revised and clarified his views, the structure is altogether different. Unlike *The World*, the *Principles* begins with an account of Descartes' first philosophy, his metaphysics. Parts II–IV correspond more closely to the contents of *The World*. Part II deals with the notions of body, motion, and the laws of motion, corresponding roughly to the rather informal exposition of chapters 6 and 7 in *The World*. Parts III and IV correspond roughly to chapters 8–15 in *The World*. As in the earlier work, Descartes presents and defends a vortex theory of planetary motion, a view that is unmistakably Copernican, despite attempts to argue that on his view, the Earth is more truly at rest than it is in other theories. But in the *Principles*, light lacks the central organizing role that it has in *The World*, and the *Principles* contains discussions of a number of topics, including magnetism, for example, that do not appear at all in *The World*. Clearly the *Principles* is something other than *The World* with a classical education.

With the *Principles* we have what can be considered a canonical presentation of Descartes' views in physics. While the earlier works present important insights, as do discussions of various issues in Descartes' correspondence, the *Principles* will be our main text in unraveling the complexities of Descartes' physical world.

3. BODY AND EXTENSION

Descartes' natural philosophy begins with his conception of body. For Descartes, of course, extension is the essence of body or corporeal substance. Or, to use the technical terminology that Descartes adopted in the *Principles*, extension is the principal attribute of corporeal substance. For Descartes, as for many others, we know substances not directly but only through their accidents, properties, qualities, etc. But among these, one is special, Descartes holds. And so, in the *Principles* Descartes writes: "And indeed a substance can be known from any of its attributes. But yet there is one special property of any substance, which constitutes its nature and essence, and to which all others are referred" (*Principles* Part I, art. 53). This special property is extension in body, and thought in mind. All other notions "are referred" to this special property insofar as it is through the notion of extension that we understand size, shape, motion, etc., and it is through the notion of thought that we understand the particular thoughts we have, Descartes claims.[24] The notion of extension is so closely bound to the notion of corporeal substance that, for Descartes, we cannot comprehend the notion of this substance apart from its principal attribute. Descartes writes in the *Principles:*

When [others] distinguish substance from extension or quantity, they either understand nothing by the name 'substance,' or they have only a confused idea of an incorporeal substance, which they falsely attribute to corporeal substance, and leave for extension (which, however, they call an accident) the true idea of a corporeal substance. And so they plainly express in words something other than what they understand in their minds.

(*Principles* Part II, art. 9)[25]

Elsewhere Descartes suggests that there is only a conceptual distinction or "distinction of reason" (*distinctio rationalis*) between corporeal substance and its principal attribute.[26] In addition to the principal attribute of body, extension, which is inseparable from body, Descartes recognizes what he calls modes, particular sizes, shapes, and motions that individual bodies can have. Although not essential to body, the modes Descartes attributes to bodies must be understood *through* extension; they are *ways* of being extended for Descartes.[27] In this way insofar as they are not modes of extension, colors and tastes, heat or cold are not really in bodies but in the mind that perceives them.

It is important to recognize that while Descartes holds that the essence of body is extension, he does not understand the notion of an essence in precisely the way his scholastic contemporaries did. Put briefly, basic to scholastic metaphysics is the distinction between a substance and its accidents.[28] Now, certain of those accidents are especially important, those that constitute the essence or nature of that substance. A human being, for example, is essentially a rational being and an animal; take either of those away from a substance, and it is no longer human. But nonessential accidents bear a completely different relation to the substance; they may be lost without changing the nature of the substance. Now, some of those accidents are the sorts of things that can only be found in human beings. Risibility and the actual act of laughing were thought to be possible only for something that has reason.[29] But many other accidents (color, size, etc.) bear no such relation to the essence; while such accidents must be understood as being in *some* substance or other, they are not necessarily connected to the essence of the human being. In this sense the Aristotelian framework allows for there to be accidents which are, as it were, tacked onto substances which are otherwise conceived of as complete. This is quite foreign to Descartes' way of thinking. For him *all* of the accidents in a corporeal substance must be understood through its essence, extension; there is nothing in body that is not comprehended through the essential property of extension. In this way Cartesian bodies are just the objects of geometry made real, purely geometrical objects that exist outside of the minds that conceive them.

Though there is every reason to believe that Descartes held the conception of body as extension from the late 1620s on, he offers little in the way of serious argument for the claim before 1640 or so.[30] But the question is taken up in depth in the writings that follow, mainly the *Meditations* (along with the *Objections and Replies*) and the *Principles of Philosophy*. Basic to the argument is the celebrated proof Descartes offers for the existence of the external world. While there are some significant differences between the versions that Descartes gives in different places, all of the versions of the argument turn on the fact that we are entitled to believe that our sensory ideas of bodies derive from bodies themselves. In the version Descartes offers in the *Meditations*, this claim is grounded in the fact that we have a great inclination to believe this, and the nondeceiving God has given us no means to correct that great inclination;[31] in the version in the *Principles* it is grounded in the fact that "we seem to ourselves clearly to see that its idea comes from things placed outside of us" (*Principles* Part II, art. 1). But, Descartes claims, the body whose existence this proves is not the body of everyday experience; when we examine our idea of body, we find that the idea we have of it is the idea of a geometrical object, and it is *this* Cartesian body whose existence the argument proves. Thus Descartes concludes the version of the argument in the Sixth Meditation as follows:

It follows that corporeal things exist. They may not all exist in a way that exactly corresponds with my sensory grasp of them, for in many cases the grasp of the senses is very obscure and confused; but indeed, everything we clearly and distinctly understand is in them, that is, everything, generally speaking, which is included in the object of pure mathemathics.

(AT VII 80: CSM II 55)

In this way the argument for the existence of the external world serves not only to restore the world lost to the skeptical arguments of the First Meditation; but also to replace the sensual world of colors, tastes, and sounds with the spare geometrical world of Cartesian physics.

But, of course, this just pushes the investigation one step back; for this argument plainly depends on the view that our idea of body is as Descartes says it is, the idea of something that has geometrical properties and geometrical properties alone. To establish this conclusion, Descartes seems to appeal to at least three separate arguments, what might be called the argument from elimination, the argument from objective reality, and the complete concept argument.

While it is suggested in the wax example in the *Meditations*,[32] the argument from elimination appears most explicitly in the *Principles*. In *Principles* Part II, art. 4, Descartes claims to show "that the nature of matter, or of body regarded in general does not consist in the fact that it is a thing that is hard or heavy or colored or affected with any other mode of sense, but only in the fact that it is a thing extended in length, breadth, and depth." The argument proceeds by considering the case of hardness (*durities*). Descartes argues that even if we imagined bodies to recede from us when we try to touch them, so that "we never sensed hardness," things "would not on account of that lose the nature of body." He concludes: "By the same argument it can be shown that weight and color and all of the other qualities of that sort that we sense in a material body can be taken away from it, leaving it intact. From this it follows that its nature depends on one of those qualities" (*Principles* Part II, art. 4, Latin version).[33] The argument seems to be that extension must be the essence of body because all other accidents can be eliminated without thereby eliminating body, and so, without extension, there can be no body.

But, interesting as this argument is, it doesn't seem to do the job. Descartes needs to establish that our idea of body is the idea of a thing whose only genuine properties are geometrical, a thing that *excludes* all other properties. But what the strategy in this argument establishes is that our idea of body is the idea of a thing at least *some* of whose properties must be geometrical. From the fact that we can conceive of a body without hardness, or color, or warmth, it does not follow that *no* body is really hard, or colored or warm, any more than it follows from the fact that we can conceive of a nonspherical body that no body is really spherical. At best the argument from elimination establishes that the essence of body is extension in the weaker Aristotelian sense, and not in the stronger Cartesian sense.

What I have called the argument from objective reality is suggested most clearly in the Fifth Meditation, whose title promises an investigation of "the essence of material things. . . ." When we examine our idea of body, Descartes claims, we find that what is distinct in our ideas of body is "the quantity that philosophers commonly call continuous, or the extension of its quantity, or, better, the extension of the thing quantized, extension in length, breadth, and depth . . ." (AT VII 63: CSM II 44). His reasoning seems to be something like this. What strikes Descartes as extremely significant about the geometrical features of our ideas of body is that we can perform proofs about those features, and demonstrate geometrical facts that we did not know before, and that we seem not to have put into the ideas ourselves. But, Descartes notes, "it is obvious that whatever is true is something, and I have already amply demonstrated that everything of which I am clearly aware is true" (AT VII 65: CSM II 45). Descartes seems to assume that whatever is true must be true of *something*, and so he concludes these geometrical features we find in our ideas of body must, in some sense, exist. At this stage in the argument we cannot, of course, conclude that they exist outside the mind. And so, Descartes concludes, they exist as objects normally exist in the mind, as objects of ideas, as objective realities. And so, Descartes takes himself to have established, our ideas of bodies really have the geometrical properties we are inclined to attribute to them.

But what does this argument really show? It certainly can be seen to establish that our idea of body is the idea of something that has geometrical properties. But Descartes wants to establish a stronger claim, that bodies not only *have* geometrical properties, but that they have geometrical properties *alone,* that is, that they *lack* all other properties. So far as I can see, the argument suggested in the Fifth Meditation falls short of establishing the essence of body, as Descartes implies it does.

Finally let us turn to what I have called the complete concept argument. This argument is, in essence, found in the celebrated argument for the distinction between mind and body in the Sixth Meditation. But the premises of the argument are considerably clarified in the *Objections and Replies* and in correspondence of the period. Behind the argument is a certain view about the concepts we have. When we examine our concepts, we note that some of them are incomplete, and require certain connections to others for full comprehensibility. Writing to Gibieuf on 19 January 1642, Descartes noted:

In order to know if my idea has been rendered incomplete or inadequate by some abstraction of my mind, I examine only if I haven't drawn it . . . from some other richer or more complete idea that I have in me through an abstraction of the intellect . . . Thus, when I consider a shape without thinking of the substance or the extension whose shape it is, I make a mental abstraction. . . .   (AT III 474–5: CSMK 202)

And so Descartes noted in the Fourth Replies, in response to an objection of Arnauld's: "For example, we can easily understand the genus 'figure' without thinking of a circle. . . . But we cannot understand any specific differentia of the 'circle' without at the same time thinking about the genus 'figure' "(AT VII 223: CSM II 157).[34] Following out this series of conceptual dependencies, from circle to shape, we are led ultimately to the idea of a thing that has the appropriately general property, since, Descartes holds, "no act or accident can exist without a substance for it to belong to" (AT VII 175–6: CSM II 124).[35] When we examine our ideas, we find that all of the concepts we have sort themselves out into two classes, those that presuppose the notion of extension, and those that presuppose the notion of thought.[36] Answering Hobbes in the Third Replies Descartes wrote:

Now, there are certain acts that we call 'corporeal', such as size, shape, motion and all others that cannot be thought of apart from local extension; and we use the term 'body' to refer to the substance in which they inhere. It cannot be imagined [*fingi*] that one substance is the subject of shape, and another is the subject of local motion, etc., since all of those acts agree in the common concept [*communis ratio*] of extension. Next there are other acts which we call 'acts of thought', such as understanding, willing, imagining, sensing, etc.: these all agree in the common concept of thought or perception or consciousness [*conscientia*], and we call the substance in which they inhere a 'thinking thing', or a 'mind' . . . .

(AT VII 176: CSM II 124)[37]

And so, Descartes observes, again to Hobbes, "acts of thought have no relation to corporeal acts, and thought, which is their common concept, is altogether distinct from extension, which is the common concept of the other" (AT VII 176: CSM II 124). Thus, Descartes concludes, the ideas we have of mind and body do not depend upon one another for their conception. But, as Descartes argues in the Fourth Meditation, whatever we can clearly and distinctly conceive, God can create. And so, things purely extended can exist without thinking substance. The thinking things are what Descartes calls souls, or minds, and the extended substance from which they are distinguished in this argument is what Descartes calls body, or corporeal substance. Souls, or minds, contain sensation, intellection, and will, but extended substance contains the broadly geometrical properties of size, shape, and motion, and those alone; insofar as sensory qualities like heat and color presuppose thought and not extension, and thus require a thinking substance in which to inhere, Descartes claims, they belong not in extended substance but in mind and mind alone. And insofar as it is body so conceived that, we are inclined to believe, is the source of our sensory ideas of body, it is body so conceived that exists in the world, Descartes concludes. The bodies of physics are, thus, the objects of geometry made real.

4. BODY AND EXTENSION: SOME CONSEQUENCES

From the doctrine of body as extension, some extremely important consequences follow for Descartes about the physical world, doctrines that concern the impossibility of atoms and the void, as well as the falsity of the scholastic doctrine of substantial forms.

The void had been a topic much discussed for some centuries when Descartes turned to it in his system. Aristotle had clearly denied the possibility of a vaccum and empty space.[38] This raised certain theological problems for Christian thinkers; as Etienne Tempier, bishop of Paris noted in his condemnation of various Aristotelian doctrines in 1277, were a vacuum impossible, then God could not move the world, should he desire to do so.[39] But despite the problems, later schoolmen continued to follow Aristotle in denying that there are empty spaces in the world, or that there could be. Indeed, the very idea of an empty space, a nothing that was something of a something, continued to be very puzzling to people well into the seventeenth century.[40] Though Descartes departed in many ways from the scholastic account of body, as we shall later see, he saw his identification of body and extension as leading him to the same conclusions that his teachers had reached, that the world is full and that there is no empty space.

While there is every reason to believe that Descartes had rejected the possibility of a vacuum as early as the late 1620s,[41] the strongest arguments for that view are found in his *Principles*. There Descartes appeals to the principle that every property requires a subject to argue that there can be no extension that is not the extension of a substance. Descartes writes:

The impossibility of a vacuum, in the philosophical sense of that in which there is no substance whatsoever, is clear from the fact that there is no difference between the extension of a space, or internal place, and the extension of a body. For a body's being extended in length, breadth and depth in itself warrants the conclusion that it is a substance, since it is a complete contradiction that a particular extension should belong to nothing; and the same conclusion must be drawn with respect to a space that is supposed to be a vacuum, namely that since there is extension in it, there must necessarily be substance in it as well.   (*Principles* Part II, art. 16)

And since, of course, extended substance is just body, it follows that the world must be full of body.

Descartes offers a graphic illustration of his position. He writes, again in the *Principles:*

It is no less contradictory for us to conceive a mountain without a valley than it is for us to think of . . . this extension without a substance that is extended, since, as has often been said, no extension can belong to nothing. And thus, if anyone were to ask what would happen if God were to remove all body contained in a vessel and to permit nothing else to enter in the place of the body removed, we must respond that the sides of the vessel would, by virtue of this, be mutually contiguous. For, when there is nothing between two bodies, they must necessarily touch. And it is obviously contradictory that they be distant, that is, that there be a distance between them but that that distance be a nothing, since all distance is a mode of extension, and thus cannot exist without an extended substance.

(Principles Part II, art. 18, Latin version)[42]

If the two sides of the vessel are separated, there must be some distance between them, and if there is distance, then there must be body. On the other hand, if there is no body, there can be no distance, and if there is no distance, then the two sides must touch.

In denying the possibility of a vacuum, Descartes rejected one of the central doctrines of the atomist tradition of Democritus, Epicurus, and Lucretius. Another central atomist doctrine fares little better on Descartes' conception of body. Important to the atomists was the view that the world of bodies is made up of indivisible and indestructable atoms. As Epicurus wrote:

Of bodies some are composite, others the elements of which these composite bodies are made. These elements are indivisible and unchangeable, and necessarily so, if things are not all to be destroyed and pass into non-existence, but are to be strong enough to endure when the composite bodies are broken up, because they possess a solid nature and are incapable of being anywhere or anyhow dissolved. It follows that the first beginnings must be indivisible, corporeal entities.[43]

Atoms are, thus, indivisible, unchangeable bodies, the ultimate parts into which bodies can be divided and from which they can be constructed.

As with the void, Descartes seems to have rejected atoms from the late 1620s,[44] and filled the universe with a subtle matter that is infinitely divisible and, in some circumstances, infinitely or at least indefinitely divided.[45] Descartes' most careful argument against the possibility of an atom appears, again, in the *Principles.* Descartes writes:

We also know that there can be no atoms, that is, parts of matter by their nature indivisible. For if there were such things, they would necessarily have to be extended, however small we imagine them to be, and hence we could in our thought divide each of them into two or more smaller ones, and thus we could know that they are divisible. For we cannot divide anything in thought without by this very fact knowing that they are divisible. And

therefore, if we were to judge that a given thing were indivisible, our judgment would be opposed to what we know. But even if we were to imagine
that God wanted to have brought it about that some particles of matter not
be divisible into smaller parts, even then they shouldn't properly be called
indivisible. For indeed, even if he had made something that could not be
divided by any creatures, he certainly could not have deprived himself of the
ability to divide it, since he certainly could not diminish his own power. . . .
And therefore, that divisibility will remain, strictly speaking, since it is
divisible by its nature.   (*Principles* Part II, art. 20)[46]

It is, then, the infinite divisibility of geometrical extension together
with divine omnipotence that undermines atomism, Descartes argues. But such an argument, in an important way, misses the mark.
While it may work for ancient versions of atomism which deny a
transcendent and omnipotent God,[47] it will not work against the
Christian atomists among Descartes' contemporaries, like Pierre
Gassendi, who believed in an omnipotent God who was surely capable of splitting even an atom, if he chose to do so.[48] What is at issue
for the atomists is *natural* indivisibility, not the possibility of *su-
pernautral* divisibility.

But despite these significant departures from atomist doctrine, Descartes still shared their mechanist view of explanation; since all there
is in body is extension, the world is made up of the same kind of stuff
and everything must be explicable in terms of size, shape, and motion. Descartes writes in the *Principles:* "I openly admit that I know
of no other matter in corporeal things except that which is capable of
division, shape, and motion in every way, which the geometers call
quantity and which they take as the object of their demonstrations.
And, I admit, I consider nothing in it except those divisions, shapes,
and motions" (*Principles* Part II, art. 64).[49] And so, like the atomists,
Descartes rejects the substantial forms of the schoolmen.

Though he often tried to hide or, at least, deemphasize his opposition to the philosophy of the schools,[50] Descartes offered numerous
reasons for rejecting substantial forms. Sometimes he suggests that
forms are to be rejected for considerations of parsimony; everything
can be explained in terms of size, shape, and motion, and thus, there
is no reason to posit them. Thus he writes in *The World:*

When it [i.e., fire] burns wood or some other such material, we can see with
our own eyes that it removes the small parts of the wood and separates them

from one another, thus transforming the more subtle parts into fire, air, and smoke, and leaving the grossest parts as cinders. Let others [e.g., the philosophers of the schools] imagine in this wood, if they like, the form of fire, the quality of heat, and the action which burns it as separate things. But for me, afraid of deceiving myself if I assume anything more than is needed, I am content to conceive here only the movement of parts.   (AT XI 7: CSM I 83)

Elsewhere he claims not to understand what a substantial form is supposed to be, calling it "a philosophical being unknown to me," and characterizing it as a chimera.[51] Elsewhere still he contrasts the fruitfulness of the mechanical philosophy with the sterility of the scholastic philosophy. In the *Letter to Voëtius* Descartes remarks: "the common philosophy which is taught in the schools and academies . . . is useless, as long experience has already shown, for no one has ever made any good use of primary matter, substantial forms, occult qualities and the like" (AT VIIIB 26).[52] All of these arguments show Descartes' clear opposition to the substantial forms that underly the natural philosophy of the schools. But, in a way, it is his very doctrine of body that most clearly and unambiguously marks his opposition to the philosophy of form and matter; it is no mystery why Descartes was loath to mention his identification of body and extension in the rather cautious *Discourse* and *Essays*. As I noted above, Descartes saw the Aristotelian substantial forms as impositions of mind onto matter. When we learn, through his philosophy, that mind and body are distinct, we discover that all of the ideas we thought we had of substantial forms and the like derive from the ideas we have of our own minds, and that they do not in any way pertain to body as such, which contains extension and extension alone.[53] In this way the Cartesian doctrine of the distinction between mind and body is intended not only to clarify the notion of the mind, but also that of the body.[54]

But as clear as Descartes' arguments seem to be, as convincing as they might have been to many of his contemporaries, and as influential as they might have been on the downfall of Aristotelian natural philosophy, there are certain deep weaknesses in the case Descartes presents against his teachers. Though he sometimes claims not to understand what a form is supposed to be, his mentalistic interpretation of the scholastic doctrine would seem to undermine that pose. And while he sometimes claims that everything in physics can be explained with only size, shape, and motion, and while he contrasts the fruitfulness of his own mechanical philosophy with that of the schools, even his most sympathetic modern reader must see more than a little bit of bravado in those claims. The fact is that Descartes' mechanical philosophy is considerably more promise than accomplishment, and, in the end, size, shape, and motion turned out to be considerably less fruitful than Descartes and his mechanist contemporaries had hoped. But most importantly, there is an embarrassing hole in the argument that is supposed to lead from the nature of body as extension to the denial of substantial forms. If we grant Descartes his arguments for the distinction between body and mind, and his characterization of both, we can agree that if there are forms, they must be tiny minds of a sort, distinct from the extended bodies whose behavior they are supposed to explain. But that by itself does not seem to eliminate forms, so far as I can see; the schoolman can just continue to claim that however Descartes wants us to conceive of them, they are still there. To make the case, Descartes must show not only that forms are tiny minds, but that outside of human (and, perhaps, angelic) minds, there are no minds at all. Descartes does address this question, though not in its full generality; he does attempt to show that one kind of form the schoolmen posited, the forms that constitute the souls of animals, do not exist.[55] But even here, in this special case, Descartes finally admits to Henry More, who pressed Descartes to admit animal souls and much more, that his arguments are just probable, and cannot establish with any certainly the impossibility of animal souls.[56] And as go animal souls, so goes the more general question of substantial forms.

5. MOTION

Motion is quite crucial to the Cartesian physics; all there is in body is extension, and the only way that bodies can be individuated from one another for Descartes is through motion. In this way, it is motion that determines the size and shape of individual bodies, and, thus, motion is the central explanatory principle in Descartes' physics.

Though it is central to his thought, Descartes resisted defining motion through much of his career. In the *Rules*, for example, Descartes held quite explicitly that motion is simply not definable. Making fun of a standard scholastic definition of motion, Descartes writes:

Indeed, doesn't it seem that anyone who says that motion, a thing well-known to all, is *the actuality of a thing in potentiality insofar as it is in potentiality* is putting forward magic words . . . ? For who understands these words? Who doesn't know what motion is?. . . . Therefore, we must say that these things should never be explained by definitions of these sorts, lest we grasp complex things in place of a simple one. Rather, each and every one of us must intuit these things, distinguished from all other things, by the light of his own intelligence [*ingenium*].   (AT X 426–7: CSM I 49)

This attitude is found also in the *The World*, and seems to continue throughout the 1630s.[57] But even though Descartes avoids formal definition, it is reasonably clear what he thinks motion is. In *The World*, for example, the motion we all immediately understand without benefit of definition is claimed to be: "that by virtue of which bodies pass from one place to another and successively occupy all of the spaces in between" (AT XI 40: CSM I 94).[58] Motion as Descartes understands it is, quite simply, local motion, the change of place, the motion of the geometers.

Behind these remarks is, again, an attack on the natural philosophy of his teachers. For the schoolmen, motion is a general term that embraces all varieties of change. As Descartes notes in *The World*: "The philosophers . . . posit many motions which they think can take place without any body's changing place, like those they call *motus ad formam, motus ad calorem, motus ad quantitatem* ('motion with respect to form', 'motion with respect to heat', 'motion with respect to quantity') and numerous others" (AT XI 39: CSM I 94). It is because of the generality of the notion of motion which they require that the schoolmen offer the very general definition of motion that Descartes is so fond of mocking, the definition of motion as the actuality of a thing in potentiality insofar as it is in potentiality. Motion conceived of in this very general way is the process of passing from one state (actuality) into another state that a body has potentially but not yet actually, from red to blue, from hot to cold, from square to round. But if Descartes is right, and all body is just extension, than all change must ultimately be grounded in change of place. And so for the obscure and paradoxical definition of change that the schoolmen offer us in their account of motion, Descartes substitutes the apparently clear and distinct notion of local motion, the motion of the geometers that we can all intuit without aid of definition.

But later, while writing the *Principles* and attempting to systemetize his thought, even the apparently clear geometric conception of local motion comes in for more careful scrutiny and formal definition. Descartes begins the account of the notion of motion in the *Principles* with a definition that is intended to capture the notion of motion as understood by the vulgar: "Motion . . . as commonly understood is nothing but the action [*actio*] by which some body passes [*migrat*] from one place into another" (*Principles* Part II, art. 24). In contrast to this, Descartes offers another definition that is supposed to capture the true notion of motion:

> But if we consider what we should understand by motion not so much as it is commonly used but, rather, in accordance with the truth of the matter, then in order to attribute some determinate nature to it we can say that it is the transference [*translatio*] of one part of matter or of one body from the neighborhood of those bodies that immediately touch it and are regarded as being at rest, and into the neighborhood of others.
>
> (*Principles* Part II, art. 25)

The positive definition that Descartes offers here is a very curious one, and in its almost baroque complexity many commentators have seen the shadow of the condemnation of Galileo.[59] But whatever external factors may have been at work in these passages, one can make reasonably good sense of what Descartes had in mind in his definition, and why he chose to define motion differently than the vulgar do.

The first important difference between Descartes and the vulgar concerns the notion of activity. According to the vulgar definition, motion is an action, an *actio*, while in the proper definition it is a transference, a *translatio*.[60] Descartes offers two different reasons for this difference. For one, if we think of motion as an action, then we are immediately led to think of rest as the *lack* of action, as Descartes notes in connection with the vulgar definition: "Insofar as we commonly think that there is action in every motion, we think that in rest there is a cessation of action . . ." (*Principles* Part II, art. 24). This, Descartes thinks, is a mistake, one of the many prejudices we acquire in our youth.[61] On the contrary, Descartes thinks, "No more action is required for motion than for rest" (*Principles* Part II, art. 26). And so, Descartes argues, the action necessary to put a body at rest into motion is no greater than the activity necessary to stop it; rest requires as much of an active cause as motion does.[62] But there is another reason why Descartes prefers transference to action. Descartes writes in the *Principles:*

And I say that [motion] is *transference,* not the force or action that transfers in order to show that it is always in the mobile thing, and not in what is moving it, since these two things are not usually distinguished carefully enough, and to show that [motion] is a mode of a thing, and not some subsisting thing, in just the same way as shape is a mode of a thing with shape, and rest is a mode of a thing at rest.   (*Principles* Part II, art. 25)[63]

It is important for Descartes to distinguish motion, a mode of body, from its cause, that which puts the body in motion, which, as we shall later see, is God, in the general case in physics.

There is another important difference between the two definitions worth noting. The vulgar definition is given in terms of the change of place, while the proper definition talks of a body passing from one neighborhood, considered at rest, and into another. This difference is connected with the obvious fact that the designation of a place is relative to an arbitrarily chosen frame of reference, and so, it is only relative to this arbitrarily chosen frame that one can say that a body is or is not changing place. Descartes writes in explanation of the vulgar definition:

the same thing can at a given time be said both to change its place and not to change its place, and so the same thing can be said to be moved and not to be moved. For example, someone sitting in a boat while it is casting off from port thinks that he is moving if he looks back at the shore and considers it as motionless, but not if he looks at the boat itself, among whose parts he always retains the same situation.   (*Principles* Part II, art. 24)[64]

And so, on the vulgar definition of motion as change of place, there is no real fact of the matter about whether or not a given body is in motion; it all depends upon the arbitrary choice of a rest frame. Descartes' intention is that his proper definition will not have this undesirable feature. He writes in the *Principles:*

Furthermore, I added that the transference take place *from the neighborhood of those bodies that immediately touch it into the neighborhood of others,* and not from one place into another since . . . the designation [*acceptio*] of place differs and depends upon our thought. But when we understand by motion that transference which there is from the neighborhood of contiguous bodies, since only one group of bodies can be contiguous to the mobile body at a given time, we cannot attribute many motions to a given mobile body at a given time, but only one.   (*Principles* Part II, art. 28)

As Descartes notes on a number of occasions, motion and rest are opposites, and, he thought, the proper definition of motion must capture this fact.[65] But even though it is clear *that* Descartes wants to eliminate the arbitrariness in the distinction between rest and motion, it is not altogether clear *why* he wants to do so, or *how* he thinks the definition has this consequence.

As for the "why", though Descartes never says anything directly about this, it is not difficult to see why, in the Cartesian physics, one would want there to be a genuine distinction between motion and rest. As I noted earlier, motion is a basic explanatory notion in Descartes' physics: "all variation in matter, that is, all the diversity of its forms depends on motion" (*Principles* Part II, art. 23). But if the distinction between motion and rest is just arbitrary, a matter of an arbitrary choice of a rest frame, as it is on the vulgar definition, then it is difficult to see how motion could fulfill this function. Or, at least, this is the way I think Descartes thought about it. Later physicists, most notably Huygens, were able to figure out how to accommodate a radically relativistic notion of motion into a physics, but, I think, for Descartes, if there is no nonarbitrary distinction between motion and rest, then motion isn't really real, and if it isn't really real, then it cannot occupy the place he sets for it in his physics.

The 'how' is a bit more difficult to see. Descartes writes:

If someone walking on a boat carries a watch in his pocket, the wheels of the watch move with only one motion proper to them, but they also participate in another, insofar as they are joined to the walking man and together with him compose one part of matter. They also participate in another insofar as they are joined to the vessel bobbing on the sea, and in another insofar as they are joined to the sea itself, and, finally, to another insofar as they are joined to the Earth itself, if, indeed, the Earth as a whole moves. And all of these motions are really in these wheels.   (*Principles* Part II, art. 31)

But on the proper definition, of course, this cannot be said; since a body has only one immediately contiguous neighborhood it has at most one proper motion. As Descartes puts it: "every body has only one motion proper to it, since it is understood to recede from only one [group of] contiguous and resting bodies" (*Principles* Part II, art. 31). This certainly eliminates some of the arbitrariness in the notion of motion; because a wheel of the watch is in motion with respect to its contiguous neighborhood, we are obligated to say that it is in motion, despite the fact that the watch as a whole is resting in the pocket of its owner. But, of course, this isn't the whole story. There are, of course, considerable difficulties in specifying exactly what the contiguous neighborhood of a given body is. But that aside, there is another obvious problem. Motion, Descartes says, is transference. But Descartes also acknowledges in the *Principles* that transference is reciprocal:

Finally, I added that the transference take place from the neighborhood not of any contiguous bodies, but only from the neighborhood of those *regarded as being at rest.* For that transference is reciprocal, and we cannot understand body AB transferred from the neighborhood of body CD unless at the same time body CD is also transferred from the neighborhood of body AB. . . . Everything that is real and positive in moving bodies, that on account of which they are said to move is also found in the other bodies contiguous to them, which, however, are only regarded as being at rest.

(*Principles*, Part II, arts. 29, 30)

And so, while there may be a sense in which a given body has only one proper motion, it would still seem to be an arbitrary decision whether to say that body AB is in motion and its neighborhood CD is at rest, or vice versa.

The doctrine of the reciprocity of transference has convinced many that Descartes' conception of motion does not allow for a genuine distinction between motion and rest.[66] But I think that this is a misunderstanding.

Crucial to understanding what Descartes had in mind is a little-known text, most likely a marginal note he wrote in his copy of the *Principles* in the mid-1640s, while the Latin edition of 1644 was being translated into French. The relevant portion reads as follows:

Nothing is absolute in motion except the mutual separation of two moving bodies. Moreover, that one of the bodies is said to move, and the other to be at rest is relative, and depends on our conception, as is the case with respect to the motion called local. Thus when I walk on the Earth, whatever is absolute or real and positive in that motion consists in the separation of the surface of my foot from the surface of the Earth, which is no less in the Earth than in me. It was in this sense that I said that there is nothing real and positive in motion which is not in rest.[67] When, however, I said that motion and rest are contrary, I understood this with respect to a single body, which is in contrary modes when its surface is separated from another body and when it is not. . . . Motion and rest differ truly and modally [*modaliter*] if by motion is understood the mutual separation of bodies and by rest the lack [*negatio*] of this separation. However, when one of two bodies which are separating mutually is said to move, and the other to be at rest, in this sense motion and rest differ only in reason [*ratione*].   (AT XI 656–7)

This commentary on the sections of the *Principles* we have been examining suggests that there is, indeed, a sense in which the distinction between motion and rest is purely arbitrary; when I lift my foot, it is in a sense correct to say both that my foot is moving and the Earth at rest, and that the Earth is moving while my foot is at rest. But this is not the only way to think about motion and rest, Descartes suggests. Motion can also be thought of as the mutual separation of a body and its neighborhood, and in this sense, there is a non-arbitrary distinction between motion and rest; if a body and its neighborhood are in mutual transference, no mere act of thought can change that and put them at rest. Because of the doctrine of the reciprocity of transference, whenever a body is in motion, we must say that its neighborhood is as well, properly speaking; a body AB cannot separate from its neighborhood CD without, at the same time, CD separating from AB. And so Descartes notes in the *Principles*: "*If we want to attribute to motion its altogether proper and non-relative nature [omnino propriam, & non ad aliud relatam, naturam]* we must say that when two contiguous bodies are transferred, one in one direction, and the other in another direction, and thus mutually separate, there is as much motion in the one as there is in the other" (*Principles* Part II, art. 29). This, indeed, is the main thrust of the doctrine of the reciprocity of transference, not to introduce relativity and undermine the distinction between motion and rest, but to emphasize that a motion properly speaking belongs equally to a body and its contiguous neighborhood. But this in no way undermines the kind of distinction between motion and rest that Descartes wants to draw. If motion is understood as the mutual separation of a body and its neighborhood, then it is impossible for a body to be both in motion and at rest at the same time insofar as it is impossible for that body both to be in transference and not in transference with respect to the same contiguous neighborhood. Understood in this way, motion and rest are different and distinct modes of body.[68]

Though Descartes' proper definition of motion thus allows us to draw a non-arbitrary distinction between motion and rest, the distinction comes at some cost, and results in a conception of motion that is not altogether appropriate to the physics that he wants to build on it. On the vulgar conception of motion as change of place, notions like speed and direction are well-defined, given the choice of a rest frame. But matters are not so clear on Descartes' preferred definition. As a body moves in the plenum, its neighborhood of contiguous bodies will change from moment to moment, and without a common frame of reference, it is not clear what sense can be made of the notions of direction and speed, basic to Descartes' mechanist physics. There is no reason to believe that Descartes saw the problems that his definition raised. My suspicion is that it was work in progress (as other aspects of his physics were), an attempt to deal with a serious problem in the foundations of his natural philosophy that had not yet been fully integrated into his full system. It is significant that when we turn to his laws of motion later in this chapter, we shall find Descartes implicitly depending not on the complex definition of motion that he puts forward, but on a conception of motion as change of place.

6. THE LAWS OF MOTION

There is one kind of body in Descartes' world, material substance whose essence is extension, and all of whose properties are modes of extension. But how does this substance behave? For the schoolmen, each kind of substance had its characteristic behavior, determined by its substantial form; water tends to be cool, fire hot, air tends to rise, and earth fall. Descartes, of course, cannot appeal to such characteristic behaviors. For him, the characteristic behavior of body as such, corporeal substance, is given by a series of laws of nature. Since, as noted above, all change is grounded in local motion, these laws of nature are, in essence, laws that govern the motion of bodies.

While there are numerous indications of Descartes' interest in the laws of motion from his earliest writings, the first attempt to present a coherent account of those laws is found in *The World*. Descartes begins his account in chapter 7 by turning directly to God. "It is easy to believe," Descartes says, "that God . . . is immutable, and always acts in the same way" (AT XI 38: CSM I 93). From this Descartes derives three laws in the following order:

[Law A:] Each part of matter, taken by itself, always continues to be in the same state until collision [*recontre*] with others forces it to change. . . . [And so,] once it has begun to move, it will continue always with the same force, until others stop it or slow it down.   (AT XI 38: CSM I 93)

[Law B:] When a body pushes another, it cannot give it any motion without at the same time losing as much of its own, nor can it take any of the other's away except if its motion is increased by just as much.

(AT XI 41: CSM I 94)

[Law C:] When a body moves, even if its motion is most often on a curved path . . . , nevertheless, each of its parts, taken individually, always tends to continue its motion in a straight line.   (AT XI 43–44: CSM I 96)

Hidden in the argument Descartes offers for the first two laws is another principle of some interest:

Now, these two rules follow in an obvious way from this alone, that God is immutable, and acting always in the same way, he always produces the same effect. Thus, assuming that he had placed a certain quantity of motions in the totality of matter from the first instant that he had created it, we must admit that he always conserves in it just as much, or we would not believe that he always acts in the same way.   (AT XI 43: CSM I 96)[69]

This, of course, is the principle of the conservation of quantity of motion, a principle that will play an explicit and important role in the later development of his laws of nature.

The laws Descartes formulated in *The World* and the basic strategy he used to prove them, by appeal to God, remained very much the same throughout his career. But when, in the early 1640s Descartes wrote the corresponding sections of the *Principles of Philosophy*, the laws took on a new and somewhat more coherent shape.

Prominent in the account of the laws Descartes gives in the *Principles* is a distinction not found in the earlier *World*. Descartes begins:

Having taken note of the nature of motion, it is necessary to consider its cause, which is twofold: namely, first, the universal and primary cause, which is the general cause of all the motions there are in the world, and then the particular cause, from which it happens that individual parts of matter acquire motion that they did not previously have.

(*Principles* Part II, art. 36)

Descartes characterizes the "universal and primary cause" as follows:

And as far as the general cause is concerned, it seems obvious to me that it is nothing but God himself, who created motion and rest in the beginning, and now, through his ordinary concourse alone preserves as much motion and rest in the whole as he placed there then.   (*Principles* Part II, art. 36)

Though it is not explicitly identified as a law, Descartes goes immediately on to state a version of the same conservation principle introduced earlier in *The World:*

Whence it follows that is most in agreement with reason for us to think that from this fact alone, that God moved the parts of matter in different ways which he first created them, and now conserves the whole of that matter in the same way and with the same laws [*eademque ratione*] with which he created them earlier, he also always conserves it with the same amount of motion.   (*Principles* Part II, art. 36)

After discussing the universal cause of motion, Descartes turns to the particular causes:

And from this same immutability of God, certain rules or laws of nature can be known, which are secondary and particular causes of the different motions we notice in individual bodies.   (*Principles* Part II, art. 37)

Descartes then introduces three laws of motion, the recognizable successors of the laws he presented earlier in *The World*, though presented in a different order. The first law corresponds closely to law A of *The World:*

[Law 1:] Each and every thing, insofar as it is simple and undivided, always remains, insofar as it can [*quantum in se est*], in the same state, nor is it ever changed except by external causes. . . . And therefore we must conclude that whatever moves, always moves insofar as it can.

(*Principles* Part II, art. 37)[70]

The second law concerns rectilinear motion, and corresponds to law C of *The World:*

[Law 2:] Each and every part of matter, regarded by itself, never tends to continue moving in any curved lines, but only in accordance with straight lines.   (*Principles* Part II, art. 39)

The third law pertains to collision, and it is a further development of Law B of *The World:*

[Law 3:] When a moving body comes upon another, if it has less force for proceding in a straight line than the other has to resist it, then it is deflected in another direction, and retaining its motion, changes only its determination. But if it has more, then it moves the other body with it, and gives the other as much of its motion as it itself loses.   (*Principles* Part II, art. 40)

Law 3 is then followed by a series of seven rules in which Descartes works out the specific outcomes of various possible cases of direct collision.[71]

Let us begin our discussion by considering Descartes' conservation principle, as given in the *Principles*. When Descartes gives this principle in *The World*, as I noted earlier, it is not given as a principle, but as part of the argument for the collision law, Law B. Furthermore, there is no numerical measure suggested; Descartes characterizes what God conserves in the world merely as a "certain quantity of motions" (AT XI 43: CSM I 96). The phrase he uses, "*quantité de mouvements*," curiously enough in the plural, may be a typographical error, but it may indicate that what Descartes' God is preserving is, quite literally, a certain number of motions, perhaps the fact that such-and-such a number of bodies is moving.[72] However, it is also quite possible that Descartes was simply unclear about what precisely it was that God was conserving at this point. In the *Principles* though, Descartes is quite clear about the numerical measure. He writes:

Although . . . motion is nothing in moving matter but its mode, yet it has a certain and determinate quantity, which we can easily understand to be able to remain always the same in the whole universe of things, though it changes in its individual parts. And so, indeed, we might, for example, think that when one part of matter moves twice as fast as another, and the other is twice as large as the first, there is the same amount of motion in the smaller as in the larger. . . .   (*Principles* Part II, art. 36)

What God conserves, Descartes suggests, is size times speed.

It is important here not to read into Descartes' conservation principle the modern notion of momentum, mass times velocity. First of all, Descartes and his contemporaries did not have a notion of mass independent of size; in a world in which all body is made up of the same kind of stuff, there is no sense to equal volumes (without pores, etc.) containing different quantities of matter.[73] And while Descartes was certainly aware of the importance of considerations of directionality,[74] directionality does not enter into the conservation principle at all. What is conserved is size times speed *simpliciter*, so that when a body reflects, and changes its direction, then as long as there is no change in its speed, there is no change in the quantity of motion.[75]

Descartes' conservation principle was exteremely influential on later physicists; a basic constraint on nature, it defined an important way of thinking about how to do physics. Unfortunately, the law turned out to be radically wrong. Though many Cartesians were very resistant to admitting it, Descartes' conservation principle led to many absurdities. In an important series of arguments in the 1680s and 1690s, Leibniz displayed some of the absurdities that follow from Descartes' principle, including the fact that if the world were governed by Descartes' principle, one could construct a perpetual motion machine.[76]

But right or wrong, the conservation principle is not, by itself, sufficient for Cartesian physics. Though in the *Principles* it is presented as a general constraint on all motion, it does not, by itself, tell us how any individual bodies behave; as long as the *total* quantity of motion in the world is conserved the conservation principle is satisfied, no matter how any individual body may happen to behave. It is in this sense, I think, that the conservation principle is taken to be the "universal and primary" cause of motion, and must be supplemented with "secondary and particular causes," a series of particular laws that, like the conservation principle, are said to follow from the immutability of God. As given in the *Principles* these laws include two laws that might be called *principles of persistence*, laws that mandate the persistence of certain quantities in individual bodies, motion in the case of Law 1, and the tendency to move in a rectilinear path in the case of Law 2. But sometimes these laws may come into conflict in different bodies; if A is moving from right to left, it may encounter a body B that is moving from left to right. Laws 1 and 2 tell us that the motions of both bodies tend to persist; Law 3 tells us how the conflicting motions in those two bodies are reconciled with one another and in that sense, it constitutes a kind of *principle of reconciliation*.

Law 1 asserts that every thing remains in the state it is in, until changed by external causes. Motion apparently enters as a special case, something that is a state of body, and, as such, must persist in just the same way as other states of body. This principle is set in direct opposition to Aristotelian accounts of motion. On the Aristotelian conception of motion, a body in motion tends to come to rest. Elaborate explanations had to be given for why a projectile continues in motion after it leaves that which gives it its initial push.[77] Descartes, of course, does not have to explain this. He writes: "Indeed, our everyday experience of projectiles completely confirms this first rule of ours. For there is no other reason why a projectile should persist in motion for some time after it leaves the hand that threw it, except that what is once in motion continues to move until it is slowed down by bodies that are in the way" (*Principles* Part II, art. 38). The Aristotelian view that bodies in motion tend toward rest is, for Descartes, an absurdity. Descartes notes that those who except motion from the general principle of the persistence of states hold that: "[motions] cease of their own nature, or tend toward rest. But this is, indeed, greatly opposed to the laws of nature. For rest is contrary to motion, and nothing can, from its own nature, proceed toward its own contrary, or toward its own destruction" (*Principles* Part II, art. 37).[78] Two things are especially noteworthy here. First, unlike the schoolmen, Descartes sees motion as itself a state of body. For the schoolmen, motion is the process of passing from one state to another;[79] for Descartes, it is itself a state, and as such, it persists. Second, for Descartes it is a state that is distinct from and opposite to that of rest. Descartes seems unambiguous here in holding that motion and rest are opposites.

This observation, that motion in and of itself persists, is one of the most important insights that grounds the new physics of the seventeenth century. Descartes did not invent it; it can be found earlier in his mentor Isaac Beeckman, and in various forms in his contemporaries Galileo and Gassendi. It received its canonical statement in Sir Isaac Newton's *Principles*, where it is enshrined as the principle of inertia.[80] Descartes is sometimes given the credit for having the first published statement of the "correct" version of this important principle, and he may deserve it. However, it is important to recognize that while Descartes was certainly an early advocate of the principle, and important in disseminating it, it was very much in the air at the time he was writing, and the version he offers, grounded as it is in the radical distinction between motion and rest, as we have seen, and in the immutability of God is in important ways different than the similar principle offered by others in his century.[81]

In the explicit statement of Law 1, Descartes is not clear about the motion that is said to persist; does it always maintain the same direction? the same speed? This is to some extent clarified by Law 2 of the *Principles*, which makes clear that what persists is rectilinear motion: "each and every part of matter, regarded by itself, never tends to continue moving in any curved lines, but only in accordance with straight lines" (*Principles* Part II, art. 39). But this law is more than just an amplification and clarification of Law 1. The real focus of Law 2 is an important consequence of the persistence of rectilinear motion, the tendency of a body in curvilinear motion to recede from the center of rotation. Consider a body rotating around a center, for example, a stone in a sling. If we consider all of the causes that determine its motion, then the stone "tends" [*tendere, tendre*] circularly.[82] But if we consider only "the force of motion it has in it" (*Principles* Part III, art. 57) then, Descartes claims, it "is in action to move," or "is inclined to go," or "is determined to move" or "tends" to move in a straight line, indeed, along the tangent to the circle at any given point.[83] And, Descartes concludes: "From this it follows that every body which is moved circularly tends to recede from the center of the circle that it describes" (*Principles* Part II, art. 39).[84] This tendency to recede, what later came to be called centrifugal force, is very important to Descartes' program in physics. Descartes held that the planets are carried around a central sun by a sworl of fluid, what he called a vortex. Light, on Descartes' view, is just the pressure that this fluid exerts in trying to recede from the center of rotation.[85] Law 2 is central to the program insofar as it establishes the existence of this centrifugal tendency that is light. Though, in a sense, it is just a consequence of the more general Law 1, it is sufficiently important to Descartes to get independent statement.

The third and last law in the *Principles* governs what happens in impact, when two bodies have states, both of which would tend to persist, but which cannot persist at the same time. The question was certainly broached in Law B of *The World*. There Descartes writes that "when a body pushes another, it cannot give it any motion without at the same time losing as much of its own, nor can it take any of the other's away except if its motion is increased by just as much" (AT X 41: CSM I 94). But although this bears on the question of impact, it falls considerably short of a genuine law of impact. The law says that if one body transfers motion to another in collision, it must lose a corresponding amount of its own. But it does not say when motion is to be transfered, and when it is, exactly how much one body gives to another. And so, from this law it is impossible to determine the actual outcome of an actual collision. Matters are a bit clearer with the impact law Descartes presents in the *Principles*. There Descartes divides the question into two cases. Consider body B colliding with body C. If B has less force for proceeding than C has force of resisting, then B is reflected, and C continues in its previous state. But if B has more force for proceeding than C has force of resisting, then B can move C, giving it as much motion as it loses. Impact, then, is regarded as a kind of contest between the two bodies. If the force for proceeding in B is less than the force of resisting in C, then C wins and gets to keep its state. If, on the other hand, the force for proceeding in B is greater than the force of resisting in C, then B wins and gets to impose its motion on C.[86]

Although the impact law in the *Principles* is a considerable advance over the parallel law in *The World*, it is still not clear how exactly it is to be applied in actual circumstances; it is by no means clear from the bare law just how force for proceeding and force of resisting are to be calculated, and how much motion is to be transfered from the winner to the loser of the contest, for example. But matters are clarified a bit through an example that Descartes works out in the *Principles*. Immediately following the statement of Law 3 (and some explanatory remarks) Descartes adds seven rules of impact, dealing with various possible cases in which two bodies moving on the same line collide directly. (The rules are summarized in the Appendix to this chapter.) From the rules Descartes gives we can infer much about how he was thinking about impact. From R1–R3, for example, we can conclude that when we are dealing with two bodies in motion, their force for proceeding and force of resisting is simply to be measured by their quantity of motion, that is, their size times their speed. Furthermore, from R2 and R3 we can also infer that when a body B wins the impact contest, it imposes just enough motion on C to enable B to continue in the same direction in which it was moving, that is, just enough motion for B and C to be able to move off in the same direction with the same speed. The cases in which one body is at rest is a bit more complex. Consider R4–R6. It is fair to assume, I think, that as in R1–R3, the force for proceeding in B is measured by B's size times its speed. But what of the force of resisting in C? In presenting these cases, Descartes argues that "a resting body resists a greater speed more than it does a smaller one, and this in proportion to the excess of the one over the other" (*Principles* Part II, art. 49). This suggests that the force of resisting C exerts is proportional to its own size, and the speed of the body that is colliding with it. This has the rather strange consequence (which Descartes fully endorsed) that a larger body at rest could never be moved by a smaller body in motion, no matter how fast that smaller body were to move.[87]

Descartes' seven rules of impact were very problematic for his contemporaries. Descartes found very quickly that he had to explain himself at some length, particularly with respect to his analysis of the case in which one body is at rest, and in the French edition of the *Principles* of 1647, these sections receive alterations more extensive than those in any other section in the book.[88] Indeed, the law of impact and the rules that follow seem to be work in progress that Descartes never really finished. Nor for that matter are they ever applied to any real problems in Descartes' physics. As late as 26 February 1649, Descartes wrote Chanut saying that "one need not" spend much time with the rules of impact, because "they are not necessary for understanding the rest" of the *Principles* (AT V 291: CSMK 369).

Later physicists quite decisively rejected Descartes' rather crude formulations.[89] But despite the obvious problems there are with the rules, they are very revealing of certain aspects of Descartes' thought. For one, the rules of impact show quite clearly Descartes' distinction between motion and rest. Consider rules R5 and R6, the case in which two unequal bodies collide, one of which is at rest. When the larger body is at rest, the smaller one is reflected (R5), but when the smaller body is at rest, both travel off at the same speed in the same direction (R6). These two cases clearly cannot be redescriptions of one another. But if the distinction between motion and rest is just arbitrary, then it should make no physical difference whether it is the smaller or larger body that we consider at rest. But even though the rules of impact embody the nonarbitrary distinction Descartes wants to draw between motion and rest, there is no hint in the rules of impact of the complex definition of motion that is supposed to enable us to draw the distinction.[90] In the rules of impact, there is no reference to the presumably separate neighborhoods of bodies assumed at rest in terms of which the proper motions of bodies B and C are defined. A common frame of reference is assumed; motion is treated almost as if it were simple local motion.

7. MOTION AND FORCE

One question that the laws of impact raise for the Cartesian metaphysics is that of force. As we discussed at some length above, for Descartes, bodies are extension and extension alone, and contain only the modes of extension. But we also saw that in Law 3 of the *Principles*, Descartes makes explicit appeal to the notion of force, the force for proceeding and the force of resisting bodies have, that, Descartes holds, determines the outcome of any collision. What sense can be made of the claim that merely extended bodies have such forces? In explicating Law 3, Descartes offers the following account of the forces to which that law appeals:

What the force each body has to act or resist consists in. Here we must carefully note that the force each body has to act on another or to resist the action of another consists in this one thing, that each and every thing tends, insofar as it can [*quantum in se est*] to remain in the same state in which it is, in accordance with the law posited in the first place.[91] Hence that which is joined to something else has some force to impede its being separated; that which is apart has some force for remaining separated; that which is at rest has some force for remaining at rest, and as a consequence has some force for resisting all those things which can change that; that which moves has some force for persevering in its motion, that is, in a motion with the same speed and toward the same direction.   (*Principles* Part II, art. 43)

Because bodies remain in their states of rest or motion in a particular direction with a particular speed, they exert forces that keep them in their states, and resist change, Descartes claims.[92] But this answer is not wholly satisfactory; for it just raises the question as to how Cartesian bodies can have the tendencies that Descartes attributes to them, a notion no less problematic than that of force.

A satisfactory answer to these questions leads us back to the ultimate ground of the laws of motion, God. As noted above, Descartes is quite explicit in holding that it is God who grounds the laws of motion in the world. Descartes, along with the tradition in Christian thought, holds that God must not only create the world, but he must also sustain the world he creates from moment to moment.[93] It is this conception of God that is explicitly introduced in justifying the conservation principle that starts the exposition of the laws in the *Principles*.

> We also understand that there is perfection in God not only because he is in himself immutable, but also because he works in the most constant and immutable way. Therefore, with the exception of those changes which evident experience or divine revelation render certain, and which we perceive or believe happen without any change in the creator, we should suppose no other changes in his works, so as not to argue for an inconstancy in him. From this it follows that it is most in harmony with reason for us to think that merely from the fact that God moved the parts of matter in different ways when he first created them, and now conserves the totality of that matter in the same way and with the same laws [*eademque ratione*] with which he created them earlier, he always conserves the same amount of motion in it.   (*Principles* Part II, art. 36)

Descartes similarly appeals to the divine sustenance in justifying his "secondary and particular causes" of motion, the three laws that follow the initial conservation principle: "From God's immutability we can also know certain rules or laws of nature, which are the secondary and particular causes of the various motions we see in particular bodies" (*Principles* Part II, art. 37). Descartes' reasoning is by no means clear here, and there is wide lattitude for interpretation. But one way or another Descartes held that it is an immutable God whose divine sustenance is responsible for the various laws Descartes posits, for the conservation of quantity of motion, for the persistence of motion, for the orderly exchange of motion in collision.

This suggests that the force Descartes appeals to in Law 3, and the tendency a body has to persevere in its state derive from God, from the immutable way in which he sustains the world he creates, in particular, from the way in which he sustains the bodies in motion in that world. In this way force is not *in* bodies themselves.[94]

The appeal to divine conservation that underlies the laws of motion in Descartes' physics suggests strongly that in the physical world, at least, it is God who is the primary cause of motion; in a world without the substantial forms of the schoolmen to do the job, God steps in directly to cause bodies to behave as they characteristically do. This comes out nicely in an exchange that Descartes had with Henry More. Writing to Descartes on 5 March 1649, More asked if "matter, whether we imagine it to be eternal or created yesterday, left to itself, and receiving no impulse from anything else, would move or be at rest?" (AT V 316)[95] Descartes' answer appears in August 1649: "I consider 'matter left to itself and receiving no impulse from anything else' as plainly being at rest. But it is impelled by God, conserving the same amount of motion or transference in it as he put there from the first" (AT V 404: CSMK 381). God, Descartes suggests, is what causes bodies to move in the physical world. But God is not the only cause of motion in Descartes' world.

But even though God is the primary cause of motion in the physical world, it is important to recognize that God is not the only such cause; Descartes does allow that finite minds, too, can move bodies. Writing again to More, Descartes notes:

That transference that I call motion is a thing of no less entity than shape is, namely, it is a mode in body. However the force [vis] moving a [body] can be that of God conserving as much transference in matter as he placed in it at the first moment of creation or also that of a created substance, like our mind, or something else to which [God] gave the power [vis] of moving a body. (AT V 403–4: CSMK 381).

What is that "something else" Descartes has in mind here? Angels are certainly included, as certain other passages in the More correspondence and elsewhere suggest.[96] It is not *absolutely* impossible that Descartes meant to include bodies among the finite substances that can cause motion.[97] But I think that it is highly unlikely. If Descartes really thought that bodies could be causes of motion like God, us, and probably angels, I suspect that he would have included them *explicitly* in the answer to More; if bodies could be genuine causes of motion, this would be too important a fact to pass unmentioned. Furthermore, Descartes' whole strategy for deriving the laws of motion from the immutability of God presupposes that God is the real cause of motion and change of motion in the inanimate world of bodies knocking up against one another. Somewhat more difficult to determine is whether or not bodies can be genuine causes of the states of sensation or imagination. Though Descartes persists in holding that mind can cause motion in bodies, he is somewhat more guarded about the causal link in the opposite direction. The argument for the existence of the external world presented in the Sixth Meditation, where bodies are said to contain the "active faculty" that causes sensory ideas in us would suggest that bodies are the real causes of our sensations. But later versions of the argument found in the Latin and French versions of the *Principles* don't make use of the notion of an active faculty in bodies, and seem to posit a progressively weaker conception of the relation between bodies and the sensory ideas that we have of them.[98] While there is room for disagreement, it seems to me that all of the important signs lead to the view that bodies (inanimate bodies, at least) have no real causal efficacy, and lack the ability to cause either changes in motion in other bodies, or sensations in minds.

With the account of the laws of motion, we complete the foundations of Descartes' program for physics. Though I shall end my account here, Descartes did not. Descartes' program extended to the explanation of all phenomena in the physical world, life included, all grounded on the simple foundations he set out, extended substance, moving in accordance with the laws of motion.[99]

APPENDIX: DESCARTES' IMPACT RULES
PRINCIPLES PART II, ARTS. 46–52

Consider bodies B and C, where $v(B)$ and $v(C)$ are the speeds B and C have before impact, $v(B)'$ and $v(C)'$ are their speeds after impact, and $m(B)$ and $m(C)$ are their respective sizes.

> *Case I: B is moving from right to left, and C is moving from left to right*

R1. If $m(B)=m(C)$, and $v(B)=v(C)$, then after the collision, $v(B)'=v(C)'=v(B)=v(C)$, B moves from left to right, and C moves from right to left (i.e, B and C are reflected in opposite directions). (art. 46)

R2. If $m(B) > m(C)$, and $v(B)=v(C)$, then after the collision, $v(B)'=v(C)'=v(B)=v(C)$, B and C move together from left to right (i.e., B continues its motion and C is reflected in the opposite direction). (art. 47)

R3. If $m(B)=m(C)$, and $v(B) > v(C)$, then after the collision, B and C move together from right to left (i.e., B continues its motion and C is reflected in the opposite direction) and $v(B)'=v(C)'=((v(B)+v(C))/2)$. (art. 48)

Case II: C is at rest and B collides with it

R4. If $m(B) < m(C)$, then after the collision, C remains at rest and B rebounds (i.e., B moves off in the opposite direction) with $v(B)'=v(B)$. (art. 49)

R5. If $m(B) > m(C)$, then after the collision, B and C move together in the direction in which B was moving before the collision, with $v(B)'=v(C)'=(m(B)v(B)/(m(B)+m(C)))$. [The formula is inferred from the example using the conservation principle.] (art. 50)

R6. If $m(B)=m(C)$, then after the collision, C moves in the direction B originally moved with $v(C)'=(1/4)v(B)$ and B would be reflected in the opposite direction, with $v(B)'=(3/4)v(B)$. (art. 51)

Case III: B and C move in the same direction, with $v(B) > v(C)$

R7a. If $m(B) < m(C)$ and "the excess of speed in B is greater than the excess of size in C," i.e., $v(B)/v(C) > m(C)/m(B)$, then after the collision, B transfers to C enough motion for both to be able to move equally fast and in the same direction. I.e., $v(B)'=v(C)'=(m(B)v(B)+m(C)v(C))/(m(B)+m(C))$. [The formula is inferred from the example using the conservation principle. In the French version, Descartes drops the condition that $m(B) < m(C)$, though he keeps the condition that $v(B)/v(C) > m(C)/m(B)$.] (art. 52)

R7b. If $m(B) < m(C)$ and "the excess of speed in B" is less than "the excess of size in C," i.e., $v(B)/v(C) < m(C)/m(B)$, then after the collision, B is reflected in the opposite direction, retaining all of its motion, and C continues moving in the same direction as before, with $v(B)=v(B)'$ and $v(C)=v(C)'$. (art. 52)

R7c. If $m(B) < m(C)$ and $v(B)/v(C)=m(C)/m(B)$, then B transfers "one part of its motion to the other" and rebounds with the rest. [This rule is only in the French edition. There is no example from which one can infer a formula, but perhaps Descartes means that B would transfer half of its speed to C, so that by the conservation principle, $v(B)' = v(B)/2$ and $v(C)' = (3/2v(C)$.] (art. 52, French version)

NOTES

1 For accounts of medieval natural philosophy, see, for example, Grant, *Physical Science in the Middle Ages*; Lindberg, (ed.), *Science in the Middle Ages*; Kretzmann, et al., (eds.), *The Cambridge History of Later Medieval Philosophy*, sect. VII.

2 For an overview of Renaissance alternatives to Aristotelianism in natural philosophy, see, for example, Ingegno, "The new philosophy of nature," in Schmitt, et al. (eds.), *The Cambridge History of Renaissance Philosophy*, pp. 236–63. It is to be emphasized that in the Renaissance there was not one single opposition to Aristotle and Aristotelianism, but a wide variety of quite different opposing programs.

3 On the persistence of Aristotelianism in the Renaissance and into the seventeenth century, see especially Schmitt, *Aristotle and the Renaissance*. For an account of the sort of education Descartes would have received in the Jesuit schools, see the notes to part one in Gilson, *Descartes: Discours de la méthode, texte et commentaire*, and C. de Rochemonteix, *Un collège des Jésuites . . .* The Jesuit schools of the time were supposed to follow the Jesuit *Ratio Studiorum*, a careful and detailed curriculum that had been worked out and approved by the Society of Jesus for use in their schools. See, for example, Fitzpatrick (ed.), *St. Ignatius and the Ratio Studiorum*. The full text of the *Ratio Studiorum* is given in Ladislaus Lukács, S.J., (ed.), *Ratio atque Institutio Studiorum Societatis Iesu*. (1586, 1591, 1599) (*Monumenta Paedagogica Societatis Iesu*, vol. V; *Monumenta Historica Societatis Iesu . . .* , vol. 129) (Rome: Institutum Historicum Societatis Iesu, 1986). For a more general account of French higher education in the period, see Brockliss, *French Higher Education in the Seventeenth and Eighteenth Centuries*.

4 See, for example, Aristotle, *Physics* I, ch. 7, particularly as interpreted in St. Thomas, *The Principles of Nature*. In practice, though, the theory could get very complex. See, for example, Maier, *On the Threshold of Exact Science*, pp. 124–42.

5 For St. Thomas, for example, substantial form is that which actualizes prime matter, and matter by itself is pure potentiality; see *On Being and Essence*, chap. 2. For other later thinkers, though, form and matter have greater autonomy from one another, and more of a capacity for independent existence. See, for example, Whippel, "Essence and Existence," in Kretzmann, et al. (eds.), pp. 385–410, esp. p. 410.

6 See also AT III 667: CSMK 219; AT V 222–23: CSMK 357–8. Descartes offers a similar interpretation of Roberval, who had proposed a kind of theory of universal gravitation; see AT IV 401. While I often borrow from the excellent translations in CSM, in most cases the translations are my own, for better or for worse.

7 See the reference cited in note 2, and Vickers (ed.), *Occult and Scientific Mentalities in the Renaissance*.

8 On seventeenth-century atomism, see especially Lasswitz, *Geschichte der Atomistik vom Mittelalter bis Newton*; Kargon, *Atomism in England from Hariot to Newton*; Marie Boas, "The establishment of the mechanical philosophy," *Osiris* 10 (1952), pp. 412–541; Jones, *Pierre Gassendi 1592–1655: An Intellectual Biography*; Joy, *Gassendi the Atomist: Advocate of History in an Age of Science*; and Meinel, "Early Seventeenth-Century Atomism: Theory, Epistemology, and the Insufficiency of Experiment."

9 Though he was later to reject the physics he had been taught, it is interesting that when in 1638 a friend asked where he should send his son for schooling, he recommended not the Dutch universities, where there were many sympathetic to Descartes' own thought, but La Flèche, singling out the teaching of philosophy for special praise. See AT II 378.

10 On the teaching of mathematics in the Jesuit schools, see Cosentino, "Le matematiche nella *Ratio Studiorum* della Compagnia di Gesù," pp. 171–213; Dainville, "L'ensengement des mathématiques dans les Collèges Jésuites de France du XVIᵉ au XVIIIᵉ siècle," pp. 6–21, 109–23; Rodis-Lewis, "Descartes et les mathématiques au collège," in Grimaldi and Marion (eds.), *Le Discours et sa méthode*, pp. 187–211; Wallace, *Galileo and his Sources: The Heritage of the College Romano in Galileo's Science*, pp. 136–48; and Dear, *Mersenne and the Learning of the Schools*, chap. 4.

11 Beeckman's complete surviving notes are published in de Waard (ed.), *Journal tenu par Isaac Beeckman de 1604 à 1634*; the passages that relate specifically to Descartes can be found in AT X 41–78. Descartes' own record of some of those conversations can be found in the notes from Descartes' "Parnasus" manuscript, as preserved by Leibniz; see AT X 219ff and Gouhier, *Les Premières Pensées de Descartes*, p. 15. It is from this period that Descartes' first completed work dates, the *Compendium musicae*, written by Descartes as a present for Beeckman. The *Compendium* can be found in AT X 88–141 and in a new, annotated edition by Frédéric de Buzon. The study of music was, of course, for Descartes' contemporaries, part of mixed mathematics, along with astronomy and mechanics, and so this work fits neatly within the context of the other things Descartes discussed with his mentor. On the place of

music in early seventeenth-century thought, see Dear, *Mersenne and the Learning of the Schools,* chap. 6.

12 In one of the discussion notes Descartes presented to Beeckman, he talks of "one atom of water [*unus aquae atomus*]" traveling twice as fast as "two other atoms"; see AT X 68. Furthermore, the problems Descartes discussed with Beeckman include the problem of free-fall in a vacuum; see AT X 58–61, 75–8. While suggestive, these are not decisive. Though Descartes used the term "atom," it is not in a context in which its indivisibility or perfect hardness is at issue, so it isn't clear that he meant the term in its strict technical usage. Furthermore, the (counterfactual) discussion of motion in a vacuum is commonplace among scholastic natural philosophers, all of whom would deny that there really could be such vacua in nature.

13 On Descartes' development in the 1620s, see Milhaud, *Descartes savant;* Rodis-Lewis, *L'Oeuvre de Descartes,* ch. II. For the dating and development of the *Rules* see Weber, *La Constitution du texte des Regulae;* and Schuster, "Descartes' *Mathesis universalis,* 1619–28," in Gaukroger (ed.), *Descartes: Philosophy, Mathematics and Physics,* pp. 41–96.

14 Magnetism is discussed in Rules XII, XIII, and XIV of the *Rules:* AT X 427, 430–1, 439: CSM I 49–50, 52, 57.

15 See particularly Rules XII and XIV of the *Rules,* AT X 419, 442–7: CSM I 44–5, 59–62.

16 The metaphysics of 1629–30 is mentioned in a letter to Mersenne: 15 April 1630, AT I 144: CSMK 22. For an account of what it might have contained, see Rodis-Lewis, *L'Oeuvre,* ch. III.

17 See, for example, AT I 13, 23, 53f, 71, 106–7, 109, 119–20, 127, 179.

18 See AT I 270–2, 285–6; the latter is translated in CSMK 42–4.

19 See AT I 314, 339; the latter is translated in CSMK 50–2. The former passage, from a letter to Morin from September or October 1634 is not altogether clear, but the implication is that Descartes may be back to work on his *Optics.*

20 See AT VI 74–77: CSM I 149–50.

21 See AT III 232–3: CSMK 156 and AT III 259–60.

22 See AT III 286, 470, 491–2; this last passage is translated in CSMK 205–6.

23 See AT IV 72–3. The book was still in the process of being printed in May 1644; see AT IV 112–13, 122–3.

24 Some mention must be made of the notions of substance, duration, order, and number, which are common to all existents and thus not understood through either thought or extension; see *Principles* Part I, art. 48. These notions appear in the *Rules* as the "common" simple natures (AT X 419: CSM I 44–5), and in the celebrated letter to Elisabeth

of 21 May 1643 as one of the groups of "primitive notions" in terms of
which everything is comprehended (AT III 665: CMSK 218). Though
they pertain to mental and material substances, these notions would not
seem to be comprehended through the principal attribute, thought or
extension.

25 Descartes seems to take a somewhat different point of view in his conversation with Burman; see AT V 156, translated in Cottingham, *Descartes' Conversation with Burman*, p. 17.

26 See *Principles* Part I, art. 63.

27 It is interesting to note here that the Latin *modus* means "way"; the
word used in the French translation of the *Principles* is *façon*, also
"way."

28 See, for example, Aristotle, *Categories*, I.2; St. Thomas, *On Being and
Essence*, ch. 2, sect. 2, and Goclenius, *Lexicon philosophicum*, pp. 26ff
and 1097–8.

29 "Risibility" is, strictly speaking, what was called a property; while not
in the essence of a human being, it belongs to all and only humans. See
Aristotle, *Topics* I.5 102a 17ff. The actual act of laughing is what was
called a proper accident, something that can only be in a human being,
but isn't in every human always. See Goclenius, *Lexicon philosophicum*, p. 28.

30 See the references given above in note 15 for the earliest suggestions of
Descartes' doctrine on the nature of body.

31 See AT VII 79–80: CSM II 55.

32 It is important to note, though, that in responding to Hobbes, Descartes
denies that the wax example is intended to establish anything about the
nature of body. See AT VII 175: CSM II 124.

33 The French version of this article adds a positive statement about their
nature: "and that its nature consists in this alone, that it is a substance
which has extension." Note also the very similar argument in *Principles*
Part II, art. 11, where Descartes is arguing that "the extension constituting the nature of a body is exactly the same as that constituting the
nature of a space."

34 See also the discussion in the *First Replies:* AT VII 120–1: CSM II 85–6.

35 "Act" (*actus*) is not to be understood as an action, but in the scholastic
sense, as an actuality, something real.

36 In the 1643 letters to Elisabeth on mind–body union and interaction,
Descartes adds a third class, those that depend on the union of mind and
body; see AT III 665–6: CSMK 218.

37 Again, "act" is to be understood as a technical term. The French translation of this passage has an interesting variant; instead of saying that all
corporeal acts "agree in the common concept of extension," the French

says that "they agree with one another insofar as they presuppose extension" (AT IXA 137). See also AT VII 121, 423–4: CSM II 86, 285–6.

38 Aristotle's main attack on the vacuum can be found in the *Physics* IV.6–9.

39 See Grant (ed.), *A Source Book in Medieval Science*, p. 48. The relevant section of the condemnation is § 49. The objection assumes a finite world, as both Aristotle and his medieval followers generally did.

40 See Grant, *Much Ado about Nothing: Theories of Space and Vacuum from the Middle Ages to the Scientific Revolution*, for an account of the history of theories of space and vacuum.

41 So far as I can see, there is no clear reason to believe that Descartes seriously confronted the problem of the vacuum before the latest stages in the composition of the *Rules*. There, in Rule XIV, he suggests that at least in imagination, there is no distinction between body and extended space. However, there is also a suggestion there that while body and space are indistinguishable in imagination, they may be distinguishable by reason. See AT X 442–6: CSM I 59–62. It seems clear that Descartes denies the vacuum by the time he was working on *The World*. But it is interesting that in ch. 4, where the topic is discussed, there are no real arguments against the vacuum; Descartes gives only weaker considerations designed to show that we cannot infer that there is empty space from the fact that we don't see a body in a given place. See AT XI 16–23: CSM I 85–8.

42 The French version is slightly different. See also AT V 194: CSMK 355 and AT V 272–3: CSMK 363–3. It is by no means easy to picture exactly what the vessel would look like the moment after God did the deed. Jammer suggests that what Descartes imagines is that the vessel would simply implode due to the pressure of the external atmosphere, though he (wrongly) claims that Descartes had no conception of atmospheric pressure. See Jammer, *Concepts of Space: The History of Theories of Space in Physics*, pp. 43–4. But surely this is not what Descartes imagined.

43 Diogenes Laertius, *Lives of Eminent Philosophers* X 41–2; see also idem, X 54 and Lucretius, *De rerum natura*, I 483ff.

44 For evidence of Descartes' possible earlier atomism, see the references cited above in note 12. Evidence on Descartes' views in the 1620s is inconclusive. The earliest text I know of in which Descartes comes out conclusively against atoms is a letter to Mersenne, 15 April 1630, AT I 139–40: CSMK 21–2.

45 See *Principles* Part II, arts. 33–4. Descartes does not claim that all bodies are in this state, of course. He recognizes three distinct elements, which are distinguished from one another by the size and shape of the particles that make them up. See *The World*, ch. 8, and *Principles* Part III, art. 52.

46 For other discussions of atomism, see also AT III 191–2; AT III 213–14: CSMK 154–5; AT III 477: CMSK 202; AT V 273: CSMK 363.

47 For the ancient atomists, the gods are themselves made up of atoms and do not have the power to split them. See, for example, Rist, *Epicurus: An Introduction*, ch. 8.

48 In his *Syntagma philosophicum*, Gassendi wrote: "There is no thing that God cannot destroy, no thing he cannot produce." See *Opera Omnia*, vol. I, p. 308 A. For general accounts of Gassendi's atomism see Jones, *Pierre Gasssendi, 1592–1655: An Intellectual Biography*; and Joy, *Gassendi the Atomist: Advocate of History in an Age of Science*, chap. 5.

49 See also *Principles*, pt. II, art. 23.

50 In advising his then-disciple Henricus Regius on how to deal with the attacks of the orthodox theologian, Gisbertus Voëtius, Descartes advises him to follow his example in the *Discourse* and *Essays*, and simply not mention that his natural philosophy does away with the scholastic forms. See AT III 491–2: CSMK 205–6. In the *Meteorology*, Descartes deftly skirts the question. See AT VI 239, translated in Olscamp, *Discourse on Method, Optics, Geometry and Meteorology*, p. 268. It is also notable that in the *Principles*, Descartes never discusses the issue of substantial forms, despite the fact that that work was originally intended as a direct answer to the scholastic textbook of Eustachius. On this, see Descartes' remarks to Father Charlet, assistant to the General of the Jesuits, to whom he sent a copy of the Latin *Principles* when they appeared in 1644; AT IV 141.

51 See AT II 364: CSMK 120; AT II 367; AT III 212; AT III 503–4, 505–6; AT III 648–49: CSMK 216. See also the French versions of *Principles* Part IV arts. 201, 203.

52 See also AT I 430, AT III 504, 506, and the introduction to the French version of the *Principles*: AT IXB 18–19: CSM I 189. This resembles Bacon's critique of the Aristotelian philosophy as all talk and no works; see, for example, the Preface to the *Great Instauration*, in Bacon, *The New Organon and Related Writings*, pp. 7–8. However, unlike Bacon, Descartes is not thinking of technological success, but of explanatory success.

53 This is a theme Descartes takes up at some length in the Sixth Replies. See AT VII 443–4: CSM II 298–9.

54 See Etienne Gilson's still classic essay, "De la critique des formes substantielles au doute méthodique," in his *Etudes sur le rôle de la pensée médiévale dans la formation du système cartésien*, pp. 141–90.

55 The main published discussion of animal souls is in Part V of the *Discourse*: AT VI 56–9: CSM I 139–41. The issue also comes up in the

Fourth Replies and in the Sixth Replies, as well as in the correspondence. See AT VII 230–1: CSM II 161–2; AT VII 426: CSM II 287–8; AT II 39–41: CSMK 99f; AT III 121; AT IV 575–6: CSMK 303–4; AT V 277–8: CSMK 365–6. For a general account of the question in Descartes and later thinkers, see Rosenfield, *From Beast-Machine to Man-Machine: Animal Soul in French Letters from Descartes to La Mettre.*

56 See AT V 276–7: CSM 365.

57 See AT XI 39: CSM I 93–4; AT II 597: CSMK 139.

58 This account of motion as change of place is also suggested in the *Rules,* where in Rule 12 Descartes points out that the ambient surface of a body can "be moved (*moveri*) with me in such a way that although the same [surface] surrounds me, yet I am no longer in the same place" (AT X 426: CSM I 49).

59 Descartes' contemporary, Henry More, was the first to claim that Descartes fashioned his definition of motion in the *Principles* specifically to allow himself to assert that the Earth could be regarded at rest, as he does in *Principles* Part III, arts. 28–9. See the "Preface General" to his *Collection of Several Philosophical Writings,* p. xi. For later discussions of this claim, see, for example, Koyré *Galileo Studies,* pp. 261, 265; Blackwell, "Descartes' Laws of Motion," pp. 220–34, esp. p. 277; Aiton, *The Vortex Theory of Planetary Motions,* pp. 33, 41–2; Dugas, *Mechanics in the Seventeenth Century,* pp. 172–3; and Westfall, *Force in Newton's Physics,* pp. 57–8. It is interesting that while many claim that Descartes fashioned the account of motion in the *Principles* specifically to deal with the problem of copernicanism, and thus that Descartes did not really believe that it is correct, hardly any two commentators agree on how precisely the definition is supposed to help. In the end, I find the claim highly implausible; see the discussion in ch. 6 of Garber, *Descartes' Metaphysical Physics.*

60 Interestingly enough, only a few years earlier Descartes himself had defined motion as an action, "the action through which the parts of . . . matter change place"; see Descartes to Morin, 12 September 1638: AT II 364.

61 See *Principles* Part II, art. 26.

62 See ibid. This also comes up in Descartes' letters to More: AT V 345–6, 348.

63 See also AT V 403–4: CSMK 382.

64 See also *Principles* Part II, art. 13, and Part III, art. 28.

65 See, for example in *The World,* ch. 6: AT XI 40: CSM I 94. Also see *Principles* Part II, arts. 27, 37, 44.

66 See, for example, Prendergast, "Descartes and the Relativity of Motion," pp. 64–72; Koyré, *Newtonian Studies,* pp. 81–2; Dugas, *Mechanics in*

the Seventeenth Century, pp. 172–3; Aiton, *The Vortex Theory of Planetary Motions*, p. 33; and Westfall, *Force in Newton's Physics*, pp. 57–8.

67 See *Principles* Part II, art. 30.

68 For a different way of drawing the distinction between motion and rest in Descartes, see Martial Gueroult, "The metaphysics and physics of force in Descartes," in Gaukroger, (ed.), pp. 196–229.

69 See also AT XI 11: CSM I 85.

70 The text given is translated from the Latin version. In the French version Descartes writes that things (bodies, presumably) change "through collision with others." Note that the formulation in the Latin version would seem to apply to mind as well as to body. Descartes, though, never makes use of this implication; indeed, it seems inconsistent with a view of the mind as active. For Descartes' follower, Henricus Regius, though, it is the ground of his account of the unity of mind and body. In the broadsheet he published declaring his views on mind, Regius writes: "the bond which keeps the soul conjoined with the body is the law of the immutability of nature, according to which everything remains in its present state so long as it is not disturbed by anything else" (AT VIIIB 344: CSM I 295). The same view can be found in Regius' *Fundamenta physices*, p. 250. Descartes rejects this application of his principle; see AT VIIIB 357: CSM I 303.

71 See *Principles* Part II, arts. 46–52. The seven rules are summarized in the appendix to this chapter.

72 This point is especially stressed in Costabel, "Essai critique sur quelques concepts de la mécanique cartésienne," esp. pp. 250–1. .

73 See *Principles* Part II, arts. 6ff.

74 For an excellent account of Descartes' notion of determination and his treatment of directionality, see Gabbey, "Force and inertia in the seventeenth century: Descartes and Newton," in Gaukroger (ed.), pp. 230–320, esp. pp. 248–60.

75 This feature has led to a "Cartesian" theory of mind–body interaction and the claim that mind acts on body by changing the direction of the motion of a body without changing its speed, in that way allowing for mind–body interaction without violating the conservation principle. For a discussion of this, as well as a discussion of the general scope of the laws of nature and the question as to whether they govern animate bodies or not, see Garber, "Mind, body, and the laws of nature in Descartes and Leibniz," pp. 105–33.

76 Leibniz' basic argument can be found in his *Discourse on Metaphysics*, art. 17, among many other places. For an account of the argument and Leibniz' debates with late seventeenth-century Cartesians, see Iltis, "Leibniz and the *vis viva* controversy," pp. 21–35.

77 For discussions of the impetus theory, a popular way of explaining the continued motion of bodies among medieval natural philosophers, see, for example, Edward Grant, *Physical Science in the Middle Ages*, pp. 48ff, and Maier, *On the Threshold of Exact-Science*, chs. 4 and 5.

78 See also AT XI 40: CSM I 94.

79 For a discussion of scholastic conceptions of the nature of motion, see Maier, *On the Threshold of Exact Science*, ch. 1.

80 In 1613 Beeckman wrote in his journal the principle that "a thing once moved never comes to rest unless impeded." See de Waard, *Journal tenu par Isaac Beeckman de 1604 à 1634*, vol. I, p. 24, and AT X 60. Descartes almost certainly learned this from Beeckman; see the use he makes of it in the solution to the problem of free-fall he sketched out for Beeckman: AT X 78. For Galileo's version in 1632, see, for example, Galileo, *Dialogue Concerning the Two Chief World Systems*, pp. 20–1, 28, 147ff. Gassendi's version can be found in his *De motu impressu a motore translato* (1640), translated in Brush, *The Selected Works of Pierre Gassendi*, pp. 141, 143. Newton's principle of inertia is Law I of the "Axioms or Laws of Motion" from Book I of his *Mathematical Principles of Natural Philosophy* (1687).

81 See especially the insightful comparison between Descartes and Newton by Gabbey, in Gaukroger (ed.), pp. 287–97.

82 See AT XI 85; *Principles* Part III, art. 57.

83 See AT XI 45–6, 85; *Principles* Part II, art. 39; idem, Part III, art. 57.

84 See also *Principles* Part III, art. 55f and AT XI 44, 84f.

85 See the references cited below in note 99.

86 For a clear exposition of the basic ideas behind Descartes' impact contest model of collision, see Gabbey, in Gaukroger (ed.), pp. 245ff.

87 Strange as this consequence is, we must recognize that Descartes does not mean to say that this is the way bodies behave in our world. As he notes, the rules explicitly omit any effects that might arise from the fact that the bodies in question are surrounded with fluid. This fluid can change the outcome drastically and allow a smaller body to set a larger resting body into motion. See *Principles* Part II, art. 53, particularly the passages added in the French version, as well as the additions to the French version of *Principles* Part II, art. 50. For general discussions of the force of rest, see, for example, Gueroult, in Gaukroger (ed.), pp. 197ff, and Gabbey, in Gaukroger (ed.), pp. 267ff.

88 Also important is a letter Descartes wrote to Claude Clerselier, 17 February 1645: AT IV 183–7. In response to Clerselier's evident puzzlement over the rules of impact in the Latin edition of the *Principles*, particularly those that involve one body at rest, Descartes introduces new ways

of thinking about the problem that seem inconsistent with the simple impact contest model in the Latin *Principles*. The development of Descartes' thought on impact in the mid-1640s is treated in some detail in ch. 8 of Garber, *Descartes' Metaphysical Physics*.

89 See especially Leibniz's careful examination of Descartes' rules of impact in his "Critical Thoughts on the General Part of the Descartes' *Principles*," translated by Loemker, *Philosophical Papers and Letters*, pp. 383–412, esp. 398–403.

90 Descartes does mention it in his letter to Clerselier, though; see AT IV 186–7.

91 See *Principles* Part II, art. 37.

92 The claim that the impact-contest forces derive from law 1, though ingenious, is not unproblematic. Leibniz, who wants to deny the Cartesian ontology of geometrical bodies and explicitly add force as something over and above extension, makes the following remark on this claim to the Cartesian De Volder:

> You deduce inertia from the force any given thing has for remaining in its state, something that doesn't differ from its very nature. So you judge that the simple concept of extension suffices even for this phenomenon. . . . But even if there is a force in matter for preserving its state, that force certainly cannot in any way be derived from extension alone. I admit that each and every thing remains in its state until there is a reason for change; this is a principle of metaphysical necessity. But it is one thing to retain a state until something changes it, which even something intrinsically indifferent to both states does, and quite another thing, much more significant, for a thing not to be indifferent, but to have a force and, as it were, an inclination to retain its state, and so resist changing (*Philosophical Papers*, ed. Loemker, p. 516).

93 See, for example, Descartes' formulation of this in the Third Meditation: AT VII 49: CSM II 33. When this is questioned by Gassendi, Descartes responds by saying that "you are disputing something which all metaphysicians affirm as a manifest truth" (AT VII 369: CSM II 254). He continues by paraphrasing the account of the doctrine found in St. Thomas, *Summa Theologiae* I, Q.104 a 1.

94 The issue of the ontological status of force in Descartes is a tangled one, though. For other views, see, for example, Guéroult, in Gaukroger (ed.), Gabbey, in Gaukroger (ed.), pp. 234–9; and Hatfield, "Force (God) in Descartes' physics," pp. 113–140.

95 See also AT V 381; Descartes evidently missed the question the first time around, and More had to repeat it.

96 AT V 347: CSMK 375; *Principles* Part II, art. 40.

97 See, for example, Hoenen, "Descartes's mechanicism," in Doney (ed.), *Descartes*, pp. 353–68, esp. p. 359.

98 Rather than identifying body as the active cause of a sensation, in the Latin *Principles* Descartes says, more vaguely, that "we seem to ourselves clearly to see that its idea comes from things placed outside of us" (*Principles* Part II, art. 1, Latin version). The French is vaguer still: "it seems to us that the idea we have of it forms itself in us on the occasion of bodies from without" (*Principles* Part II, art. 1, French version). It is, by the way, important not to conclude that Descartes was an occasionalist on the basis of this and other similar uses of the term "occasion," which did not seem to become a technical term until later in the seventeenth century.

99 There is relatively little in the way of secondary literature on Descartes' physics, when one gets beyond the foundations. Scott, *The Scientific Work of René Descartes*, offers a summary of Descartes' main scientific writings, but nothing more than that. For a general discussion of Descartes' science, with particular attention to its later influence, see Mouy, *Le Développement de la physique Cartésienne: 1646–1712*. For more specialized studies, see the essays collected in Milhaud, *Descartes savant*; and Costabel, *Démarches originales de Descartes savant*. For more recent work, see the essays by Crombie, Armogathe, Pessel, Rodis-Lewis, and Costabel in Grimaldi and Marion (eds.), *Le Discours et sa méthode* and the essays by Costabel, Wickes and Crombie, Zarka, and Rodis-Lewis in Méchoulan (ed.), *Problématique et réception du Discours de la méthode et des essais*. On questions relating to light and optics, see especially Sabra, *Theories of Light from Descartes to Newton*, and Shapiro, "Light, pressure, and rectilinear propagation: Descartes' celestial optics and Newton's hydrostatics." On Descartes' vortex theory of planetary motion and its later fate, see Aiton, *The Vortex Theory of Planetary Motions*.

11 Descartes' physiology and its relation to his psychology

Descartes understood the subject matter of physics to encompass the whole of nature, including living things. It therefore comprised not only nonvital phenomena, including those we would now denominate as physical, chemical, minerological, magnetic, and atmospheric; it also extended to the world of plants and animals, including the human animal (with the exception of those aspects of human psychology that Descartes assigned solely to thinking substance). In the 1630s and 1640s Descartes formulated extensive accounts of the principal manifestations of animal life, including reproduction, growth, nutrition, the circulation of the blood, and especially sense-induced motion. In connection with the latter he discussed at length the bodily conditions for psychological phenomena, including sense perception, imagination, memory, and the passions. He also examined the mental aspects of these phenomena, sometimes by way of complementing his physiological discussions and sometimes as part of his investigation into the grounds of human knowledge.

Philosophical readers may be curious about the relation between these scientific pursuits (Descartes would have called them natural philosophical or physical) and Descartes' philosophy, where the latter is conceived as his contribution to metaphysics and epistemology. Descartes' physiological and psychological writings bear directly on central topics in his philosophy, notably on the relation between mind and body and on the theory of the senses. With respect to the first, they exemplify Descartes' attempt to distinguish mind (or soul) from body and they raise the question of mind–body interaction. With respect to the second, they explain the functioning of the senses that conditions their use in acquiring knowledge, and they exemplify the metaphysics of sense percep-

335

tion as expressed in Descartes' version of (what Boyle and Locke later called) the distinction between primary and secondary qualities. Study of Descartes' physiological and psychological writings thus might illuminate the topics that English-speaking philosophers of the twentieth century have taken to be of philosophical interest in his work.

It would, however, be a mistake to approach Descartes' physiological and psychological writings merely by way of the usual descriptions of his philosophical problematic. Study of these writings provides an opportunity to approach Descartes' philosophy anew, working from his own understanding of what was important in it. And indeed, judging from the attention that he devoted to physiological and psychological topics, they, along with the rest of his physics, formed the raison d'être of his philosophical program. Consider Descartes' picture of the relationship between these topics and his more standardly "philosophical" work in metaphysics, as depicted in his "tree of knowledge": metaphysics forms the roots, physics the trunk, and medicine (along with mechanics and morals) are the branches of the tree (AT IX 14: CSM I 186). Although the metaphysical roots support and give sustenance to the physical trunk, Descartes did not believe that he or his followers should spend much time rummaging about down there. Indeed, he considered metaphysics as an (admittedly essential) propaedeutic that should be undertaken only once in one's life, in order to secure the proper foundations of natural philosophy by removing the Aristotelian "prejudices" of childhood and discovering that the essence of matter is identical with the object of pure geometry.[1] This metaphysical study was to provide the grounds not only for his approach to the physics of nonliving things, but, significantly, for his approach to vital phenomena and animal behavior, and indeed Descartes is credited with having virtually initiated the micromechanical approach to physiology.[2] In the course of Descartes' own intellectual development this work in metaphysics did not precede his natural philosophical project, but began after the project was underway; as the French scholar Etienne Gilson has observed, Descartes first turned to metaphysics only in 1629, when he had already been pursuing questions in mathematical physics for more than a decade and had been thinking about the physiology of animal motion and of human sense perception for several years.[3]

Every one of Descartes' major works, those he published and those printed posthumously, contain some discussion of topics in physiology or in the physiology and psychology of the senses. The doctrine of the "animal machine" is already stated in the *Rules*, which also touches briefly on the physiology of the senses and imagination (AT X 412–17: CSM I 40–3). Descartes' first attempt at a general statement of his physics in *Le Monde* was to have been divided into three parts: a general physics of the heavens and earth, entitled the *Treatise on Light*; a second part devoted entirely to the physiology of vital phenomena, sensory processes, and animal motion, entitled the *Treatise on Man*; and a separate discussion of the rational soul in a third part that no longer exists or was never written. The *Discourse* contains, in Part V, a sketch of Descartes' physiological results – which he exemplified through an extensive account of the motion of the heart in producing the circulation of the blood – and, in Part VI, a hint at Descartes' medical program (along with a plea for funds); Parts IV to VI of the *Optics* (one of the three essays for which the *Discourse* was a preface) contain an extensive discussion of the physiology and psychology of vision. The *Meditations*, with which Descartes hoped surreptitiously to introduce "all the foundations of [his] Physics,"[4] include an extensive discussion of the interplay between nervous physiology and bodily sensation, in the Sixth Meditation. The *Principles* contain some discussion of the metaphysics of sense perception in Part I and were to have included two separate parts devoted exclusively to physiological and psychological topics, one on "living things" (plants and animals) and one on "man"; out of these projected parts Descartes covered a portion of the physiology of the senses in Part IV of the printed work (AT IX 315–23: CSM I 279–85). The *Passions of the Soul* contains a summary of Descartes' physiology of sensory processes and animal motion, along with extensive discussion of the brain processes that produce appetites and passions. Descartes undertook to revise and complete his *Treatise on Man* in 1647–8, producing part of a new treatise entitled *Description of the Human Body*.[5] Finally, his letters include numerous discussions of anatomical and physiological matters attesting to Descartes' periodic examination of animal parts obtained from local butchers as well as his attendance at an autopsy, and his papers contain a draft essay on the formation of the foetus and extensive notes on anatomical topics.[6]

DID PHYSIOLOGY AND PSYCHOLOGY EXIST IN DESCARTES' TIME?

To this point I have spoken of Descartes' "physiology" and "psychology" even though Descartes only rarely used the first term (and then with a meaning slightly different from ours) and never used the second. Unreflective application of current disciplinary categories to past thinkers distorts their thought and can be especially confusing when, as in the present case, the terms that we now use were used in the past with different meanings. We shall therefore consider briefly the use of these terms by past authors; at the same time, we shall ask whether our present terms "physiology" and "psychology" – understood to mean the science of the functions and vital processes of organisms and the science of the mind, respectively – are appropriate for describing portions of Descartes' works.

The term "physiology" had two related meanings in the seventeenth century, both of which were inherited from antiquity and neither of which squares precisely with our usage. First, it meant the theory of nature in general. It had been used with this sense in both ancient Greek and Latin, and continued to be used with this meaning throughout the seventeenth century and into the eighteenth.[7] Second, it meant the portion of medicine that explains the nature of the human body by applying the theory of nature in general. The program of physiology in this second sense was to give an account of the structure of the body by using the elements recognized in the theory of nature (usually, earth, air, fire, and water) to account for the elements of living things (such as the traditional four humors of ancient medicine: yellow bile, blood, phlegm, and black bile); the latter elements were in turn used to account for the "homoeomerous" parts of the body (such as bone, nerve, ligament, heart, brain, and stomach). Galen used the term in this manner: he defined "physiology" as the study of the nature of man, including the elements out of which the body is composed, the formation of the foetus, and the parts of the body as revealed through dissection. Jean Fernel (1497–1558), whose work was known to Descartes (AT I 533), also used the term in this way.[8] Even with this second meaning, the term "physiology" had a broader scope than we now give it. However, authors such as Galen and Fernel did engage in analysis of the functions of bodily structures and processes; they did so under the rubric of examining "the uses of the parts" or their "functions," and our term "physiology" may appropriately be applied to this part of their work.

The term "psychology" apparently was first coined in the sixteenth century to refer to the theory of the soul, and more specifically to the subject matter covered in Aristotle's *De anima* and *Parva naturalia*. The term itself was seldom used during the seventeenth century, but *De anima* and the associated literature were regularly taught in the arts curriculum as a division of philosophy, in connection not only with natural philosophy but also with metaphysics and ethics.[9] This literature in fact contained very little that we would retrospectively label "psychology" considered as a branch of natural science. In addition to biological topics such as growth and nutrition, Aristotelian discussions of the soul included the sensory reception of "species" and the subsequent intellectual processes of abstraction; in the first case the emphasis was on the ontology of sensible species, not on topics that we should consider psychological – such as the means by which distance is judged – and in the second case the focus was on the ontological, logical, and epistemic status of the intelligible species or substantial forms abstracted from sensible species.[10] Nonetheless, a full discussion of the functions of the sensitive soul and the attendant "motive power" would include an account of how the senses and appetites serve to mediate between sense perception and motor action, and thus would include a wide range of psychological topics pertaining to the explanation of animal and human behavior, topics that were in fact discussed in the medical literature.[11] Furthermore, the perception of distance was discussed in a literature taught under the rubric of "mixed mathematics," the so-called "perspectivist" literature stemming primarily from Alhazen, Pecham, and Vitello. Book Two of Alhazen's *Opticae thesaurus* contains an extensive treatment of psychological topics; corresponding discussions occurred in seventeenth-century optical treatises, such as that by the Jesuit Frances Aguilon, published in 1613.[12] Thus, the medical and optical literatures included much that is appropriately described as "psychological" (in our sense of the term).

What was Descartes' relation to the actual terminology and to the work that we may retrospectively denominate as physiological and psychological? His extant writings reveal only two uses of the term "physiology," both in the second, medical sense, and both to describe theses discussed in the schools (AT III 95; IV 240). Nonetheless, he undertook extensive work that he called the study of the "functions" of the parts of the body,[13] and which we may reasonably denominate as physiological. Similarly, although he did not use the term "psychology" at all, he discussed sensory perception and other psychological phenomena in ways that should be distinguished from his purely mechanistic physiology on the one hand and from his concern with the status of sensory knowledge on the other. Indeed, he himself drew a sharp distinction between the "natural" functions of the mind–body complex in ordinary sense perception and the epistemically privileged deliverances of so-called natural light, a distinction to which we shall return when examining the relation between Descartes' psychology and his metaphysics.

DESCARTES' PHYSIOLOGICAL PROGRAM AND ITS RELATION TO PREVIOUS PHYSIOLOGY

Descartes' program in physiology was an extension of his generally mechanistic approach to nature. Where previous physiologists had invoked powers, faculties, forms, or incorporeal agencies to account for the phenomena of living things, Descartes would invoke only matter in motion, organized to form a bodily machine. His aim was:

> to give such a full account of the entire bodily machine that we will have no more reason to think that it is our soul which produces in it the movements which we know by experience are not controlled by our will than we have reason to think that there is a soul in a clock which makes it tell the time.
> (AT XI 226: CSM I 315)

Never timid in speculating about micromechanisms in nature, Descartes claimed that he had observed no part of the body in his many dissections which he could not explain through purely material causes – both as to its formation and its mode of operation (AT II 525–6: CSMK 134–5). Thus, where previous physiology invoked the vital force of the soul to explain the formation of the foetus and the subsequent growth and nutrition of the body, Descartes projected an entirely mechanistic account based upon the assertion that, in forming the parts of the body, "Nature always acts in strict accordance with the exact laws of Mechanics" (ibid.), reducing the "vital force" to the heat of the heart (understood as matter in motion; AT V 278–9:

CSMK 366). And where previous physiology accounted for the actions of the nerves in transmitting sensory stimulation to the rational soul by positing subtle matter endowed with the faculty of sentience or informed by a sensitive soul, Descartes attempted to explain the functions of nervous transmission by mechanistic means alone, invoking the soul only to account for conscious awareness in the reception of sensations.

Nonetheless, it would be an error to describe Descartes' physiological program as if it were a new fabrication, cut from whole cloth. Descartes was familiar with the major texts of the medical tradition, which he freely invoked in his correspondence; he even claimed to have adopted no structure that was controversial among the anatomists.[14] Indeed, whether wittingly or by oversight, he followed the Galenic tradition – as did the authorities with which he was familiar – even on matters that had been corrected by Vesalius, and particularly on the attribution of a *rete mirabile* to the brain of humans, a structure Vesalius had shown was present in simians but not in humans. Moreover, Descartes' debt to traditional physiology did not stop with anatomy: his conceptions of the functions of the bodily parts were largely drawn from previous work. He accepted not only descriptive "facts" from scholastic and Galenic physiology, but also their conceptions of the basic functions of the heart, brain, nerves, blood, and the notorious "animal spirits."[15] His innovation, which was truly radical, came in his reliance on mechanistic categories alone in explaining how bodily functions are performed. To a large extent his physiology may be seen as a straightforward translation of selected portions of previous physiology into the mechanistic idiom.

It is not surprising that Descartes' physiology should follow Galen's in these ways, for Galenic physiology was by far the most influential in the period prior to Descartes.[16] Galen's philosophy of nature shared many features with the prevailing Aristotelian natural philosophy, including an appeal to the four elements to explain the basic properties of bodily constituents and the association of life with heat (which as virtually universal in ancient thought). But Galen went far beyond the descriptions of bodily functions provided in the Aristotelian corpus. Where the two overlapped on specifics, he differed with Aristotle on several points, and in particular he made the brain, not the heart, the center of mental function, and he assigned the cause of the pulse to the heart and arteries themselves, rather than to the "ebullation" of the blood through its own heat. Among medical writers known to Descartes even those who explicity adopted an Aristotelian ontology followed Galen on many points. Thus, Fernel followed Galen in making the brain the center of nervous action; important Aristotelian commentators, such as those at Coimbra, cited Fernel in adopting the Galenic position.[17] However, both Fernel and the commentators followed Aristotle on other matters, for example in their account of sense perception (discussed below).

Descartes' relation to the physiological tradition is exemplified in his account of the beating of the heart and the circulation of the blood. As a case study, this topic is in fact atypical, inasmuch as Descartes adopted Harvey's novel position that the blood circulates and therefore rejected the traditional view of a slow ebbing of venous blood and a separate arterial distribution of rarefied blood or of nonsanguinous vital spirits. Descartes was, in fact, an important early defender of Harvey on circulation.[18] He disagreed, however, with Harvey's account of the motion of the heart and in the explanation of the efficient cause of the circulation. On these points of disagreement he followed tradition in opposition to Harvey.

According to the Galenic account, diastole and systole are simultaneous in the heart and the arteries, and indeed are the consequence of active expansion and contraction by the *vis pulsans* located in cardiac and arterial substance. In diastole these organs expand, drawing in vital spirit, and in systole they contract, forcing the vital spirit along the channel of the arteries; the "thump" of the heart against the chest occurs as a consequence of the expansion of the heart during diastole. Harvey contended that the traditional account made a fundamental error in its description of diastole, systole, and the thump. Specifically, it mistook systole for diastole in the heart, and it mistakenly explained the pulse of the arteries as an arterial diastolic action that occurs simultaneously with diastole in the heart.[19] According to Harvey, the heart actively contracts during systole and thereby pumps the blood into the arteries; thus, systole in the heart is simultaneous with diastole in the arteries. Further, he contended that the heart hits the chest during systole as a consequence of muscular contraction. He thus radically challenged previous doctrine not only on the flow of the blood, but also on the identification of diastole and systole, the most fundamental of cardiac phenomena.

Descartes apparently accepted Harvey's postulated circulation of the blood after hearing it described but before reading Harvey's book; at the same time, he formulated his own account of the motion of the heart, which he did not change after reading Harvey.[20] Descartes' account of the motion of the heart accords completely with the traditional description: he holds that diastole in the heart is simultaneous with the beating of the heart against the chest and the arterial pulsation. However, Descartes differs from the Galenic account and from Harvey (but agrees with Aristotle) in ascribing the cause of the motion of the heart to the expansion of the blood, rather than to the expansive and contractive action of the heart itself. And indeed, it is difficult to see how else he could mechanize the phenomena of the heart: having rejected bare "powers" such as the *vis pulsans*, he needed to give a mechanistic accound of the power of the heart to force the blood into arteries, for indeed he was to use the force of the blood to drive the machine of the body as a whole. The expansion of the blood through heating could be readily mechanized through his equation of heat with particulate motion. As commentators have observed, he left unexplained the energy source of the "fire without light" that burns in the heart; but he may have felt comfortable doing so because he could compare this fire with apparently nonvital phenomena, such as fermentation or the heat generated in a stack of moist hay.[21] In any case, it is hard to imagine where Descartes could have turned for a motive force in his machine if he had been required to provide a source of power to drive the heart conceived as a mechanical pump. The episode with Harvey may perhaps be seen as an example of how Descartes picked and chose – from among the available descriptions of vital phenomena and conceptions of vital functioning – those most suited for translation into the mechanistic idiom.

Considered systematically, Descartes' aim was to mechanize virtually all of the functions that had traditionally been assigned to the vegetative and sensitive souls. Galenists and Aristotelians agreed that there were three domains of phenomena that must be explained by the postulation of a soul: vital or vegetative, sensitive, and rational (the last pertaining only to humans).[22] Although they disagreed over the precise ontology of the soul or souls commanding these phenomena, and in particular over whether there are three different souls or one soul with three powers, they agreed on the functions assigned to each power: the vegetative soul controls growth, nutrition, and reproductive generation; the sensitive soul governs sense perception, appetites, and animal motion; and the rational soul is the seat of intellect and will. Given that animals were granted only vegetative and sensitive souls, the sensitive soul was attributed sufficient powers to guide the animal motions that achieve the satisfaction of appetite across a variety of circumstances. The sensitive power in both animals and humans thus controlled learned responses as well as mere automatic or instinctual behavior.[23] In humans, reason and the will were attributed the power to direct behavior against the pull of the appetites.

Notoriously, Descartes agreed with his predecessors in according reason and will a special status. But he claimed to be able to account for all vegetative and sensitive phenomena mechanistically, leaving only consciousness, intellection, and volition proper to the soul or mind. Thus, the fact that Descartes separated the rational soul from matter did not release him from the requirement to explain "cognitive" phenomena (such as adaptive responses to a variety of circumstances) through bodily mechanisms alone; such was the implication of his claim that he could explain those phenomena attributed to the sensitive soul of beasts – and the same phenomena in humans (so long as conscious volition did not intervene) – through appeal to organized matter.

THE RELATION BETWEEN PHYSIOLOGY AND PSYCHOLOGY IN DESCARTES

Consider the list of phenomena that Descartes claimed to have explained mechanistically in his *Treatise on Man:*

the digestion of food, the beating of the heart and arteries, the nourishment and growth of the limbs, respiration, waking and sleeping, the reception by the external sense organs of light, sounds, smells, tastes, heat and other such qualities, the imprinting of the ideas of these qualities in the organ of the common sense and the imagination, the retention or stamping of these ideas in the memory, the internal movements of the appetites and passions, and finally the external movements of all limbs (movements which are so appropriate not only to the actions of objects of the senses, but also to the pas-

sions and the impressions found in the memory, that they imitate perfectly
the movements of a real man).   (AT XI 201–2: CSM I 108)

The first four belong to the vegetative soul; the rest belong to the
sensitive soul and are such as we would denominate "psychological."
Moreover, as the examples make clear, the phenomena allegedly explained by clockwork mechanism (more accurately, by mechanisms
modeled after hydraulically powered automata) include psychologically complex responses to objects, conditioned by the passions and
by memory. Nor was this ambitious list a reflection of the early date
of the *Treatise:* Descartes made no less ambitious claims in reply to
Arnauld's skepticism that a purely mechanical sheep – devoid of a
sensitive soul – could respond appropriately when light from a wolf
was reflected into its eyes (AT VII 229–30: CSM II 161). Here in print
he made clear that the actions of both humans and other animals
could be explained mechanistically, dropping the pretense of the *Treatise* in which he putatively explained the functions of artificial creatures that only outwardly resembled real humans.

For purposes of exposition we may divide Descartes' discussion of
the physiology of human perception and motion into two branches:
those processes that he conceived to take place without any influence from or upon the mind, and those that involve mind–body
interaction. This division in fact accords with Descartes' program as
stated in the *Treatise:* He proposed to explain there only those actions that could take place without the intervention of the mind,
leaving for the third (unavailable) part his discussion of the soul.

Descartes considered many of the actions of humans and animals
to have a common explanation. He could maintain that there are
such explanations despite the fact that he believed humans have
minds and animals do not because he also held that many human
actions take place without mental guidance. In fact, one might consider the chief aim of the *Treatise* to have been that of providing a
purely mechanistic account of the way in which sensory stimulation causes the motion of the limbs – taking into account the effects
of instinct, memory, and the passions – without invoking mind. It
would thus provide an integrated account of the behavior of the
"animal machine," where "animal" is defined – as it was by Descartes on occasion – to include both humans and other animals.[24]

Descartes' animal machine is driven entirely by the "fire without light" in the heart, which creates pressure in the arteries. The movements of the limbs (and internal muscular motions such as breathing) are driven by the "animal spirits" (subtle matter) filtered out of the arteries at the base of the brain and distributed through the pineal gland, which Descartes located in the center of the cerebral cavities.[25] These spirits flow out from the pineal gland and enter various pores lining the interior surface of those cavities, whence they proceed down nervous tubules to the muscles, which they cause to inflate and contract, thereby moving the machine.[26] Descartes compared the mechanical control of the muscular motion to the operations of a church organ, the keys of which are depressed by external objects. The heart and arteries, he observed, are like the bellows of the organ. Further, just as the harmony of an organ depends entirely on "the air which comes from the bellows, the pipes which make the sound, and the distribution of the air in the pipes," so too the movements of the machine depend solely on "the spirits which come from the heart, the pores of the brain through which they pass, and the way in which the spirits are distributed in these pores" (AT XI 165–6: CSM I 104). The distribution of the spirits into these pores itself depends on three factors: the character of the spirits themselves (whether lively or sluggish, coarse or fine), the effects of sensory activity on the opening of the pores, and the character of the matter of the brain itself, which is determined by its innate constitution together with the effects of previous sensory excitation.[27] In Descartes' own psychological terms, the distribution of the spirits depends on the current state of the *passions* (abundant spirits "exciting movements in this machine like movements that give evidence in us of *generosity, liberality,* and *love,*" etc.), current *sensory* excitation (including internal senses such as that of hunger), the *natural* (or innate) plumbing of the brain (which mediates all responses and is by itself sufficient for instinctual responses), and the effects of *memory* and *imagination*.[28]

Let us focus on the role of sensory stimulation in directing the spirits down one tubule or another. Like most of his predecessors, Descartes assigned single nerve fibers both sensory and motor functions. The motor function is carried out by the flow if spirits down the tube; the sensory by a thin fibril stretching like a wire from the sense organs to the brain (these are cushioned within the flexible sheath of the nerve by the ever-present animal spirits). Sensory activity causes tension in the fibril, which opens up the corresponding pore on the inner surface of the cavity of the brain, initiating a flow of spirits outward from a corresponding location on the pineal gland. This flow can have several effects besides causing a motor response; it can, for instance, alter the structure of the brain around the tubules through which it flows, thereby altering its characteristics and so affecting subsequent behavior.

Descartes illustrated the coupling of sensory input and motor response with a simple example of automatic movement, presumably governed by the innate structure of the brain in the manner that he termed "instinctual" (AT XI 192: Hall 104: *suivant les instincts de notre nature*). He portrays a humanlike machine with its foot near a fire. The agitated particles of the fire move the skin of the foot, causing a nerve fiber from the foot to open a pore in the brain. Spirits flow into the pore and are directed "some to muscles which serve to pull the foot away from the fire, some to muscles which turn the eyes and head to look at it, and some to muscles which make the hands move and the whole body turn in order to protect it" (AT XI 142: CSM I 102).[29] In fact, as Descartes later observes, depending on how close the bodily part is to the fire, the tugging of the nerve will open the pore differently and effect different paths of the spirits through the brain and into the nerves to the muscles, producing a smile of pleasure in one case and a grimace of pain along with limb retraction in another (AT XI 191–3: Hall 102–5). Although the account is short on detail about the specifics of neuroplumbing, it presents a clever means of yoking motor response to sensory input in a purely hydraulic machine.

Descartes' ambitious program required him to envision subtle mechanisms for allowing the machine to respond differentially to objects under varying environmental conditions and in a manner contingent upon previous "experience." Unfortunately, the extant *Treatise* does not develop the account of learning that it promises (AT XI 192: Hall 103–4); it does, however, make the surprising claim that on the basis of corporeal memory alone, independent of the soul, the machine is able "to imitate all [*tous*] the movements of real men" (AT XI 185: Hall 96). In the service of this bold claim (which he qualified in other writings) Descartes gave close attention to mechanisms for allowing the visual sense to direct the spirits differentially depending on an object's size, shape, and distance from the body. Thus, he presented a mechanism that allegedly would cause the optical apparatus to focus on near objects. The resulting pattern of flow contained elements corresponding to the shape of the visual object (at least in two dimensions) and to its distance as determined by the settings of the eye musculature necessary to focus on the object. These characteristics of the pineal pattern, depending on their slight differences and on other factors influencing the flow of spirits and antecedently affecting the structure of the brain – such as whether the machine is in a state of hunger, whether it has eaten apples before, and so on – putatively cause the limbs of the machine to move differentially and, if the object is an apple (or perhaps if it is only sufficiently "applelike" – Descartes does not raise this problem here), to grasp it and convey it toward the mouth. In general, Descartes imagined a precise relation between the tubes leading to the members of the body and the pores from which the spirits flow out of the pineal, such that tubes correspond to members and pores correspond to directions of movement in those members.[30] He thereby intimated that all motions of the limbs result from a specific mechanical contrivance that is activated solely by the direction of the spirits leaving the pineal gland, which would mean that those motions governed by the soul must be effected solely by influencing the direction of the motion of the spirits.[31]

The mechanisms depicted in the *Treatise* for mediating between sensory excitation and subsequent movements are artfully clever. Less charitably, they are the product of sheer fantasy. For the most part they are described in a manner that confidently couples patterns of spirit-flow with external movements but that is short on engineering detail. Moreover, to the extent that the central mechanisms of pineal control are described sufficiently for the reader to grasp their mode of operation, it is certain that they would not work.

Nonetheless, the picture of an animal machine that behaves differentially depending on whether it has eaten recently and contingent on its past experience, and does so on the basis of mechanical structures alone, has proven powerful in the subsequent history of psychology, or at least of psychology's metaphysics.[32] And indeed the significance of Descartes' project should not be missed because the details are absent, or, when present, largely implausible. In his physiology, just as in his physics overall, the general vision Descartes presents is more important than his particular explanatory proposals.

Two aspects of Descartes' physiological program are of particular interest. The first is his radical mechanism, which I have stressed throughout. In comparing Descartes' work with prior physiological literature, it may indeed be difficult to see just how radical a step he took. In the hundred years before Descartes it was in fact quite common to speak of wholly "corporeal" animal spirits distributed from the brain through the hollow tubes formed by the nerves.[33] Bernardino Telesio (1509–88), whose name was familiar to Descartes (AT I 158), wrote in this manner. Telesio even said that the spirits flowing outward cause the muscles to contract or expand, thereby moving the limbs in a machinelike fashion.[34] But we must be careful not to read these pre-Cartesian statements with post-Cartesian eyes. Key differences between Telesio and Descartes – differences that distinguish between a truly mechanistic physiology and a modified physiology of powers – occur in their respective conceptions of the operation of the senses, of the processes mediating between sensory excitation and motor action, and of the operation of the nerves on the muscles. Descartes posited a fully mechanized loop between senses and muscles. Telesio referred the operation of sense perception to a "sensitive power," which, if "corporeal," was realized in a material substance endowed with powers and qualities.[35] And indeed his conception of the influence on the muscles of the "animal spirits" flowing along the nerve fibers is not mechanical, but appeals to immaterial qualitative agents, in the form of the two primary qualities he posited, viz., heat and cold.[36] These qualities, far from being mechanical themselves (that is, far from being reducible to matter in motion), were described as incorporeal agents by Telesio himself.[37] In effect, he has simply reduced the ancient pantheon of four primary qualities (including wet and dry, as well as heat and cold) to two. In the period prior to Descartes a purely "corporeal" sensitive soul need not have been a sensitive soul reducible to purely extended substance in motion.[38]

The second aspect of Descartes' program of interest here is his particular conception of the relation between bodily states and their mental effects. Descartes of course held that the human body is joined with a rational soul, a fact that was to account not only for certain acts of "general intelligence" he considered incapable of mechanistic explanation, but also for the conscious experience that accompanies the bodily processes of sense perception, imagination, memory, voluntary motion, and the appetites and passions. He designated the pineal gland the seat of mind–body interaction, citing a variety of reasons, including the fact that the gland is unitary (as is consciousness), is centrally located, and can be easily moved by the animal spirits.[39] Beyond that, he generally treated the mind-body relation as a mystery. When he explained the relation between a bodily state and its mental effect (or vice versa), he appealed to an "institution of nature," which in effect is a relationship established by God and is such as to account for the fact that an "appropriate" mental state occurs on the occasion of a given bodily configuration.[40] His treatise on the *Passions* is based on this conception (AT XI 356–7: CSM I 342). In the *Meditations* he describes the appetites and sensations resulting from the mind–body union as "teachings of nature"; here, the natural institution of the mind–body union assumes the role of the sensitive soul in producing "natural" impulses that serve for the preservation of the mind–body complex (AT VII 38–9, 80–9: CSM II 26–7, 56–61).

After these discussions of the passions, the combined physiological and mental phenomenon to which Descartes devoted the largest measure of attention was sense perception, and vision in particular. Execution of his mechanistic program required that he provide a replacement theory of the senses for the one he rejected. His program of accounting for as much of the psychology of the sensitive soul as possible by corporeal processes alone led to some interesting speculations on the physiological basis of sense perception, speculations we will consider in connection with Descartes' account of both the bodily and mental conditions of visual experience.

PHYSIOLOGY AND PSYCHOLOGY OF VISION

In the sixth set of *Replies* Descartes divided sense perception into three "grades" in a manner that provides a general framework for discussing the relative contributions of mind and body in his theory of perception (AT VII 436–9: CSM II 294–6). The first grade consists in "the immediate stimulation of the bodily organs by external objects," and amounts to "nothing but the motion of the particles of the organs"; in the case of vision, it includes the excitation of the optic nerve by light reflected from external objects and the resulting pattern of motion in the brain. (This grade exhausts the sensory faculty in animals.) The second grade "comprises all the immediate effects produced in the mind as a result of its being united with a bodily organ which is affected"; in vision this amounts "to the mere perception of the color and light" reflected from the external object. Finally, the third grade includes "all the judgments about things outside us which we have been accustomed to make from our earliest years – judgments which are occasioned by the movements of these bodily organs," which in the case of vision includes judgments about the size, shape, and distance of objects. These judgments are made "at great speed because of habit," or rather previous judgments are rapidly recalled. Because of their speed they go unnoticed, and hence a rational or intellectual (and therefore in actuality *non-sensory*) act is assigned to the third grade of sensory response (in accordance with common opinion, as Descartes observes).

These three grades correspond with the causal (and temporal) sequence in sense perception as Descartes understood it. As an account of the direction of causation, Descartes' description agrees with the intromission theory attributed to Aristotle, according to which the causal chain in vision runs from objects to the sense organ, rather than with the extramission theory endorsed by Plato and Galen, according to which the causal process initially proceeds from eye to object.[41] On this issue, Descartes sided with the mainstream of the optical tradition (stemming from Alhazen through Pecham and Vitello), as did the scholastic authors with whom he was familiar.[42]

Descartes' division into three grades is not, however, a mere summary of the causal chain in perception, but a division based on the ontology of the three grades: The first grade is wholly material, the second involves mind–body interaction, and the third is wholly mental. Considered in this light, the division differs from Aristotelian intromission theories in the following respects. The process of transmission and of reception at the organ of sight previously had been understood, not as the transmission of mere matter in motion (as sound had been, which was commonly understood as a percussion in the air), but of a "form without matter." Descartes himself unfairly criticized previous theories for being committed to "intentional species" conceived as unified images transmitted through the air; although Epicurean theories posited such images (in material form), Renaissance Aristotelian accounts known to Descartes typically analyzed vision in terms of rays transmitted to the eye and received in a two-dimensional cross-section of the visual pyramid at the surface of the crystalline humor. Once the form was received in the eye, the usual description maintained a "quasi-optical" transmission of this cross-section along the optic nerves, conceived as hollow tubes filled with transparent "visual spirit." This process itself was not devoid of soul-dependent attributes: according to received doctrine, the spirit present in the crystalline humor, vitreous body, and optic nerve is endowed with the power of sentience, and the light and color received and transmitted are at the same time sensed. Thus one might say that the correlate to Descartes' "second grade" occurs at the surface of the cyrstalline humor, except that this "sensing," unlike Descartes' second grade, does not involve consciousness. Finally, according to many authors this transmitted form (conveying a cross-section in two dimensions) is the subject of a judgment by the "estimative power" of the sensitive soul, which determines size according to distance and angle, or distance from size and angle, and so on. In this also Descartes departs from previous doctrine, for he assigns such judgments to the rational soul, having banished from existence the sensitive soul with its estimative power.[43]

Care must be taken in characterizing what is radically different in Descartes' conception of the sensory process and what is a creative adaptation of previous theory. Thus, although his conception of the ontology of the sensory processes was novel, considered from the standpoint of geometrical optics Descartes' theory may be seen as a translation of previous doctrine into the mechanistic idiom – taking into account, of course, differences required by the discovery of the retinal image. These differences were not as large as one might expect. Indeed, the problems confronting pre- and post-Keplerian theorists were similar: each had to show how a point-for-point relation could be established between objects in the field of vision and the sensitive surface in the eye, and each had to show how the pattern established at the sensitive surface could be transmitted to the seat of judgment (or how the results of a judgment "on the spot" were centrally conveyed). Previous optical writers invoked the crystalline's special receptivity for rays normal to its surface to achieve the former, whereas Descartes invoked the optics of image formation. And where previous theorists posited a quasi-optical transmission of the received pattern, Descartes explained the transmission of the pattern by appealing to the arrangement of the nervous fibrils and, in

his full theory as presented in the *Treatise,* the flow of pineal spirits
(AT XI 175–6: CSM I 105–6). He in effect translated the quasi-
optical transmission of previous optics into a mechanical transmission serving the same function, a function which he described (in
the *Optics*) as the transmission of an image: "the images of objects
are not only formed at the back of the eye but also pass beyond into
the brain" (AT VI 128: CSM I 167).[44] At the same time, the entity so
transmitted is conceived in a radically new fashion: although the
ontological differences entailed by Descartes' mechanistic program
do not alter the geometrical similarity of the transmitted entities in
the two theories, Descartes denied that the transmitted entity contains the form of color, for he denied that color is a "real quality."[45]
Having done so, he needed an account of how material objects cause
sensations of color, an account he provided in connection with
mind–body interaction: various properties of objects (their "physical colors," so to speak) impart various spins to particles of light,
which variously affect the nervous fibrils, causing different patterns
of flow from the pineal gland, and thereby causing various colors to
be perceived by the soul in the second grade of sensory response.[46]

The text from the *Sixth Replies* not only provides a summary of
the ontology of sense perception according to Descartes; it also contains some quite interesting – though problematic – remarks characterizing the mental processes in grades two and three. Descartes
tells us that the second grade "extends to the mere perception of the
color and light reflected from" an external object, and that "it arises
from the fact that the mind is so intimately conjoined with the body
that it is affected by the movements which occur in it" (AT VII 437:
CSM II 295). This wording suggests that the second grade includes
only the perception of light and color but does not include any representation of the shape or form projected onto the retina and conveyed into the brain; the focus on light and color might also suggest
that the relation between the brain activity and the resulting sensations is of the "natural institution" sort. The same passage soon
renders both suggestions problematic. Descartes continues by in-
structing the reader to "suppose that on the basis of the extension of
the color [in the visual sensation] and its boundaries together with
its position relative to the parts of the brain, I make a rational calculation about the size, shape and distance" of the object. It thus appears that whether or not the second grade includes a perception of

the projected shape of the object, the sensations present a bounded area of color from which the shape of the object could, in conjunction with other information pertaining to size and shape, be inferred. Moreover – and this is particularly astonishing – the quoted sentence says that the position of the color sensation is determined relative to the parts of the brain, implying a comparison between the shape presented within a mental event (a sensation) and actual spatial locations in the material brain.

This passage is an instance of a persistent tension in Descartes between two conceptions of mind–body interaction: a conception according to which mental events are paired with bodily processes in an arbitrary fashion by an "institution of nature," and a conception according to which the content of the mental event is determined by what the mind "sees" in the body, by direct inspection of a pattern in the brain (as it were). These may be termed the "interaction" and "inspection" conceptions.[47] Descartes invoked interaction often; the question of interest is whether he seriously proposed the inspection view, or was simply careless in his wording here and there.

Descartes should not be saddled with a naïve inspection view, for he warned against such a view himself in the *Optics*, where he cautioned that although the image or picture transmitted into the brain "bears some resemblance to the objects from which it proceeds," nonetheless

we must not think that it is by means of this resemblance that the picture causes our sensory perceptions of these objects – as if there were yet other eyes within our brain with which we could perceive it. Instead, we must hold that it is the movements composing this picture which, acting directly upon our soul in so far as it is united to our body, are ordained by nature to make it have such sensations.   (AT VI 130: CSM I 167)

But what has Descartes actually cautioned against here, and how does this relation between bodily motions and sensations, a relation "ordained by nature" (*institué de la Nature*), actually work? It is sure that he means to deny that the colors of objects are perceived by means of resemblance, because he denies that the image transmitted in the brain contains color as a "real quality"; this point is foremost in his "no resemblance" view (AT VI 113: CSM I 165). He also observes that the shapes represented in the brain image need not precisely resemble the shapes they make us see; thus, in an engraving a circle must often be represented by an ellipse in order for us to experience it as a circle (AT VI 113: CSM I 165–6). This latter warning against thinking in terms of resemblance is, however, irrelevant to the passage from the *Replies;* for in the *Optics* Descartes is speaking of the relation between the image in the brain and our experience of the visual world (the third grade of sense), whereas in the *Replies* he is describing the characteristics of the sensation from which this experience is to be constructed through an unnoticed process of reasoning. Thus, the second grade of sense should include ellipses for circles, etc.; but that would mean that the boundary of the color sensation should correspond precisely to the shape of the brain image.

It is not an accident that Descartes' position should be difficult to interpret precisely at this point, for space perception raises serious metaphysical difficulties for him. In particular, it raises the question of how extended matter can act upon a nonextended mind, and can do so over an extended area (as would be necessary if we assume that an extended brain pattern collectively and simultaneously produces the sensation of a bounded color patch), and it also raises the question of how a nonextended mind can "contain" an imagistic representation (as opposed to a mere conceptual understanding) of extension and its modes.[48] There are no easy solutions to these problems, but the perspective provided by Descartes' physiological work in general offers a way of understanding his conception of the image on the pineal gland. In particular, one could see his early talk of "corporeal ideas" (AT X 419: CSM I 44; see also AT XI 176: CSM I 106; AT VI 55: CSM I 139), and his recollection of such talk in the second set of *Replies* (AT VII 160–1: CSM II 113), as another instance of the creative adaptation of previous doctrine, this time pertaining to the physiology of sensory processes and intellection. In the Aristotelian tradition, the operation of the intellect requires an image in the corporeal imagination. Now Descartes certainly rejected the slogan that all thought must be directed upon an image; but he may in fact have had in mind that spatially articulated sensations result from the body "informing" the mind. And indeed that is the very language that he uses on occasion to describe the relation between "corporeal ideas" and ideas in the mind. Thus, when he says that an idea is "the form of any given thought" (AT VII 160: CSM II 113), he may mean that in the case of a sense perception or an imagination of a shape, the mind possesses the appropriate form only by virtue of its direct contact with a real shape in the body (the corporeal idea, so he says, "gives form" to the mind).[49] In this way we could make some sense of his talk of the mind "turning toward" and even "inspecting" bodily images (AT III 361: CSMK 180; AT VII 73: CSM II 51), without having to attribute to Descartes the naive position that the mind literally looks at the body. Of course, we are left with the mystery of how a bodily state can serve as the form of a mental state, but that was not something easily understood in Aristotelian thought, nor did Descartes have a ready proposal for understanding mind–body union and interaction generally, as he ultimately admitted to Elizabeth (AT III 690–5: CSMK 226–9).

Whatever the relation between the pineal image and the attendant sensation, Descartes' theory of visual perception could not end with the creation of a sensation that simply represented the spatial features of that image, for the image varied in only two dimensions and, as Descartes recognized, our phenomenally immediate visual experience – the third grade of sensory response – is of a world of objects distributed in three dimensions.[50] According to the passage from the Sixth Replies, the processes that yield the third grade are judgmental and hence depend on the activity of the mind or soul. In the portion of the passage last quoted, Descartes speaks of making a "rational calculation" of the size, shape, and distance of an object; he goes on to say that he "demonstrated in the Optics how size, distance and shape can be perceived by reasoning alone, which works out any one feature from the other features" (AT VII 438: CSM II 295). The account of size and distance perception he here recalls from the Optics follows the optical tradition in explaining that size can be judged from visual angle plus perceived distance, distance from visual angle plus adjudged size, and shape from projected shape and perceived distance to various parts. Such accounts make size and distance perception seem always to depend on judgment, and hence to depend on a rational, or at least an estimative, power. And yet in the Treatise Descartes had claimed to mechanize the functions of the sensitive soul. Did he do so for vision merely by transferring the activities of the estimative power to the rational soul?

As far as the Replies can tell us, that is what he did. But in both the Optics and the Treatise on Man he presents an alternative account of the perception of distance, an account which may be described as purely psychophysical. In the *Optics* Descartes contends that "as we adjust the shape of the eye according to the distance of objects, we change a certain part of our brain in a manner that is ordained by nature to make our soul perceive this distance" (AT VII 137: CSM I 170), thus effectively ascribing one means of distance perception to the second grade of sense; that is, to the direct effect of a brain state on the soul, unmediated by judgment. He goes on to indicate that convergence too causes us to perceive distance, "as if by a natural geometry" (AT VI 137: CSM I 170). Although some readers, perhaps influenced by the intellectualist wording of the Latin *Optics*, have understood natural geometry to involve rational judgment, Descartes tells us that in fact this process occurs "by a simple act of imagination."[51] And whether or not he meant to exclude judgment from natural geometry in the *Optics*, it is clear that he did so in the *Treatise*, where he explains that the (corporeal) "idea of distance" consists in the degree to which the pineal gland leans away from the center of the brain as a consequence of the physiological process of converging the eyes (AT XII 183: Hall 94). This purely psychophysical account of distance perception, in which the idea of distance is caused by a brain state without judgmental mediation, represents the height of Descartes' attempt to mechanize the office of the sensitive soul, in this case, of the estimative power.[52]

Finally, the passage from the *Sixth Replies* demarcates not only three grades of sense perception – the third of which actually comprises judgments of the intellect – but it also indicates that the merely habitual judgments of the third grade should be distinguished from the considered judgments of the mature understanding. The passage as a whole arose in response to an objection that the intellect does not correct the errors of the senses, as Descartes had written, but one sense corrects another; the objectors gave as an example touch correcting vision in the case of a stick in water looking bent (AT VII 418: CSM II 282). Descartes replies that in the first place it is not truly the senses that err – he denies falsehood (and by implication, truth) to both the material process of transmission and to the sensations of the second grade. The error lies in the habitual judgment of the third grade. Touch itself delivers the product of such an habitual judgment when it reports that the stick is straight: although this judgment is again assigned to the third grade of "sense," it is really an unnoticed intellectual judgment. In effect, Descartes here assigns a portion of the office of the sensitive soul to the intellect acting in an habitual manner. In his view, such merely habitual judgments ("assigned to sense") do not provide sufficient grounds for deciding whether to trust sight or touch: the reflective intellect of the mature reasoner makes the decision. The mature intellect in this case does not correct the senses proper; rather, it corrects the habitual intellect, which has produced what we mistakenly take to be a simple sensory experience (AT VII 439: CSM I 296).

The carefully cultivated judgments of the mature intellect provide the metaphysical foundations upon which Descartes built his mechanistic physics, including his physiology. These judgments ostensibly provide the basis for the metaphysical doctrine that the essence of matter is extension (AT VII 440–3: CSM II 296–8), a doctrine upon which Descartes relies in banishing substantial forms, real qualities, and ultimately the vegetative and sensitive souls. Let us consider the relation between these judgments and Descartes' physiological and psychological doctrine.

THE RELATIONS OF DESCARTES' PHYSIOLOGY AND PSYCHOLOGY TO HIS METAPHYSICS

Although Descartes' image of the tree of knowledge places metaphysics prior to physics in the order of justification, one may suspect that in the order of Descartes' intellectual development metaphysics was developed as an afterthought to physics, at a time when Descartes was considering ways to gain acceptance for the principles of his physics among an audience likely to be skeptical of corpuscularism. On this view, his project of mechanizing the nutritive and sensitive powers would have arisen with his physico-mathematical project. Although this interpretation of the origins of Descartes' metaphysics has enjoyed some favor,[53] it should be rejected. As Gilson has argued, Descartes' physics was not fully completed prior to his metaphysical turn in 1629; his mature physics developed in interaction with his metaphysics, each influencing the other.[54] But even Gilson attributes to Descartes a "piecewise," but general, rejection of substantial forms prior to 1629.[55] Let us examine the extent to which Descartes had rejected substantial forms, real qualities, and vital powers prior to his metaphysical turn, especially in physiology and sensory psychology.

In the period before 1629 Descartes had developed the view that the powers of the sensitive soul could be divided between purely corporeal and purely spiritual agencies. Already in the *Rules*, abandoned prior to (or with) the metaphysical turn, Descartes expressed the thesis that we can "understand how all the movements of other animals can come about, even though we refuse to allow that they have any awareness of things, but merely grant them a corporeal imagination." As in the later *Treatise*, he ascribed the power of moving the nerves to the "corporeal imagination" or "common sense"; he also attributes to the common sense a "motive power" (*vis motrix*) that possesses "a purely corporeal mode of operation" (AT X 415: CSM I 42). It would be tempting to suppose that here Descartes not only expressed the thesis of animal automatism inasmuch as this implies a purely corporeal explanation of animal motion, but that he also formulated the position that all corporeal powers – including motor and nutritive powers as well as the primary causal powers of matter – can be reduced to matter conceived as pure extension.[56] But such is not the case. For although Descartes assigned the motive power a purely corporeal mode of operation, that assignment is not equivalent to the thesis that matter is extension; in order to find that thesis here we must supply it ourselves.[57] However, as mentioned earlier, we must take care not automatically to read the position of the mature Descartes into earlier works, including his own. In the *Rules* Descartes did not equate matter with extension and its geometrical modes. Although he implied that it pertains to the essence of bodies to be extended (AT X 444: CSM I 60), he also attributed weight to bodies as a real property; thus, in Rule 14, he expressly stated that "the weight of a body is something real," contrasting it with other measurable dimensions of nature, such as the day as divided into hours and minutes, that are not (AT X 448: CSM I 63). Without the thesis that matter is extension (or extended substance), we cannot assume that the *vis motrix* of Rule 12 must be reduced to merely extended matter, instead of its being a proper power of the animal body. Similarly, there is no basis in the *Rules* for concluding that Descartes had already conceived his project of reducing the nutritive power to matter in motion.

Leaving aside the precise route that Descartes took to the equation of matter with extension, let us consider further the implications of his new ontology for his physics. In histories of seventeenth-century science and metaphysics, prodigious conceptual import is ascribed to this equation: it is made responsible for the distinction between primary and secondary qualities, the banishment of mind from nature, and the rejection of final causes – in short, for the "mechanization of the world picture."[58] And rightly so. But we need to see how closely these hallowed features of the metaphysics of modern science fit Descartes' doctrine in physiology. Granting him the primary–secondary quality distinction, let us examine the banishment of the mind and the rejection of final causes.

Descartes' mechanics of matter in motion, governed by three impersonal laws of motion (and seven rules of impact), suggests a wholly "mechanical" set of interactions – interactions that are the product of aimless efficient causation. Descartes holds to this sort of explanation in his discussion of impact, of the formation of the earth, of the action of minerals, and so on throughout Parts III and IV of the *Principles*. There are, however, two domains of phenomena that draw mentality and final causes back into the picture.

The first domain of phenomena simultaneously reintroduces the mind and final causes, but in a way that is explicitly acknowledged. To discharge the office of the Aristotelian sensitive soul in preserving the human organism by judging short-range benefits and harms, Descartes introduced the "teachings of nature." These are lessons that come unbidden from mind–body interaction, as when a dryness in the throat causes a jiggle in the brain which in turn changes the flow of spirits and, via the institution of nature, makes one feel thirsty and hence directs one toward drink. These "teachings of nature" are instituted by God for the preservation of the body. They are not perfect, for they must make the best of a fallible bodily mechanism, as when pain is felt in a limb that does not exist because the central portion of the nerve fiber is stimulated and the "institution of nature" governing the mental effects of nervous activity remains unchanged (AT VII 84–9: CSM II 58–61). These teachings are distinguished from clear and distinct perceptions received via the light of nature: whereas the latter are a true guide to the natures of things, the "proper purpose" of the former "is simply to inform the mind of what is beneficial or harmful for the composite of which the mind is a part" (AT VII 83: CSM II 57). Final causes are of the essence here: these teachings are instituted by God for our good.

Ostensibly, the situation is better if we consider only animals and those processes in humans that depend upon mechanism alone. To do so, however, we must consider the punning sense of the word "mechanism" that has been used hitherto without remark. For "mechanism" means not only blind causation according to natural law – it also means machinelike. And indeed Descartes' "mechanism" is in one sense a natural philosophy of machines. But machines are artefacts; the structure of a machine is identified by virtue of a conception of what counts as its proper functioning and what counts as its being broken.[59] It may be possible to ignore this aspect of the machine metaphor in Descartes' treatments of salt or wind: these explanations do not trade on the notion of well-functioning implicit in the concept of a machine. But the case of animal bodies is different, for Descartes treats such bodies as well-functioning wholes.[60]

The fabular character of the *Treatise* allowed Descartes to finesse this problem by treating his machine as a creation of God, thereby making the finality expressed in the skillful organization of its parts God's handiwork. But his mechanistic program as expressed nonfabularly does not allow such a move. This program requires that the universe develop from chaos, unguided by divine intervention, totally in accordance with the efficient causality of impact (AT XI 34–5: CSM I 91; AT IX 101–3: CSM I 257–8). And yet Descartes provides no hint of what plays the role of artificer of his *Man* when his *World* develops from chaos; he apparently did not adequately resolve the problem of the origin or the ultimate status of his animal machine. By his own account, the universe includes machines characterized by a well-functioning disposition of parts; it thus includes entities with that degree of finality implied by the notions of well-functioning and malfunctioning. In his physiological writing and thinking he clearly acknowledged the organism to be an integrated whole, in which the parts and their relations show a certain integrity, are suited to certain "uses" or "functions."[61] And yet in the Sixth Meditation he would seem to degrade talk of "well-functioning" – when it does not make specific reference to the admittedly teleological "institution of nature" involved in the mind–body union – to the status of a mere "extraneous label" or (fictional) creature to thought (AT VII 85: CSM II 59). As he observes, a poorly functioning clock follows the laws of nature just as fully as does a clock that performs in accordance with the intentions of its maker (AT VII 84: CSM II 58). Similarly, he reasons, the human body follows the laws of nature even when its mechanisms drive it to behavior that is destructive of the whole. Here the body is presented as a mere collection of corpuscles, not as an organized machine.

Perhaps it should not surprise us that the tension in Descartes' thought between the "mechanism" of efficient causation and the "mechanism" of machines apparently went unresolved, for this tension persists in the metaphysics of our own time. But here we pass beyond the limits of a philosophical companion to Descartes' writings. Indeed, in the face of such unresolved philosophical problems, we should seek to become philosophical companions to Descartes, and to address the problems of our own time just as he addressed those of his. In order properly to understand the problems that Descartes saw before him, we have had to examine the historical context in which they arose. It may help us to understand our own philosophical circumstances if we recognize that our problems cannot be precisely the same as his, even if some are his bequest, precisely because the context that shaped his questions has been eclipsed by his response to it. For Descartes – like other philosophers whose works continue to repay study – altered the problem space of philosophy in such a way that his failures bequeath problems that take their peculiar shape only against the background of his enormous success.[62]

NOTES

1 For Descartes' teaching that metaphysics should be pursued "once in one's life," see his letter to Elizabeth of 28 June 1643: AT III 695: CSMK 228. See also Hatfield, "The Senses and the fleshless eye: the *Meditations* as cognitive exercises," in A. O. Rorty (ed.), *Essays on Descartes' Meditations*, pp. 45–79; and Garber, "*Semel in vita*: the scientific background to Descartes' *Meditations*," in A. O. Rorty (ed.), *Essays on Descartes' Meditations*, pp. 81–116.

2 Hall, *History of General Physiology*, vol. 1, ch. 18; Rothschuh, *Physiologie: Der Wandel ihrer Konzepte, Probleme und Methoden vom 16. bis 19. Jahrhundert*, ch. 1.

3 Gilson, *Etudes sur le rôle de la pensée médiévale dans la formation du système cartésien*, pp. 163–84.

4 A famous passage from Descartes' letter to Mersenne, 28 January 1641 (AT III 298: CSMK 173; see also AT III 233: CSMK 157).

5 On the date of composition and subsequent publication of this treatise, see AT XI 219–22; an abridged translation is provided in CSM I 313–24.

6 Letters: AT I 102, 137, 263, 377–8, 522–7; II 525–6, 621; III 49, 139, 445; IV 247, 326. Draft: *Primae cogitationes circa generationem animalum* (AT XI 499–538). Notes. AT XI 543–639, 651–3.

7 Aristotle, *Physics*, trans. Richard Hope (Lincoln: University of Nebraska Press, 1961), Book 3, ch. 4, 203b15 (pp. 47, 211); Marcus Tullius Cicero, *De natura deorum*, trans. H. Rackham (London: Putnam, 1933), i.20 (p. 23); Goclenius, *Lexicon philosophicum* (Frankfurt and Marburg, 1615; reprint, Hildesheim and New York: G. Olms, 1964), 828b; Alexander Gottlieb Baumgarten, *Philosophia generalis* (Halle and Magdeburg: Hemmerde, 1770), sec. 148 (p. 65); Immanuel Kant, *Critique of Pure Reason*, trans. Smith, A ix (p. 8).

8 Galen, *Introductio seu medicus*, ch. 7, in his *Opera omnia*, vol. XIV, 689; Jean Fernel, *Universa medicina*, 6th ed. (Frankfurt: Marnium and Aubrii, 1607), Part I, "Physiologiae libri VII." On the development of the concept of physiology, see Rothschuh, *Physiologie*, ch. 1.

9 Katharine Park and Eckhard Kessler, "The concept of psychology," in Schmitt, Skinner, and Kessler (eds.), *Cambridge History of Renaissance Philosophy*, ch. 13; Eckart Scheerer, "Psychologie," in Joachim Ritter and Karlfried Gründer (eds.), *Historisches Wörterbuch der Philosophie*, vol. VII (Basel: Schwabe, 1989), pp. 1,599–601. Park and Kessler (pp. 456–7) document the place of *De Anima* in the curriculum.

10 See, e.g., Suarez, *De Anima*, Book III, ch. xvi, art. 8, and Book IV, chs. i–v, vii–viii, in his *Opera omnia*, vol. III, pp. 669b–670a, 713a–733b, 738b–745a.

11 See Hall (ed. and trans.), *Treatise on Man*, p. 34, n.60, for a summary of Bartholin's account of the processes mediating sense perception and action. On the medical literature more generally, see Katharine Park, "The organic soul," in Schmitt et al. (eds.), *Cambridge History of Renaissance Philosophy*, pp. 464–84.

12 Alhazen's *Perspectiva*, which circulated widely in manuscript, was published in 1572 under the title *Opticae thesaurus*. On Alhazen's psychology of vision, see Sabra, "Sensation and inference in Alhazen's theory of visual perception," in Machamer and Turnbull (eds.), *Studies in Perception*, pp. 160–85; and Hatfield and Epstein, "The sensory core and the medieval foundations of early modern perceptual theory." Aguilon discusses distance perception in *Opticorum libri sex, Philosophis juxta ac mathematicus utiles* (Antwerp: Plantiniana, 1613), Bk. III, pp. 151ff.

13 AT I 263; II 525; IV 566; V 261. Functional language is used throughout

the *Treatise on Man* and the *Description of the Human Body* (the title of which continues: *and of All Its Functions*), as Descartes describes the "functions" that the parts of the body "serve," or the "uses" of the parts.

14 Descartes to Mersenne, 25 May 1637: AT I 378. In various places Descartes mentioned several anatomists and physiologists by name, including Galen, Fernel, Harvey, Bartholin, Bauhin, Fabricius of Aquapendente, and Riolan; historians of physiology think he was also acquainted with the writings of Columbus, Fallopius, van Helmont, and Piccolhomini: see the indexes of proper names and of books cited in AT V, and Hall pp. xvii–xxii, xxxii.

15 Gilson (*Etudes*, 99–100) maintains that Descartes accepted only "facts" from Fernel and scholastic authorities, which he then explained via a novel theory. Hall (pp. xxxi–xxxiii, and in assorted textual notes) is closer to the mark when he characterizes Descartes' relation to his predecessors as the creative adaptation of their theoretical conceptions into his mechanistic theory. Descartes conceived "animal spirits" as subtle matter, devoid of any qualities but size, shape, position, and motion.

16 Hall, *Treatise on Man*, pp. xxvi–xxviii; Owsei Temkin, *Galenism: Rise and Decline of a Medical Philosophy* (Ithaca, N.Y.: Cornell University Press, 1973), chs. 3–4. esp. pp. 164–79.

17 Fernel, *Universa medicina*, Part. I, bk. I, ch. 2, p. 3; for quotations from the Coimbrans, see Gilson, *Index Scholastico-Cartésien*, selections 171, 173, 174.

18 See Gilson, *Etudes*, Part. I, ch. 2, on which my discussion draws.

19 See Harvey, *Anatomical Studies*, ch. 2, p. 31.

20 AT I 263; Gilson, *Etudes*, pp. 73–6.

21 Commentators: Gilson, *Etudes*, pp. 84–5; Georges Canguilhem, *La Formation du concept de réflexe aux xviie et xviiie siècles* (Paris: Presses Universitaires de France, 1955), p. 34. Descartes, *Principles*, trans. Miller, Book pt. IV, art. 92 (pp. 225–6).

22 On Galenist and Aristotelian accounts of the powers/faculties/parts of the soul, see Hall, *History of General Physiology*, I 107–13, 142–4. On the three souls in Galen, see Temkin, *Galenism*, p. 44. An Aristotelian statement on the three powers of the soul is Thomas Aquinas, *Summa Theologiae*, Pt. I, Q. 78, art. 1 (vol. 11). See Fernel, *universa medicina*, Part. I, Book 5, ch. 1 (p. 171), on the three parts of the soul.

23 For Aquinas on the estimative power, see *Summa Theologiae*, Part. I, Q. 78, art. 4 (vol. 11). Suarez describes the estimative power (*De Anima*, Book III, ch. 30, art. 7; vol. III, p. 705) and argues that it is not really distinct from imagination and common sense (arts. 13–15; III 707–8), and thus that the internal senses are one (art. 16; III 708–9). Summers, *Judgment of Sense: Renaissance Naturalism and the Rise of Aesthetics*,

provides a history of theories of the estimative power in relation to aesthetics.

24 Descartes describes a portion of his *Monde* (surely the *Treatise on Man*) as a treatise on the "animal in general" (AT II 525–6: CSMK 134–5); it is most likely the *Treatise* that he refers to elsewhere as his "treatise on animals" (e.g., AT IV 326: CSMK 274).

25 The idea that the animal spirits are filtered out of the blood near the base of the brain was a commonplace, and some authors even granted the pineal gland a role in controlling the flow of the spirits between the cavities of the brain. Galen dismisses this view in *On the Usefulness of the Parts*, trans. Margaret T. May, bk. VIII, ch. 14 (Kühn, I 489–90). Hall samples various Renaissance positions (Hall, p. 86, n. 135). Descartes' particular conception of the sense-controlled mechanism for this distribution apparently was unique.

26 Descartes, again following the Galenic tradition (Hall, p. 25, n. 48), described muscle action as antagonistic; he described an elaborate shunting system by which one muscle would inflate and contract while another deflates and elongates (AT XI 133–7: Hall, pp. 24–9).

27 Descartes explicitly states that the arrangement of the fibers may be either "natural" or "acquired" (AT XI 192: Hall, p. 103). The actions "incited" by objects impinging on the senses are determined by six factors in all, which Descartes lists at AT XI 190 (Hall, 101).

28 The italicized terms are scattered throughout the *Treatise*; see esp. AT XI 163–78, 184–97 (Hall, pp. 68–88, 96–108).

29 On the basis of this passage and others, Descartes is sometimes described as the inventor of the concept of the reflex. Although he did describe as automatic some movements that we consider to be reflexes, he did not explicitly distinguish such movements from other automatic movements such as those depending on habit. For a discussion of the origin of the concept of reflexive motion, see Canguilhem, *La Formation du concept de réflexe*.

30 Descartes equated the outflow of spirits that causes muscular motion with the corporeal idea of that motion: "the movements of the members, and the ideas thereof, can be reciprocally caused the one by the other" (AT XI 182: Hall, 94). In a machine endowed with a rational soul, the outflow of the spirits could serve to give the soul a mental idea of the position of the bodily parts (AT XI 160–1: Hall 63–5).

31 AT XI 182: Hall 94; see also AT VII 229–30: CSM II 161. According to Descartes' mechanics, changes in direction did not count as a change in the quantity of motion (AT IX 65–6: CSM I 242–3); hence, the mind's influence on the direction of the pineal spirits would not alter the quantity of motion in the universe. Leibniz remarked on this aspect of Des-

cartes' mechanics and physiology in his "Considerations on Vital Principles and Plastic Natures," in Leibniz's *Philosophical Papers and Letters*,
trans. Loemker, p. 587; the paper first appeared in the *Histoire des
ouvrages des savants* (May, 1705).

32 On the reception of the idea of the "beast-machine," see Balz, "Cartesian doctrine and the animal soul"; Rosenfield, *From Beast-Machine to
Man-Machine*; Vartanian, *Diderot and Descartes*; see also Thomas
Henry Huxley, "On the hypothesis that animals are automata, and its
history," in his *Animal Automatism and Other Essays* (New York:
Humboldt, 1884), pp. 1–16. The program of reducing humans and other
animals to physicalistically conceived micromechanisms is still confidently described and still short on plausible detail: W. V. Quine, *Roots of
Reference* (La Salle, Ill.: Open Court, 1973), pp. 10–11.

33 Canguilhem, *Formation du concept de réflexe*, p. 21; Park, "Organic
Soul," pp. 483–4.

34 Telesio, *De rerum natura juxta propria principia*, BK. V, xi–xiv (pp. 190–
7); xxii–xxiii (pp. 205–6). He compared the action of muscles and joints
to that of a machine (i.e., a simple machine like a hoist).

35 Ibid., BK. V, x–xi (pp. 188–91).

36 Ibid., BK. V, xxii–xxiii (pp. 205–6).

37 Ibid., BK. I, iv (pp. 6–8).

38 Consider further that although Galen distinguished the "pneuma" in
the nerves from the soul and described it as the "first instrument" of the
soul, he nonetheless attributed sentience to the pneuma itself: *On the
Doctrines of Hippocrates and Galen*, trans. Phillip de Lacy, 3 vols. (Berlin: Akademie Verlag, 1980), vol. 2, pp. 445, 447, 473–5 (Kühn, V 606,
609, 642). Specht, *Commercium mentis et corporis*, pp. 7–12, discusses
the crucial differences between Descartes and several alleged precursors
of his mechanistic program.

39 AT III 19–20, 47–9, 123, 263–5, 361–2: CSMK 143, 145–6, 149, 162,
180.

40 On the "Natural Institution" theory, see M. D. Wilson, *Descartes*, pp.
207–18. In my view, Descartes' talk of such an "institution" or "ordination" is consistent with both occasionalist or interactionist readings of
mind–body interaction; Specht, *Commercium mentis et corporis*, ch. 3,
discusses the occasionalist tendencies in Descartes' writings.

41 Lindberg, *Theories of Vision*, ch. 1, discusses extramission theories.

42 Lindberg, *Theories of Vision*, follows the intromission theory to its eventual triumph. Although both positions were discussed in the scholastic
literature, intromission typically came out on top, e.g., Suarez, *De
Anima*, Book III, ch. 17 (III, 670a–673b).

43 On the quasi-optical transmission see Lindberg, *Theories of Vision*, pp.

81–5; on the unnoticed judgment of what Alhazen termed the "discriminative power," see Sabra, "Sensation and inference," pp. 170–7.

44 On Descartes' relation to previous optical theory, see Hatfield and Epstein, "Sensory core."

45 Descartes held that there need be no "resemblance" (*ressemblance*) between the images transmitted into the brain, or, at least that the resemblance may be "very imperfect" (*Optics*: AT VI 112–14: CSM I 165–6). He denied resemblance in two ways. First, in the case of color, he rejected all resemblance between the images in the eye and color as experienced; the images are bodily states possessing only the properties of size, shape, position, and motion (*Principles*, Part. IV, art. 198: AT IX 322: CSM I 285). Second, in the case of shape, he allowed that there is a "real resemblance" but explained that it can be imperfect, as in perspective drawings (to be discussed).

46 Descartes did allow that color is a property of physical objects, as when he said that "in the bodies we call 'colored' the colors are nothing other than the various ways in which the bodies receive light and reflect it against our eyes" (AT VI 85: CSM I 153; see also AT VI 92: CSM I 156; AT IX 34: CSM I 218; AT IX 322–3: CSM I 285).

47 Descartes introduces the idea of an arbitrary "institution" or "ordination" of nature in a passage from *Optics* soon to be quoted. Smith, *New Studies in the Philosophy of Descartes*, ch. 6, collects and discusses passages in which Descartes emphasizes the mind's "inspection" of corporeal images.

48 George Berkeley, *Principles of Human Knowledge* (Dublin, 1710), Part I, art. 49, raises the problem of how the mind can have an idea *of* extension (or have an idea with extension as its "content") without itself being extended.

49 AT VII 161: CSM II 113; see Smith, *New Studies*, p. 149, n. 2.

50 Descartes described the phenomenon of shape constancy: "the images imprinted by objects very close to us are a hundred times bigger than those imprinted by objects ten times farther away, and yet they do not make us see the objects a hundred times larger; instead they make the objects look almost the same size, at least if their distance does not deceive us" (*Optics*: AT VI 140: CSM I 172). The phenomenon had previously been described by Ptolemy and Alhazen, among others (Hatfield and Epstein, "Sensory core," pp. 366, 368–9).

51 The phrase "par une action de la pensée, qui, n'estant qu'une imagination toute simple, ne laisse point d'envelopper en soy un raisonnement tout semblable a celuy que sont les Arpenteurs, lors que, part le moyen de deux differtes stations, ils mesurent les lieux inaccessibles" (AT VI 138), was rendered into Latin as "per actionem mentis quae, licet simplex judicium

videatur, rationationem tamen quamdam involutam habet, simili ili quâ Geometrae, per duas stationes diversas, loca inaccess dimetiuntur" (AT VI 609–10). The Latin translation (1644) was by Etienne de Courcelles (AT VI v) and was advertised as having been reviewed and emended by Descartes (AT VI 517); if the quoted phrase is Descartes' emendment, perhaps he introduced it in order to render the *Optics* consistent with the sixth *Replies* (1641).

52 George Pitcher, *Berkeley* (London: Routledge & Kegan Paul, 1977), pp. 19–20, discusses the general characteristics of a psychophysical account, without attributing such an account to Descartes. Descartes did not propose an extension of his psychophysical account to size perception. One might envision that a pineal image of a given physical size yields a larger or smaller perceived size depending open the lean of the pineal gland (which serves to indicate distance). This proposal faces the problem, though, that various parts within the pineal image must be referred to different perceived distances; Descartes implies that the perception of some objects' "distance and the position of their parts" is sufficient for size and shape perception (AT VI 140: CSM I 172), but he does not explain how the various parts of objects (lying in various visual directions) are variously referred to different distances during a single perceptual act.

53 Caton, *The Origin of Subjectivity: An Essay on Descartes*, esp. chs. 1, 3; Kenneth Dorter, "Science and Religion in Descartes' *Meditations*," *The Thomist* 37 (1973), 313–40.

54 Gilson, *Etudes*, Part. II, ch. 1, esp. pp. 165–8.

55 Ibid., pp 167–8. According to Gilson, after 1629 Descartes conceived substantial forms as like little souls that were needed to explain the causal powers of an otherwise "mathematical" matter; he was repulsed by this ontology (ibid., pp. 162–3) and, having formulated the real distinction between soul and body (pp. 163–8), he applied it to substantial forms, exorcizing them from matter and driving them to oblivion (pp. 173–84).

56 Even in his mature physics and metaphysics, Descartes did not claim to reduce the causal agency of matter either to motion or to a force indwelling in matter, but referred it to God (AT XI 37–8: CSM I 92–3; AT IX 61–6: CSM I 240–3); but he restricted the properies of matter to size, shape, position, and motion (AT XI 33: CSM I 90–1; AT IX 52–4: CSM I 232–3).

57 Gilson is, I think, correct in his assertion that Descartes' rejection of substantial forms had largely to do with his reconceiving matter rather than mind, but his emphasis on the role of the mind–body distinction per se obscures the significance of Descartes' insight (Gilson, *Etudes*, Part. II, ch. 1). The mind–body distinction implies the rejection of sub-

stantial forms and real qualities only if one already has the conception of matter as qualityless extension or of qualities as soullike entities: that is Descartes' conclusion, and should not be built into his starting point. Gilson's argument rests upon two questionable claims: that Descartes was intimately acquainted with only two bodies of physical doctrine, his own and that of thirteenth-century scholasticism (Gilson, *Etudes*, p. 143); and that he had developed the physics of qualityless extension prior to affirming the mind–body distinction in 1629 (Gilson, *Etudes*, pp. 149, 166). As regards the latter, Descartes treated weight as a real quality through the period of the *Rules*, as he had in his mathematical treatment of weight-driven motion in conjunction with Beeckman (AT X 68). Moreover, Descartes undoubtedly was familiar with other bodies of doctrine portraying a variety of relations among body, soul, qualities, incorporeal agencies, and matter. Within the scholastic tradition itself, the treatment of the human soul as an incomplete being had been challenged; the soul was sometimes treated as a substance in its own right, which governed the body "like the captain of a ship" (Kessler, "Intellective Soul," in Schmitt [ed.], *Cambridge History of Renaissance Philosophy*, pp. 523–9). Of even greater interest is the variety in the available conceptions of matter. According to one standard sixteenth-century source, Democritus reduced matter to size and shape, but he also posited the void and "the incorporeal"; Epicurus attributed weight to matter in addition to size and shape; and the Stoics posited two principles in the universe: an active incorporeal one (God) and a passive, extended matter (pseudo-Plutarch, "Les opinions des philosophes," in vol. 2 of *Les Oeuvres morales et meslées de Plutarche*, trans. Jacques Amyot, 2 vols. [Paris, 1572; reprint, New York: Johnson, 1971], Book 1, chs. 2, 9). Furthermore, as the physiological literature has shown us, simply equating the sensitive soul with corporeal substance did not amount to reducing it to matter in motion.

58 E. A. Burtt, *The Metaphysical Foundations of Modern Physical Science: A Historical and Critical Essay*, rev. ed. (London: Routledge & Kegan Paul, 1932), chs. 1, 4, 8; Alfred N. Whitehead, *Science and the Modern World* (New York: Macmillan, 1926), 79–80.

59 Ludwig Wittgenstein, *Philosophical Investigations*, trans. G. E. M. Anscombe, 3d ed. (New York: Macmillan, 1969), secs. 193–4, observes that, when machines are regarded in a certain way, their motion seems completely determined in a way that ignores the possibility that the parts of a given machine might bend or break (thereby yielding a motion different from the one foreseen).

60 On the philosophical implications of the machine metaphor for Descartes' philosophy and physiology, see Rodis-Lewis, "Limitations of the

mechanical model in the Cartesian conception of the organism," in Hooker (ed.), *Descartes: Critical and Interpretive Essays*, pp. 152–70, and Gisela Loeck, *Der cartesische Materialismus*, esp. ch. 7.

61 Descartes in his physiological writings regularly speaks of the "functions" of the body (e.g., AT XI 121, 201: Hall, pp. 5, 113; AT XI 224: CSM I 314) or of what its parts "serve" to do (AT XI 154: Hall, p. 54). Rodis-Lewis "Mechanical model," pp. 161–5, discusses Descartes' treatment of the body as a functioning whole. Descartes most typically discusses the unity of the body into a functioning whole in connection with its union with the mind (AT VII 85: CSM II 59; AT IV 166–7).

62 In preparing this chapter I received support from the Centre for Interdisiplinary Research of the University of Bielefeld (Germany). I am grateful to the Landesbibliothek in Oldenburg, and the Bodleian Library in Oxford for permission to consult rare books in their possession.

12 Descartes on thinking with the body

What difference, if any, does the specific character of an individual's body make to the way that individual thinks, to his thoughts and to the sequence or association of his thoughts? What must the body be like, so that its contribution to thinking is reliable, and perhaps even useful? What nonepistemic benefits does the body bring to the mind? Although Descartes did not himself ask these questions in just these terms, answering them is central to the success of his enterprise. In any case, he provided the materials for addressing those issues, which he would have formulated as a problem about how divine epistemic benevolence – a guarantee of the possibility of demonstrative scientific knowledge – is expressed in the way that the body is structured, as it affects the mind.[1]

A familiar caricature represents Descartes as having the grossly simplified, nearly grotesque features attributed to Platonists who allegedly locate the source of confusion and error in the body, while treating the pure intellect as rational, truth-bound. According to this multiple distortion, the possibility of knowledge depends on there being some mode of thought that is not determined by, and that is capable of being corrected independently of, the general character of an individual's body, and even of its particular condition at any given time. On this view, the power of an individual mind depends on its autonomy, on its power to distinguish its purely intellectual clear and distinct ideas from the confused ideas caused by the body.

Like all caricatures, this gross distortion of Descartes' views conveys some features of the original. While he was himself largely focused on attacking scholastic science and on constructing the metaphysical foundations for mathematical physics, Descartes acknowledged the contributions of bodily based thought to the sciences, particularly to kinematics and the biological sciences. It is the medium and the messenger by which the imperial will realizes many of its operations: the retrieval of certain kinds of memory (*Passions* Part I, art. 44), the determination of what is valuable and important. Even when the will elicits perceptual memories or images, it does so through the active cooperation of the pineal gland, the nerves and animal spirits (*Principles*, Part IV, art. 189–96; *Passions*, Part I, art. 42). Bodily based thought, following the promptings of nature, is necessary to guide the will's determinations in directing a soundly constructed life, since the body not only affects the content, but the sequence and association of perceptual ideas (*Passions*, Part I. art. 44). It is, after all, Descartes who ends his *Treatise on the Passions* by saying, "It is on the passions alone that all the good and harm of this life depends. . . . They dispose us to want those things which nature deems useful to us . . ."

In Part I, I shall characterize the functions of the various ideas that are produced in the mind by the action of the body. Part II investigates the relation between the body's epistemological contributions and its homeostatic maintenance system. Part III sketches some of the therapeutic and moral functions of the passions; and Part IV addresses some criticisms of Descartes' analysis.

We will take part of the project of the *Meditations* as established: The hypothesis of the deceiving demon has been defeated, the existence of an epistemically benevolent deity has been demonstrated, deductive mathematical demonstrations have been well-grounded and well-developed. To establish the rough epistemic reliability of perceptions, and the trustworthiness of the passions, Descartes need not – and by his lights should not – be prepared to answer the skeptic by showing that each and every turn of confused and misleading body-based thought can be transformed or translated into the clear and distinct ideas of high science. Just as it was sufficient in the first two Meditations to cast doubt on classes of ideas – on sense perception, on memory, on mathematical claims – so it is only necessary to establish the conditions for the reliability of classes of ideas. Descartes need not commit himself to supplying a method for doing what cannot be done, for testing individual bodily based ideas seriatim, in isolation.

I

Descartes distinguishes three classes of passions; that is, three classes of ideas that are caused by the body: perceptual ideas are referred or attributed to their external causes; bodily sensations are referred or attributed to our own bodies; and passion–emotions (narrowly speaking) are referred or attributed to the soul, but caused by physical objects acting on our bodies (*Passions*, Part I, art. 12, 13, 23).[2]

1.1. Perceptual ideas

There are, then, to begin with, perceptual ideas, that "refer to things outside us, the objects of our senses . . . that cause certain movements in the organs of the external senses, and by means of the nerves produce other movements in the brain, which cause the soul to have sensory perception of the objects" (*Passions*, Part I, art, 23; see also *Principles*, Part IV, art. 191).

Taken in isolation, perceptual ideas are, to be sure, confused: They are neither veridical nor informative. Even in their confused forms, they need to be interpreted by the mind, which uses its innate geometric ideas (of size, shape, location) to form and organize them into judgments. (Cf. *Optics* for a detailed account of the way that the mind mathematizes and geometrizes perceptual sensations. The explanation of the causes of perceptual ideas falls within a theory of mechanics.) Nevertheless, although perceptual ideas do not resemble their causes, they bear the traces of those causes and stand in a lawlike relation to them. A mind equipped with high science – with the mathematico-deductive physics that demonstrates the necessary properties of *extension* – can decipher perceptual ideas to form judgments about the size, shape, location and motions of physical objects.

Whereas innate mathematical ideas are required to interpret their contributions, bodily perceptions present essential, decipherable clues about the properties of physical objects. It is, for example, not only the geometry, but also the physiology of binocular vision that provides the material for judging the distance and size of particular objects (*Optics* VI: AT VI 137). Although the proximate cause of perceptual ideas is nothing more than the motion of the pineal gland, inclining this way or that, perceptual ideas are affected by the structure of the eye, of the nervous system and of the brain, presumably because these structures determine just that motion, in that direction, at that angle; and the structure and patterns of the flow of the animal spirits outward from the gland also serves as the proximate cause of perceptual ideas, again, because they determine the motion of the pineal gland.

1.2. Ideas of motion

Let us examine the contribution of one perceptual bodily based idea – that of the motion of a specific physical object – to thought, and indeed to high science.

We should distinguish: The innate philosophical idea of motion as an idea of a mode of physical objects; the idea of a specific motion of a specific physical body that provides initial conditions for the application of laws of motion; and the formulation and demonstration of specific laws of motion in kinematic mechanics.

Descartes defines motion in this way: "Motion is the transfer of one piece of matter, or one body, from the vicinity of the other bodies which are in immediate contact with it, and which are regarded as being at rest, to the vicinity of other bodies" (*Principles*, Part II, art. 25). This innate philosophical idea is also a geometrical idea: It is used to define lines, planes, curves. "In order to trace the curved lines which I intend to introduce here, we need assume nothing except that two or three more lines can be moved through one another. . . . Complex lines [are] described by continuous movements or by several successive movements" (*Geometry* II, "Of the Nature of Curved Lines," Olscamp, 190–1). Despite the fact that Descartes characterizes the idea of motion as an innate geometrical idea, he attributes it to physical objects; and he insists that locomotion – a change in the relative location of a physical body – is the only kind of motion. The philosophical definition of motion and its application in geometry does not, as it stands, presuppose observation or experiment. Nevertheless, Descartes also distinguished geometry from mechanics and kinematic physics, suggesting that while the kinematic idea of motion presupposes the philosophic/geometric idea, it cannot be derived from it, presumably because it includes reference to perceptual ideas. "But it seems to me that . . . we understand by 'geometry' that which is precise and exact, and by 'mechanics' that which is not" (*La*

Géométrie, Bk. II, AT VI 389: Olscamp, p. 191). In discussing whether a body could be both at rest (relative to some bodies) and in motion (relative to others), Descartes remarks that a man sitting still on the deck of a moving ship is 'more properly said to be at rest than in motion, since he does not have any sensory awareness of action in himself" (*Principles* Part II, 24). Despite Descartes' ad hoc claim that "the countless different kinds of motion can be derived from the infinite variety of different shapes," (*Principles*, Part II, 24) the motion of a particular physical object cannot be derived from its own geometrical qualities. "Strictly speaking," Descartes says, "the same portion of matter always takes the same amount of space . . . and absolutely speaking, there is . . . only a single motion which is the proper motion of each body" (*Principles*, Part II, art. 31–3). But this means that the motion of a physical object cannot be specified independently of a determination of its size, shape and location; and it certainly cannot be specified by the intellect alone.

But of course it should not be surprising that we need perceptions to determine the motion of a particular physical body. Such an admission need not, it might be thought, jeopardize Descartes' primary project of providing a philosophical account of, and the a priori principles for, a deductive mathematical physics. Can Cartesian theoretical physics be constructed without reference to bodily based ideas? The question is: What functions do perceptual ideas play in the development of theoretical physics and kinematic mechanics?

Descartes certainly attempts to derive the principles that govern the law of motion from metaphysical considerations about the nature of God (*Principles*, Part II. art. 36–52). Indeed he thinks that the physical world just is the mathematical world as realized by God, who sets the physical world in motion but preserves the same quantity of motion in matter, continuously recreating the world according to the same laws by which he originally created it.[3] But from all this, it does not follow that the detailed laws of acceleration and impact can be derived from the properties of God and the laws of geometry. It is one thing to classify the philosophical idea of motion as an innate geometrical idea, and quite another to claim that all the kinematic sciences are deducible from geometry, or even from the general principles that constrain the laws of motion as assured by divine benevolence.

Gary Hatfield and Marjorie Grene have, I think, convincingly argued that even if it were possible to get a mathematico-deductive theoretical physics and even if that physics were the physics of physical bodies as well as that of Extension, still the greater part of the science of nature – the explanation of natural phenomena – must come from mechanics and kinematics.[4] It is, after all, Descartes himself who says that "All the variety in matter, and all the diversity of its forms, depends on motion" (*Principles*, Part II, art. 23). While this claim might itself be an a priori philosophical claim, the variety and diversity of matter is not actually derived from the philosophical idea of motion, even as it might be extended by divine benevolence to the principles of the laws of motion. Hatfield and Grene argue that the laws of motion serve only as background principles for mechanics; that mechanics does the lion's share of the work in explaining natural phenomena; and that the demonstrations of kinematic physics, needing as it does to be supplemented by mechanics, depends on observation and experiment.[5] As Hatfield puts it:

Various particular mechanistic explanations cannot be defended on the basis of metaphysics alone, since mathematical intuition per se gives no direct insight into the particular geometrical configurations of actually existing bodies. The latter must be determined by sensory observation and experiment; by positing particular mechanistic hypotheses, and checking the empirical plausibility of the posit. Metaphysics reveals what kinds of properties can be used in constructing hypotheses; sensory observation and experiment must be used to determine which of these constructions fit the actual order of things.[6]

There appears to be at least one powerful argument against an interpretation that assigns a significant role to perception in the construction of science. In the Second Meditation, Descartes claims to have shown that "It is not the faculty of the imagination that gives me my grasp of the wax as flexible and changeable. . . . Take away everything which does not belong to the wax and see what is left: namely something extended, flexible and changeable" (AT VII: 31 CSM II 21). Descartes accepts the Platonic argument that forming a judgment about the identity of a changing physical object ("judging that it is *the same thing* that now has this shape and then that") presupposes a set of purely intellectual ideas. But this does not entail that the idea of a particular change in location is a purely intellectual idea. In the *Meditations* passage, Descartes is primarily concerned to show that the *general* ideas of extension and of its essential properties are intellectual ideas, independent of the imagination as a faculty of the embodied mind. Because imagination-ideas about physical objects logically presuppose intellectual ideas, the general properties of extension are best analyzed by an investigation of intellectual ideas. But this thesis is compatible with Descartes' later acknowledging that judging *particular* claims about motion, even claims about the *laws* of motion and acceleration requires the co-operation of bodily based perceptual ideas. It is, in short, because we have bodily based ideas that we distinguish between the development of two branches of theoretical physics, between algebraicized solid geometry on the one hand, and kinematic physics and mechanics on the other.

Since the development and verification of the laws of kinematic physics requires the support of perceptions, it is necessary to establish their reliability. The ending of the Sixth Meditation is meant to assure us that perceptions are not in principle misleading: properly understood, "what nature teaches us" through the action of the body on the mind is genuinely informative. But how are we to determine when such teachings *are* properly understood? Descartes needs a criterion for identifying an epistemically reliable perceiver, whose perceptual system provides the kind of information that supports the development of a kinematic mechanics. He does not of course need to establish the reliabiity of every perceiver. As long as variant perceptual systems stand in continuous lawlike correlations to the initial model, their perceptions are also reliable when they are suitably uncoded and carried through the system of correlations.

1.3. Ideas of bodily sensations and the emotion–passions

I believe that the functions of the two remaining classes of bodily based ideas – bodily sensations and emotion–passions – provide a way of identifying an epistemologically reliable perceptual system, because they provide a way of identifying a soundly functioning healthy physical body. The motto of my reconstructive hypothesis is this: find a healthy body type and you'll find a reliable perceiver; analyze the perceptual system of a healthy perceiver and you have the ground base for the reliability of any perceptual system that stands in a lawlike relation to the model.

Without getting involved in the mechanics of Cartesian dualism, and without prejudicing the case, let us call the external sense organs and everything directly involved in their presenting perceptual ideas of the properties of physical objects to the mind (the brain, the filaments that connect the nerve system to the brain, the animal spirits, the pineal gland) *the information system*. But there is more to our bodies than our information systems. Like other complex machines, institutions, and organizations, many of the parts and operations of our bodies (like those of the digestive and circulatory systems, for example) are directed to its survival and maintenance. Let us call all those parts and their functions *the maintenance system*.

The maintenance system includes the emotion–passions and most bodily sensation – thirst, heat, pain, weariness – that indicate some of the conditions of the individual's own body. In *Principles*, Part IV, art. 190, Descartes characterizes bodily sensations as "natural appetites, whose function is to keep our natural wants supplied." They involve the excitation of the nerves of the stomach, throat, etc. Sensations of this kind produce changes in the muscles, changes that lead to the bodily motions that are normally appropriate to satisfying natural wants. When those changes affect the brain and the pineal gland, they produce ideas that can in turn form a desire to modify or check the natural motions begun by inner bodily sensations. The functions of the sensations of the body resemble those of the passion–emotions, which also generate the body's protective and maintenance motions.

The emotion–passions, narrowly speaking, comprise the third class of ideas caused by the body. Unlike perceptions and bodily sensations, the emotion–passions are not referred or attributed to their causes but are rather predicated directly of the mind. The body, not the mind, is hot or parched; but it is the mind, not the body, that loves, fears, hates. Emotion–passions do not even confusedly present or represent properties of their ultimate causes or of the body as a mediating or transmitting cause of ideas. They express or signal heightened or lowered bodily functioning. So for instance, the physiological reactions which produce the idea–passion of fear are caused by the motion of the optic nerves, stimulated by the light reflecting from (say) a charging lion. This motion is communicated to the brain (which has presumably also been perceptually activated to retrieve memories of dangers and harms caused by charging lions) and thence to the pineal gland, where it "arouses," as Descartes puts it, "the passion of anxiety in the soul" (*Passions*, art. 35–6). But even if it is individuated by its cause, fear does not itself indicate whether the thought of danger has been caused by (the motions of) a charging lion, or by (brain motions involved in) the memory of an avalanche, or by (the brain motions of) imagining a Martian invasion. And in any case, even a charging lion does not generate fear in every person: whether it does – and how it affects subsequent ideas and behavior – varies with individual constitutions and individual experience (*Passions*, art. 36). But all emotion–passions produce a sequence of other associated ideas; and all but wonder produce a sequence of associated ideas that form a characteristic desire-type that, in the absence of an intervening volition, is registered in the body in such a way as to generate the motions that standardly would avoid what is harmful or pursue what is beneficial. In any case, even without the intervention of a specific desire formed by the association of ideas, the physical condition that caused a passion–idea automatically begins to produce muscular movements characteristically appropriate for avoidance or pursuit. The bodily condition that is the cause of the emotion–passion of fear also causes the beginning motions of flight. It does so, without a mediating judgment or even a mediating association of ideas, desires or volitions. Because all kinds of internal and external physical causes can affect the brain to produce the motions that are characteristic of emotion-passions, the emotion-passions do not always signal the body's real and present benefits or harms. Unless the mind actively judges or evaluates them, attempting to trace their proper etiology, such passions are not only confused, but potentially dangerous. They can produce motions and actions that are not appropriate to the individual's actual condition. But corrigibility is always in principle possible. The beginning motion of flight associated with fear can be accentuated, directed, or redirected, or stopped by another bodily motion caused by the movements associated with a contravening desire.

II

With this brief functional characterization of the varieties of bodily based ideas in mind (or in hand), let's see how they affect the mind's thoughts, and particularly, its epistemic functions.

Bodily sensations are two-faced. On the one hand, insofar as they represent the condition of the body, the sensations of thirst, cold, pressure are part of the information system. Both perceptions and bodily sensations are registered in the brain through the movement of the pineal gland, which does not by itself distinguish external from internal sources of motion. As Descartes puts it:

At the same time and by means of the same nerves we can feel the cold of our hand and the heat of the nearby flame. . . . This happens without there being any difference between the actions which make us feel the cold in our hand and those which make us feel the . . . heat outside us.

(*Passions*, art. 24)

Because all perceptual ideas are mediated through bodily sensations, they all have a kind of double-entry bookkeeping, as registering a condition or change of the body and as characteristically indicating something about the motions of physical objects impinging on us.[7] Because Descartes is eager to attribute all such differentiations to the *judgment* of the mind, rather than to the information provided by the internal and external senses themselves, he is content to differentiate the two by the functional roles they play in thought and reactions. "In the case of the cold of the hand and the heat of the nearby flame, we judge that the first is already in us and that its successor is not yet there, but in the object which causes it" (*Passions*, art. 24).

But bodily sensations also function in another system of double-entry bookkeeping. Besides being part of the information system, the sensations of hunger, thirst, pain are also part of the maintenance system (*Principles*, Part IV, art. 190). Along with the emotion-passions, they generate a set of motions that protect and enhance the body's activities. In their causes, bodily sensations are, like perceptions of external bodies, part of the information system; in their effects, they are, like the emotion–passions, part of the maintenance system. As we shall see, there is a good reason for this instability: Bodily sensations play a crucial role in identifying an epistemologically reliable body, and in establishing the particular lawlike correlations that connect the body's information system with high science.

2.1. How do we identify a reliable information system?

Suppose divine epistemic benevolence guarantees that, against the background of high science, the mind can use the information system to determine something about the size, shape and motion of objects that affect the human body. Consider this bootstrap problem: *Just how do we initially establish the details of such a coded translation system?* Because perceptual claims, taken at face value, remain confused and unreliable, it is not clear how science can initially establish even a rough correlation between perception types and the physical properties of physical objects. How is an epistemically reliable body identified? It would be circular to identify a reliable information system as one that conforms to the predictions of high mathematico-deductive science, since the predictions of high science are generated as predictions of what *would be* realized by an epistemically reliable body. (The mathematical science of optics cannot, for instance, *by itself* initially predict the color sensations of a normal body. It is *first* necessary to identify a reliable information system, to serve as the control model by reference to which the predictions of mathematical optics can be projected.)[8]

2.2. The solution: The reliability of the information system is assured by the effective functioning of the maintenance system

Descartes intimates his answer to this problem in the Sixth Meditation. We have a rough notion of a normal and reliable healthful body, as one whose interactions with other bodies produces changes that enable it to maintain and enhance its functioning. It is a body whose maintenance system operates so that it feels hunger and moves toward food at times when its body is depleted, a body that is, furthermore, nourished by the food it eats. It is a body that feels pain and moves away from harmful stimuli, experiences pleasure at and moves toward physically beneficial interactions. It inclines the mind to fear what is dangerous, to hate what injures it, to love what benefits it.

A body's maintenance system either enhances its survival and self-regulating functioning or it doesn't. Because the criterion for its reliability is independent of the criterion for epistemological reliability, it can help solve the circularity problem: An analysis of the operations and structures of a healthy body might provide a prima facie guide to the characterization of an epistemologically reliable body.

2.3. A further problem

But we are obviously not yet on safe territory. As we saw, the information system and the maintenance system are functionally interdependent: A sound information system needs a relatively sound maintenance system to keep it in working order; and a relatively sound maintenance system relies on a sound information system to recognize and avoid what is dangerous. We might have hoped to turn to the emotions to help us with our bootstrap problem of identifying a sound maintenance system. After all, as Descartes put it: "The function of all the passions consists solely in this, that they dispose our soul to want those things which nature deems useful for us, and to persist in this volition" (Passions, art. 52). "It is on the passions alone that all the good and the evils of this life depend" (Passions, art. 212). A sound maintenance system is one that inclines the mind to have reliable, health-oriented emotion–passions. Unfortunately:

The ultimate and most proximate cause of the passions . . . is simply the agitation by which the spirits move the little gland in the middle of the brain. . . . It appears that the passions are excited by objects which stimulate the senses and which . . . are their principal and most common causes. . . . But they may sometimes be caused by an action of the soul when it sets itself to conceive some object or other, or by the mere temperament of the body or by the impressions which happen to be present in the brain . . . [In order to distinguish] between the various passions [and to evaluate their motivational promptings] we must investigate their origins and examine their first causes.   (Passions, art. 51)

But because the emotions are not representational, their causs cannot, even with the aid of a translation manual, be deciphered or inferred from their presentations. The emotions, cannot, after all, provide us with an independent route to identifying a sound informtaion system. A person's emotions are only as good as her perceptions; and they are only as trustworthty as her capacity to determine their real causes. While the emotions are necessary to maintenance, their guiding messages are often difficult to decipher.

2.4. Resolution

Still what seemed to be an overwhelming difficulty – the interdependence of the information system and the maintenance system –

turns out to be a blessing in disguise. The functional or operational interdependence of the two systems doesn't entail the interdependence of the criteria for their respective soundness. As long as the *criterion* for a sound survival system is independent of the *criterion* for the soundness of the information system, a healthy body can be identified independently of the epistemological reliability of its information system. Once that is done, it is precisely the *functional* interdependence of the two systems that allows a healthy body to serve as the standard model for investigating the structure and operations of a reliable information system.

It turns out that divine epistemic benevolence is very generous indeed. The correlation between a medically sound and an epistemically reliable body in principle allows a wide range of variations, as long as those variations stand in a chain of lawlike correlations to the model body. Consider that there might be a correlation between diabetes and certain patterns of color blindness. As long as there is a way of identifying a diabetic body, and as long as the chain of diabetic effects on perception is continuously lawlike, such variations need not jeopardize the reliability of the information system. Whenever there are lawlike rather than an erratic string of correlations between variant maintenance and information systems, there is a way of identifying a reliable perceptual system.

The model healthy body which initially identified a reliable perceptual system does not serve as a norm against which variations are marked as epistemologically unreliable. It rather provides a baseline for establishing the reliability of variations that stand in a string – and it can be quite a long string – of lawlike correlations to the model.

But divine epistemic generosity goes even further. Even if a medically abnormal body has *erratic* effects on the information system, so that its information cannot be reliably integrated into high science, everything is not lost, epistemologically speaking. Consider the ways in which a body that produces a high rate of testesterone might suffer damages to its information system. It might, for instance, suffer olfactory and auditory hypersensitivity that leaves the nerves permanently irritated, or it could produce emotions that typically generate harmful motions and actions. As long as an individual can be brought to recognize deviations of this kind and to acknowledge that their effect on his information system is erratic, he need not be misled. "There is," Descartes says, "no mind so weak that it cannot, if well directed, acquire an absolute power over its passions. . . . [even for ideas which nature inclines it to accept and affirm]" (*Passions*, art. 50). When we discover the patterns of standard – and sometimes erratic – perceptual illusions, we can restrain though not always correct our usual inclinations to belief. A man whose erratic hormonal malfunction leads him to imagine insults or injuries that conduce to anger and hate, can, when he recognizes his condition, attempt to set in motion the bodily changes that would check his reactions, or at least check his actions. Sometimes "the most the will can do while this disturbance is at its full strength is not to yield to its effects and to inhibit many of the movements to which it disposes the body" (*Passions*, art. 46). Even when a person's condition is so erratic that he lacks a corrective translation manual (of the sort that enables the color-blind person to form sound judgments about colors), he can at the very least suspend judgment and attempt to check his behavior. At best he can retrieve the memories whose physical realization would check his deviant perceptions and actions; at worst he can simply refrain from forming a judgment. (It is here – in Descartes' relentless optimism about the autonomy and power of the will – that the parody clichés about Descartes' pure intellectualism have their ground and justification.) While admitting that "it is to the body alone that we should attribute everything that can be observed in us to oppose our reason" (*Passions*, art. 47), Descartes nevertheless also shows how will depends on the cooperation of the body to correct or check its deviations. There is nothing about the body that in itself resists or opposes the guidance of the rational will. On the contrary, it is the body's information system that provides the will with whatever material it can have to make a sound judgment about how to redirect the motion of the body. Perceptual judgments that are not directly reliable can often be corrected; those that cannot be corrected, can often be checked.[9]

2.5. A further difficulty: Dual criteria for bodily health

But we are not yet home safe: There is another serious difficulty. The will is offered two different standards to guide its correction of the passions and their functions in bodily maintenance. One standard weights sheer bodily survival and the avoidance of pain while the other weights heigher level maintenance and the pursuit of bodily benefits. The five basic passions – love, hatred, desire, joy, and sadness – are all, Descartes says, "ordained by nature to relate to the body . . . Their natural function is to move the soul to consent and to contribute to actions which may serve to preserve the body or render it in some way more perfect" (*Passions*, art. 137). But the two – preserving the body, on the one hand, and rendering it more perfect, on the other – might sometimes diverge: A body that primarily serves one, might be different from one that primarily serves the other. Which should be taken as the norm of a medically sound body, and used as the initial exemplar of an epistemically reliable body? Descartes' initial answer is: "Sadness is in some way more primary and more necessary than joy, and hatred more necessary than love; for it is more important to reject things which are harmful and potentially destructive than to acquire those which add some perfection we can subsist without" (*Passions*, art. 137). This is what he says, speaking of the *bodily* functions of the passions. But the weighting could also go in the other direction, if we emphasize the function of the passions in guiding the relevant association of ideas as serving the information system. The criteria for identifying a medically sound body might sometimes vary, depending on whether the body is considered primarily and solely as a homeostatic machine, or as a homeostatic machine designed to serve an epistemically sound information system. One way of solving this thorny problem is to recognize the necessity for another extension of divine benevolence so that it guarantees the general and typical coincidence or at least the correlation between the physically and the epistemologically oriented criteria for medical soundness.

When the two criteria for medical health diverge, it falls to the free will to determine which criterion for medical health – one that serves sheer survival or one that serves epistemologically oriented survival – should have priority in different sorts of circumstances. But how is the will to be guided in making such judgments? No a priori considerations are available; and no "experiments" can allow the will to appeal to the judgment of an epistemologically sound mind to determine the priority of conflicting standards for medical health. It seems we must yet turn again to divine benevolence to support the will's appropriate judgment. But this time, divine benevolence underwrites the connection between criteria for the epistemic and the *moral* soundness of the will.

III

3.1. The passions as motivating the directions of the intellect

We have so far concentrated on determining conditions for assuring the epistemological reliability and corrigibility of body-based ideas. Let us now turn to some of the general benefits and joys of the various body-based ideas. We've sketched some of the contributions of perceptual ideas and perceptual judgments to the development of high science. The utility of bodily sensations, particularly those that are associated with bodily maintenance, is manifest. Keeping the body alive is a very good way of keeping the mind at work. To be sure the mind is immortal. But an immortal mind just sitting there being immortal is one thing, and an immortal mind that is also live enough to contribute to the construction of high science is another. It is, of course, the emotions and not the pure intellect that help us to appreciate this difference. The essence of the mind is thought: From the point of view of the mind's expressing its essence, it doesn't matter whether it thinks about God, about the mind, or about extension. None of its body-based ideas are essential to the mind as mind. It is the passions that indicate good and harm, and that provide us with a sense of what is important to us. Indeed, it is the emotions that make life interesting. They provide the principles of association of thought, the principles of direction and relevance in thought. They provide the motives for doing this or that science, rather than, say, running through the proofs for the existence of God over and over, over and over and over. Because all intellectual thought is equally a realization of that essence, nothing about the mind as such impels us to think one thought rather than another. It is the emotions, and particularly the emotion of wonder, that energize science and give it directions.

3.2. The passions, morality, and the will

And it is, finally, the emotions that – if anything does – bring us the benefits of morality. It is they that expand medical health to moral soundness. In the Part III of the *Treatise on the Passions of the Soul*, Descartes attempts to evaluate the individual passion types by con-

siderations of their appropriateness and their rationality. This section of the *Treatise* is tantalizingly evocative, cryptic, and brief. But
it is, I believe, meant to present a model of the kinds of considerations that the will might use in determining which of the various
criteria for medical health should have dominance in various sorts of
situations. For instance, Descartes classifies the *passion-habitude* of
nobility of mind (*generosité*) and proper self-esteem (one based on
"the exercise of the free will and the control we have over our volitions") as virtues, contrasting them with the vices of vanity and
abjectness (*Passions*, Part III, art. 151–9). All four are passions, and
like all passions, they each involve characteristic motions of the
animal spirits, motions that strengthen specific thoughts, presumably by acting on certain parts of the brain. Passions that strengthen
ill-founded thoughts are vices; those that strengthen well-founded,
appropriate, and beneficial thoughts are virtues. For instance, the
passion-habitude of nobility of mind inclines us to a "firm and
constant resolution to use the will and to use it well. Nobility of
mind inclines a person to believe that [others] have a similar free
will" (*Passions*, Part III, art. 153). Cartesian nobility of mind is, I
believe, one of the ancestors of the principle of charity, used as an
instrument for interpreting the beliefs and actions of others. It is a
passion because its exercise involves bodily changes, the movements of animal spirits to various regions of the brain; it is an
habitude because it is dispositional, it disposes us to have certain
types of thoughts about ourselves and others. And it is a *virtue*
because it is based on and continues to generate well-founded ideas,
and because nobility of soul requires the active cooperation of the
will, to set itself to thinking ideas whose motivational associations
go beyond the benefits assured by a homeostatically well-regulated
machine. Like all passions, nobility of mind involves ideas caused
by the motions of the body; but the bodily motions of nobility of
mind are, like those of other virtues, elicited by a decision of the will
to form ideas that can generate appropriate motivating passions.

There is a troubling question: "But what determines which ideas
are appropriate? What *should* guide the will in its determinations
when the interests of developing science are opposed to those of the
community, when wonder and desire go in one direction, and love
and *generosité* in another?" The austere answer is: "Values are not
metaphysically grounded. Since it is the emotions which give us our

sense of what is important, the will has nothing like clear and distinct ideas to ratify – or even to support – its inclinations." This aspect of Descartes' position – his insistence on the absolute unconditioned character of the will – leads to Sartre's view that values are constituted by radical choice. The less austere answer is: The body provides some central and strong inclinations (e.g., fear); and the *emotion-habitudes* of self-respect and *generosité* provide others. Because divine benevolence underwrites the reliability of "what nature teaches us," these inclinations can reliably guide the determination of the will. But they cannot do more than provide rules of thumb for the will; and when there is real conflict between the inclinations to promote scientific development and the inclinations to protect the community, they cannot even do that. Divine benevolence goes very far indeed; but it does not go so far as to provide a metaphysical ground for ethical principles, let alone a rational ground for their relative priority in situations where they might conflict.

IV

It is time to address several natural complaints. There's been, it might be said, an overgenerous splashing of such expressions as "typically cause," "charactersitically produce," and "are naturally correlated with." But isn't it the legitimacy of just such sorts of locutions that an investigation of the intellectual and psychological benefits of the body is meant to supply? Time and again we've appealed to divine epistemic benevolence to solve circularity and bootstrap problems. Descartes might be charged with writing the worst sort of melodrama, one in which all the problems are resolved, the strings tied together by a final appearance of a *deus ex machina,* except that in this case it is a *deus pro machina.* But we can charitably read all this in another way. These appeals can be translated into talk about the preconditions for the possibility of knowledge. In locating the points – exactly the points – where it is necessary to appeal to divine epistemic benevolence, we have located the conditions for the possibility of knowledge and health, and for the possibility of the correlation between knowledge and health. Because the criteria for medical health are distinct from those of epistemological soundness, a medically sound maintenance system can conditionally be used to identify a reliable information system. The interdependence of the operations of the maintenance and the informational systems give us a rule of thumb: Find a sound body, and you'll be likely to find a sound mind. Analyze the workings of a sound body, and you'll have some part of the analysis of the physical conditions for a sound mind. This provides no foundational certainty, no clear and distinct ideas, no demonstrations, no self-certifying criteria for perceptual reliability. No more than rules of thumb can be promised, no more delivered. Why should Descartes provide a more secure grounding than the one we actually have? Why should he give criteria for reliability in a place where we do not have it?[10]

NOTES

1 Early Enlightenment philosophers – empiricists and rationalists alike – were clearly aware that a great deal hangs on the answer to this question, and that much of it is political as well as theological. Indeed it seems likely that they did not elaborate on them because they were aware of the highly charged theological and political consequences of their views. A vivid awarenes of this kind may well have prompted Descartes to assure the authorities that his philosophical and scientific investigations would not and should not affect the judgments and practices of daily life. For Descartes, the implicit question is that of whether an ordinary person, with no more than the standard issue, ordinary physical and intellectual equipment is in a position to contribute to high, mathematico-deductive science; or failing that, whether he – or perhaps even she! – has all the equipment necessary to evaluate the claims of high science; or failing that, whether she is equipped to avoid intellectual error and to lead a safe and reasonably formed life by trusting the promptings of her nature, her ordinary reactions and beliefs, without herself being able to demonstrate the truth of her opinions. For late Enlightenment and rationalist philosophers – that is, for us – the answers to these questions affect the assessment of racism, sexism, ageism. It is likely to influence access to advanced education and to the power accorded to privileged professions and responsible positions.

2 In Meditation VI, Descartes classifies hunger, thirst, and pain together with those physiological conditions which involve avoiding harm and pursuing what is beneficial. This class includes some (but not all) bodily sensations and some (but not all) passion-emotions. It is contrasted with the class of intellectual ideas that includes both perceptual sensations and clear and distinct ideas (AT VII 64–70). In *Principles* Part IV, art. 190,

however, Descartes distinguishes sensation (*sensum perceptiones, sensus:* the five external senses); appetites (*appetitus*) such as hunger and thirst; and passions (*affectus*). The passions are caused by the actions of the body, and are felt as certain sorts of sentiments (*sensus*) as, for instance, a sense of joy. And they also produce *commotiones* specific to each passion. In the *Treatise on the Passions of the Soul*, the general class of passions (all ideas that are caused in the mind by the action of the body) is subdivided into perceptual sensations, bodily sensations, and passions proper (*Passions*, art. 23–5: AT XI 346–7). The differences in these classificatory schemes do not represent any major change in Descartes' views, save that he has become interested in dropping the Scholastic term *appetitus*, which carries connotations of a natural movement for species preservation incompatible with his mechanistic physiology. The differences in classification can be explained by the differences in contexts. In the *Meditations*, Descartes is primarily concerned with reestablishing the rough reliability of what nature and experience teach us. While the legitimation of sense perception is ensured by its absorption into pure science, the reinstatement of the promptings of thirst and fear must take another route. For this purpose, the differences between such bodily sensations as thirst and such passions as fear are irrelevant. In *Principles* Part IV, however, Descartes is presenting an account of human physiology: for these purposes, the distinctions between bodily sensations and passions are of no interest. It is only in the *Passions of the Soul* that Descartes turns his attention to the psychological distinctions between passions and bodily sensations; it is only there that it is important for him to distinguish their functional roles." "Cartesian passions and the union of mind and Body," in A. O. Rorty (ed.), *Essays on Descartes' Meditations*, pp. 531–2.

3 I am grateful to Daniel Garber for stressing this point. Cf. his "Descartes and Experiment in the *Discourse* and *Essays*," in Voss (ed.), *René Descartes: Metaphysics and Classification of the Sciences in 1637.*

4 Cf. Gary Hatfield, "The senses and the fleshless eye," in A. O. Rorty (ed.) *Essays on Descartes' Meditations*, pp. 58–9, for a nice account of the layering of this process. Marjorie Grene develops a related idea in the extremely suggestive and interesting last chapter of her recent book, *Descartes*. A full development of this idea would track the way in which Descartes goes back and forth in the *Optics*, between the geometric ideas that the mind uses to *judge* sensations, and the essentially *tactile* bodily sensations whose *changes* register the motions of external bodies. See my "Formal Tracers in Cartesian Functional Explanation."

5 Hatfield, "The senses and the fleshless eye."

6 Ibid., p. 69.

7 The beneficial functioning of the two systems – the information system and the maintenance system – could in principle and within limits vary independently. What serves maximal information might in principle lower the probability of survival by setting perceptual thresholds at such a low, finely grained level as to overload and endanger the maintenance system. Or a maximally sound maintenance system might frequently but erratically interfere with the information system, endangering its reliability. It is, of course, just these possibilities that are ruled out by the defeat of the hypothesis of the malignant demon.

8 There is a further philosophical-epistemological problem: it takes a sound information system to determine whether health *has* been assured by this or that maintenance inclination. Still, there is some reason to think the marked experience of pain provides some sort of certification, at least of malfunction. It is for this reason – because he is in the middle of a thought experiment designed to identify a sound maintenence system to help him characterize the details of the structure of a reliable information system – that Descartes worries about phantom limbs and misleading pains.

9 Although Descartes is an epistemological egalitarian about some kinds of knowledge, he also distinguishes the epistemological powers of individual minds. Any and every mind is capable of evaluating the claims of mere authority and superstition; and any mind is capable of recognizing confused ideas, and suspending judgment about what they signify. Any and every mind is capable of the *Cogito* and of following the proof for the existence of God. But very few minds are capable of engaging in high science and high philosophy. In principle, more are capable of correcting some of the errors of high science, and many more are capable of a critical evaluation of the claims of high science.

There are no general rules that can guide the will in its project of eliciting the ideas that can replace inappropriate with appropriate emotions. To counteract fear, one person might best elicit ideas that would generate pride; whereas another might best elicit ideas that would generate shame. Furthermore, individuals vary radically in the ways that specific ideas can predictibly generate specific emotions, the motions that might be appropriate to countervail an undesirable emotion. And, obviously, individuals vary greatly in the kind of self-knowledge that is necessary for a successful project of emotional self-manipulation. Descartes' claim about the strength of the will is carefully hedged: there is no will that is not *in principle* strong enough to redirect or control its emotions.

10 An earlier version of this chapter was presented at an NEH Summer Institute on seventeenth- and eighteenth-century philosophy, at Brown

University, Summer 1988, and to colloquia at the University of New Hampshire and at Duke University. I am grateful to the participants in those seminars, and to Stephen White and David Wong for stimulating and lively discussions. John Cottingham, Daniel Garber, and Gary Hatfield generously gave me extensive and helpful comments.

13 The reception of Descartes' philosophy

At the height of his enthusiasm for Locke, Voltaire delivered a characteristically witty verdict on his great compatriot:

Our Descartes, born to uncover the errors of antiquity, but to substitute his own, and spurred on by that systematizing mind which blinds the greatest of men, imagined that he had demonstrated that the soul was the same thing as thought, just as matter, for him, is the same thing as space. He affirmed that we think all the time, and that the soul comes into the body already endowed with all the metaphysical notions, knowing God, space, the infinite, having all the abstract ideas, full, in fact, of learning which unfortunately it forgets on leaving its mother's womb.[1]

Voltaire's portrait of Descartes is instantly recognizable today; indeed his estimate of Descartes is one on which many of us have been brought up, especially in the English-speaking world. Descartes is the father of modern philosophy, but he was led astray by his passion for system; he tried to derive factual truths about the world from principles that are supposedly known a priori. In short, although, Voltaire does not use the term, his Descartes is very much a rationalist. Moreover, like many modern readers, Voltaire tends to associate Descartes primarily with a distinctive set of doctrines in the philosophy of mind.

Voltaire's verdict on Descartes may have become standard, but it was not the verdict passed by Descartes' first readers. A century earlier Descartes was criticized, not for building a metaphysical castle in the air, but rather for advancing doctrines that were dangerous for the Christian faith. Further, Descartes' name was associated less with the specific teachings cited by Voltaire than with mechanism and the rejection of substantial forms: Descartes was the archenemy

393

of scholasticism. Of course the charge that Descartes' philosophy is dangerous for the faith is not formally incompatible with the charge that it is a castle in the air, but in practice these two kinds of criticism were not often combined; instead, the one gave way to the other. By the time of Voltaire there were few who were willing to attack Descartes on grounds of theological heterodoxy. Indeed the Descartes described by Voltaire had become an establishment figure, at least in France. Descartes might still be criticized by those who, like Voltaire, were themselves outsiders and rebels, but the basis of the criticism has undergone a remarkable transformation.

The structure of the chapter is as follows. We shall begin by looking at official reactions (Section 1) and the reactions of the religious orders (Section 2). Next, Sections 3 and 4 examine the views of Cartesians and anti-Cartesians respectively. We shall conclude the chapter by discussing the reactions of the three most influential "modern" philosophers of the seventeenth century after Descartes: Spinoza, Leibniz (Section 5) and Locke (Section 6).

I. OFFICIAL REACTIONS: CHURCH, STATE, AND UNIVERSITY

Descartes' philosophy and science made rapid advances, but they did so only in the face of official persecution by church, state, and universities. Not surprisingly, persecution was especially severe under the Catholic absolute monarchy of Louis XIV; during this period France was experiencing its own delayed version of the Counterreformation. But official persecution was not confined to Catholic countries or to absolute monarchies; even in liberal Holland Descartes' teaching ran into trouble from the authorities. The grounds of official opposition, however, were affected by the religious differences between the two countries. In both France and Holland Descartes' rejection of scholasticism was regarded as a threat by conservative opinion, but as we shall see, French Catholics had concerns which were not shared by Dutch Protestants.

In Holland persecution broke out in 1641, the year in which the *Meditations* was published. At the newly founded University of Utrecht Descartes' philosophy fell foul of the rector, Gisbert Voetius, a scholastic in philosophy and Calvinist in theology. Voetius began by attacking Descartes' protégé, Regius, who was professor of medicine at Utrecht.[2] Voetius's envy and hostility were aroused by the popularity of the lectures on Cartesian philosophy, which Regius was offering. Voetius was particularly incensed by Regius's incautious claim that a human being is not a substantial unity, but only an *ens per accidens*[3]; this claim clearly derived from Regius's reading of Descartes, but Descartes himself never approved of it. The generally conservative tenor of Voetius's own views can be gauged from three "corollaries," which he published as an appendix to an academic tract. In these corollaries Voetius attacked not merely the doctrine that a human being is an *ens per accidens* but also the theory of the movement of the earth and the "philosophy which rejects substantial forms." Voetius's denunciation of the new philosophy was nothing if not comprehensive: "This philosophy is dangerous, favourable to Scepticism, apt to destroy our belief concerning the reasonable soul, the procession of divine persons in the Trinity, the Incarnation of Jesus Christ, original sin, miracles, prophecies, the grace of our regeneration, and the real possession of demons."[4] Subsequently, Voetius turned to attacking Descartes directly. With the assistance of a young protégé, he published a work called *Philosophia Cartesiana* in which he charged that Descartes' philosophy led to skepticism and atheism.[5] Much to Descartes' disgust, his name was coupled with that of a notorious atheist, Vanini, who had been burned at the stake earlier in the century.

Voetius was not content to conduct a private campaign against Descartes and Regius; he also sought to use his position as rector to secure the official condemnation of the new philosophy by the university senate. Indeed, if we are to believe Descartes' account, Voetius intimidated his colleagues into voting for the motion. The terms of the condemnation are revealing:

The professors reject this new philosophy for three reasons. First, it is opposed to the traditional philosophy which universities throughout the world have hitherto taught on the best advice, and it undermines its foundations. Second, it turns away the young from this sound and traditional philosophy and prevents them reaching the heights of erudition; for once they have begun to rely on the new philosophy and its supposed solutions, they are unable to understand the technical terms which are commonly used in the books of traditional authors and in the lectures and debates of their professors. And lastly, various false and absurd opinions either follow from the new philosophy or can rashly be deduced by the young – opinions which are in conflict with other disciplines and faculties and above all with orthodox theology.[6]

This judgment reveals the mentality not just of the embattled conservative but also of the academic administrator: the content of the traditional syllabus is valued as an end in itself, rather than as a means to the discovery of truth.

In Holland the universities were not subject to any central authority but they were responsible to the local city councils, who indeed administered them. It is not surprising, then, that the civil authorities were directly involved in the persecution of the new Cartesian philosophy, especially when a powerful figure such as Voetius campaigned against it. At Utrecht the involvement of the city fathers may have been reluctant, and at times they acted as a restraining influence on Voetius; his attempts to get Regius deprived of his chair were thwarted by a burgomaster sympathetic to Descartes' protégé. But they did carry out significant repressive measures on several occasions. At Voetius's assistance and in order to placate him, the magistrates forbade Regius to teach anything other than medicine. In 1643, after Voetius had attacked Descartes personally, the civil authorities intervened again; they took direct action against Descartes himself. The open letters Descartes had published in his own defence were officially declared defamatory[7]; two years later all publications either for or against Descartes were banned. At one stage in the affair Descartes was even ordered by the city magistrates to appear in person to answer a charge of libel; at this point Descartes may have been in some real personal danger. Descartes was able to deflect these charges by appealing to the French ambassador; the ambassador spoke to the Prince of Orange who in turn used his influence to have the charges quashed.

Descartes' philosophy also encountered serious opposition at the University of Leiden, the most distinguished of Dutch universities in the seventeenth century. Two professors of theology, Revius and Triglandius, scurrilously attacked Descartes' teachings in their lectures. Revius travestied methodic doubt by saddling Descartes with the claims that "one must doubt that there is a God, and . . . one can deny absolutely for a time that there is one."[8] With equal inaccuracy and even less coherence, Triglandius charged Descartes with asserting not merely that God is an impostor but also that our free will is greater than God himself.[9] Triglandius's intention seems to have been to smear Descartes as a crypto-Jesuit. The implicit theme of his attack was that Descartes sympathized with the Pelagian tendency to stress the freedom of the will in theological controversies over grace; Pelagianism was the charge frequently leveled against the Jesuits by their Catholic and Calvinist enemies. When Descartes protested against such slanders, the university authorities responded by forbidding all mention of his philosophy in lectures and disputations. Here, as at Utrecht, the authorities seem to have resorted to censorship, not out of any great conviction, but because it was the line of least resistance in a troublesome situation.

Official censorship was much more concerted and enthusiastic in absolutist France. Unlike Holland, which was a federation of states, the France of Louis XIV was a highly centralized country where all universities were subject to the same royal and ecclesiastical authority. Of course, in France, as in Holland, Descartes' philosophy made enemies for many of the same reasons; conservative forces were offended by both its antischolasticism and the methodic doubt which seemed to license freethinking. But in France the fact that Catholicism was the official religion introduced complicating factors; Catholic opinion was troubled by the question of whether Descartes' philosophy of matter could be reconciled with the dogma of transubstantiation. For most readers today the issue is a remarkably sterile one, but for many seventeenth-century Catholics it was anything but sterile; this central dogma of the Catholic faith had been traditionally explained in terms of scholastic principles, and there were many who believed that the dogma could not survive the rejection of those principles. Unfortunately, Descartes may not have helped his cause in this matter; instead of contenting himself with saying that the dogma was a mystery that must simply be accepted on faith, Descartes attempted to explain it in terms of his own philosophy.[10] Descartes' possibly misguided efforts were to be taken up by his overzealous disciples.

The issue of the Eucharist was centrally involved in the persecution Descartes' philosophy suffered in France over ten years after his death. Clerselier and other loyal disciples made strenuous efforts to gain acceptance for Descartes' views on the Eucharist, and these efforts completely backfired. The Eucharist affair seems to have been behind the first major setback, an event which took place in

Rome but nonetheless had major ramifications in France itself. In 1663 the works of Descartes were placed on the *Index Librorum Prohibitorum* with the enigmatic proviso: *donec corrigantur* (until they are corrected). How the author was supposed to correct his works ten years after his death the Inquisitors did not explain. One of Clerselier's correspondents blamed him directly for this untoward development: "it must have been the Eucharist affair which brought about the censure. You see how prophetic I was when I told you, a long time ago, that your commerce with Father Bertet [about Descartes' views on the Eucharist] would deal a fatal blow to Descartes' philosophy."[11] Four years later, in 1667, Clerselier's propaganda campaign on Descartes' behalf received another setback, this time in France itself. Central to Clerselier's campaign was a plan to rebury Descartes in the capital of his native country. The reburial went ahead with great ceremony, but the service was interrupted by an order from the court forbidding the public delivery of a funeral oration. A great symbolic opportunity for eulogizing Descartes was lost.

This ban was a presage of things to come. In 1671 the "Eucharist affair" broke out again and resulted in a major wave of persecution. A little book by the Benedictine, Desgabets, which offered a Cartesian interpretation of the Eucharist, had been published without his consent; the king had been given a copy by his Jesuit confessor who told him that it was a "heretical and very pernicious work."[12] In the decade that followed, the king, acting in concert with the academic authorities, mounted a major campaign against Cartesianism in the universities. In the same year (1671), the University of Paris was informed of, and complied with, a royal ban on the teaching of Descartes' philosophy. Other French universities followed suit. At the University of Angers the authorities complained to the king that traditional teachings were being replaced by "a new and erroneous Cartesian heresy, injurious to Faith, the Sovereign, and the State."[13] Louis replied by ordering the professors to discontinue the teaching of Descartes' philosophy "since in due course that could cause disorder to our kingdom."[14] In human terms the consequences of dissent could be serious. Bernard Lamy, a Cartesian professor of philosophy at Angers, was exiled from the town and forbidden to teach or preach anywhere in the country.[15]

Even in absolutist France, however, the censors did not have it all their own way. One body in France which was invested with powers of censorship did not engage in the persecution of Descartes' philosophy: this was the Parlement of Paris. In 1671 the Parlement came under pressure from the University of Paris to renew an earlier decree banning the teaching of non-Aristotelian philosophy. But the Parlement refused to yield to this pressure. Their decision may have been influenced by a powerful satire by Nicolas Boileau and François Bernier, which ridiculed the use of censorship in science: "The Sovereign Court of Parnassus . . . expressly prohibits the blood from wandering or circulating in the human body, under pain of being abandoned to the last drop, to the Faculty of Medicine".[16] A more probable influence on the Parlement's decision was Antoine Arnauld; in his pamphlet entitled *Plusieurs Raisons pour empêcher la Censure ou la Condemnation de la Philosophie de Descartes*, he had defended Descartes' philosophy on theological grounds, and in a more serious vein than Boileau and Bernier he had also exposed the futility of attempts to persecute philosophical and scientific opinions.

2. RELIGIOUS ORDERS: JESUITS, JANSENISTS, AND ORATORIANS

Catholic religious orders tended to follow the lead of the universities in matters of censorship: the Oratorian order, for instance, imposed an official ban on the teaching of Descartes' philosophy in 1678. But the hierarchical, authoritarian structure of the Catholic church should not obscure the ideological differences and even rivalries among the orders; the Jesuit–Jansenist rivalry, in particular, was notorious in late seventeenth-century France. Where attitudes to Descartes' philosophy are concerned, it is important to isolate three groups for special attention: Jesuits, Jansenists, and Oratorians.

Descartes had been educated by the Jesuits, and the literary model for his masterpiece, the *Meditations*, was in part at least the *Spiritual Exercises* of St. Ignatius Loyola.[17] Moreover, throughout his life Descartes maintained good relations with individual Jesuits such as his former teachers. *Pace* Leibniz, it does not seem that Descartes ever sought to "enter the lists" with the Jesuits.[18] It is true that Descartes was understandably angered by the Seventh Objections of the Jesuit Bourdin, and he feared that because of Jesuit solidarity Bourdin's reaction would become the standard one in the order.[19] But contrary to Leibniz, Descartes seems rather to have sought acceptance of his philosophy by the Society of Jesus. He hoped, for instance, that his *Principles of Philosophy* would be adopted as a textbook by Jesuit schools.

Descartes' efforts to win favor with the Jesuits were largely unavailing; in general the Jesuits reacted with hostility to Descartes' philosophy. This hostility of the society hardened after Descartes' death; indeed, they became the leaders of Catholic opposition to Descartes' philosophy. Jesuit intrigues lay behind the decision to put Descartes' works on the *Index;* and it was a Jesuit confessor who prompted Louis's campaign against Descartes' philosophy in 1671. The Jesuits suspected the Cartesians of favoring a Calvinist – i.e., purely symbolic – interpretation of the Eucharist. For this reason, as one contemporary noted, they were determined to cling to their traditional scholasticism: "Believe me, once and for all, they'd sooner stop teaching than reject the philosophy of Aristotle."[20] The strength of Jesuit opposition to Descartes' philosophy is suggested by the fate of one Père André. André was the rare example of a Jesuit who was also a Cartesian and indeed a disciple of Malebranche. André paid dearly for his attachment to Descartes' philosophy; he was persecuted and even imprisoned in the Bastille.

By contrast, the Jesuits' arch rivals, the Jansenists, have often been seen as the champions of Descartes' philosophy.[21] Certainly this was the view of at least one contemporary: the French Protestant theologian, Pierre Jurieu, notoriously remarked that the theologians of Port-Royal had as much attachment to Cartesianism as to Christianity.[22] As the taunt of a hostile critic Jurieu's remark must be treated with some caution, and no one would accept it uncritically; but the substance of Jurieu's claim has often been adopted by historians. Recently, however, this traditional picture of Port-Royal as a bastion of Cartesianism has been challenged by a number of scholars.[23]

The main evidence for a natural alliance between Port-Royal and Cartesianism is the life and writings of Antoine Arnauld. Arnauld is perhaps most famous to readers of Descartes as the author of a penetrating set of objections to the *Meditations;* his criticisms of Descartes' proof of the real distinction between mind and body, to say nothing of the Cartesian circle, have always been admired, and are still widely discussed. But unlike Hobbes or Gassendi, Arnauld was a sympathetic critic of Descartes' philosophy; his aim was to make the system more watertight. Arnauld in fact was a fairly orthodox Cartesian, and he became a champion of Descartes' philosophy, not merely against its outright enemies, but also against unorthodox interpreters such as Malebranche. For Arnauld, Descartes' philosophy offered the best philosophical support of the Christian faith; it provided the best arguments for the existence of God and the spirituality of mind. Given these convictions, Arnauld was understandably dismayed by Catholic attempts to censor Descartes' philosophy. He was shocked, in particular, by the *Index* condemnation of 1663; to him it seemed perverse and unjust that Descartes should be condemned while Gassendi's Epicurean philosophy escaped censorship.[24] As we have seen, Arnauld was also active, and more successful, in the campaign to prevent the Parlement of Paris from banning the teaching of Descartes.

But Arnauld's enthusiasm for Descartes seems to have been the exception rather than the rule at Port-Royal. In fundamental respects the spirit of Descartes' philosophy was alien to Jansenist thought. Descartes' basic confidence in the power of human reason to understand the world was not calculated to win many adherents at Port-Royal; Cartesian optimism was in conflict with the pessimistic Jansenist belief that human reason had been corrupted by the Fall. In this respect Nicole's attitude to Descartes is revealing. Nicole had collaborated with Arnauld on the Port-Royal *Logic*, a textbook that was thoroughly Cartesian in inspiration, but Nicole admired Descartes most for exposing the vanity of previous attempts to understand nature, and hence for supporting his own belief in the impotence of reason: "What is most real [in the Cartesian philosophy] is that it makes one know very well that all the people who have spent their lives in philosophizing about nature had entertained the world and entertained themselves with guesses and chimeras."[25] In its positive aspect Cartesianism fared poorly: "all that it proposes to us reduces to some probable suppositions which contain nothing absolutely certain."[26] Pascal's famous judgment: "Descartes useless and uncertain" is probably more characteristic of Port-Royal than Arnauld's enthusiasm.[27]

On broadly theological grounds Jansenists were disturbed by other, more specific aspects of Descartes' philosophy. Le Maistre de Sacy was offended by Descartes' new conception of the physical world; in language reminiscent of Berkeley, he observed that the mechanistic account of nature detracted from the grandeur of God's creation:

God created the world for two reasons . . . one, to provide an idea of his greatness; the other to depict invisible things in the visible. M. Descartes has destroyed the one as well as the other. 'The sun is a lovely piece of work,' one says to him. 'Not at all', he replies, 'it is a mass of metal filings.' Instead of recognizing invisible things in the visible, such as the God of nature in the sun, and seeing an image of his grace in all that he has produced in plants, he insists, on the contrary, on providing a reason for everything.[28]

Another member of Port-Royal, Du Vaucel, perceived the dangers of the beast-machine doctrine. The doctrine was not only opposed to Scripture, but it would also encourage people to believe that a completely materialist account could be given of human beings as well as beasts.[29] Du Vaucel was a true prophet; in the eighteenth century the beast-machine doctrine was indeed developed in the direction of the man-machine.

Despite an official ban on the teaching of his philosophy, Descartes found a number of disciples in the Oratory. The Oratory was a new religious order, which had been founded in 1611 by Cardinal de Bérulle to rival the Jesuits.[30] One of the principal aims of the Oratory was to revive the study of Augustine's philosophy and theology. In their devotion to Augustine the Oratorians resembled Port-Royal, but the Augustinianism of the Oratory was of a different character. The Oratorians were devoted to the distinctively Augustinian project of "Christian philosophy"; in other words, they sought to revive Augustine's conception of the intimate relationship between philosophy and theology which is expressed in the slogan: "Believe in order that you may understand." On this conception, the doctrines of revealed theology can serve as a basis for philosophical speculation, and philosophy in turn can illuminate revealed truths. For the Jansenists, by contrast, devotion to Augustine meant above all the defence of his doctrine of grace against the deformations of the Jesuits. Unlike the Oratorians, the members of Port-Royal expressed no real interest in the Augustinian project of Christian philosophy. On the contrary, the Jansenists tended to distinguish rather sharply between the provinces of faith and reason.

The Augustinian project of "Christian philosophy" is alien to the spirit of Descartes' enterprise; although he is not fully consistent in this area, Descartes, like the Jansenists, characteristically stresses the distinction between faith and reason. Nonetheless, in spite of this divergence in spirit, Descartes' philosophy appealed strongly to many members of the Oratory, and the fact of this appeal is historically important; some Oratorians made strenuous efforts to legitimate Descartes' philosophy in the eyes of the Catholic Church by showing its conformity with Augustinian teaching.[31] They thus sought to impress on the Church that there were powerful alternatives to Aristotle and scholasticism within its own tradition. One Oratorian made a systematic attempt to synthesize the teachings of Descartes and Augustine; this of course is Malebranche, whom we shall discuss below.

3. CARTESIAN DEVELOPMENTS

According to his biographer, Baillet, within a few years of Descartes' death it was no more possible to count the number of his disciples than the stars of the sky or the grains of sand on the seashore.[32] There is no doubt that, despite official persecution, Descartes' philosophy and science rapidly made many converts. In Holland Cartesian ideas penetrated the universities at an early date; the newly founded University of Breda was Cartesian from the beginning. In France Cartesians labored under various official bans in the universities and religious orders, and committed Cartesians were excluded from the Academy of Sciences; nonetheless Cartesian views circulated freely in more informal settings such as the salons of Paris. Moreover, even in the universities professors were able to devise strategies for spreading Cartesian ideas while technically complying with official bans; either they taught Descartes' ideas without mentioning him by name or they ascribed them to other philosophers, such as Aristotle.

Cartesians were not a homogeneous group. At one end of the scale there were loyal disciples who were dedicated to spreading the pure gospel of Descartes' philosophy. Clerselier and perhaps Rohault may be ranked among the number of these. Clerselier oversaw the publication of Descartes' works after his death, and he campaigned tirelessly to get Descartes' philosophy accepted by the Catholic Church. Sometimes, as we have seen, he was incautious in his zeal; his efforts to promote Descartes' views on transubstantiation helped to bring about the *Index* decision of 1663. Clerselier's son-in-law, Rohault, was a writer and physicist who played a major role in popularizing Descartes' physical theories. He was famous for his Wednesday lectures in which he expounded the basic principles of Cartesian physics and even performed experiments. Rohault's *Traité de Physique* achieved the status of a classic as a textbook exposition of Descartes' physics. Rohault also provides a noteworthy example of the tactics employed by loyal Cartesians to gain acceptance for the new ideas in the face of conservative opposition. At first Rohault was inclined to champion Descartes' physics at the expense of Aristotelian science. Later, in response to opposition, he adopted a different tack; he ingeniously minimized the differences between the physical theories of Descartes and Aristotle.[33]

At the other end of the scale were philosophers who modified Descartes' teaching in significant respects. Some of them were so independent-minded that it is difficult to know whether they should be classified as Cartesians at all; Malebranche is an obvious example. A full survey of these Cartesians is obviously far beyond the scope of this chapter, but we cannot afford to ignore them altogether, for by seeing how Cartesians departed from strict orthodoxy we can gauge their estimates of the strengths and weaknesses of Descartes' philosophy. In some cases, Cartesians agreed with anti-Cartesians in rejecting some fairly central tenets of Descartes' thought; Malebranche, for instance, rejects the doctrine that the mind is better known than body,[34] and both he and Régis, for different reasons, reject the doctrine of innate ideas.[35]

Central to the thought of the less orthodox Cartesians is the development of Descartes' philosophy in the direction of occasionalism. Occasionalism is a much misunderstood doctrine which has often been presented in textbooks as an ad hoc response to the problem of mind–body interaction, which Descartes supposedly left unsolved. But this picture is doubly misleading.[36] In the first place, occasionalism is not a seventeenth-century invention but a doctrine with a long history; its origins are found in Arabic thought of the middle ages. Secondly, occasionalism is not characteristically proposed simply as a solution to the mind–body problem. It is perfectly true that Descartes' successors worried about his account of mind–body interaction; to that extent the received picture is correct. But occasionalism is a doctrine of much more general application; it holds that no finite created substance is ever the genuine cause of a change of state in any other finite substance; God alone is the true cause. The stone's hitting the window, for instance, is the occasional cause of the window's breaking in the sense that it is merely the occasion on which God's causal power is exercised. But occasionalists such as Malebranche do not deny that changes in the world are law-governed; what they deny is that these laws are genuinely causal.

Occasionalism was most fully developed by Malebranche, but versions of the doctrine, with varying degrees of explicitness, were advanced by a number of Cartesians.[37] Individual philosophers differed in the weight they attached to particular arguments. Geulincx laid great stress on an argument which relies on the principle that if A is the cause of B, then A knows how to bring about B; Malebranche, by contrast, made little use of this argument.[38] However, for our present purposes the important point is that occasionalists were responding to perceived problems in Descartes' general teaching concerning causality. La Forge, for instance, proposed an argument for unqualified occasionalism from Descartes' doctrine of continuous creation. He argued that if this doctrine is thought through, no room is left for causal activity on the part of a finite substance; all causal activity must be ascribed to God alone.[39] La Forge's argument clearly relies on the assumption that there can be no causal overdetermination.

Occasionalism is fueled not just by philosophical argument but by theological motives. The tendency of occasionalism is clearly to push Descartes' metaphysics in a theocentric direction; it thus appealed to thinkers such as Malebranche who were independently convinced of the Pauline doctrine that in God "we live, move and have our being."[40] On a more mundane level such philosophers might believe that the best way of legitimating Cartesian philosophy, broadly conceived, was to stress its theological advantages. This combination of philosophical argument and theological motives is also at work in Malebranche's doctrine of vision in God.

In philosophical terms Malebranche's doctrine of vision in God is a response to perceived weaknesses in Descartes' theory of ideas and indeed his whole theory of mind. As Malebranche sees it, Descartes proposed a new mechanistic theory of the physical world, and then classified everything as mental which did not qualify as physical by the austere standards of the new theory; thus concepts (e.g., the concept of a triangle) were treated as straight forwardly mental items on a par with occurrent thoughts and sensations. If we leave the issue of occasionalism on one side, Malebranche has no serious quarrel with Descartes' theory of the physical world, and he does not challenge the thesis that the mental and the physical are exclusive categories; what he does challenge is the claim that these categories are exhaustive. Against Descartes, Malebranche wants to insist that the immediate objects of thought are neither mental nor physical but abstract entities whose locus is God.[41] In other words, Malebranche protests against Descartes' tendency to conflate logic and psychology, a tendency he believes is at the root of Descartes' doctrine of the creation of the eternal truths.[42] In candor it must be admitted that Malebranche wants to pursue the doctrine of vision in God further than this. He wishes to argue that, not just in thinking, but even in sense perception the mind is directly related to abstract entities (ideas) in God.[43] But the doctrine of vision in God is perhaps best approached as a response to Descartes' tendency to conflate logic and psychology.

Vision in God is no less motivated than occasionalism by theological considerations; indeed, vision in God may be seen as an epistemological parallel of the metaphysical doctrine of occasionalism. According to occasionalism, human beings are causally powerless by themselves; according to vision in God, human minds are, as it were, cognitively powerless unless they are illuminated by the light of God's ideas. In developing Descartes' thought in this direction, Malebranche is self-consciously reviving and extending the Augustinian doctrine of divine illumination. But Malebranche could also claim to be developing Cartesian themes. In the Fifth Meditation Descartes argues that all knowledge depends on the prior knowledge of God (AT VII 71: CSM II 49). Descartes had also given a theological twist to his doctrine of innate ideas by claiming that they are implanted by God himself (AT VII 51: CSM II 35).

The differences between more and less orthodox Cartesians could sometimes erupt into bitter controversy. A celebrated case in point is the debate between Malebranche and Arnauld over the nature of ideas. In *On True and False Ideas* (1683) Arnauld vehemently attacked Malebranche's doctrine of ideas as what he called *êtres représentatifs* over and above mental states. Arnauld argued that this interpretation of ideas was both unfaithful to Descartes' teaching and philosophically unsound in itself; such *êtres représentatifs* were both useless and unnecessary in explaining the nature of perception.[44] Malebranche could have defended his theory on philosophical grounds while simply pleading guilty to the charge of deserting Descartes. In fact, Malebranche's response to the latter charge was somewhat equivocal; at times he admitted that he found Descartes' theory of ideas unsatisfactory, but at others he tried to show that he was in fact being faithful to Descartes' own teaching.[45] To that extent even Malebranche thought of himself as a loyal Cartesian.

4. ANTI-CARTESIANS

Committed anti-Cartesians are perhaps an even more varied group than committed Cartesians. As we have seen, Cartesianism found enemies among such religious groups as the Jesuits and Jansenists; philosophically its enemies range from scholastics and skeptical fideists among the conservatives to atomists and outright materialists among the moderns. What is surprising is the extent to which conservatives and radicals could find common ground; for one thing, they tend to agree in assimilating Descartes' views to traditional philosophical positions.

Some of Descartes' sharpest critics were fellow moderns who were intent on pursuing their own philosophical agenda. It is striking that Descartes' most acrimonious exchanges in the first six sets of *Objections and Replies* are not with the conservative theologians but with Hobbes and Gassendi. Leibniz believed that, on Descartes' side at least, professional jealousy was responsible for the acrimonious tone of these exchanges; Descartes feared Hobbes and Gassendi as rivals whose philosophies might overshadow his own, and for this reason he treated their objections with less respect than they deserved.[46] However this may be, the sharpness of Descartes' reactions only served to increase the hostility of Hobbes and Gassendi, although they reacted in markedly different ways. After the cool reception of his objections by Descartes, Hobbes never afterward mentioned Descartes' philosophy in his published writings; Gassendi, by contrast, expanded his original objections into a large volume, the *Disquisitio Metaphysica* (1644). In this work Gassendi not merely amplifies his original criticisms, but constantly complains of his treatment at the hands of Descartes.

According to John Aubrey, Hobbes admired Descartes as a mathematician, but dismissed him as a philosopher; he gave him credit for neither philosophical ability nor intellectual integrity:

Mr Hobbes was wont to say that had Descartes kept himselfe wholy to Geometrie that he had been the best Geometer in the world but that his head did not lye for Philosophy. He did very much admire him, but said that he could not pardon him for writing in the Defence of Transubstantiation, which he knew to bee absolutely against his judgement and donne meerly to putt a compliment on the Jesuites.[47]

It is not difficult to see what lies behind this unfavorable judgment on Descartes' philosophical ability. In the Third Objections Hobbes' main objection focuses on what may seem like an argument for dualism; Hobbes criticizes Descartes' inference from "I am thinking" to "I am thought" on the ground that it confuses the mere act of a subject with the essential nature of the subject (AT VII 172: CSM II 122). At most of course Hobbes has refuted only one argument for Descartes' dualist theory of mind, and arguably he has not even done that; for Descartes insists that it is not until the Sixth Meditation that he proves the real distinction of mind and body. But as one writer has said, for Hobbes, the Cartesian conception of the mind as an immaterial substance seems to have been so obviously absurd as to be scarcely worth refuting.[48]

One feature of Descartes' philosophy Hobbes did not admire was his use of skepticism in the First Meditation; Hobbes expressed surprise that Descartes should decide to publish this ancient material (AT VII 171: CSM II 121). Gassendi was similarly insensitive to Descartes' use of skepticism, but there is a difference in their reactions. Unlike Hobbes, Gassendi seems to see that there is a novel element in the skepticism of the First Meditation, but he does not regard the novelty of Descartes' contribution as something to be admired.[49] On the contrary, Gassendi takes Descartes to task for perversely misunderstanding the ancient Greek skeptics such as Sextus Empiricus. For Gassendi, the whole point of skeptical arguments is to show that we cannot know the true inner natures of things. As Gassendi says, the ancient skeptics differ from Descartes in that they do not question what he calls "phenomena," or appearances.[50] In other words, they accept that honey tastes sweet to some and bitter to others, and on this basis they argue that it is difficult to determine the true nature of the honey; but they do not question that there really is something – honey – which tastes differently to different people. Unlike Descartes, the ancient skeptics do not call into question the existence of the external world.

Gassendi may appear to us to have missed the point of Descartes' skepticism about the senses, but it is only fair to note that, from his perspective, it is Descartes who has missed the point of the skeptical challenge. In the eyes of Gassendi, Descartes has perversely failed to grasp the force of the skeptical attack on the power of the human intellect. Descartes claims to have discovered the internal natures of things, but if he is challenged as to the basis of this knowledge, he must appeal to the reliability of clear and distinct ideas. If Descartes is then challenged on the issue of how he knows that these clear and distinct ideas are true, he can only appeal to the existence of a nondeceiving God. But in that case, as other critics also charge, his argument seems blatantly circular.[51]

Of all Descartes' critics the scholastics might be expected to be most aware of his novelty; surely, in their eyes Descartes must appear a dangerous revolutionary. Curiously, however, this reaction seems to have been less common than one might imagine. The case of one scholastic, Libert Froidmont, is instructive in this respect. When the *Discourse on Method* first appeared, Froidmont correctly saw that Descartes is a mechanist, and predictably enough, it is Descartes' mechanism that offends him: "this composition of bodies from parts of different shapes seems excessively crass and mechanical."[52] But in other ways Froidmont's reaction is surprising. For Froidmont sees Descartes not merely as a mechanist but as an atomist in the tradition of Democritus and Epicurus. This of course is a misunderstanding; Descartes explicitly rejected atomism. But it is interesting to see Descartes attacked, not as an innovator, but as a reviver of old heresies that have long been solidly refuted. Indeed, in the eyes of Froidmont, atomism had been refuted by Aristotle in advance of Epicurus himself.[53]

The charge that Descartes was an unoriginal thinker did not die out in the seventeenth century when his philosophy became better known. Descartes' lack of originality is one of the central charges brought by Pierre-Daniel Huet against Descartes in his immensely influential *Censura Philosophiae Cartesianae* (1689). Huet was a patron and protector of the Jesuits, and like the Jesuits he had a deep respect for the philosophy of Aristotle. But he was also sympathetic to the tradition of philosophical skepticism deriving from the Greeks, and like some other figures in the seventeenth century he combines skepticism in philosophy with a fideistic approach to religion.[54]

For Huet, Descartes was something of a poseur. Descartes claimed to be the first to establish philosophy on firm foundations, and he boasted of his ignorance of the philosophical tradition, but these claims were largely fraudulent. Descartes' claim to be ignorant of the tradition was a device for persuading people that he was more original than he really was.[55] In fact, for Huet, there was little that was truly new in Descartes' philosophy. On the contrary, almost everything in it has been borrowed from the philosophical past. Indeed, Huet catalogues Descartes' borrowings in detail: his doubt is taken from the Greek skeptics, his Cogito from Augustine, the ontological argument from Anselm, and so on.[56] Huet comes close to charging Descartes with outright plagiarism; at the very least he takes him to task for disingenuously concealing his debts to other philosophers. Huet thus seems to give the lie to the claim, often made today in Descartes' defence, that in the seventeenth century it was simply not the custom to footnote other authors. Huet at least saw Descartes as doing something reprehensible.

Somewhat predictably, a major theme of Huet's critique is that Descartes' philosophy is a threat to the Catholic faith. Huet acknowledges Descartes' professions of respect for Catholic teachings, but he charges that his arrogance leads him to adopt a perverse strategy with regard to the faith. Descartes should have accepted the Catholic dogmas as given, and then adapted his philosophy to them; instead, he treats his own philosophical opinions as certain and then tailors Catholic dogmas to fit them.[57] Huet makes it clear that he has in mind Descartes' attitude towards transubstantiation and creation *ex nihilo*.

On this basis Huet offers an interesting diagnosis of Descartes' motives for introducing his strange doctrine of the creation of the eternal truths. According to Huet, Descartes sets up his own intellect as a standard of what is and is not in conformity with reason. But he is forced to recognize that there are Catholic dogmas, such as transubstantiation, which do not meet this standard. Descartes then infers that God can do things that are not merely above, but even contrary to reason.[58] Instead, says Huet, Descartes should have regarded it as axiomatic that Catholic dogmas are never contrary to reason. If he had taken that line, he would have been forced to conclude that his own philosophical intuitions are not the standard of rationality.

Huet's *Censura* does not just attack Descartes' lack of originality and theological heterodoxy; it also offers a detailed philosophical commentary on Descartes's thought from a viewpoint sympathetic to skepticism. Unlike some other conservative critics, Huet does not oppose Descartes' methodic doubt per se; in fact, for Huet, this is the best thing about Descartes' philosophy. Instead Huet criticizes Descartes for not consistently carrying through the project of methodic doubt. In other words, Descartes lays down a rule for himself of not accepting anything that is not certain, but he soon abandons it, and admits propositions that are either merely probable or actually false.[59] Among other criticisms, Huet claims that Descartes has not succeeded in showing that the Cogito is indubitable. In the words of one commentator, "Huet argued that not only is 'I think therefore I am' an inference but also that it involves a time sequence from the moment when thinking is occurring to the moment when on realises that he thought, and that memory may be inaccurate."[60]

It has been claimed that in his philosophical critique Huet is heavily dependent on Gassendi.[61] This is perhaps an exaggeration, but it is certainly true that Huet and Gassendi attack many of the same doctrines, and that sometimes Huet reproduces Gassendi's actual objections. Thus Huet follows Gassendi in criticizing Descartes for saying that he intends to reject all his previous opinions as false; this is not doubting but acquiring a new belief, and this new belief is almost certainly false, for among the old opinions are presumably some true ones. Thus the enterprise of methodic doubt cannot be characterized in these terms.[62] Moreover, like Gassendi, Huet mounts a broadly empiricist attack on the doctrine of innate ideas and the thesis that the mind is better known than the body.[63] The important point for our purposes is that Huet and Gassendi could find so much common ground. Whereas Huet is a conservative, Gassendi is one of the moderns; indeed, he is engaged in a project, not unlike Descartes' own, of advancing an anti-Scholastic, mechanistic philosophy of nature.

To speak of Cartesians and anti-Cartesians is in one way misleading, for it overlooks the fact that some philosophers could change their party affiliation. Even Huet, despite his later hostility, had been a Cartesian at one stage of his career. Perhaps the most conspicuous example of seeming apostasy from the Cartesian faith is Henry More, the Cambridge Platonist. More had corresponded with Descartes, and at one time he had been one of his most ardent admirers, but like Huet, he became one of his bitterest enemies.

More's apostasy has puzzled scholars, and its exact nature has been debated. It does not seem that More's own philosophical position changed, or even that his purely philosophical estimate of Descartes moved from initial acceptance to final rejection.[64] From the beginning More had philosophical reservations about Descartes' views, and these reservations remained fairly constant; for instance, he never accepted the thesis that extension is the essence of matter, and even in correspondence with Descartes he was a harsh critic of the beast-machine doctrine.[65] What does seem to have changed is the nature of More's fundamental preoccupations; the defence of religion against atheists came to assume greater importance in relation to his purely philosophical interests. As a result, Descartes' austere mechanistic account of the physical world seemed to offer too much comfort to the enemies of religion; in the words of one writer, it was "tailor-made for the atheist's purposes."[66]

5. SPINOZA AND LEIBNIZ

Spinoza composed an exposition of Descartes' *Principles of Philosophy*, and Leibniz wrote a critical commentary on the same work.[67] Descartes' philosophy was indeed of primary importance to his two leading "rationalist" successors, but neither Spinoza nor Leibniz can be classified as straightforwardly Cartesian or anti-Cartesian; their attitudes to Descartes are complex and ambivalent. Despite the enormous differences in their philosophical motivations, in many respects their attitudes to Descartes tend to run parallel. Spinoza and Leibniz famously agree that Descartes created a problem of mind–body interaction which he was unable to solve; as Leibniz put it, "Descartes gave up the struggle over this problem, so far as we can know from his writings."[68] More generally, Spinoza and Leibniz sympathize with the project of a priori metaphysics, but they both agree that Descartes failed in the execution of the project. Indeed, in this respect, Leibniz's reaction complements Spinoza's, for if Spinoza claimed that Descartes had not gone far enough toward his own system, Leibniz held, on the contrary, that Descartes had gone too far in that direction; at the very least, Descartes had made Spinozism possible. As Leibniz memorably puts it, "Spinoza merely cultivated certain seeds in Descartes' philosophy."[69]

The characteristic ambivalence of Spinoza's attitude to Descartes is caught in the Preface to his exposition of Descartes' *Principles*; this Preface was written by one Lodewijk Meyer, but it received Spinoza's blessing. On the one hand, Descartes is eulogized as "that brightest star of our age";[70] it was Descartes who had "uncovered firm foundations for philosophy, foundations on which a great many truths can be built, with mathematical order and certainty."[71] Yet, as Meyer indicates, although in this textbook exposition Spinoza feels obliged to follow Descartes, this does not mean that he agrees with Descartes in everything; on the contrary, there are a great many doctrines of Descartes' that he rejects as false. As an example of such disagreement, Meyer singles out Spinoza's inability to accept Descartes' commitment to the existence of a faculty of free will distinct from the intellect.[72]

In the eyes of Spinoza, Descartes had failed to pursue his principles to their logical conclusion. For Spinoza, it seems, there is no real mystery about the source of Descartes' failure in this respect. Descartes had been influenced by theological politics; he had been afraid of flying in the face of Church doctrine. In particular, Descartes had made concessions in his system in order to accommodate traditional Christian beliefs about God, freedom, and immortality. For instance, Descartes had defined "substance" in such a way as to imply that only God satisfied the definition, but he had shied away from drawing out this consequence (*Principles*, Part I, art. 51). Again, in order to find room in his system for free will and immortality, Descartes had embraced an incoherent account of the human mind as exempt from the reign of natural causality; Descartes and others conceive of man in nature as a "kingdom within a kingdom."[73] If Descartes had stuck consistently to his principles, he would have been led to the kind of naturalistic metaphysics Spinoza expounded in the *Ethics*.

Leibniz's mature view of Descartes is powerfully shaped by his awareness of Spinoza, and his concern with the threat of Spinozism leads him to give a new twist to the familiar complaint that Descartes' philosophy is a danger to religion. Leibniz stops short of questioning Descartes' sincerity; he accuses him rather of embracing principles that have "strange" – i.e. Spinozistic – consequences.[74] As we have said, Descartes' definition of "substance" could be seen as having Spinozistic implications, and Leibniz did not hesitate to point this out.[75] But Leibniz's charge of incipient Spinozism against Descartes goes further than this; he draws on other doctrines in Descartes' philosophy in order to support his charge. One such doctrine is particularly prominent in Leibniz's critique: Descartes' banishment of final causes in physics prepares the ground for Spinoza's outright rejection of all forms of teleological explanation.[76] Sometimes Leibniz seems to go out of his way to tar Descartes with the brush of Spinozism. Leibniz was fond of quoting an obscure passage from the *Principles of Philosophy*, where Descartes states that "matter assumes successively all the forms of which it is capable" (Part III, art. 47: AT VIIIA 103: CSM I 258). Leibniz comments:

I do not believe that a more dangerous proposition than this one could be formulated. For if matter takes on, successively, all possible forms, it follows that nothing can be imagined so absurd, so bizarre, so contrary to what we call justice, that it could not have happened and will not one day happen. These are precisely the opinions which Spinoza has expounded more clearly.[77]

Descartes might have replied that he was merely expounding a version of the so-called Principle of Plenitude, and that far from being a dangerous innovation, this is a principle that goes back to Aristotle. Or if acceptance of this principle makes him a Spinozist, then he is in respectable company.

The other main theme of Leibniz's critique aligns him with Huet whose *Censura* he is known to have admired.[78] Like Huet, Leibniz mounts a general attack on Descartes' claims to originality, and again like Huet, he mingles philosophical criticism with personal attacks on Descartes' character; in particular, he attacks Descartes for his "strange ambition to become the leader of a sect."[79] The substance of Leibniz's critique of Descartes' originality is really twofold. First, Descartes owes much more to the philosophical tradition than he is willing to admit; Leibniz follows Huet in cataloguing Descartes' unacknowledged borrowings from earlier philosophers. [80]

Leibniz is perhaps particularly impressed by Descartes' debt to Plato; at times, he seems to regard him as a sort of wayward Platonist.[81] Secondly, those things on which Descartes chiefly bases his claims to originality do not amount to much. Descartes' rules of method are criticized for their vacuity, and indeed are the subject of one of Leibniz's most memorable gibes: "they are like the precepts of some chemist: take what you need, do what you should, and you will get what you want."[82] Similarly, Descartes' criterion of truth – Whatever I clearly and distinctly perceive is true – is useless unless criteria of clarity and distinctness are provided; and Leibniz thought that Descartes had not succeeded in providing adequate criteria.[83]

In one way even Leibniz's critique of Cartesian physics can be seen as a commentary on Descartes' rules of method. The value of a method must be judged by its results; if Descartes' method were of any real value, then its application to problems in physics would have resulted in genuine, and only genuine, discoveries. But in fact Descartes' physics is full of errors, and Leibniz delighted in pointing them out; as Leibniz showed, Descartes' laws of impact are seriously at odds with the empirical data.[84] So if we assume that Descartes was true to his own principles, it follows that the method is of no value. As we have seen, Leibniz's view is not so much that the rules of method are substantive but erroneous, as that they are devoid of any real content.

Leibniz's critique of Descartes is very comprehensive; it embraces his physical theories as well as his metaphysics, theory of knowledge and methodology. It is no wonder, then, that Leibniz fell foul of committed Cartesians; he was accused by Regis, for instance, of seeking to building his reputation on the ruins of Descartes'.[85] Yet, as Leibniz was quick to point out, his attitude to Descartes' philosophy was by no means entirely negative. On the contrary, Leibniz says he is accustomed to call Descartes' philosophy the antechamber of truth.[86] Presumably, with this comment Leibniz seeks to draw attention to his sympathy with the Cartesian enterprise of natural theology; Leibniz thoroughly approves of Descartes' attempts to prove the existence of God and the immateriality of the soul, even though he thinks that Descartes' proofs are flawed or incomplete. Indeed, Leibniz is in many ways engaged in a creative reinterpretation of Cartesian doctrines such as innate ideas and the thesis that the mind always thinks.

6. LOCKE

The first books (as Mr Locke himself has told me) which gave him a relish of philosophical studies were those of Descartes. He was rejoiced in reading of these because though he very often differed in opinion from this writer, yet he found that what he said was very intelligible; from whence he was encouraged to think that his not having understood others had, possibly, not proceeded altogether from a defect in his understanding.[87]

Lady Masham's remark brings out a truth that has often been lost sight of since; Locke, like Leibniz and Spinoza, was ambivalent in his attitude to Descartes. For Locke, Descartes was the first, or one of the first, to emancipate people's minds from their bondage to the unintelligible doctrines of Aristotle and the scholastics. But Descartes was also a dogmatist, and dogmatism was almost as much of a danger to the advance of knowledge and science as the "rubbish" of scholasticism, which Descartes had helped to bury.

Lady Masham refers modestly to Locke's differences of opinion from Descartes, and Locke is perhaps as famous as anyone for having differences of opinion with Descartes. Yet if we concentrate on specific issues, it may seem that there is little that is new in Locke's critique of Descartes. Indeed, on almost every issue, Locke's particular criticisms are anticipated by others; Gassendi is perhaps the chief precursor, for Gassendi, like Locke, opposed Cartesian dogmatism in the name of a tentatively atomistic account of nature. Although he is far removed from him philosophically, even Locke's compatriot, More, anticipates some of Locke's criticisms; as we have seen, More constantly opposed the Cartesian doctrines of animal automatism and extension as the essence of matter, and these criticisms are present in Locke's Essay.[88]

When all such allowances are made, it is difficult to escape the feeling that Locke introduces a new stage in the reception of Descartes' philosophy. Locke seems to promote a view of Descartes that was to be popularized by Voltaire in the eighteenth century and thus become the common currency of the Enlightenment. For one thing, whereas Huet, Leibniz, and some scholastics claimed to see little that was original in Descartes, Locke seems implicitly to accept that with Descartes philosophy begins again; Locke may not use the phrase, but he would hardly quarrel with the claim that Descartes is the "father of modern philosophy." There are further features of Locke's attitude to Descartes, which, taken together at least, set him apart from his contemporaries and look forward to the century that followed.

Locke is of course not the first to accuse Descartes of being ensnared by the "vanity of dogmatizing"; Huet had brought the same charge.[89] Yet there is a difference between Locke and Huet in the way they handle this charge. In the case of Huet it is sometimes difficult to tell whether he is attacking the pretensions of the human intellect or the pretensions of Descartes' intellect; in other words, philosophical points about the limits of human cognitive faculties are mingled, or even conflated, with personal attacks on Descartes' arrogant confidence in his own arguments. By contrast, Locke's charge of dogmatism against Descartes is free from this kind of conflation. For Locke, to say that Descartes is a dogmatist is to say that he is in the grip of a mistaken belief about the powers of human reason; what is at issue is a philosophical error rather than a personal failing. In his discussion of the mind–body problem, for instance, Locke's clear, if implicit, view is not so much that Descartes trusts his own arguments for dualism at the expense of others that might fare better, but rather that Descartes is committed to the dubious assumption that human reason must be able to solve this problem.[90]

For many seventeenth-century figures, Descartes is primarily a philosopher–scientist in revolt against the scholastic philosophy of nature. Descartes was famous, or notorious, as the enemy of substantial forms and occult qualities, and as the champion of purely mechanical explanations. In other words, it was Descartes' science and his ontology of the physical world that were at the center of attention and controversy. This side of Descartes is of course not absent from Locke's discussions, for Locke's charge of dogmatism embraces Descartes' claims about *res extensa* no less than his claims about *res cogitans*. But there is little doubt that Locke is more concerned with Descartes the philosopher of mind than with Descartes the natural scientist. Indeed, it would seem that, for Locke, Descartes is above all the proponent of a dogmatic theory of mind from which he deduced such supposed truths as that the soul always thinks and that it is stocked with innate ideas. This change of emphasis is subtly reflected in Voltaire's writings about Descartes. Pascal had accused Descartes of writing a "novel of nature";[91] Voltaire appropriates this phrase and transforms it by implicitly accusing Descartes of having written a "novel of the soul."[92] From the time of Voltaire, it is Descartes' "novel of the soul," rather than his "novel of nature," which is of most concern to philosophers.

From Louis XIV downward, seventeenth-century critics of Descartes had charged that his philosophy was dangerous to the Christian faith. In Locke, by contrast, such charges make no appearance. Of course, as a Protestant, Locke did not have the distinctively Catholic concerns of a Huet; he did not have to worry about the compatibility of Descartes' philosophy of matter with the dogma of transubstantiation. But, as we have seen, the cry that Descartes' philosophy was dangerous for the Christian faith was not raised exclusively by Catholics; it had been heard from such Protestants as Voetius, Leibniz, and More. It might be pointed out that, as one who refused to exclude the possibility of thinking matter, Locke was not strategically well placed to accuse Descartes of undermining Christian beliefs even if he had wanted to do so.[93] But Locke surely had no interest in mounting the kind of theological smear campaign that appealed to so many of his contemporaries. As a latitudinarian, Locke was deeply opposed to the sectarian spirit that characteristically underlay such attacks. It is not too much to say that Locke was seeking to bring about a change in the currency of philosophical discourse.

In 1741, exactly a hundred years after the publication of the *Meditations*, a writer surveyed the position of Cartesianism in France:

It is true that Cartesianism is not prohibited any more these days, nor persecuted as it was formerly; it is permitted, even protected, and perhaps it is important that it should be in certain respects; but it has grown old, it has lost the graces that it acquired from unjust persecution – graces even more piquant than those of youth.[94]

By the middle of the eighteenth century, Cartesianism had passed, in the words of one scholar, from opposition to power; in France at least, Descartes had become an establishment figure.[95] This change in Descartes' reputation was not without its ironies. In 1751 the Sorbonne was prompted to uphold the Cartesian doctrine of innate ideas against the new empiricism of Locke.[96] A century earlier, by contrast, the same Sorbonne had attacked innate ideas in the name of the Aristotelian–scholastic tag: "There is nothing in the intellect which was not previously in the senses." Thus within a century there had been a complete reversal of positions. Innate ideas had become the new orthodoxy, and empiricism was now the radical doctrine. A further irony of the new situation was noted by Voltaire. Descartes was being accepted by the academic establishment in France at the very time when his physics was being superseded by Newton. As Voltaire put it: "What a revolution in the opinions of men! The philosophy of Descartes was proscribed in France while it had some appearance of truth, and its ingenious hypotheses were not given the lie by experience, and now that our eyes demonstrate its errors, it will not be allowed to abandon them."[97]

What were the reasons for this dramatic change in Descartes' fortunes? A full discussion of this issue is beyond the scope of the present essay, but two possible factors are worth mentioning here. First, we have seen that various thinkers campaigned to legitimate Descartes in the eyes of the Catholic Church by associating him with Augustine; they sought to remind the orthodox of a nonscholastic tradition in Christian philosophy and theology with which Descartes could be plausibly linked, and of which indeed he might seem the modern representative. This campaign no doubt achieved a degree of success; it succeeded in focussing attention on that side of Descartes which provided support for the defence of the Christian faith. A second factor is perhaps more important. By the eighteenth century Descartes had been outflanked on the philosophical left by other moderns; Hobbes and Spinoza were especially notorious, but even Locke had defended the possibility of thinking matter. Conservatives turned to Descartes with relief because the alternatives seemed so much worse. But, as Voltaire says, by the middle of the eighteenth century such a move was really too late; Descartes' philosophy had been overtaken by Locke, and his physics had been demolished by Newton.

NOTES

1 Voltaire, *Letters on England*, trans. Tancock, letter 13, p. 63.
2 Henricus Regius, or Henri Le Roy, (1598–1679) was one of Descartes' first disciples, but he later developed materialist views of which Descartes strongly disapproved.

3 *Ens per accidens:* "accidental entity" (literally, "entity through accident"). Regius is saying that, in Descartes' philosophy, a human being is only an accidental unity of two heterogeneous substances, mind and body, which are not substantially united. Such a claim ran counter to the scholastic doctrine that the soul, as the substantial form of the body, conferred a genuine unity on a human being.

4 Baillet, *La Vie de M. Des-Cartes*, vol. II, p. 146.

5 Ibid., p. 188.

6 Letter to Father Dinet; AT VII 592f; CSM II 393 note. Cf. Cottingham, *Descartes*, p. 4.

7 The writings in question are the letter to Voetius: AT VIIB 3–194, and the letter to Father Dinet: AT VII 563–603: CSM II 384–97.

8 Baillet, *Vie*, vol. II, p. 314.

9 Ibid., p. 315.

10 For Descartes' views on the Eucharist, see Fourth Replies: AT VII 248–56: CSM II 173–8; letter to Mesland, 9 February 1645: AT IV 163–70: CSMK 241–6. The account of transubstantiation that Descartes gave in the letter to Mesland was regarded as particularly suspect. Descartes did not publish the letter, but it was circulated in manuscript after his death.

11 Vinot to Clerselier, 1664; quoted in McClaughlin, "Censorship and defenders of the Cartesian faith in mid-seventeenth-century France," p. 572. In this section I am heavily indebted to this excellent and informative article.

12 McClaughlin, "Censorship and defenders," p. 572.

13 Ibid., p. 567.

14 Bouillier, *Histoire de la philosophie cartésienne*, vol. I, pp. 460–1. Although dated and often tendentious, this is still a valuable book.

15 McClaughlin, "Censorship and defenders," p. 567.

16 Quoted in McClaughlin, "Censorship and defenders," p. 566.

17 See Z. Vendler, "Descartes' Exercises," *Canadian Journal of Philosophy* 19 (1989): 193–224.

18 Untitled essay, Gerhardt, vol. IV, p. 304.

19 See letter to Father Dinet: AT VII 564: CSM II 384.

20 McClaughlin, "Censorship and defenders," p. 571.

21 The Jansenists were disciples of Cornelius Jansen, or Jansenius, Bishop of Ypres, whose *Augustinus* (1640) expounded an Augustinian doctrine of grace that, in the eyes of orthodox Catholics, was uncomfortably close to Protestantism. Port-Royal des Champs, near Paris, was the leading community of Jansenists.

22 Jurieu's remark occurs in his *La Politique du clergé de France* (1681). See Rodis-Lewis, "Augustinisme et cartésianisme à Port-Royal," in Dijksterhuis (ed.), *Descartes et le cartésianisme hollandais*, p. 131.

23 See, for instance, S. M. Nadler, "Arnauld, Descartes, and transubstantiation; reconciling Cartesian metaphysics and real presence," *Journal of the History of Ideas* 49 (1988): 229–46; Rodis-Lewis, "Augustinisme et cartésianisme."

24 Nadler, "Arnauld, Descartes," 239.

25 Quoted in Rodis-Lewis, "Augustinisme et cartésianisme," 149.

26 Ibid.

27 Pascal: *Pascal, Pensées*, trans. Krailsheimer, p. 300.

28 Quoted in Nadler, "Arnauld, Descartes." 229.

29 Unpublished article by Du Vaucel, "Observations sur la Philosophie de Descartes," in Dijksterhuis (ed.), *Descartes*, p. 124.

30 Cardinal de Bérulle was a powerful, mystical personality who was known to Descartes himself; it was Bérulle who exhorted Descartes to make full use of his God-given talents.

31 Apart from Malebranche, the chief figures here are André Martin (Ambrosius Victor), Nicolas Poisson, and Bernard Lamy. See Gouhier, *Cartésianisme et Augustinisme au XVIIᵉ siècle*, esp. ch. IV.

32 Baillet, *Vie*, vol. II, p. 449.

33 McClaughlin, "Censorship and defenders," pp. 578–9. Cf. Clarke, *Occult Powers and Hypotheses*, ch. 1.

34 Malebranche, *Search after Truth*, ed. and trans. Lennon and Olscamp, 3.2.7, pp. 237–9.

35 Ibid., 3.2.4, pp. 226–7; for Régis, see Clarke, *Occult Powers*, pp. 43–4.

36 For a good account of occasionalism, see McCracken, *Malebranche and British Philosophy*, ch. 3.

37 The chief figures here are Géraud de Cordemoy (1626–84), Johannes Clauberg (1622–65), Arnold Geulincx (1624–69), and Louis de la Forge (1632–66). For a useful study of some Cartesians, see Balz, *Cartesian Studies*. See also Clarke, *Occult Powers*.

38 See Bouillier, *Histoire*, vol. I, pp. 286–7.

39 See Garber, "How God causes motion: Descartes, divine sustenance, and occasionalism," *Journal of Philosophy* 84 (1987): 567–80. Cf. Malebranche, *Dialogues on Metaphysics*, Dialogue VII, pp. 156–9.

40 Acts, 17:28.

41 See Jolley, *The Light of the Soul: Theories of Ideas in Leibniz, Malebranche, and Descartes*.

42 See, for example, Malebranche to Régis, Malebranche, *Oeuvres Complètes de Malebranche*, vol. XVII–1, p. 308.

43 Malebranche, *Search after Truth*, 3.2.6, esp. p. 234.

44 See Nadler, *Arnauld and the Cartesian Philosophy of Ideas*, esp. ch. IV.

45 See, for instance, *Trois Lettres I, Oeuvres*, ed. Robinet, vol. VI, pp. 214–18.

46 Leibniz, "Remarques sur l'abrégé de la vie de Mons. de Cartes," in Gerhardt (ed.), *Philosophischen Schriften* IV 321.

47 O. L. Dick (ed.), *Aubrey's Brief Lives* (Penguin: Harmondsworth, 1972), p. 185.

48 J. W. N. Watkins, *Hobbes's System of Ideas*, 2nd ed. (Hutchinson, London, 1973), pp. 86–7.

49 On this issue see R. Walker, "Gassendi and Skepticism," in Burnyeat (ed.), *The Skeptical Tradition*, pp. 319–36.

50 Gassendi, *Disquisitio metaphysica*, Rochot, ed. Meditation 2, Doubt 1, Instance, pp. 68–9.

51 Ibid., Meditation 3, Doubt 1, Instance 1, pp. 204–5.

52 Fromondus (Froidmont) to Plempius, 13 September 1637: AT I 406. See Garber, "Descartes, the Aristotelians, and the revolution that did not happen in 1637," 475.

53 Garber, "Descartes, the Aristotelians," 475–7.

54 On Huet, see Bouillier, *Histoire*, vol. I, ch. 27.

55 P.-D. Huet, *Censura philosophiae cartesianae*, pp. 195–6.

56 Ibid., pp. 201–20.

57 Ibid., pp. 172–3.

58 Ibid., pp. 174–5.

59 Ibid., p. 13.

60 R. Popkin, "Pierre-Daniel Huet," in P. Edwards (ed.), *Encyclopedia of Philosophy* (New York, 1967), vol. 4, p. 67. See Huet, *Censura*, pp. 19–21.

61 Bouillier, *Histoire*, vol. I, p. 584.

62 Huet, *Censura*, p. 13; Gassendi, Fifth Objections: AT VII 257–8: CSM II 180.

63 For the rejection of innate ideas, see Huet, *Censura*, pp. 90–6; Gassendi, Fifth Objections: AT VII 279–90: CSM II 195. For the rejection of the claim that the mind is better known than body, see Huet, *Censura*, pp. 81–5; Gassendi, Fifth Objections: AT VII 275–7: CSM II 192–3.

64 See Gabbey, "Philosophia cartesiana triumphata: Henry More (1646–1671)," in Lennon, Nicholas, and Davis (eds.), *Problems of Cartesianism*, p. 195.

65 See More to Descartes, 11 December 1648: AT V 243.

66 Gabbey, "Philosophia cartesiana," p. 233.

67 Spinoza, *Parts I and II of Descartes' Principles of Philosophy*, in Gebhardt (ed.), *Opera* I, 127–281, in Curley (ed.), *Collected Works* I, 224–346; Leibniz, "Critical remarks concerning the general part of Descartes' principles," Gerhardt IV 350–92; in Loemker (ed.), *Leibniz, Philosophical Papers and Letters*, 383–412. Spinoza's work contains an appendix entitled *Metaphysical Thoughts* in which he expounds his own philosophical views.

68 "New System of the Nature and Communication of Substances," Gerhardt IV 483, Loemker 457.

69 Leibniz to Nicaise, 15 February 1697: Gerhardt II 563.

70 Gebhardt I 128, Curley I 226.

71 Ibid.

72 Gebhardt I 132; Curley I 229.

73 *Ethics* III, Preface: Gebhardt II 137: Curley I 491.

74 See, for example, Leibniz to Nicaise, 15 February 1697: Gerhardt II 562.

75 "Conversation of Philarete and Ariste": Gerhardt VI 582, Loemker 620.

76 Leibniz to Nicaise, 15 February 1697: Gerhardt II 562; Leibniz to Philippi, undated: IV 281.

77 Leibniz to Philippi, January 1680: Gerhardt IV 283.

78 Leibniz even hoped that his own criticisms of Descartes could be included in a future edition of Huet's *Censura* (Gerhardt I 421). See Brown, *Leibniz*, p. 47 n. 2.

79 For example, "Remarques sur l'abrégé," Gerhardt IV 320.

80 Untitled essay, Gerhardt IV 305.

81 See "On the correction of metaphysics and the concept of substance," Gerhardt IV 468–9, Loemker 432. Cf. Brown, *Leibniz*, pp. 37–8.

82 Untitled essay, Gerhardt IV 329.

83 Ibid., 331. See Belaval, *Leibniz, critque de Descartes*, esp. ch. 1.

84 In the *Acta Eruditorum* of March 1686, Leibniz published an important article, critical of Descartes' laws of impact, entitled "A brief demonstration of a notable error of Descartes", Loemker 296–302.

85 Gerhardt IV 333.

86 Leibniz to Philippi, undated: Gerhardt IV 282; "Réponse aux Reflexions," 337.

87 Quoted in M. Cranston, *John Locke: A Biography* (London, 1957), p. 100.

88 See *Essay* II.xi.11; II.xiii.11.

89 *The Vanity of Dogmatizing* (1661) is the title of a work by Joseph Glanvill. Glanvill was closely associated with the early Royal Society.

90 See *Essay* IV.iii.6.

91 Pascal, *Pensées*, p. 356.

92 Voltaire, *Letters on England*, p. 63.

93 See *Essay* IV.iii.6.

94 Quoted in Bouillier, *Histoire*, vol. II, p. 547.

95 Ibid.

96 Ibid., p. 624.

97 Ibid., p. 563.

BIBLIOGRAPHY

TEXTS AND EDITIONS: DESCARTES

Adam, C., and Milhaud, G. (eds.), *Descartes, Correspondence* (Paris: Presses Universitaires de France, 1936–63).

AT: Adam, C., and Tannery, P. (eds.), *Œuvres de Descartes*, revised ed., 12 vols. (Paris: Vrin/CNRS, 1964–76).

Alquié, F. (ed.), *Descartes, Œuvres philosophiques*, 3 vols. (Paris: Garnier, 1963).

Buzon, F. (ed.), *Descartes, Abrégé de Musique, avec présentation et notes* (Paris: Presses Universitaires de France, 1987).

Cottinham, J. G. (ed.), *Descartes Conversation with Burman* (Oxford: Clarendon, 1976).

CSM: Cottingham, J. G., Stoothoff, R., and Murdoch, D. (eds.), *The Philosophical Writings of Descartes*, 2 vols. (Cambridge University Press, 1985); CSMK: Volume three of the preceding, by the same translators and Anthony Kenny (Cambridge University Press, 1991).

Crapulli, G. (ed.), *Descartes: Regulae ad directionem ingenii* (The Hague: Nijhoff, 1966).

Gilson, E., *René Descartes, Discours de la méthode, texte et commentaire* (Paris: Vrin, 1925; 4th ed., 1967).

Hall, T. S. (ed.), *Descartes, Treatise on Man* (Cambridge: Harvard University Press, 1972).

Mahoney, M. S. (trans.), *Descartes, The World* (New York: Abaris, 1979).

Marion, J.-L. (ed. and trans.), *Règles utiles et claires pour la direction de l'esprit* (The Hague: Nijhoff, 1977).

Miller, V. R., and Miller, R. P., (eds.), *Descartes, Principles of Philosophy* (Dordrecht: Reidel, 1983).

424

Olscamp, P. J. (trans.), *Discourse on Method, Optics, Geometry and Meteorology* (Indianapolis: Bobbs-Merrill, 1965).

Rodis-Lewis, G. (ed. and trans.), *Lettres à Regius et remarques sur l'explication de l'esprit humain* (Paris: Vrin, 1959).

Verbeek, T. (ed. and trans.), *René Descartes & Martin Schook, la querelle d'Utrecht* (Paris: Les Impressions Nouvelles, 1988).

Voss, S. (ed.), *The Passions of the Soul* (Indianapolis: Hackett, 1989).

TEXTS AND EDITIONS: OTHER PRE-TWENTIETH CENTURY WRITERS.

Aquinas, Saint Thomas, *Summa Theologiae*, Latin text with English translation, 61 vols. (Cambridge: Blackfriars, 1964–81).

Albert of Saxony, *Quaestiones super quatuor libros de caelo et mundo* (Rome, 1567).

Bacon, Francis, *The New Organon and Related Writings*, ed. F. H. Anderson (Indianapolis: Bobbs-Merrill, 1960).

Baillet, A., *La Vie de M. Des-Cartes* (Paris: Horthemels, 1691; photographic reprint, Hildesheim: Olms, 1972).

Balzac, Guez de, *Le Socrate chrétien* (Paris: Courbé 1652).

Barbier, A., *Trois Médecins poitevins au XVIe siècle* (Poitiers: Marche, 1899).

Beeckman, I. *Journal tenu par Isaac Beeckman de 1604 à 1634*, ed. C. de Waard, 4 vols. (The Hague: Nijhoff, 1939–53).

Bellarmine, R., *Louvain Lectures*, trans. U. Baldini and G. V. Coyne (Studi Galileani, 1984).

Borel, P., *Renati Cartesii . . . vita* (Paris, 1653; 2nd ed. 1656).

Bouillier, F., *Histoire de la philosophie cartésienne* (Paris: Durand, 2 vols., 1854; 3rd edn., 1868).

Coimbran Commentators, *Commentarii in tres libros de anima Aristotelis* (Coimbra, 1598).

Eustachius a Sancto Paulo, *Summa philosophica quadripartita* (Paris, 1609).

Galen, *Opera omnia*, ed. Kühn (Leipzig: Cnoblock, 1821–33).

Galileo Galilei, *Siderius nuncius* [Venice 1610], trans. Van Helden, (Chicago: Chicago University Press, 1989).

Dialogue Concerning the Two Chief World Systems [1632], trans. S. Drake (Berkeley and Los Angeles: University of California Press, 1967).

Gassendi, Pierre, *Disquisitio metaphysica* [1644], ed. B. Rochot (Paris: Vrin, 1962).

Opera Omnia (Lyons, 1658).

The Selected Works of Pierre Gassendi, trans. C. Brush (New York: Johnson Reprint, 1972).

Gaultruche, P., *Institutio totius mathematicae* (Caens, 1656).

Goclenius, R., *Lexicon philosophicum* (Frankfurt, 1613).

Harvey, William, *De motu cordis* [1628], trans. C. D. Leake, *Harvey, Anatomical Studies on the Motion of the Heart and Blood* (Baltimore: Thomas, 1931).

Huet, P. D., *Censura philosophiae cartesianae* [Kempen, 1690] (repr. Hildesheim: Olms, 1971).

Hume, David, *A Treatise of Human Nature* [1739–40], ed. L. A. Selby-Bigge, rev. P. H. Niddich (Oxford: Oxford University Press [Clarendon], 1978).

Enquiry into the Human Understanding [1748], ed. L. A. Selby-Bigge, rev. P. H. Nidditch (Oxford: Oxford University Press [Clarendon], 1975).

Kant, Immanuel, *Critique of Pure Reason* [1781], trans. N. Kemp Smith (London: Macmillan, 1929).

La Forge, Louis de la, *Traité de l'âme humaine* (Paris: Girard, 1666), reprinted in Clair, P. (ed.), *Louis de la Forge, Œuvres Philosophiques* (Paris: Presses Universitaires de France, 1974).

Lasswitz, K., *Geschichte der Atomistik vom Mittelalter bis Newton* (Hamburg and Leipzig: Leopold Voss, 1890).

Le Bossu, R., *Parallèle des principes de la physique d'Aristote et de ce de Descartes,* (Paris, 1674).

Le Grand, A. *An Entire Body of Philosophy* (London, 1694).

Leibniz, G. W., *Die philosophischen Schriften,* ed. C. I. Gerhardt, 7 vols. (Berlin: Wiedmann, 1875–90).

Philosophical Papers and Letters, ed. L. E. Loemker, 2nd ed. (Dordrecht: Reidel, 1969).

Martin, R. N. D., and Brown, S. (eds.), *Leibniz: Discourse on Metaphysics* (Manchester: Manchester University Press, 1988).

Lipstorp, D., *Specimina philosophiae cartesianae* (Leiden: Elzevier, 1653).

Locke, John, *An Essay Concerning Human Understanding* [1689], ed. P. H. Nidditch (Oxford: Oxford University Press, 1975).

Malebranche, Nicolas, *Œuvres complètes de Malebranche,* ed. A. Robinet, 20 vols. (Paris: Vrin, 1958–67).

Dialogues on Metaphysics, trans. W. Doney (New York: Abaris, 1980).

Search after Truth, trans. T. M. Lennon and P. J. Olscamp (Columbus: Ohio State University Press, 1980).

Mersenne, M., *Correspondence*, ed. de Waard (Paris: Beauchesne, 10 vols., 1932–67).

Millet, J., *Descartes, sa vie, ses travaux, ses découvertes* (Paris: Didier, 1867).

More, Henry, A *Collection of Several Philosophical Writings* (London: 1662).

Newton, Isaac, *Mathematical Principles of Natural Philosophy and His System of the World* [1687], trans. A. Motte, 1729; revised F. Cajori (Cambridge University Press, 1934).

Oresme, N., *Livre du ciel et du monde*, ed. and trans. A. D. Menu and A. J. Denomy (Madison: University of Wisconsin Press, 1968).

Pascal, B., *Œuvres complètes*, ed. J. Mesnard (Paris Bloud et Gay, 1970). *Pensées*, trans. A. J. Krailsheimer (Harmondsworth: Penguin, 1966).

Poisson, N. J., *Commentaire ou remarques sur la méthode de M. Descartes* (Paris, 1671).

Regius, H., *Fundamenta physices* (Amsterdam: Elsevier, 1646).

Rochemonteix, Camille de, *Un Collège des Jésuites au XVIIᵉ et XVIIIᵉ siècles: le Collège Henri IV de la Flèche*, 4 vols. (Le Mans: Leguicheux, 1889).

Rohault, J., *A System of Natural Philosophy* [1671], trans. J. Clarke (London, 1723).

Scipion Dupleix, *Corps de philosophie contenant la logique, l'éthique, la physique et la métaphysique* (Geneva, 1627).

Sextus Empiricus, *Outlines of Pyrrhonism* (Loeb edition, London: Heinemann and New York: Putnam, 1933).

Spinoza, *Opera*, ed. C. Gebhardt, 4 vols. (Heidelberg: Winters, 1925; repr. 1972).
Collected Works, trans. E. Curley (Princeton, N.J.: Princeton University Press, 1985).

Suarez F., *Disputationes metaphysicae* (Salmanticae, 1597).
Opera omnia, ed. M. André, 28 vols. (Paris: Vives, 1856–78).

Telesio, B., *De rerum natura juxta propria principia*, libri ix, (Naples: Salvianum, 1586).

Tepel, J., *Historia philosophiae cartesianae* (Nuremburg, 1674).

Voltaire, *Letters on England*, trans. L. Tancock. (Harmondsworth: Penguin, 1980).

BOOKS PUBLISHED AFTER 1900

Aiton, E. J., *The Vortex Theory of Planatary Motions* (New York: Neale Watson, 1972).

Alquié, F., *La Découverte métaphysique de l'homme chez Descartes* (Paris: Presses Universitaires de France, 1950; 2d ed. 1987).

Armogathe, J.-R., *Theologiaa cartesiana: l'explication physique de l'Eucharistie chez Descartes et Dom Desgabets* (The Hague: Nijhoff, 1977).

Ayer, A. J., *Language, Truth and Logic* (New York: Dover, 1936).

Ayers, M., and Garber, D. (eds.), *Cambridge History of Seventeenth Century Philosophy* (Cambridge University Press, forthcoming).

Balz, A. G. A., *Cartesian Studies* (New York: Columbia University Press 1951).

Beck, L. J., *The Metaphysics of Descartes: A Study of the Meditations* (Oxford: Oxford University Press [Clarendon] 1965).

Belaval, Y., *Leibniz, critique de Descartes* (Paris: Gallimard, 1960).

Beyssade, J.-M., *La Philosophie première de Descartes* (Paris: Flammarion, 1979).

Brockliss, L. W. B., *French Higher Education in the Seventeenth and Eighteenth Centuries: A Cultural History* (Oxford: Oxford University Press [Clarendon], 1987).

Brophy, S. (ed.), *The Cartesian and Newtonian Revolution; Essays on Matter, Motion and Mechanism* (Dordrecht: Reidel, forthcoming).

Brown, S., *Leibniz* (Brighton: Harvester, 1984).

Burnyeat, M. (ed.), *The Skeptical Tradition* (Berkeley and Los Angeles: University of California Press, 1983).

Caton, H., *The Origins of Subjectivity: An Essay on Descartes* (New Haven, Conn.: Yale University Press, 1973).

Chisholm, R., *Person and Object* (London: Allen & Unwin, 1986)

Chomsky, N., *Language and Mind* (New York: Harcourt Brace and World, 1968).

Churchland, P., *Neurophilosophy* (Cambridge, Mass.: MIT Press, 1986).

Clarke, D. M., *Occult Powers and Hypotheses* (Oxford: Oxford University Press [Clarendon], 1989).

Cohen, G., *Les Ecrivains français en Hollande* (Paris: Champion, 1920).

Costabel, P., *Démarches originales de Descartes savant* (Paris: Vrin, 1982).

Cottingham, J., *Descartes* (Oxford: Blackwell, 1986).
    The Rationalists (Oxford: Oxford University Press, 1988).

Crapulli, G., *Mathesis universalis: Genesi di una idea nel XVI secolo* (Rome: Ateneo, 1966).

Curley E., *Descartes against the Skeptics* (Oxford: Blackwell, 1978).

Dainville, François de, *L'Education des Jésuites* (Paris: Editions de Minuit, 1987).

Dear, P., *Mersenne and the Learning of the Schools* (Ithaca, N.Y.: Cornell University Press, 1988).

Dijksterhuis, E. J., (ed.), *Descartes et le cartésianisme hollandais* (Paris: Presses Universitaires de France, 1950).

Doney W. (ed.), *Descartes: A Collection of Critical Essays* (New York: Doubleday, 1967).

Dugas, R., *Mechanics in the Seventeenth Century* (Neuchatel: Griffon, 1958).

Fitzpatrick, E. A. (ed.), *St. Ignatius and the Ratio Studiorum* (New York: McGraw Hill, 1933).

Frankfurt, H. G., *Demons, Dreamers, and Madmen* (Indianapolis, Ind.: Bobbs-Merrill, 1970).

Garber, D., *Descartes' Metaphysical Physics* (Chicago: University of Chicago Press, 1992)

Gaukroger, S. (ed.), *Descartes: Philosophy, Mathematics and Physics.* (Sussex: Harvester, 1980).
Cartesian Logic (Oxford: Oxford University Press [Clarendon], 1989).

Gilson, E., *Etudes sur le rôle de la pensée médiévale dans la formation du système cartésien,* 4th ed. (Paris: Vrin, 1975).
Index Scolastico-Cartésien (Paris: Alcan, 1913).
La Doctrine cartésienne de la liberté et la théologie (Paris: Alcan, 1913).

Gouhier, H., *Cartésianisme et augustinisme au XVIIᵉ siècle* (Paris: Vrin, 1978).
La Pensée métaphysique de Descartes (Paris: Vrin, 1962).
La Pensée religieuse de Descartes (Paris: Vrin, 1924).
Les Premières Pensées de Descartes (Paris: Vrin, 1958).

Grant, E., *Much Ado about Nothing: Theories of space and vacuum from the Middle Ages to the Scientific Revolution* (Cambridge University Press, 1981).
Physical Science in the Middle Ages (New York: John Wiley & Sons, 1971).
(ed.), *A Source Book in Medieval Science* (Cambridge, Mass.: Harvard University Press, 1974).

Grene, M., *Descartes* (Minneapolis: University of Minnesota Press, 1985).

Grimaldi, N., and Marion, J.-L. (eds.), *Le Discours et sa méthode* (Paris: Presses Universitaires de France, 1987).

Gueroult, M., *Descartes selon l'ordre des raisons* (Paris: Montaigne,

1953). English translation by R. Ariew, *Descartes' Philosophy Interpreted According to the Order of Reasons* (Minneapolis: University of Minnesota Press, 1984).

Hall, T. S., *History of General Physiology*, 2 vols. (Chicago: University of Chicago Press, 1975).

Hamelin, O., *Le Système de Descartes* (Paris: Alcan, 1911).

Heilbron J., *Electricity in the Seventeenth and Eighteenth Centuries. A Study of Early Modern Physics* (Berkeley and Los Angeles: University of California Press, 1979).

Holland, A. J. (ed.), *Philosophy: Its History and Historiography* (Dordrecht: Reidel, 1985).

Hooker, M. (ed.), *Descartes: Critical and Interpretive Essays* (Baltimore: Johns Hopkins University Press, 1978).

Jammer, M., *Concepts of Space: The History of Theories of Space in Physics*, 2nd ed. (Cambridge, Mass.: Harvard University Press, 1969).

Jolley, N., *The Light of the Soul: Theories of Ideas in Leibniz, Malebranche and Descartes* (Oxford: Oxford University Press, 1990).

Jones, H., *Pierre Gassendi, 1592–1655: An Intellectual Biography* (Nieuwkoop: B. De Graaf, 1981).

Joy, L. S., *Gassendi the Atomist: Advocate of History in an Age of Science* (Cambridge University Press, 1987).

Kargon, R., *Atomism in England from Hariot to Newton* (Oxford: Oxford University Press, 1966).

Kenny, A., *Descartes: A Study of His Philosophy* (New York: Random House, 1968).

Klein, J., *Greek Mathematical Thought and the Origin of Algebra* (Cambridge, Mass.: MIT Press, 1968).

Kneale, W., and Kneale, M. *The Development of Logic* (Oxford: Oxford University Press [Clarendon], 1962).

Knorr, W. R., *The Evolution of the Euclidean Elements* (Dordrecht: Reidel, 1975).

Koyré, A., *Galileo Studies*, trans. J. Mepham (Atlantic Highlands, N.J.: Humanities Press, 1978).

   Newtonian Studies (Cambridge, Mass.: Harvard University Press, 1965).

Kretzmann, N., Kenny, A., and Pinborg, J. (eds.), *The Cambridge History of Later Medieval Philosophy* (Cambridge University Press, 1982).

Laporte J., *Le Rationalisme de Descartes* (Paris: Presses Universitaires de France, 1945; 3rd ed. 1988).

Lennon, T. M., Nicholas, J. M., and Davis, J. W. (eds.), *Problems of Cartesianism* (Montreal: McGill Queens University Press, 1982).

Lenoble, R., *Mersenne ou la naissance du mécanisme* (Paris: Vrin 1943).

Lindberg, D., *Theories of Vision from al-Khindi to Kepler* (Chicago: University of Chicago Press, 1976).

(ed.), *Science in the Middle Ages* (Chicago: University of Chicago Press, 1978).

Lindeboom, G. A., *Descartes and Medicine* (Amsterdam: Rodopi, 1978).

Loeck, G., *Der cartesische Materialismus: Maschine, Gesetz und Simulation* (Frankfurt and New York: Lang, 1986).

Lukács, L. (ed.), *Ratio atque Institutio Studiorum Societatis Jesu (1586, 1591, 1599) [Monumenta Paedagogica Societatis Jesu,* vol V; *Monumenta Historica Societatis Jesu,* vol. 129.] (Rome: Institutum Historicum Societatis Jesu, 1986).

Machamer, P. K., and Turnbull, R. G. (eds.), *Studies in Perception* (Columbus: Ohio State University Press, 1978).

McCracken, C. J., *Malebranche and British Philosophy* (Oxford: Oxford University Press, 1983).

McGinn, C., *The Subjective View* (Oxford: Clarendon, 1983).

Maier, A. *On the Threshold of Exact Science,* trans. S. D. Sargent, (Philadelphia: University of Pennsylvania Press, 1982).

Marion, J.-L., *Sur la théologie blanche de Descartes* (Paris: Presses Universitaires de France, 1981; 2nd edn. 1991).

Sur le prisme métaphysique de Descartes (Paris: Presses Universitaires de France, 1986).

Sur l'ontologie grise de Descartes (Paris: Vrin, 1975; 2nd edn. 1981).

Questions Cartésiennes (Paris: Presses Universitaires de France, 1991).

Markie, P., *Descartes's Gambit* (Ithaca, N.Y.: Cornell University Press, 1986).

Méchoulan, H. (ed.), *Problématique et réception du Discours de la méthode et des Essais* (Paris: Vrin, 1988).

Merylees, W. A., *Descartes, An Examination of Some Features of his Metaphysics and Method* (Melbourne: Melbourne University Press, 1934).

Milhaud, G., *Descartes savant* (Paris: Alcan, 1921).

Mouy, P., *Le Développement de la physique cartésienne, 1646–1712.* (Paris: Vrin, 1934).

Nadler, S., *Arnauld and the Cartesian Philosophy of Ideas* (Manchester: Manchester University Press, 1989).

Nagel, T., *The View from Nowhere* (Oxford: Oxford University Press 1986).

Perini, E., *Il problema delle fondazione nelle Regulae di Descartes* (Rimini: Maggiri, 1983).

Rist, J. M., *Epicurus: An Introduction* (Oxford: Oxford University Press, 1972).

Rodis-Lewis, G., *Descartes* (Paris: Libraire Générale Française, 1984).

Idées et vérités éternelles chez Descartes et ses successeurs (Paris: Vrin, 1985).

L'œuvre de Descartes (Paris: Vrin, 1971).

L'antropologie cartésienne (Paris: Presses Universitaires de France, 1991).

Rorty, A. O. (ed.), *Essays on Descartes' Meditations* (Berkeley and Los Angeles: University of California Press, 1986).

Rorty, R., *Philosophy and the Mirror of Nature* (Oxford: Blackwell, 1980).

Rosenfield, L. C., *From Beast-Machine to Man-Machine: The Theme of Animal Soul in French Letters from Descartes to La Mettrie* (New York: Oxford University Press, 1941).

Rothschuh, K. E., *Physiologie: Der Wandel ihrer Konzepte, Probleme und Methoden vom 16 bis 19 Jahrhundert* (Freiburg and Munich: Alber, 1966).

Sabra, A. I., *Theories of Light from Descartes to Newton* (London: Oldbourne, 1967).

Schmitt, C. B., *Aristotle and the Renaissance* (Cambridge: Harvard University Press, 1983).

Schmitt, C. B., Skinner, Q., and Kessler, E. (eds.), *Cambridge History of Renaissance Philosophy* (Cambridge University Press, 1988).

Scott, J. F., *The Scientific Work of René Descartes* (London: Taylor and Francis, 1952).

Sirven, J., *Les Années d'apprentissage de Descartes* (Albi: Imprimerie Coopérative du Sud Ouest, 1928; repr. New York: Garland, 1987).

Smith, N. Kemp, *New Studies in the Philosophy of Descartes* (London: Macmillan, 1966).

Specht, R., *Commercium mentis et corporis* (Stuttgart: Frommann, 1966).

Summers, D., *Judgment of Sense: Renaissance Naturalism and the Rise of Aesthetics* (Cambridge University Press, 1987).

Swinburne, R., *The Evolution of the Soul* (Oxford: Oxford University Press, [Clarendon], 1986).

Szabó, A., *The Beginnings of Greek Mathematics* (Dordrecht: Reidel, 1978).

Tomas, V. (ed.), *Charles S. Pierce, Essays in the Philosophy of Science* (Indianapolis: Bobbs Merrill, 1957).

Vartanian, A., *Diderot and Descartes: A Study of Naturalism in the Enlightenment* (Princeton, N.J.: Princeton University Press, 1953).

Verbeek, T., *Descartes and the Dutch: Early reactions to Cartesianism* (Journal of the History of Philosophy Monographs, Carbondale: Southern Illinois University Press, 1992).

Vickers, B. (ed.), *Occult and Scientific Mentalities in the Renaissance* (Cambridge University Press, 1984).

Voss, S. (ed.), *René Descartes: Metaphysics and the Classification of the Sciences in 1637* (proceedings of the conference at San Jose State University, Calif., 1988).

Vuillemin, J., *Mathématiques et métaphysique chez Descartes* (Paris: Presses Universitaires de France, 1960; 2nd edn., 1987).

Wahl, J., *Du rôle de l'idée d'instant dans la philosophie de Descartes* (Paris: Alcan, 1920).

Wallace, W., *Galileo and His Sources: The Heritage of the Collegio Romano in Galileo's Science* (Princeton, N.J.: Princeton University Press, 1984).

Weber, J.-P., *La Constitution du texte des Regulae* (Paris: Société de l'édition de l'enseignement supérieur, 1964).

Westfall, R. S., *Force in Newton's Physics* (New York: Neale Watson, 1971).

Williams, B., *Descartes: The Project of Pure Inquiry* (Penguin: Harmondsworth, 1978).

Wilson, C., *Leibniz's Metaphysics* (Manchester: Manchester University Press, 1989).

Wilson, M. D., *Descartes* (London: Routledge, 1978).

Wright, J., *The Sceptical Realism of David Hume* (Cambridge University Press, 1985).

ARTICLES

Anscombe, E., "The first person," in S. Guttenplan (ed.), *Mind and Language: Wolfson College Lectures 1974* (Oxford: Oxford University Press, [Clarendon], 1975), pp. 45–65.

Ayer, A. J., "I think therefore I am," in *Descartes, A Collection of Critical Essays*. See Doney (ed.).

Balz, A., "Cartesian doctrine and the animal soul," in Columbia Philosophy Dept. (ed.), *Studies in the History of Ideas* (New York: Columbia University Press, 1935), vol. 3, pp. 117–77.

Becco, A., "Première Apparition du terme de substance dans la Méditation III de Descartes," *Annales de l'Institut de Philosophie* (ULB: Brussels, 1976).

"Remarques sur le 'Traité de la substance' de Descartes" *Recherches sur le XVIIᵉ siècle* 2 (Paris: CNRS, 1978).

Bennett, J., "Truth and stability in Descartes's *Meditations*," *Canadian Journal of Philosophy*, supp. volume 16 (1990), 75–108.

Blackwell, R., "Descartes' Laws of Motion," *Isis* 57 (1966): 220–34.

Boas, M., "The establishment of the mechanical philosophy," *Osiris* 10 (1952): 412–541.

Cosentino, C., "Le matematiche nella *Ratio Studiorum* della Compagnia di Gesu," *Miscellanea Storica Ligure* (Istituto di Storia Moderna e Contemporanea, Universita di Genova) 2 (1970): 171–213.

Costabel, P., "Essai critique sur quelques concepts de la mécanique cartésienne," *Archives Internationales d'Histoire des Sciences* 80 (1967): 235–52.

Cottingham, J. G., "A brute to the brutes? Descartes' treatment of animals," *Philosophy* (1978): 551ff.

"Cartesian trialism," *Mind* (1985): 218–30.

"Descartes on thought," *Philosophical Quarterly* (1978): 208ff.

"The Cartesian legacy," *Proceedings of the Aristotelian Society*, supp. vol. LXVI (1992).

Dainville, F. de, "L'enseignement des mathématiques dans les Collèges Jésuites de France du XVIᵉ au XVIIIᵉ siécle." *Revue d'Histoire des Sciences* 7 (1954), pp. 6–21, 109–23.

Doney, W., "The Cartesian Circle," *Journal of the History of Ideas* 16 (1955): 324–38.

"Descartes's conception of perfect knowledge," *Journal of the History of Philosophy* 8 (1970): 387–403.

Etchemendy, J., "The Cartesian Circle: *circulus ex tempore*," *Studia Cartesiana* 2 (1981): 5–42.

Feldman, F., "Epistemic appraisal and the Cartesian Circle," *Philosophical Studies* 27 (1975).

"On the performatory interpretation of the Cogito," *Philosophical Review* 82 (1973).

Feldman, F., and Levison, A., "Anthony Kenny and the Cartesian Circle," *Journal of the History of Philosophy* (1971): 491–6.

Frankfurt, H., "Descartes' discussion of his existence in the Second Meditation," *Philosophical Review* 75 (1966).

"Descartes' validation of Reason," *American Philosophical Quarterly* 2 (1965): 149–56.

"Memory and the Cartesian circle," *Review* 71 (1962): 504–11.

Gabbey, A., "Force and inertia in the seventeenth century: Descartes and Newton," in *Descartes: Philosophy, Mathematics and Physics*. See Gaukroger (ed.).

Garber, D., "Descartes, the Aristotelians and the revolution that did not happen in 1637," *Monist* 71 (1988): 471–87.

"Mind, body, and the laws of nature in Descartes and Leibniz," *Midwest Studies in Philosophy* 8 (1983): 105–33.

Garns, R. L., "Descartes and indubitability," *Southern Journal of Philosophy* (1988): 83–100.

Gaukroger, S., "Aristotle on intelligible matter," *Phronesis* XXV (1980): 187–97.

Gewirth, A., "Clearness and distinctness in Descartes," *Philosophy* 18 (1943), reprinted in *Descartes, A Collection of Critical Essays*. See Doney (ed.).

"The Cartesian Circle," *Philosophical Review* 50 (1941) 368–95.

"The Cartesian Circle reconsidered," *Journal of Philosophy* 67 (1970): 668–85.

"Descartes: Two disputed questions," *Journal of Philosophy* 68 (1971): 288–96.

Gombay, A., "Mental conflict: Descartes," *Philosophy* 54 (1979): 485–500.

Grant, E., "Celestial orbs in the Latin Middle Ages," *Isis* (1987): 153–7.

Gueroult, M., "The physics and metaphysics of force in Descartes," in *Descartes: Philosophy, Mathematics and Physics*. See S. Gaukroger (ed.).

Hatfield, G., "First philosophy and natural philosophy in Descartes," in *Philosophy, Its History and Historiography*. See A. J. Holland (ed.).

"Force (God) in Descartes' physics," *Studies in History and Philosophy of Science* 10 (1979): 113–40.

Hatfield, G., and Epstein, W., "The sensory core and the medieval foundations of early modern perceptual theory," *Isis* 70 (1979): 363–84.

Hintikka, J,. "Cogito ergo sum: Inference or performance," in *Descartes, A Collection of Critical Essays*. See W. Doney (ed.).

"Cogito ergo sum as an inference and a performance," *Philosophical Review* 72 (1963).

Hoenen, P. H. J., "Descartes's mechanism," in *Descartes, A Collection of Critical Essays*. See W. Doney (ed.), pp. 353–68.

Iltis, C., "Leibniz and the *vis viva* controversy," *Isis* 62 (1971): 21–35.

Kenny, A., "A reply to Feldman and Levison," *Journal of the History of Philosophy* 9 (1971): 497–8.

"The Cartesian Circle and the eternal truths," *Journal of Philosophy* 67 (1970).

Larmore, C., "Descartes' psychologistic theory of assent," *History of Philosophy Quarterly* (1984): 61–74.

Lehrer, K., "Why not scepticism," *Philosophical Forum* 2 (1971).

Levett, M. J., "Note on the alleged Cartesian Circle," *Mind* 46 (1937): 206–13.

Loeb, L., "Is there radical dissimulation in Descartes' *Meditations?*" in *Essays on Descartes' Meditations*. See A. O. Rorty (ed.).

"The priority of reason in Descartes," *Philosophical Review* 98 (1990): 243–70.

Lohr, C. H., "Renaissance Latin Aristotle Commentaries," *Renaissance Quarterly* (1974, 1975, 1976, 1980, 1982).

McClaughlin, T., "Censorship and defenders of the Cartesian faith in mid-seventeenth-century France," *Journal of the History of Ideas* 40 (1979).

McRae, R., "Descartes: The project of a universal science," in *The Problem of the Unity of the Sciences, Bacon to Kant* (Toronto, 1963).

Marion, J.-L., "The essential incoherence of Descartes' definition of divinity," in A. O. Rorty (ed.), *Essays on Descartes' Meditations*.

Markie, P., "The Cogito puzzle," *Philosophy and Phenomenological Research* 43 (1982).

Meinel, C., "Early seventeenth-century atomism: Theory, epistemology and the insufficiency of experiment," *Isis* 79 (1988): 68–103.

Noonan, H., "Identity and the first person," in C. Diamond and J. Teichman (eds.), *Intention and Intentionality* (Ithaca, N.Y.: Cornell University Press, 1979).

O'Neil, B., "Cartesian simple natures," *Journal of the History of Philosophy* 10/2 (1972).

Parsons, C., "Review of Frankfurt, *Demons, Dreamers, and Madmen,*" *Journal of Philosophy* (1972): 38–46.

Parsons, K., "Mistaking sensations," *Philosophical Review* 79 (1970).

Prendergast, T. L., "Descartes and the relativity of motion," *Modern Schoolman* 49 (1972): 64–72.

Review of Frankfurt, Demons, Dreamers, and Madmen, *International Philosophical Quarterly* (1972): 303–5.

Reif, P., "The textbook tradition in natural philosophy 1600–1650," *Journal of the History of Ideas* 30 (1969): 17–32.

Rodis-Lewis, G., "Du doute vécu au doute suprême," *Actas del III Congreso de Lenguages natureles y lenguages formales* (Barcelona: Vide, 1988), pp. 865–85.

"L'alto e il basso e i sogni di Descartes," *Rivista di Filosofia* (1989): 189–214.

"Le dernier fruit de la métaphysique cartésienne: la générosité," *Etudes philosophiques* (1987): 43–5.

"Le premier régistre de Descartes," *Archives de Philosophie* (1991): 353–77; 639–57.

"On the complimentarity of Meditations III and V," in *Essays on Descartes' Meditations*. See A. O. Rorty (ed.).

Rorty, A. O., "Cartesian Passions and the Union of Mind and Body," in A. O. Rorty (ed.) *Essays on Descartes' Meditations*.

"Formal Tracers in Cartesian Functional Explanation," *Canadian Journal of Philosophy*, 1984.

"The Structure of Descartes' *Meditations*," see A. O. Rorty (ed.).

Rubin, D., "Descartes's validation of clear and distinct apprehension," *Philosophical Review* (1977): 197–208.

Sanford, D. H., Review of Frankfurt, Demons, Dreamers, and Madmen, *Philosophical Review* (1973): 120–4.

Shapiro, A., "Light, pressure and rectilinear propagation: Descartes' celestial optics and Newton's hydrostatics" *Studies in History and Philosophy of Science* 5 (1974): 239–96.

Sievert, D., "Descartes' self-doubt," *Philosophical Review* 84 (1975).

"Sellars and Descartes on the fundamental form of the mental," *Philosophical Studies* 37 (1980).

Stout, A. K., "The basis of knowledge in Descartes," *Mind* 38 (1929): 330–42, 458–74. Reprinted in *Descartes, A Collection of Critical Essays*. See W. Doney (ed.).

Stubbs, A. C., "Bernard Williams and the Cartesian Circle," *Analysis* 40 (1980): 103–8.

Tlumak, J., "Certainty and Cartesian method," in *Descartes, Critical and Interpretive Essays*. See M. Hooker (ed.).

Unguru, S., "On the need to rewrite the history of Greek mathematics," *Archive for History of Exact Sciences* XV (1975–6): 67–114.

Van Cleve, J., "Foundationalism, epistemic principles, and the Cartesian Circle," *Philosophical Review* 88 (1979) 55–91.

"Conceivability and the Cartesian argument for dualism," *Pacific Philosophical Quarterly* 64 (1983).

Vendler, Z., "Descartes' exercises," *Canadian Journal of Philosophy* 19 (1989).

Watson, R. A. "Descartes and Cartesianism," *Encyclopaedia Britannica,* vol. 15 (1989).

Williams, B., "Descartes' use of skepticism," in *The Skeptical Tradition.* See M. Burnyeat (ed.).

Wolz, H. G., "The Double guarantee of Descartes' ideas," *Review of Metaphysics* 3 (1950): 471–89.

Zemach, E., "*De Se* and Descartes: A new semantics for indexicals," *Nous* 19 (1985).

INDEX

439